ANNAPOLIS GOES TO WAR

ANNAPOLIS GOES TO WAR

THE NAVAL ACADEMY CLASS
OF 1940 AND ITS TRIAL
BY FIRE IN WORLD WAR II

by
CRAIG L. SYMONDS

OXFORD
UNIVERSITY PRESS

Oxford University Press is a department of the University of Oxford.
It furthers the University's objective of excellence in research, scholarship,
and education by publishing worldwide. Oxford is a registered trade mark of
Oxford University Press in the UK and in certain other countries.

Published in the United States of America by Oxford University Press
198 Madison Avenue, New York, NY 10016, United States of America.

© Craig L. Symonds 2025

All rights reserved. No part of this publication may be reproduced, stored in a retrieval system,
transmitted, used for text and data mining, or used for training artificial intelligence, in any form or
by any means, without the prior permission in writing of Oxford University Press, or as expressly
permitted by law, by license or under terms agreed with the appropriate reprographics rights
organization. Inquiries concerning reproduction outside the scope of the above should be sent
to the Rights Department, Oxford University Press, at the address above.

You must not circulate this work in any other form
and you must impose this same condition on any acquirer

Library of Congress Cataloging-in-Publication Data
Names: Symonds, Craig L., author.
Title: Annapolis goes to war : the Naval Academy class of 1940 and its
trial by fire in World War II / by Craig L. Symonds.
Other titles: Naval Academy class of 1940 and its trial by fire in World War II
Description: New York : Oxford University Press, [2025] |
Includes bibliographical references and index.
Identifiers: LCCN 2025000257 (print) | LCCN 2025000258 (ebook) |
ISBN 9780197752678 (hardback) | ISBN 9780197752692 (epub)
Subjects: LCSH: United States Naval Academy. Class of Forty—Biography. |
United States. Navy—Officers—Biography. | World War, 1939–1945—Naval
operations, American.
Classification: LCC V415 .S96 2025 (print) | LCC V415 (ebook) |
DDC 940.54/59730922—dc23/eng/20250305
LC record available at https://lccn.loc.gov/2025000257
LC ebook record available at https://lccn.loc.gov/2025000258

DOI: 10.1093/oso/9780197752678.001.0001

Printed by Sheridan Books, Inc., United States of America

Dedicated to
The Members of the Naval Academy Class of 1940
Who Lost Their Lives during the Second World War

Arthur Alexander

Robert Thomas Allsopp

Ralph O. Anderson, Jr.

Daniel Eugene Arnold

Donald Francis Banker

William Henry Beck, Jr.

Clarence Frederick Blair

John Taylor Blodgett

Donald Raymond Bried

Jack B. Brown

William Wilson Burgan

William Mann Butler

Richard B. Campbell

Fred Beatty Cannon, Jr.

Leon Edmond Chabot

Edward Blanchard Cloues

Arthur Barton Cross, Jr.

Marshall Eugene Darby, Jr.

Edward Emmet DeGarmo

Charles E. Deterding, Jr.

Robert Lee Dodane

Dolive Durant, Jr.

Thomas Bayliss Earle

Henry Forester Graham, Jr.

William Frank Greene

William Lee Guice, Jr.

Benjamin C. Hall

John Carlyle Hanna

Burton Roaklvan Hanson

John Daniel Harris

Richie Neale Henderson

Joseph Parker Hittorff, Jr.

William Philip Hodnet, Jr.

Robert Huntley Hurst

Milton L. Jarrett, Jr.

Ralph Karl John, Jr.

John Joe Keough

Fraser Sinclair Knight

Frank Stuart Lomax

Virgil W. Lusk

Fred Ferguson Mallory

Charles P. Mason, Jr.

Richard Keeble Mason, Jr.

William H. Mathews, Jr.

Thomas P. McCann

Thomas Patrick McGrath

Howard Deal Merrill

Raymond James Murray

Alva Freeman Nethken

Jay Alvin Noble, Jr.

Edward Francis O'Brien, Jr.

Merlin Paddock

James Tate Preston

Reginald John Proseus, Jr.

Carlton F. Rees

Thomas Michael Roddy

David G. Rodger

Charles Haddon Sawyers

Donald Stone Scheu

Alan H. Schirmer

Coleman Sellers, IV

Walter Lewis Shaffer

Carthel Hill Smith, Jr.

Orville Stanley Smith

John Pratt Spears

Robert C. Stimson

Warren P. Strong, Jr.

Irvin Andrew R. Thompson

Paul V. Thompson

Donald Keith Tripp

Carl Alfred Weeden

Ulmont R. Whitehead, Jr.

George Vincent Williams

David Spencer Wilson

Charles Mills Wood, Jr.

Eric Reed Young

"Only Forty is 4.0"

Contents

Prologue: Reef Points   ix

PART I: MIDSHIPMEN

1. Appointment   3
2. Plebe Year   16
3. Youngster Cruise   34
4. Youngsters   44
5. Beat Army   53
6. Firsties   64

PART II: JUNIOR OFFICERS

7. The Real Navy   81
8. The Cusp of War   96
9. Infamy   103
10. Retribution   116
11. U-Boats, Convoys, and Matrimony   132
12. The Coral Sea and Midway   145

PART III: ON THE OFFENSIVE

13. Savo Island   163
14. Ironbottom Sound   175
15. Flight Training   184
16. The Med   196
17. Submarine Warfare   208
18. "Moored as Before"   225

viii CONTENTS

PART IV: VALEDICTION

19. Semper Fidelis 237

20. The Atlantic Again 252

21. The Battle of Leyte Gulf 264

22. Iwo Jima and Okinawa 278

23. Culmination 294

Epilogue 305

Acknowledgments 317
Notes 321
Bibliography 345
The Forties Index 351
General Index 355

Prologue
Reef Points

They arrived in Annapolis in the summer of 1936: 750 young men (and boys) aged sixteen to twenty who aspired to become "midshipmen." The term had originated in the Royal Navy in the seventeenth century to designate "young gentlemen" (some as young as eleven) who went to sea to learn to become naval officers and who often served "amidships." Such on-the-job training was also the route to officer status in the US Navy until 1845 when the Naval Academy was founded in Annapolis, Maryland, on the banks of the Severn River, which empties into Chesapeake Bay. Though aspiring officers no longer served "amidships," the term survived.

By the standards of 1936, the new arrivals constituted an eclectic group. As one midshipman from an earlier class described it: "We were a strange and assorted lot: the nasal down-easter, the Irish Catholic Bostonian, the hearty Westerner, the big-framed and a little awkward boy from the Middle West, the sophisticated New Yorker, the slow drawling Southerner." Some had come to honor a family tradition, some were drawn by a sense of adventure, many merely hoped for a free college education, a rare and precious thing in Depression America. Some of them had been enlisted sailors, scraping paint on battleships; others came from the most exclusive prep schools in the country. Some were from second- or third-generation navy families; some had never seen the ocean. They were athletes, musicians, readers, and poets. Despite their differences, they were in many ways remarkably homogeneous. They were all men (women were not admitted until 1976), and, with one notable exception, they were all white. A statistically unlikely number had blue eyes and light brown hair. Almost to a man, they embraced—even embodied—their society's values of manliness, stoicism, and loyalty.[1]

The differences among them were reflected mostly in regional accents or differing food preferences. Alone and away from home, some for the first time, many found a lifeline in meeting someone from his home state. "It sure is interesting," one wrote home, "to meet all these boys and find out where there [*sic*] from, and if you're from the same part of the country, there is a sort of bond between you right away." Pride of place was also reflected in the tendency of some of those from the South who insisted, only partly tongue in cheek, that "Yankees" were worthless. One Virginia-born class member accepted punishment from an upperclassman rather than commit the sin of singing the Union song "Marching Through Georgia." Eventually, many of these differences were smoothed away by their subsequent shared experience in the incubator of Bancroft Hall, the enormous dormitory where they lived together for four years. There they were channeled into an even narrower path of sameness, partly by a regimented daily schedule, partly by institutional principles. Because of that, it was only logical that, as a professor in the Department of English put it, "the same ideas, same convictions, and same prejudices are likely to follow." They learned that they were responsible for themselves, of course, but also that they were responsible for others: their roommate, their team, their company, the regiment, the navy, the country. That near-universal view became a part of them, a source of great strength at times, though it also solidified their tribalism.[2]

For those who had come seeking adventure, it was a historically fateful moment. Just three months before, the German chancellor, Adolf Hitler, had sent the German army, recently renamed the Wehrmacht, marching into the previously demilitarized Rhineland. It was his first open violation of the Versailles Treaty, though it would not be his last. And only weeks after the new midshipmen arrived, a civil war broke out in Spain. Elsewhere in the world, the Japanese were in Manchuria, and the Italians in Abyssinia. For the most part, the young men who reported to the Naval Academy that summer were too focused on their own uncertain and unnerving circumstances to pay much attention to these historic events. From the moment they arrived they were taken forcefully in hand by the second classmen (juniors), whose job it was to strip away any veneer of civilian life and replace it with an entirely new set of customs and mores.

To aid them in that transformation, each of the new arrivals was handed a small booklet, two inches wide, three inches high, and bound in navy-blue leather. It was called *Reef Points*, a term from the old sailing navy when sailors

PROLOGUE   xi

clewing up a sail used short lengths of line called reef points to secure the sail to the yardarm. The booklet described itself as "The Plebe Bible," and it enjoined the new midshipmen to "Read it; 'bone' it; learn it; live by it." During any break in their busy days, they were instructed to pull out their copy of *Reef Points* and study it—indeed, to memorize it. As one new plebe described it: "It was the book of books, it was our Bible and our law, our mentor and our judge."[3]

A lot of the information in *Reef Points* was mundane: the history and traditions of the navy and the Naval Academy, the layout of the campus (called "the Yard"), the schedule of religious services, the location of the drill field, the Academy's athletic teams, and the station ship *Reina Mercedes*. (*Reef Points* query: "What is the fastest ship in the Navy?" Answer: "The *Reina Mercedes*, for she has been tied fast to the dock for 24 years.") *Reef Points* also included what were labeled the "Laws of the Navy," including such bromides as "On the strength of one link in the cable dependeth the might of the chain." Or: "Thou shalt not criticize, but obey."[4]

Reef Points also included nonsensical ditties that every midshipman was required to memorize for no other reason than the fact that his predecessors had been compelled to do so. At any time, an upperclassman could pick out a plebe (as first-year midshipman were called) and require him to recite on demand. To this day, every living graduate of the Naval Academy can answer the question: "How's the Cow?" Keeping his eyes "in the boat," that is, staring straight ahead and avoiding eye contact with his questioner, the plebe responded, word for word:

> She walks, she talks, she's full of chalk.
> The lacteal fluid extracted from the female of the bovine species
> Is highly prolific to the nth degree.[5]

Or the upperclassman might ask: "How long have you been in the navy?" To which the plebe must respond:

> All me bloomin' life, sorl.
> Me mother was a mermaid; me father was King Neptune.
> I was born on the crest of a wave and rocked in the cradle of the deep.
> Seaweed and barnacles are me clothes.
> Every tooth in me head is a marlinspike;
> The hair on me head is hemp.
> Every bone in me body is a spar,
> And when I spits, I spits tar.
> I'se hard, I is, I am, I are.[6]

xii PROLOGUE

If the upperclassman was satisfied with the reply, he might growl, "Carry on" and continue his stroll. If not—if the plebe stumbled or hesitated, or if the upperclassman was not happy with his demeanor—he could say, "Come see me." That was called a "Come Around," and it meant that the hapless plebe had to report in uniform to the upperclassman's room that evening to be subjected to more strenuous questioning and quite possibly some punishment.

Whatever that punishment might be, the worst aspect of it was that it took more time, and time was the most precious commodity of all. William "Lanny" Lanier from Birmingham, Alabama, who was destined to become the class poet laureate, put it this way: "No time to dress, no time to eat, no time to get from pressing here to urgent there, no time to read, no time to rest, no time to relax. No time ever to slip, stumble, or err."[7]

Of the 750 young men and boys who arrived that summer, 456 made it to graduation and earned a diploma, though not all of them received a commission. Thirty were designated as NPQ: not physically qualified, nearly all of them because their eyesight—20/20 upon arrival—had deteriorated, and perfect eyesight was a requirement for commissioning. Of those who did get commissions, 401 became US Navy ensigns and 25 others became second lieutenants in the US Marine Corps. By December 7, 1941, they had been commissioned officers for eighteen months and held positions of responsibility on battleships and cruisers, aircraft carriers and destroyers. Due to the emerging world conflict, theirs was the last prewar class to complete a four-year program.

When they arrived in Annapolis, they were filled with confidence and eagerness, innocents who embraced and internalized the conventional values of their era. Four years later, they graduated into a world already at war, and eighteen months after that, the war caught up with them. Four years of often brutal conflict challenged their received values and in many ways completed their transformation from ingenuous youths to hardened, wary adults. It also mirrored the country's transformation, for Americans would never again be quite as guileless as they were in the days before Pearl Harbor, confident of their unique place in the world and convinced that the broad oceans on both coasts provided both safety and security. As for the new midshipmen, most remained steadfast in their commitment to the virtues of duty, hard work, responsibility, compassion, and, despite the horrors and traumas of war, the essential goodness of humanity.

This book offers a pointillist view of many of the young men who made up that Naval Academy class. It is the story of a journey: of four transformative years at the Naval Academy, followed by four more annealing years in the cauldron of war. These young men were not the political leaders who contrived global strategy or the admirals and generals who orchestrated the war. They were the ones who stood the watch, flew the planes, conned the subs, and led their platoons onto enemy beaches. Seventy-six of them died in that war. It was the highest mortality rate of any class at either Annapolis or West Point in the history of those institutions. Their names are listed on the dedication page.

This book is for them.

PART I

Midshipmen

The questions asked by the upper-classmen must be considered as orders to find the answers. The knowledge you thus acquire will be of value to you.

—*Reef Points*, 1936

I

Appointment

In the United States of the 1930s, graduating from high school was a notable achievement—only about half of Americans managed to do so—and in 1936, even those who reached that milestone faced grim prospects. With a fifth of the nation out of work, there were a dozen applicants for every job, and with no minimum wage, what few jobs there were seldom paid more than twenty-five cents an hour. The average annual salary that year was $500. And if jobs were scarce, the prospect of a college education was infinitesimal. Less than 5 percent of Americans went to college at all in 1936, and far fewer than that finished. Moreover, the cost of a college education put it beyond the reach of all but the privileged few.[1]

In March 1933, during the depth of the Depression, a new president, Franklin Roosevelt, had sought to lift the spirts of a demoralized America by asserting, "The only thing we have to fear"—then pausing for effect—"is fear itself: nameless, unreasoning, unjustified terror." The words helped, and some of the programs he initiated helped, too. Despite the president's defiant cheerleading, however, the Depression ground on relentlessly. Three years later, the mood in the country had indeed shifted, but only from fear and terror to a kind of glum resignation.

In that environment, an appointment to either the Military Academy at West Point or the Naval Academy at Annapolis offered an escape for the new high school graduates by providing free room and board, a college education, prestige, security, and a career. The competition for such an opportunity was fierce, and for most it required a nomination from a sitting congressman or senator. A generation earlier, and throughout the nineteenth century, obtaining an appointment had often been a matter of family connections. Friends of a congressman, political supporters, or the sons of generous donors expected—and often received—special consideration. Even in the 1930s, there were a few congressmen who still used appointments to West Point or Annapolis as a way to reward friends and supporters. The problem with doing so was that while it might please one or two stalwart supporters, it left many more disappointed—even resentful. So, by 1936, most congressmen determined their selections by sponsoring a written examination and then appointing the individual who received the highest score. That allowed him to spread his hands at the disappointed aspirants and insist that it was beyond his control. Even with a congressional appointment in hand, however, an applicant still had to pass the Academy's own admissions test: a six-part ordeal that included English, US and ancient history, algebra, geometry, and physics, though the Academy would waive the exam if the nominated candidate had successfully completed a year or more at an accredited college or university.[2]

Most aspirants, therefore, had to take—and pass—two exams: one to win the nomination from his district and then another for admission to the Academy. Given that, candidates who were serious about it—and who could afford it—often enrolled first at one of several privately run prep schools that existed specifically to prepare young men (and in 1936 they were all men) for the Academy exams. It was something of a gamble: paying fees to a prep school for a year in the hope that it would result in a four-year education at government expense.

Another route to the academies was through the enlisted ranks. The controlling statute allotted one hundred appointments each year to enlisted men from the navy and Marine Corps, and another twenty-five to members of the Navy or Marine Corps Reserves, though they had to have joined up at least a year prior to their appointment. Consequently, some aspirants for the academies who signed up for a prep school also joined the reserves in the hope of increasing their chances. And finally, there were a handful of *presidential* appointments for those candidates who were not represented by a congressman or a senator (such as residents of the District of Columbia) as well as for the sons of soldiers, sailors, and marines who had been killed in the Great War.

During the summer of 1936, thousands of hopefuls—in high schools, in colleges, and in uniform—sought to navigate this maze of opportunities and pitfalls, in the hope of grasping the golden ticket to either West Point or Annapolis.[3]

Some had a leg up. Though family influence was no longer a guaranteed path to appointment, it could still play a role, as was evident in the application odyssey of sixteen-year-old Philip Glennon of Washington, DC. Young for his grade with a plain open face and prominent ears, Glennon was perceived as "quiet and sincere" by his peers. Because he was a resident of the District, he needed a

APPOINTMENT 5

presidential appointment, and to get it he benefited from family connections. His father was Navy Captain Harrison Glennon (Naval Academy, 1911), and his uncle was Captain James Blair Glennon (class of 1909). Even more importantly, his grandfather was Rear Admiral James Henry Glennon (class of 1878). It also did not hurt that Glennon's aunt was the daughter of war hero and former Marine Corps Commandant John A. Lejeune (Naval Academy class of 1888). And finally, both of his older brothers were already at the Academy in the classes of 1937 and 1938, and his cousin was in the class of 1939. Given all that, young Phil never really had much of a choice about where he would go to college. From earliest boyhood, he later wrote, "The only place I wanted to go to college was the Naval Academy. It was only a matter of whether or not I could get in."[4]

Glennon's grandfather helped see to that by sending him to what he considered the best of the prep schools: Columbian Prep, in Washington, DC. To attend Columbian Prep, Philip, along with two other Academy aspirants, boarded in his grandfather's house, attending classes by day and receiving private lessons from the admiral by night. Admiral Glennon was an expert on ballistics, about which he had written a book, and he grilled Philip nightly on the physics of gunnery, among other things.

Glennon and the two other boarders took the Academy exam that spring, and he was both excited and relieved to learn that their scores earned all three of them presidential appointments. As it turned out, the other boys also won the competitive exams in their districts, which they accepted, so in the end Glennon was the only one of the three who used his presidential appointment.

He was thrilled. "I had taken the first step toward achieving the only goal I had in life," he wrote, "becoming a naval officer." There was a recalled hint of uncertainty, however—perhaps even trepidation—in his next comment: "I was young, having just turned 17 in February of that year, and very impressionable."[5]

Other candidates had no connection to the navy at all—some had never heard of the Naval Academy, and simply hoped for a college education. At first glance, Robert Harris seemed an unlikely candidate. His passions were music and books, and he was something of an idealist, convinced that global unity could end all wars and introduce an era of world peace. Graduating in 1934 near the top of his class from Mount Lebanon High School in a suburb of Pittsburgh, he was both an excellent student and a pretty good athlete, and he was determined to go to college. He was grateful when his father took out a

6   ANNAPOLIS GOES TO WAR

loan from the local bank so he could enroll at the University of Pittsburgh. Living at home and commuting into the city each day, he earned high grades at Pitt, but the financial strain proved unsustainable.[6]

One day during his second year at college, his father told him he had read in the paper that if he got into the Naval Academy, all his college expenses would be paid by the government. Harris knew nothing about the Naval Academy, but, as he noted, "The price was right." An additional enticement was that it offered a chance to escape the small town where he had grown up and still lived. "Mount Lebanon was a very nice place," he recalled, "but there was a big wide world out there!" So, after two years at Pitt, he decided to try for an appointment to the Naval Academy.

Aware that he needed a congressional appointment, Harris began by trying to meet with his congressman, Benjamin Focht. That proved difficult. He made many trips to the congressman's office, but never found him. He then sought to track him down at his known haunts, which included a popular local restaurant and—despite the fact that Focht claimed membership in the Prohibition Party—his favorite bar. Harris never did find Focht, though he did manage to sign up for the competitive exam. He felt confident in both math and science, which he had studied at Pitt. However, he hadn't taken a history course since the ninth grade, so he borrowed a history textbook from his uncle and studied it zealously. It paid off, for not only did he score the highest grade on the exam, he did especially well in history, which put him over the top. He became Focht's nominee, and because of his grades at Pitt he did not need to take the Academy exam.[7]

Similar circumstances brought John William Myers Montgomery to the Naval Academy. Montgomery—most often called "Myers"—was from the small (population two thousand) town of Malden in the southeast "bootheel" of Missouri, ten miles from the Arkansas border. He attended public school in the same two-story brick building from elementary school through high school. Like Robert Harris, he was not especially drawn to things nautical or martial. His interests were music, journalism, typing (he won the county typing championship), and especially photography (he won a national award for a photograph he took at the Chicago World's Fair in 1933). The only quasi-martial activity that interested him was the Boy Scouts, into which he threw himself with enthusiasm. He was a founding member of the local troop, earned seventy-six merit badges, and became an Eagle Scout with both bronze and gold palms. Late in life, when asked what he considered his greatest

APPOINTMENT 7

accomplishment, he answered at once that it was being an Eagle Scout. Having skipped two grades, he graduated from high school at sixteen, the youngest member of his class, and got a music scholarship to Southwest Missouri State Teachers College, twenty-five miles north of Malden in Cape Girardeau, where he played saxophone in the marching band and the school symphony. After class, Montgomery worked at the local Boy Scout office.

It was his father who suggested that he might look into the Naval Academy. The younger Montgomery welcomed the idea, and his father wrote their congressman, Orville Zimmerman, to submit his son's "qualifications and record for your consideration." Zimmerman named young Myers as the second alternate, and when the two ahead of him dropped out, Montgomery got the appointment. He was grateful, dutifully writing the congressman to thank him "very much for the appointment affording me this wonderful opportunity."[8]

Robert Weatherup of Watertown, New York, was a handsome young man with a Cary Grant cleft in his chin who had quite specific motives for applying to the Academy. He wanted to fly. He was ten years old in 1927 when Charles Lindbergh made headlines by flying solo from New York to Paris. Weatherup acknowledged that part of his fascination with aviation was "hero worship," but he was also interested in the science of flight, the impact it was likely to have on the future, and of course, the adventure of it, which he saw as "a new medium for men to demonstrate their skill and courage." From his earliest memory, he wrote later, "I wanted to be a pilot!" Since army aviation was then still in its infancy—its future uncertain—he believed his best opportunity to learn to fly, and be paid for it, was in the navy. After all, it was a navy team that had first flown across the Atlantic (with one stop in the Azores) in 1919, thus paving the way for Lindbergh's solo fight eight years later. Then, too, like Robert Harris, an additional incentive was that "The Navy also offered the best chance to 'see the world.'"

Rather than seek immediate admission, however, Weatherup sought to pad his résumé by enrolling first at St. Lawrence University in 1935. He did well in math and physics, though he was weaker in English and history. Still, his grades were good enough that he could expect the Academy to accept his college transcript in lieu of taking the entrance examination, if he could secure the necessary appointment. In pursuit of that, he signed up for his congressman's competitive exam for both West Point and Annapolis. He scored the highest mark on both and opted at once for the Naval Academy.[9]

Ray Hundevadt was no Cary Grant, and he had no particular interest in flying. It was the ships that fascinated him. If Bob Weatherup remembered 1927 as the year Lindbergh flew the Atlantic, nine-year-old Hundevadt remembered it as the year the US Navy's battleship fleet visited New York City. He learned about it from his father, who told him that, according to the local newspaper, the visiting navy ships would anchor in the Hudson River the following day and remain there for twelve days. Since it was only a few miles from the Hundevadt home in Bergen, New Jersey, Ray got up early the next morning and rode his bicycle to the Jersey Palisades.

And there they were: six big battleships anchored from Sixty-Fourth Street all the way up to Ninety-Sixth Street. Eighteen sleek destroyers were moored off Staten Island. It was a vista Hundevadt never forgot. As he watched, small boats motored back and forth between the ships, and from the ships to the shore. He tried to imagine what important missions activated their movements. He watched all afternoon, and he came back again the next day. "I would sit there for hours," he recalled, "totally absorbed." One day as he watched, it was evident that the big ships were getting under way. Black smoke billowed from their stacks; the battleships raised their anchors; the destroyers cast off their lines and eased out into the stream. And down the river they went, "down past the ferry boats and the Statue of Liberty." He watched until they were gone from sight. For years afterward, he talked of nothing but the Naval Academy. His father, who knew the local congressman, secured him an appointment, and Hundevadt figured his future was set.[10]

Then he failed the entrance exam. It was, he acknowledged later, "a rude awakening." And despite his years-long goal, he concluded that it was not meant to be. So, after graduating from high school in 1934, he enrolled at Rutgers, forty miles to the south. There he took general engineering classes, joined the water polo team, and got a girlfriend. "Life," he decided, "was just fine."

Until it wasn't. Like Robert Harris, Hundevadt learned from his father during his second year of college that the family had run out of money. He had a choice to make: There was money enough for either one more year at Rutgers or for one year at a prep school where he could try to improve his score on the Academy entrance exam. He opted for the prep school.

The school was in a private home on East Seventy-Fifth Street in New York City, and Hundevadt commuted there every day. There were fifteen other aspirants at the school, and he knew the competition would be fierce. So, to give him one more route to admission, he enlisted in the Navy Reserves. While

APPOINTMENT 9

taking classes at the prep school, he also attended weekly drills of his Navy Reserve unit. In the summer, he took a two-week cruise on the battleship *Arkansas*. This time, instead of watching from the Palisades as the battleships headed out to sea, he was on board one of them as it streamed past the Statue of Liberty and turned north toward Halifax, Nova Scotia. It was a working cruise and not a pleasure trip, but it did nothing to dampen his enthusiasm for a life at sea.[11]

Hundevadt's father convinced the congressman to give his son another shot at the exam. As Ray was completing the forms to take it, he saw that his academic record at Rutgers was enough—he didn't have to take the exam. With an appointment in hand, and his grades from Rutgers, he was in.

John Lacouture (pronounced LOCK-a-tur) was a child of privilege with movie star looks. The scion of a prosperous and well-connected Boston family with a summer home in Hyannisport, he attended the prestigious Roxbury Latin School, founded in 1634, the oldest private school in the country. Lacouture was in the ninth grade there in 1931 when his family took a vacation to Newport, Rhode Island. There he saw a navy battleship floating majestically in Narragansett Bay, and decided at once that the Naval Academy was for him. The curriculum at Roxbury Latin School was a classical one, with an emphasis on Greek and Latin texts, and he knew that his mastery of the ancient languages would be little help on the Academy entrance exam. So, like Weatherup and Hundevadt, he enrolled in an Academy prep school. In his case, it was Randle's Annapolis Prep on N Street in Washington, DC, not far from DuPont Circle. And to improve his odds, he, too, enlisted in the Navy Reserves. It was a shock when the Reserves rejected him. Lacouture had an overbite—officially a "malocclusion"—and the Navy declared him NPQ (not physically qualified). Distraught, he turned to the marines, who, as it turned out, were happy to have him. So, after graduation from Roxbury Latin, he headed down to Quantico, Virginia, for boot camp. It was, in his understated phrase, "an eye-opening experience."

After boot camp, Lacouture went directly to Randle's prep school, where the method of instruction was straightforward: drill, drill, drill, or as Lacouture put it: "frequency, recency, and intensity." That, plus the study habits he had internalized at Roxbury Latin, allowed him to earn the highest score on his congressman's district exam in October. Having secured an appointment, he could have left Randle's at once, but the school administrator asked him to stay until the spring and take the national exam given to all navy and Marine Corps reservists. The schoolmaster hoped that Lacouture's score would raise the average of his students and enhance the reputation of his school. Lacouture agreed to do it, and in April 1936 he tied one other candidate for the highest score in the country. He turned down the presidential appointment that came with it, however, accepting instead the one from his congressman because, as he said later, it made room "for another hard-working reserve to get in."[12]

Some members of the class of 1940 stumbled on the opportunity by mere chance, or through the agency of patrons and benefactors. Richard Robert Dupzyk, called "RR" by his friends, grew up near Sacramento in California's Central Valley. Like Myers Montgomery, he skipped two grades and completed high school at sixteen in 1933. He then enrolled in Sacramento Junior College, where he took courses in chemistry, physics, and calculus. Though he aced all of them, he did not think he was getting an education, or at least not the education he wanted. His goal was to go to the University of California at Berkeley. Tuition at Berkeley was free for California residents, but RR would have to live away from home and pay for his books and his meals. So he hatched a plan to save money by enlisting in the navy. He calculated that if he served a two-year hitch and saved every dollar, he would have enough money to get through four years of college.[13]

He joined the navy in 1934, and after boot camp the navy sent him to the battleship *Oklahoma*. What happened next was pure serendipity. He was polishing brass one Friday afternoon, an unremitting activity on a peacetime warship—especially a battleship—when "the white shoes and white trousers of an officer's uniform" intruded on his peripheral vision. He jumped to his feet, squared his hat, and saluted. It was the junior officer of his division who told him: "They are giving exams for the Naval Academy tomorrow. I've looked over your record and you might make it. Why not go down and take the examination." One thing Dupzyk had learned in the navy was that when your officer made a suggestion, there was only one reply: "Aye aye, sir." Then he went back to polishing the brightwork.[14]

He showed up for the exam the next day, still not sure what it was for. The officer in charge told him it was "to select those who would attend a five-month Naval Academy preparatory course to take the Naval Academy Entrance Examinations in the spring of 1936." That didn't make things much clearer. Dupzyk had never heard of the "Naval Academy," and because he was working toward a rating as an electrician's mate, he thought it might be some sort of electrician's school. Still, he applied himself to the exam, passed it, and received orders to report to the navy's prep school in Norfolk, Virginia. There, for the

APPOINTMENT 11

first time in his life, he had to focus seriously on his studies, and in the end he was one of fifty-eight enlisted men admitted to the Naval Academy for the class of 1940.[15]

Ralph Paul Desmond, who went by his middle name, took a similar route. Another Californian, from San Francisco, Desmond remembered watching the big navy ships sailing under the Golden Gate Bridge when it was still under construction (it opened for traffic in 1937). After he graduated from high school in 1934, he went to work on the San Francisco docks as a stevedore. Though he was small of stature and weighed only 150 pounds, he spent six days a week unloading 110-pound sacks of sugar for sixty cents an hour. There were no hydraulic forklifts then, and Desmond humped those sacks on his back for ten hours a day. After six months of that, he decided that unless he wanted to do that for the rest of his life or until his body broke down, "I had better get some more education." Despite indifferent high school grades, he wrote to his congressman and to both of his senators to ask about an appointment to the Naval Academy. They didn't even answer.[16]

Desmond learned from the navy recruiter, however, that it was sometimes possible to gain entrance to the Academy as an enlisted man, so in May 1935 he joined the navy. After boot camp in San Diego, he was one of twenty recruits who reported aboard the battleship USS *Maryland*. When the new recruits lined up aboard ship, the junior officer of the deck, Ensign Jim Brown, himself a 1935 Annapolis grad, asked if any of them were interested in going to the Naval Academy. Ten hands shot up, including Paul's. Brown looked at the group and then, with no explanation of why, pointed to three of them: "You, you, and you." The last of them was Desmond. "Report to the F-Division." When Desmond had a chance to think about it later, he wondered if the criteria Brown had used was height. Brown, who was only about five foot five himself, may simply have picked the three shortest men. Whether or not that was the case, for Desmond it was a life-changing moment.[17]

Ensign Brown organized what amounted to an on-board prep school for the Academy exam. Other junior officers pitched in, among them Ensign Noel Gayler (subsequently a four-star admiral and director of the National Security Agency). They held classes five days a week, two hours in the morning and two more in the evening after the workday. Classes were suspended for any all-hands evolution, such as provisioning ship or loading munitions, but day by day, week, by week, Desmond and a handful of others got the education they had failed to get in high school.

That fall, when the *Maryland* put into the Bremerton Navy Yard in Puget Sound for a refit, eight products of Ensign Brown's ersatz prep school took the Naval Academy entrance exam. Five of them passed it, including Desmond. Soon afterward, he received orders to report to Annapolis.

He traveled by train. Trains and buses were the only practical forms of cross-country travel then—flying was for the privileged few. The train's passenger cars were not air conditioned, and Desmond remembered that "if you opened a window, you got a face full of cinders." So he leaned on his elbow and looked out the window at the countryside. After passing through the Bitterroot Mountains, the Pacific Northern ran on a long, straight stretch of track through Montana and North Dakota. It was the height of the "dust bowl," and the weather-beaten cabins of farmers were cheerless and dispiriting. One image in particular remained with him for the rest of his life: a string of clothes flapping forlornly in the dust outside an isolated and unpainted wooden farmhouse on the wide prairie. Sleeping intermittently (and uncomfortably) in his seat, he arrived in Baltimore four days later.[18]

Desmond remembered the Baltimore train station as an unsavory place and was glad to board the Washington, Baltimore, and Annapolis spur, the W. B. and A. (or as the midshipmen dubbed it, the "Wobble, Bounce, and Amble"). Arriving in Annapolis, he walked the short distance to the Academy, very likely carrying his seabag. He was temporarily berthed aboard the Academy's station ship *Reina Mercedes*, a relic from the Spanish-American War, and sworn in as a midshipman along with several others on July 4, 1936.

Late as he was, Desmond was not the last member of the class of 1940 to arrive in Annapolis. Another late arrival was Michael Joseph Hanley Jr. of Washington, DC, who, because he was a "junior" went by his middle name, Joe. The six-foot, two-inch Hanley had been named the center on Washington's all-city basketball team in 1935. He was also an academic star at Western High School, earning nearly all A's. In addition to that, he was the number-two ranking cadet officer in the citywide corps of cadets. His goal was to attend West Point. He told a reporter from the *Washington Post* that he had wanted to attend West Point "ever since I can remember." His uncle, as it happened, was a friend of the Naval Academy's football coach, Lieutenant Tom Hamilton, and he urged his nephew to travel the twenty miles or so over to Annapolis to talk with him first.[19]

Neither West Point nor the Naval Academy recruited athletes in the days before college sports became big business. The academies did well in college athletics simply because they were populated by hundreds of physically fit and

APPOINTMENT 13

disciplined young men, most of whom had been high school athletes. Of course, coaches at both academies were happy to encourage particularly talented athletes to try to be admitted, though they had to meet the same academic requirements as everyone else, including passing the competitive exams.

When Joe Hanley met with Lieutenant Hamilton, the officer made him no promises, though he did say that he thought Hanley would have a better chance of getting into the Naval Academy if he first enlisted in the reserves. Thus encouraged, Hanley turned down a scholarship to Catholic University and, on his seventeenth birthday, enlisted in the Marine Corps Reserves.

The marines sent him to boot camp at Quantico, where he met John Lacouture, who was there on the same mission. After two weeks of stressful indoctrination, both Hanley and Lacouture headed up to Washington to Randle's Prep School. They were among the five hundred or so reservists nation-wide who took the exam that spring, only the top twenty-five of whom would be offered an appointment. As we have seen, Lacouture tied for the highest score in the nation, and Hanley placed thirty-third. That was certainly a creditable perfor-mance out of five hundred, but he missed getting an appointment by eight places.

Then others began to drop out. Some, like John Lacouture, accepted other appointments; some decided the Academy was not for them after all; a few failed the physical. Slowly, one by one, Hanley moved up the list. As he remem-bered it, "I entered the Academy as the 25th and final selection from the reserves in late July 1936."[20]

One candidate for the class of 1940 who commanded particular attention and scrutiny was James Lee Johnson Jr., who was Black. Or at least he was "Black" by the standards of 1936, which is to say he had some African American ances-tors. With his light skin and short haircut, he was all but indistinguishable from the sandy-haired white midshipmen who made up the rest of the class. Inconspicuous as he was, word of his presence got around, and many of his classmates—especially those from the South—were horrified. To them, his presence corrupted and contaminated the whole class.

Johnson was not the first Black midshipman admitted to the Academy. More than half a century earlier, in 1872, during Reconstruction, a Black congressman from South Carolina, Robert B. Elliott, had appointed James H. Conyers to Annapolis. Conyers was only sixteen years old and barely five feet, three inches tall. Academy authorities sought to protect him from the worst of the physical hazing, even dismissing a dozen white midshipmen who were found guilty of physically assaulting him. In the end, it was a more subtle kind of abuse that drove Conyers out. He was shunned by his classmates, and the cumulative psychological pressure wore him down. At the end of two brutal years, he was found "academically deficient" and dismissed.[21]

A year later, in 1873, a different Black congressman appointed another Black candidate to the Academy. That candidate, Alonzo McClennan, was blond-haired and blue-eyed, but he was nevertheless "Black" by the nineteenth-century "one drop" rule. His classmates had no idea of his race until it was published in the newspapers. Then, like Conyers, he was shunned and driven out. He later graduated from Howard University Medical School and became a practicing physician in Charleston, where the McClennan-Banks Hospital was named for him.[22]

A third Black candidate, Henry E. Baker, arrived the next year. Isolated like the others, he was also attacked with barrel staves by two southern-born classmates for daring to speak to them. The two white midshipmen were dismissed, though one of them was later reinstated and eventually became a rear admiral. Baker, on the other hand, was expelled for allegedly calling another midshipman a "god damned son of a bitch." After that, and for the next sixty-two years—that is, from the end of Reconstruction to the onset of the Great Depression—no other Black candidate was admitted to the Naval Academy—until the arrival of James Lee Johnson Jr. in June 1936.[23]

Johnson was there because Congressman Arthur W. Mitchell of Chicago, at that time the only Black member of Congress, had made it a particular goal to find and enroll qualified Black applicants for both West Point and the Naval Academy. Benjamin O. Davis, later the US Army's first Black general, graduated from West Point that year, and Mitchell nominated two other Black men (George A. Johnson and Robert M. Jones) for the West Point class of 1940. For the Naval Academy, he looked outside the district and indeed outside the state. Mitchell worried that the segregated and underfunded Black schools in South Chicago did not prepare young men for the rigorous entrance exam at the Naval Academy, so he looked to Dunbar High School in Washington, DC, widely held to be the best Black high school in the country. At Dunbar, Johnson's nickname had been "Socks" for Socrates, and after graduating with honors in 1933, he had spent three years at Case Institute of Technology (now Case Western Reserve University) in Cleveland, where he took mostly technical courses. Because of the Academy policy that a congressionally nominated candidate with satisfactory marks at a reputable college did not have to take the entrance exam, Johnson was sure to be admitted as long as he passed the physical. But would he accept?[24]

Johnson had been enamored of ships and boats most of his life. He had built model ships as a boy and aspired to a career as a naval architect. When Mitchell's

APPOINTMENT

representative contacted him in Cleveland to ask if he would accept an appointment to the Naval Academy, he agreed. He would have to start college all over again, he knew, and he also knew it would be challenging personally, but he believed he could handle it and that it was his duty to represent his race. So, on June 15, 1936, James Lee Johnson Jr. was one of fifty-two new appointees who showed up at the Naval Academy.[25]

There was one other person of color in the class: Abraham Campo, who was Filipino. Campo graduated second in his high school class in Manila in 1935 and was awarded a one-year scholarship to the University of the Philippines. At the end of that year, he applied to the Philippine Military Academy in Baguio. In the Philippines, as in the United States, admission required an appointment from the local assemblyman. Campo dutifully walked the four miles to his assemblyman's office, waited there in vain all day, and then walked back again. He returned the next day with similar results. After a week of disappointment, he gave up. Then, a few days later, a friend invited him to the movies. The film was *Shipmates Forever*, a sappy 1935 musical in which an aspiring singer (Dick Powell) tries to prove to his father, a navy admiral and the Academy superintendent, that he could make it at the Naval Academy. Ruby Keeler provided the love interest. A number of scenes featured midshipmen marching through the impressive grounds of the Academy, though it was not especially realistic about Academy life. For one thing, Dick Powell spent a lot of time singing and Ruby Keeler dancing. Inspired nonetheless, Campo subsequently learned that one spot at the Naval Academy was reserved for a Filipino national each year. He would not be eligible for a US Navy commission, but he would get a diploma. Campo decided to take the exam. Afterward, the five individuals with the highest scores—including Campo—were invited to report to the Cavite Navy Yard near Manila to be interviewed. The authorities wanted to ensure that whoever was picked would be a good representative of the Philippines. Despite running a high fever—or maybe because of it—Campo answered all the questions (in his words) "jubilantly and creditably," and was selected.[26]

Thus, in the summer of 1936, as civil war broke out in Spain, and Stalin began the Great Purge in the Soviet Union, as Japanese troops consolidated their control of Manchuria, and Italian troops goosestepped through Abyssinia, 750 members of the US Naval Academy class of 1940, each with his own personal odyssey, prepared to embark on their great adventure, which would begin with an ordeal called Plebe Summer.

2

Plebe Year

The new plebes did not arrive all at once. In later years, the members of each new class would show up on the same day—Induction Day, or I-Day—and be sworn in as a group. But in 1936 the new midshipmen arrived serially in groups of ten or a dozen, even individually, all through early June and into August. The official induction date was June 15, and one large group of fifty-two did arrive on that date. Their experience was a template of the reception everyone got, even if it was not simultaneous.

It was hot in Annapolis on June 15, as it often was in midsummer. The thermometer topped out at 87 degrees, a damp, sticky 87 due to the humidity that was—and is—characteristic of Annapolis summers. (One new plebe from New Hampshire found the climate "almost unbearable.") The new arrivals looked about themselves and at one another with varying degrees of curiosity, anticipation, and trepidation. Some had never seen the Academy until this moment, the grounds of which were called not a "campus," but "the Yard"—as if it were, actually and not just metaphorically, a Navy Yard.[1]

The Yard was arranged in a triangle that was symbolic of the component parts of a midshipman's experience. To the east, toward the Severn River, was the sprawling stone edifice of Bancroft Hall, which, according to *Reef Points*, was "the largest unit dormitory in the world." It had been designed by the New York–born, Paris-educated architect Ernest Flagg in the Beaux Arts style and dedicated thirty years earlier in 1906, though two "new" wings had been added in 1920. Named for Secretary of the Navy (and historian) George Bancroft, who had presided over the founding of the Naval Academy in 1845, it encompassed twenty acres of floor space and included a tailor shop, barbershop, laundry, post office, and mess hall. It was, *Reef Points* declared proudly, "a miniature community." It was there that for the next four years the members of the class of 1940 would sleep, eat, study, and learn, not only the academic subjects but also about each other and, critically, about themselves.[2]

PLEBE YEAR

Three hundred yards to the west, across an expanse of grass shaded by a score of mature oak, buckeye, and holly trees, was a group of three more gray stone buildings, arranged in a U shape, that housed the academic classrooms: Maury Hall, where English, history, and government (E, H, & G) classes were held; Sampson Hall, which hosted natural philosophy and science classes; and Mahan Hall, which had a large auditorium on the ground floor and the Academy's library on the second floor. Beyond Mahan Hall were two more gray stone buildings, Isherwood and Griffin Halls, where engineering classes were held. These academic buildings were linked to Bancroft Hall by Stribling Walk, named for Cornelius Stribling, who had been the third superintendent at the Academy in the 1850s. (Upperclassman: "How many bricks are there in Stribling Walk?" Plebe: "Sir, there are 11,880 bricks in Stribling Walk, sir!")

The third vertex in the architectural geography was the Chapel, whose dome rose 210 feet from aisle to cupola and which, along with the steeples of the Maryland State Capitol and St. Mary's Catholic Church, dominated the Annapolis skyline. Religious services were still mandatory in 1936, and midshipmen marched, company by company, carrying their guide-on flags, to services every Sunday morning in their dress-blue uniforms. The services were high-church Episcopalian, which Baptists, Methodists, and other Protestants were simply expected to tolerate. Catholics and Jews were allowed to go into town to attend services of their choice.

The arrangement of these three sets of buildings was intentionally allegorical. In addition to athletics, it represented the divergent aspects of Academy life. In Bancroft Hall, discipline and professionalism dominated, with plebes required to square their corners (calling out "Beat Army!" as they did) and brace to attention on command as they responded to questions barked at them by upperclassmen. In the academic buildings at the other end of Stribling Walk, they were encouraged to solve problems, think, and even ask questions, though there, too, the emphasis was on rote learning rather than philosophical musing. The Chapel represented the spiritual strength that all midshipmen were expected to internalize and exhibit.

Upon their arrival in the Yard, the new plebes were first directed to Dahlgren Hall, a large, all-purpose building that was adjacent to Bancroft Hall. Named for a Civil War admiral who had specialized in ordnance, it housed several large naval weapons that were used in teaching gunnery. It was also where basketball games were played and the site of formal and informal dances—called hops. On June 15, the new arrivals dutifully lined up outside that building in front of a pair of heavy glass doors, sweating in their civilian clothes, many of them carrying suitcases that would soon prove entirely superfluous. The moment they passed through those doors into the cavernous expanse of Dahlgren Hall, they were met by second class midshipmen (third-year students) who took swift control, barking out orders: "Toe that line!" "Stand up straight!" "No talking!" "Eyes front!" Though these supervisors were only two years away from being plebes themselves, they exuded an authoritative (and, to some, intimidating) bearing. They hustled the new plebes from one station to another, shouting orders almost continuously.

The first stop was a phalanx of barbers, who performed what one new plebe called "tonsorial catastrophe": applying electric clippers to give every new plebe a buzz cut and leaving piles of hair on the floor continuously swept up by enlisted sailors. Then, at one station after another, they were handed a dizzying amount of gear: a half-dozen uniforms consisting of white trousers and a middy blouse; a raincoat and overshoes; six sheets, three bedspreads, and two blankets; a wastebasket, broom, soap, towels, shirts, collars, ties, and a gym outfit, plus a laundry bag, which they used to carry everything else. The cost of all these items would be deducted over the next year from their meager pay, which the midshipmen called their "monthly insult." It felt like "mass confusion," especially because the constant orders echoed off the high, rounded ceiling. ("That's *not* a ceiling, plebe, it's an overhead!") In addition to the shouting, there was a "constant ringing of bells, and people running about to and fro." It may have seemed chaotic, but the frenzied environment was deliberate and carefully choreographed, designed to mark the sharp break from easygoing civilian life to the strict discipline of the Academy.[3]

Relieved of their suitcases, which were eventually sent to their home address, the new plebes stuffed their new paraphernalia into their laundry bags. Then, "loaded like mules" and urged on by the second classmen, they ran with the laundry bags bouncing on their backs to their assigned rooms in Bancroft Hall. The rooms were pretty bleak: "a rough wooden table...a sad white chandelier...two unpainted wooden chairs...two iron bedsteads...and two coffin-like clothes lockers." They were provided with brown cardboard stencils and ink and told to label all the gear they had just been issued, assisted in some cases by members of the class who had arrived earlier.[4]

Some handled this stressful metamorphosis better than others. Those who had endured Navy or Marine Corps boot camp were not especially intimidated. Ernest Peterson, from Council Bluffs, Iowa, who had spent a year as an enlisted sailor, thought "the yells, commands, and admonitions of lordly

Second Classmen could not begin to compare with the 'dressing down' delivered by an irate Drill Instructor." Indeed, those who had come from the fleet believed they had a great advantage over their classmates since they already knew the manual of arms, drill maneuvers, semaphore signaling, and other skills of Navy life. Others, including most of those who had one or more years of college, were mature enough not to take it all too seriously. Conrad Carlson, who had spent two years at Harvard, took it all in stride and thought it was "a marvelous adventure."[5]

For most, however, and especially those who had come straight from high school, it was a radical, even terrifying, adjustment. Four members of the class were still only sixteen, and for them the new environment was a dizzying sequence of rules to remember—and recite on demand—as well as the inevitable punishment if they confessed ignorance. ("Sir, I will find out, sir!") One of the sixteen-year-olds was Albert H. "Pat" Clancy of Albuquerque, New Mexico, who, only a few days after arriving, noted forlornly in his diary: "Scared, lost, and homesick." Though physical punishment had largely been banned, upperclassmen were still authorized to "swat" an offending plebe with the broom (mandatory equipment in every room). A more typical punishment, though, was "sitting on infinity," which involved assuming a sitting position, sometimes against a wall but always without a chair, until the offending plebe's quivering thigh muscles gave way. There was an endless sequence of "Yes, sir," "Aye aye, sir," and punitive pushups. Even John Lacouture, who had survived two weeks of Marine Corps basic training at Quantico found it "no fun."[6]

After they donned their white pullover uniform tops with their names and numbers now stenciled on the front, they were herded up a wide set of stone stairs to a large and magnificent room inside Bancroft Hall. It had a high ceiling and a hardwood floor buffed to a bright sheen. It was Memorial Hall (or Mem Hall, as they learned to call it) and hosted a marble case with the names of those graduates who had been killed in combat since 1845. They could not have known it, of course, but within a decade, scores of their own names would be included in that case. Lined up on the polished hardwood floor and all but indistinguishable from one another in their identical outfits and haircuts, they raised their right hands and swore to "support and defend the Constitution of the United States against all enemies foreign and domestic." When they shouted, "I do!" in unison, Commander Walter S. Delaney looked out at them and said: "Gentlemen, you have now joined the finest fraternity in the world: the United States Navy."[7]

Over the next six weeks, as more members of the class arrived to be greeted similarly, the plebes were kept busy—marching, standing at attention, sitting on infinity, and memorizing Navy lore from *Reef Points*. There were inspections almost every day. They learned that there was a prescribed way to do almost everything. "We had to learn a lot in a few short weeks," one recalled. "How to get out of bed and into the corridor in five seconds; how to shave, shower, shine, and shampoo in between formation and late bells." Another remembered that "it was an awful shock when we discovered that we didn't even know how to walk, and had to learn all over again."[8]

Indeed, it was the marching they remembered most. Day after day, week after week, they practiced close order drill: "eight men to a squad, four front rank and four rear, and four squads to a platoon." At first, they maneuvered by following footprints painted on the large concrete area, called "the grinder," adjacent to Thompson Stadium, where home football games were played.* Soon enough, though, they graduated to the grassy expanse of Worden Field, named for the Civil War captain who had commanded the USS *Monitor* against the Confederate *Merrimack* (or *Virginia*) in the Battle of Hampton Roads in 1862. Eventually, the maneuvers became habitual and instinctive: "Squads right!" and "Squads left!" It was tedious in the oppressive heat of an Annapolis summer. During the first full parade, eight plebes passed out flat on the turf and lay there like battle casualties. Yet Robert Harris, for one, felt "a feeling of pride and accomplishment" when his platoon executed a complex maneuver flawlessly. The second classmen who supervised them were determined that their charges would make a good showing when the first classmen (rising seniors) returned from their summer cruise in the fall.[9]

And of course, there was physical training, or PT: squats, sit-ups, pushups, and rope climbs, all conducted under the direction of a grizzled veteran named Manz, whose Brooklyn accent brought smiles to the plebes' faces despite their exhaustion, especially when Manz instructed "the thoid platoon of the foist company" to begin a particular exercise.[10]

Trips to the rifle range offered a welcome break. The rifle range was on the other side of the Severn River, so the plebes marched down to the sea wall, where they boarded fifty-foot motor launches. The cool sea breeze on the river offered a respite from the summer heat. Then as the boats approached the landing, the chief gunners mate instructed them: "Do not disembark until I say disembark, but when I say disembark, DISEMBARK!" At the range, they

---

* The concrete "grinder" occupied the ground where Halsey Field House stands today.

fired ancient 1903 Springfield bolt-action rifles that had been manufactured for the Philippine "insurrection" thirty years before and had been widely used in the First World War. The recoil from repeated shooting left most of the plebes with discernible bruises on their chins, and the occasional swollen lip or black eye.[11]

All midshipmen had to prove that they could swim by passing a test at the indoor pool in Macdonough Hall. One of the largest indoor pools in the country, it was a hundred feet long and sixty feet wide and had a uniform depth of ten feet. (Upperclassman: "How many gallons of water are in Macdonough Hall Natatorium?" Plebe: "Sir, I will find out, sir.") The plebes, fully dressed, had to tread water in the pool for fifteen minutes, then swim three lengths (one hundred yards) in a designated time. Growing up in the 1930s during the polio scare, many of their mothers had prohibited them from using community pools, and consequently a number of the plebes—even star athletes like Joe Hanley—could not swim. And many who could swim could not meet the time requirement. If they didn't pass the test, they were assigned to what was called the "sub squad" and required to devote an extra hour every evening to swimming instruction in an already crowded day.[12]

Far more pleasant were sailing lessons in the Academy's fleet of single-masted knockabouts, lessons that most found quite enjoyable. They also took dancing lessons since it was assumed that all young gentlemen should be able to acquit themselves on the dance floor. Midshipmen were expected to master the two-step, fox trot, and of course, the waltz, doing so by dancing with one another, which of course meant that half of them had to do it backward. With the passage of time, even the younger plebes adjusted to the schedule. Pat Clancy, who had pronounced himself "scared, lost, and homesick" on July 9, noted a month later: "homesick at first, but in the routine now." He turned seventeen on August 2 and shaved for the first time on August 9.[13]

In September, the first class midshipmen ("firsties," in the Academy vernacular) returned from their summer cruise and watched critically as the new plebes paraded before them, executed the manual of arms, and passed in review. The firsties were judging the second classmen who had run plebe summer as much as the plebes themselves. Grudgingly, they acknowledged that the new arrivals looked enough like midshipmen not to embarrass them. Still, they were determined to add their own heavy-handed harassment to the new arrivals. By tradition, each plebe was assigned to a particular first classman for indoctrination and instruction. Some of the firsties were protective—a kind of "sea daddy"—while others proved tyrannical. For the most part, however, the plebes learned that the hazing they had received so far paled next to the "the real hazing" that began with the return of the firsties. At any hour of the day or night, a firstie might barge into a plebe's room and demand forty pushups and forty pull-ups (to honor the class of 1940). If a plebe did not fulfill the demand to his complete satisfaction, the firstie could apply an equivalent number of "swats" to his posterior with the broom. Most of the plebes were philosophical about it. "The upperclassmen are not *too* hard on us," one wrote to his father. "Just hard enough to make us realize that all our life in the Navy we have to take orders from someone above us. . . . They're just breaking us in."[14]

There were occasional hijinks—expected when teenaged boys were crowded together, no matter how tired they were. On one occasion, a group of plebes unreeled the firehose in the passageway, pointed the nozzle in the door of the targeted room, and turned on the water. Another night, someone put a dead fish in a plebe's pillowcase. Both events led to early formation and threats from the authorities that they would stand at rigid attention all day until someone confessed, though no one did.[15]

Then classes began. Reformers, including Rear Admiral Thomas Hart, who had been superintendent from 1931 to 1934, had sought to introduce more humanities and literature into the curriculum. He increased the official percentage of time devoted to what the *Annual Register* called "so-called cultural subjects" from 21.6 percent to 31.6 percent. Hart's successor, Rear Admiral David Sellars, who was the superintendent when the Forties arrived, changed it back. Sellers insisted that any subject that took time away from professional training was a waste of valuable time. Consequently, the plebe curriculum in the fall of 1936 consisted of only five subjects: math, marine engineering (called "steam"), electrical engineering (called "wires" or "juice"), English and history (called "bull"), and foreign language, which regardless of the language was called "Dago." Everyone took the same courses and at the same level. There were no majors and no electives. The only choice they had was which foreign language they studied (French, Spanish, or German), and even then, in order to spread out the teaching load, midshipmen were "encouraged" to take a specific one. One member of the class expressed disappointment that "there seemed to be no encouragement for developing originality and adaptability to situations outside the Service," which is very likely exactly what Sellers had in mind.[16]

Some, especially those who had come straight from high school, found the academic material challenging, even daunting. Others who had taken the same or a similar course at another college or university found much of it redundant. Pat Clancy was delighted to discover that his math class was "precisely the same course that I had at the University of New Mexico with the same book." He found that academics were "not as bad as I expected." What bothered him was "the monotony of it." Conrad Carlson, who had been a math major at Harvard, thought "academics were a breeze." All he had to do was underline the key points in the text and review them before class.[17]

The civilian professors who taught math, foreign language, or English and history (which were combined into a single class) were often the object of amused commentary by the midshipmen. The plebes bestowed nicknames on many of them that supposedly reflected their personalities. There was the prim and proper "Scoutmaster," "Slip Stick Willie" (a whiz with the slide rule), "Pig Boat Bennie," and chain-smoking "Smokey Joe." Roughly half of the faculty was composed of serving officers who taught professional courses such as mechanical and electrical engineering and who wore uniforms: summer whites when classes began, then shifting into dress blues in the fall. A few of them got nicknames, too, such as "Altimeter Al," who taught ordnance.

The midshipmen were graded in every class every day. There were fifteen to eighteen students in each section, and a prescribed routine to most of the classes. It generally began with the instructor asking if anyone had a question about the assignment. If not, he would order them to "draw slips and man the boards." That meant they were to take a problem off the top of a stack on the instructor's desk, carry it to the chalkboard, and solve it (see frontispiece). The instructor observed passively while the student worked the problem and then explained it to the class. During his recitation, the instructor made enigmatic marks in his gradebook. It was more than a little intimidating since the instructors seldom revealed the grade assigned the student for the day. If the presentation went flawlessly, the student might hope to get a "forty" (4.0) or at least be "sat" (above 2.5), or he might "bilge" (any grade below 2.5). Not knowing how he had scored was frustrating. On one occasion, a professor told his class that someone in the section was "unsat," but he didn't say who, thereby encouraging study—or provoking alarm, or both.[18]

Robert Harris remembered being "a little surprised" by this "down-to-earth academic approach," so different from the kind of instruction he had received at the University of Pittsburgh. Others also chafed at the emphasis on rote learning, especially in math and engineering. Looking back on it at the end of his career, Bill Braybrook believed that a stronger emphasis on "teaching people to think" would have been better preparation for aspiring naval officers.[19]

After morning classes, they all marched back on Stribling Walk to Bancroft Hall for a communal lunch, then marched back again for afternoon classes. Late afternoons were reserved for physical activity, which meant practice with their chosen athletic team. Then they hit the showers and executed another uniform change for dinner.

Dinner was another trial. The plebes sat with their squad mates and their squad leader: a firstie who grilled them on their "rates," which included everything from the chain of command or the orders of the day to trivia from *Reef Points*. The plebes sat on the front six inches of their chairs with their backs straight and their "eyes in the boat," that is, staring straight ahead. Stewards (almost all of them Filipino) served the food on large trays, which the plebes then passed and served to the upperclassmen; they could not touch it themselves until the questioning was over. If the plebe got the question wrong or confessed ignorance, the upperclassman might tell him to "shove out." That meant pushing away from the table and sitting on air until the squad leader relented. If the squad leader was satisfied with their responses, he might tell them to "carry on." That did not mean they could slouch back in their chairs; it simply meant they could eat what was on offer, which often meant "sea gull" (chicken) that might be accompanied by "shiverin' Liz" (jello), or, if the jello was topped by whipped cream, "shiverin' Liz in a snowstorm." On those evenings when pie was the dessert, the plebes were expected to say, "Goodie, goodie, pie race." Then the squad leader would put a slice of pie on each of their plates, the plebes would put their hands behind their backs, and at the word "go!" bend forward to gobble their piece of pie. The first to finish and then successfully whistle, got "carry on" for the rest of the meal. At the end of the meal, the plebes asked permission to leave the table, and some squad leaders took the opportunity to ask a few more questions before telling them to "shove off."[20]

After dinner came study hours, during which the academically proficient, including many who had taken a particular course elsewhere, might assist those who were struggling. It was another element in the bonding process that turned seven hundred or so separate individuals into a cohesive group. "Lights out" was at 10:30, though many found ways to extend their study hours surreptitiously, after which quiet descended on Bancroft Hall until 6:30 the next morning, when it started all over again.[21]

So insistent were these quotidian demands that the new plebes were mostly oblivious to events outside the yellow brick walls of the Academy. In July, an attempted coup in Spain triggered a bloody civil war; in August, Jesse Owens won four gold medals in the Berlin Olympics, putting the lie to Hitler's claims of Aryan supremacy; in September, Hitler held a rally in Nuremberg to celebrate Germany's remilitarization of the Rhineland; and that same month, Josef Stalin began the Great Purge as his secret police (NKVD) began killing thousands of government officials or Army leaders whom Stalin suspected of disloyalty. In November, Franklin D. Roosevelt was re-elected to a second term as president in a record-breaking landslide. And throughout it all, life in "the Yard" continued its carefully prescribed course: reveille, formation, breakfast, class, lunch, athletics, dinner, study, lights out. Repeat.

Reef Points encouraged all new plebes to try out for an Academy sports team, cheerfully suggesting that the new plebes should "Come on out and try your hand." In fact, the culture of the institution made participation in sports all but mandatory. One mid insisted that "Athletics at the Academy are a fetish." The coaching staff looked over the new plebes as they arrived and encouraged likely prospects to try out for one team or another. The coaches were themselves mostly naval officers who rotated in and out, doing a three-year tour before going back to the fleet. That made it difficult, if not quite impossible, to build and sustain a long-term athletic program since it meant that a new coach had to start over from scratch every three years.[22]

Joe Hanley naturally signed up for basketball and was immediately elected captain of the plebe team. He was excited about its prospects, especially after the plebes beat the junior varsity in a scrimmage—or as Hanley put it, "We waxed them." That augured well for the coming season.[23]

Other plebes signed up for football, soccer, cross country, wrestling, crew, or boxing. Two members of the class showed special ability in football: Emmett Wood from Wilkinsburg, Pennsylvania, and Ulmont Whitehead, who had been a member of the class of 1939 but had been "turned back" for academics. John Lacouture, who had been a three-sport star at Roxbury Latin, also went out for football, though he weighed only 135 pounds and was cut from the team after only a few days. He next tried soccer and, no more successful there, joined the boxing team—until his nose was broken—then he went out for track. Bob Weatherup also joined the boxing team and stayed on it all four years, though he later acknowledged that his greatest contribution was allowing himself to be regularly pummeled by the others during practice. Pat Clancy, the homesick plebe from New Mexico, went out for cross country and discovered that he was good enough to remain on the team. "Quite unexpected success in Cross-Country," he wrote in his diary.

"Sure makes me feel good." Ray Hundevadt, who had played water polo at Rutgers, made the Navy team in that sport. Ernest Peterson, who had served on the battleship *Nevada* and had captained the ship's rowing team that competed with boats from other battleships, naturally decided that crew would be a good fit for him, but the coach took one look at his five-foot, ten-inch frame and excused him.[24]

Those, like Peterson, who did not make a varsity or junior varsity team joined one of the four battalion teams—what today would be called intramurals. Peterson acknowledged that rowing for the battalion team yielded less glory than varsity competition, but the races were fiercely contested and endowed the winners with bragging rights in the Hall.[25]

Varsity football games dominated the fall sports agenda, and the whole brigade of midshipmen turned out for them, not only for home games on Thompson Field but also away games at Harvard, Yale, and Princeton, Navy's traditional rivals. On Fridays before football games, the plebes were expected to show their spirit by standing on their chairs in the mess hall and singing or leading cheers. There was always a rally on Friday nights, and the next morning they all assembled in front of Bancroft Hall. If it was a home game, they marched, company by company, into Thompson Stadium behind Bancroft Hall. If it was an away game, they marched through the streets of Annapolis to the train station. They generally had box lunches on the train and after disembarking formed up again to march into the home team's stadium.[26]

The designated cheers printed in *Reef Points* were utterly unimaginative. One was "Ray! Ray! Ray! Team! Team! Team!" Another was "Whoop! Rah! Team!" There were also songs, the most ubiquitous of which is still sung by midshipmen today:

> The goat is old and gnarly,
> And he's never been to school,
> But he can take the bacon
> From the worn-out Army mule.[27]

In 1936, the game against Notre Dame was in Baltimore. Notre Dame was favored to win, but although the Fighting Irish had several first-and-goal opportunities, the Navy defense held, and Navy came away with a 3–0 upset victory. The midshipmen leaped out of the stands and stormed the field to tear down the goalposts. When the brigade re-boarded the train for the ride back to Annapolis, Emmett Wood climbed on board triumphantly carrying the large tin numeral 3 that he had taken from the scoreboard as a trophy.[28]

PLEBE YEAR

The big game, of course, was the annual match with Army, held in Philadelphia two days after Thanksgiving on November 28. From their very first day in Annapolis, the plebes had been reminded of the importance of the Army game, chanting "Beat Army!" every time they squared a corner in Bancroft Hall. More than bragging rights were on the line, for the plebes knew that if Navy won the game, they were likely to be released from many (if not all) of the humiliations of plebe life.

The game attracted national attention that year and had to be moved from Franklin Field at the University of Pennsylvania (capacity thirty thousand) to Municipal Stadium, which held one hundred thousand. In another tough defensive struggle, Navy won 7–0. To the ecstatic plebes, that meant they would have "carry on" until Christmas break. The plebes were so focused on the game and its outcome that few noticed that immediately adjacent to the newspaper account of the game in the *Philadelphia Inquirer*, Walter Lippmann discussed the "strange partnership" that was emerging between Germany and Japan. Lippmann wrote that "Japan is asking for control of China" and wondered if this was what Hitler had in mind for Poland. At the time, though, beating Army seemed far more important than events in China or Poland.[29]

By now, many—very likely most—of the plebes were homesick, even if they did not show it or admit it. They were young, after all—their average age was barely over eighteen, and many of them were still seventeen. And they were far from home, many for the first time. Abraham Campo, the Filipino national, was farthest from home, and R. R. Dupzyk, who befriended him, noted that Campo was "homesick, bewildered, and frightened" for much of the first term. Despite that, Dupzyk admired the fact that Campo "overcame each obstacle and grew in stature," partly because of strong support from his classmates.[30]

The plebes got leave for Christmas, and many of them—those who could afford it and were not on academic probation—actually did leave, going home for a glorious week away from the strictures of the Yard. Even those who stayed behind found that it was "peaceful and pleasant" in the Yard with nearly all of the upper class away. At least they got to sleep through reveille.

It was tough coming back, especially after scores of them almost immediately came down with the flu. Indeed, there were so many cases of flu in January 1937 that the hospital had to open extra rooms to hold them all. Most of the affected midshipmen spent the time there sleeping, and after a few days of rest, they were all "back in harness."[31]

One of the most memorable events of the year was marching in the parade for Franklin Roosevelt's second inauguration. It was the first time the inauguration took place on January 20 instead of March 4. Rain was predicted, but Academy authorities wanted to ensure that the midshipmen made a smart impression, so instead of the nondescript raincoats, they mandated bridge coats as the uniform of the day. These were heavy, wool overcoats with two rows of bright gold buttons down the front, which made a splendid show.

The midshipmen boarded a train for the short trip to the nation's capital, then disembarked into a freezing rain and waited in the staging area for over two hours for the parade to begin. As one remembered it, they "stood, and stood, and stood." Every fifteen minutes or so, "We would be called to attention, right shoulder our rifles, and march 2–3 minutes then stop again." Throughout, the rain never let up. As Bob Harris noted, "Midshipman overcoats weigh a ton when they are wet." At last they formed up into companies and the parade began. In spite of the rain, it was "a colorful, patriotic occasion marching from the Capitol down Pennsylvania Avenue." At the reviewing stand in front of the White House, each company executed the traditional salute to the commander-in-chief, though one company commander was horrified when, in executing the sword salute, he caught the brim of his cap on his sword point, and when he swept the sword downward in salute it sent his hat "careening across the wet pavement." They marched on nonetheless, and all the while the rain pounded down, soaking through their wool bridge coats to their dress-blue uniforms, through their underwear, to their skin.[32]

When the parade ended, they were at loose ends because the train back to Annapolis was not scheduled for several more hours. They tried to make the best of it. Some wandered the capital in groups despite the rain to see what they could of the sights, including the Lincoln and Jefferson Memorials. John Lacouture and several others went to Gunston Hall, a local junior college for women just across the Potomac River in Alexandria, and there Lacouture "fell madly in love at first sight" with a Gunston coed. He was well and truly smitten and kept in touch with her all through his plebe year and the next year as well. When restrictions were loosened in his second year, they saw each other whenever they could.[33]

As a DC native, Joe Hanley could escape the elements by simply going home. He and his roommate made their way to Twenty-Fourth Street, where Hanley's mother took one look at them and ordered them to strip, which they did, donning bathrobes. She spread out their sopping coats and uniforms (underwear included), over chairs in the kitchen, turned the oven on, and left the door open. As their clothes dried, Hanley and his roommate consumed totally illicit tumblers of whiskey.[34]

Myers Montgomery, who was still recovering from the flu, had been excused from the parade. Initially he had been disappointed, but he counted his blessings as he watched his classmates stagger back into Bancroft Hall, wet, cold, and bedraggled. Once again, the hospital was crowded with flu cases.

Final exams followed, and not long after that, the publication of first-term grades, which occasioned a great sorting. There was a long list of individuals whose overall marks were below the 2.5 threshold required to be satisfactory (or "sat")—a total of 134 of them, all of whom were designated for "separation," the Academy term for expulsion. Two of Hanley's basketball teammates had previously quit the plebe team in order to focus on academics. It wasn't enough. They were both declared "unsat" and dismissed. Hanley was distraught. Though he had earned a respectable 3.1 himself, he mourned the loss of his two teammates, one of whom, he testified later, was the best basketball player he had ever seen. The loss of so many reduced the total class size from 750 down to 626.[35]

A particularly notable departure was that of James Lee Johnson Jr., whose experience at the Academy that fall had been excruciating. He had been assigned to a room by himself on the third floor of an otherwise unoccupied part of Bancroft Hall. Those midshipmen—almost exclusively from the South—who believed that it was an abomination for a Black man to be at the Naval Academy took it upon themselves to make Johnson's life as difficult as possible. Upperclassmen assigned him extra duties; others sabotaged his uniform just before personnel inspection or disarranged his effects before room inspection. They found ways to ensure that he was late to formation. That earned him demerits, which had to be worked off with extra marching, parading back and forth for hours with his weapon on his shoulder. And that kept him from his studies. Though Johnson's skin was no darker than Campo's, the Filipino was accepted as "white," while Johnson was "black."

Not everyone joined in the abuse. "We were all very conscious that we had a colored boy in the class," Joe Hanley recalled, though he professed not to be troubled by that. "I grew up in a neighborhood where there were colored families," he said, "and this did not bother me." Perhaps not. But even if Hanley and most others refused to participate in the campaign of sabotage against Johnson, neither did they come to his active defense. Most plebes did not want to call attention to themselves, and, as a result, the minority who were determined to make Johnson's experience intolerable effectively imposed their will on the majority who weren't bold enough, or didn't care enough, to confront them.[36]

Johnson was one of the 134 who was found deficient at the end of the first term and ordered to resign. Hanley smelled a rat, convinced that the dismissal "was rigged." He was not alone. Congressman Mitchell, who had appointed Johnson to the Academy, told a Black newspaper in Chicago, "There is no doubt in my mind that the boy is being railroaded out," and he openly accused the Academy of "skullduggery." He was so agitated he went to see President Roosevelt about it. Roosevelt ordered Secretary of the Navy Claude Swanson to conduct an investigation. The midshipmen were certainly aware of it. Montgomery recorded in his diary that there was a "big row" over the "darky Johnson" and that the Academy was "holding [an] investigation." Pending the outcome, all 134 of those who had been found "unsat" remained at the Academy awaiting the verdict.[37]

Claude Swanson was not an objective mediator. Born in 1862 in Virginia, where his father was a plantation master, his earliest memories were of the Civil War, during which his father had served as an officer in the Confederate Army. Now, seventy-five years later, Secretary Swanson reviewed Johnson's record and noted that Johnson had been late to formation seven times in the few weeks before the end of term, though he made no effort to find out why. He concluded that there was nothing to warrant a reconsideration of Johnson's dismissal and that "there can be no further appeal." All 134 of the "bilgers" left the next day.[38]

Angry but undaunted, Mitchell appointed two other Black candidates to the class of 1941: James Minor and George J. Trivers, both of them Dunbar High graduates. Minor was on academic probation at Howard at the time and was not accepted; Trivers, who was attending a Black teacher's college, was accepted, though his stay at the Academy was even shorter than Johnson's. After only a few days of plebe summer, he resigned of his own accord. He made no complaint of his treatment at the time, though he later told a Black reporter that he had suffered "insults and studied punishment at the hands of white youths." His departure meant that the members of the class of 1940 never saw another Black midshipman during their four-year tenure.[39]*

---

* The first African American graduate of the Naval Academy was Wesley A. Brown, another Dunbar product, who was appointed to the Academy in 1945 by Congressman Adam Clayton Powell of New York. Brown graduated from the Academy on June 3, 1949. An accomplished cross country and track athlete, the indoor track facility at the Academy is named for him.

Many of the 626 who remained at the Academy after the "great removal" lost their roommate and had to find a new one for the second term. That mattered, because such was the codependency of roommates in the challenging environment of plebe year that it encouraged an almost spousal relationship between them. Indeed, the Academy vernacular for roommates was "wives." The reshuffling in January 1937 meant that new bonds had to be formed, some of which lasted, some of which did not.

February 22 was Washington's Birthday. It was also one hundred days away from the date when the Forties would complete their plebe year. By tradition, the midshipmen observed "100th Nite," during which the plebes exchanged uniform coats with the firsties and, with mock serious expressions, took command during morning formation, ordering the firsties to brace up and recite doggerel from *Reef Points*. At evening meal, they sat at the head of the tables and "ran" the upperclassmen, asking them questions and then ordering them to "shove out" when they didn't know the answers. It was all done in good spirits, and the plebes were not so foolish as to press too hard, aware that the natural order would soon reassert itself. In fact, the high jinks devolved rather quickly into what Montgomery called "the worst chow fight in the history of the Academy." Afterward, "The messhall [*sic*] looked like a cyclone had hit it." If nothing else, it taught the kitchen staff that even on Washington's Birthday it was probably not a good idea to serve cherry pie for dessert on 100th Nite.[40]

Spring came eventually, and morning formations moved from inside to outside. As the weather improved, the Forties looked forward with excitement to the end of their plebe year. After grades were announced at the end of the second term, another, smaller, group of plebes were found "unsat" and ordered to leave. Class size dropped again, though more modestly, to 616. Conrad Carlson easily placed in the top 5 percent at 34th. Others were happy to find themselves settled comfortably somewhere in the middle. Indeed, Bob Weatherup found himself almost literally in the middle, ranking 321 of 616. For many, the most difficult class had been Mechanical Engineering in which Bob Harris ranked 476th and Joe Hanley 532nd. That was only eighty-four places from the bottom, but it was still "sat."[41]

In addition to academic grades, there was also something called "Aptitude for Service," which was a subjective evaluation made by the first class midshipmen in consultation with the company officer and was popularly called "grease." It was all but impossible to guess what your grease grade might be, though a steady accumulation of demerits was a good indicator that it was not

ANNAPOLIS GOES TO WAR

likely to be stellar. The happy-go-lucky John Lacouture ranked in the top hundred academically, but his irreverent and sometimes wayward behavior put him in the *bottom* hundred in grease.

From literally their first day in Annapolis, every member of the class had kept track of the number of days left until their plebe year came to an end. That date was June 3, 1937, when the firsties graduated. The moment that happened, the members of the class of 1940 would cease to be plebes and become what were called "youngsters," authorized to wear one thin diagonal stripe on their uniform sleeve. They would no longer be subject to the bullying harassment of upperclassmen. The night before that long-anticipated event, if they had their windows open in Bancroft Hall, they could hear the music from the First Class Ball wafting in from nearby Dahlgren Hall. It was a welcome sound, for it meant that a release from the miseries of plebe year was only hours away. At the same time, however, they were very much aware that some upperclassmen might seize the opportunity to inflict one last humiliation.

Like everyone else in the class, Gene Hemley, a dark-eyed, piano-playing native of Brooklyn, was eager for the moment of his release from plebe status. To hasten its arrival, he went to bed promptly at 10:30, turning out the lights in the hope that a sleeping plebe would be a less tempting target than a plebe in the passageway. It didn't work. Barely fifteen minutes after he had climbed into his rack, two upperclassmen came noisily into the room, banging open the door and flipping on the lights. Hemley covered his head with his blanket, but one of the intruders, laughing, grabbed the broom and proceeded to pummel him with it through the blanket. The strokes were so regular it felt like they were keeping time to the music coming in through the window. After they left, still laughing, to seek another victim, Gene got out of bed and hid the broom behind his locker in case any others had the same idea. He could hear upperclassmen harassing the plebe on duty in the passageway, but eventually Gene fell asleep.[42]

At 1:30, his door banged open again. Because the intruders couldn't find the broom, they grabbed Hemley's sandals lying next to his bed and beat him with those. Then they ordered him to get out of bed and spend the rest of the night sleeping on top of his locker. Annoying as that was, it could have been worse. When he exchanged stories with his classmates the next morning, a few of them were so badly bruised their posteriors were "colored with every shade of the rainbow."[43]

Then, suddenly, it was over. The next morning at 10:00 a.m., the members of the class of 1937 received their diplomas in Dahlgren Hall, gave three cheers for those they left behind, and threw their midshipman caps into the air. When they did, by tradition, the former plebes tumbled out of the stands to form a conga line that weaved around the grounds in a "snake dance" as they chanted, "Taint no mo' plebes."*

---

* Only a few years later, the termination of plebe year came to be signified by a collective effort by the plebe class to ascend a twenty-one-foot marble obelisk named for William Lewis Herndon, who had lost his life attempting to save others during a shipwreck in 1857. The challenge was to remove a sailor's "dixie cup" cap from atop the obelisk and replace it with a midshipman's combination cover. The first recorded "Herndon climb" was in 1940 during the Forties graduation week.

3

Youngster Cruise

The arrival of summer did not mean vacation for members of the class of 1940. They were ordered to pack everything they would need for three months into small footlockers, two feet square, and the next morning six hundred brand-new "youngsters," wearing white jumpers and black neckcloths, jostled themselves into groups on the wooden dock alongside the *Reina Mercedes*. Amid joyful confusion, they clambered into a score of fifty-foot Boston Whalers that carried them out to three large battleships anchored over the horizon at the entrance to the Chesapeake Bay. One year earlier, almost to the day, they had been anxious and uncertain plebes facing unknown challenges. Now they were confident and boisterous, not only because they had survived plebe year but because their "youngster cruise" would take them to Europe: to Spain, Italy, Greece, Germany, and England. As one recalled, "We could hardly wait."[1]

The battleships were the *New York*, *Arkansas*, and *Wyoming*, all of them older ships, built before the Great War. They had served with the Royal Navy as part of Battleship Division 9, though none of them had ever fired a shot in anger. Still, here at last was the real navy, and the midshipmen looked forward to "three months of adventure and romance in foreign lands."[2]

Their actual experience did not quite live up to those expectations, at least not at first. To begin with, the ships were quite crowded. A battleship had a crew of over a thousand men, and adding an additional three hundred—half of them rising first-ies from the class of 1938, and half youngsters from the class of 1940—made it quite congested. The Forties saw at once why they had to fit everything into a single footlocker: there was no room for more. There were not enough bunks for everyone, and the Forties had to sling hammocks in the berthing spaces. It took some of them a lot of practice to get the knack of "how to swing a hammock and to get into it, without having it roll over and throw you out." Once they did, they found that sleeping in a hammock was actually quite comfortable.[3]

In addition to the crowding, the youngsters perceived pretty quickly that rather than being treated as officers in training, they were instead assigned the duties of enlisted sailors. That included mopping, painting, and polishing brightwork, plus what was called "holy-stoning"—using a brick-sized block of sandstone to smooth the wooden deck. Gene Hemley described a typical day in a letter to his parents: "The day starts at six o'clock," he wrote, "and the first thing is scrubbing and swabbing the decks." After breakfast there was brightwork polishing, with formation at 9:00 when the officer of the deck read the orders for the day. At 9:25 there was often a formal lecture. It usually concerned "some nautical or gunnery subject," though at least one of them included a film with graphic depictions of sexually transmitted diseases. On the *New York*, the ship's doctor even commandeered several enlisted men as props, requiring them to drop their trousers and display the lesions that had resulted from their having contracted VD. It was enough to convince Joe Hanley that under no circumstances would he even touch a girl in any of the ports they visited, which was, of course, exactly the objective.[4]

On most days the youngsters were called to battle stations at 10:30 for the exercise of the "great guns," the big twelve- or fourteen-inch naval guns that were the ships' main armament. There was a meal at noon, followed by another hour of scrubbing decks, and then a second lecture at 2:30. On the other hand, they were generally finished for the day by 3:45, which left ample leisure time to explore the ship. In the evening, there was often a concert by the ship's band, and after it was full dark, a movie outside on the open deck with the entire ships' crew—those not on duty—in attendance.[5]

The Forties were also required to stand watches. Watch-standing is an important part of every officer's professional life at sea, and to accustom the midshipmen to it, each of them was required to stand a two- or four-hour watch every ten hours. Naturally, that broke up the day and made it difficult, if not impossible, to get a continuous night's sleep, though of course, that, too, was part of an officer's routine. One problem was that in order to ensure that all the midshipmen had watch-standing responsibility, it was necessary to invent assignments for them, such as standing watch over a lifeboat, a buoy, even the foremast. Some found the assignments undignified and the make-work watches annoying and silly. Joe Hanley, for one, "did not like hammocks or our very small lockers, not to mention scrubbing the decks every morning at 6 o'clock," and he began to have "serious doubts" about his decision to go to the Academy at all. More typical, however, was the reaction of Bill Debie of Oakland, California, for whom the cruise was "a real joy."[6]

36   ANNAPOLIS GOES TO WAR

After several days at sea, a rumor circulated—later proven accurate—that because of the ongoing Spanish Civil War, the planned visits to Mediterranean ports in Spain, Italy, and Greece would be scrapped. As a disappointing replacement, they would instead make a port visit to Funchal in Portuguese Madeira, some 540 miles off the coast of Morocco. At least the visits to Germany and England were still on the schedule.[7]

After six days at sea, the American battleships crept slowly up the English Channel through a fog so thick that virtually nothing could be seen from the deck. Finally, it began to lift, and Gene Hemley, who was on lookout, sighted "a long dark outline" through the mist. At first, he thought it was a bank of clouds, then the sun broke through long enough for him to recognize the White Cliffs of Dover. When he called the sighting down to the deck, the regular ship's crew did not even look up, but the midshipmen, familiar with Mathew Arnold's "Dover Beach" and Shakespeare's *King Lear*, ran excitedly to the port rail to peer at this legendary site. As the fog continued to lift, the ships increased speed, passing a flotilla of Royal Navy destroyers engaged in battle practice, the sound of the guns clearly perceptible on the American battleships, as well as several merchant vessels, many of them flying the bright red, white, and black German flag with its prominent swastika.[8]

Germany was their first port of call. On June 20 the three battleships eased in toward the mouth of the Elbe River and the entrance to the Kiel Canal, which cut through the peninsula of Denmark to connect the North Sea to the Baltic. Though it had rained all afternoon, when the *New York* entered the first canal lock there was a huge crowd to welcome the visitors. The mids noticed that almost everyone was in uniform; even the small boys wore military-style caps. The men all sported mustaches, and while a few of them were the old-fashioned handlebar or walrus style, more of them were the brush style made popular by Adolf Hitler.

A pilot came on board to guide them through the canal. Piloting a dreadnought-type battleship through the Kiel Canal was a bit like threading the proverbial needle. The canal had been widened to 107 feet in 1914, but with a beam of 95 feet, the American battleships had a margin of just 6 feet on either side. Moreover, though the canal's official depth was 36 feet, and the battleships drew 32 feet, the *New York* touched bottom no fewer than thirty-eight times during the transit. Also, in order to squeeze under the railroad bridges, all three battleships had to lower their masts, and even then they cleared the spans by mere inches. While the pilot was keeping track of these hazards, the midshipmen pestered him with questions about Hitler's "New Germany." The pilot explained to them that "formerly there were many parties and nothing was done, but now there was only one party and action was being taken." He did suggest, though, that when they went ashore, if they saw something they did not agree with, it would be wise of them not to say so.[9]

It felt odd to steam through pastures and fields, even "people's back yards," for most of a day, but at the end of it the three battleships arrived at the eastern (Baltic) end of the canal and dropped anchor in Kiel, not far from the new German "pocket battleship" *Graf Spee*. While the American officers prepared to pay the necessary social call on the *Graf Spee*, the midshipmen were granted shore liberty. The visit to Kiel was scheduled to last twelve days, and the midshipmen were determined to take full advantage of it.

One of them, Al Bergner of Kankakee, Illinois, who had been a star on the plebe football and lacrosse teams, had an aunt and uncle who lived in Kiel, and he set out to visit them. When he showed up at their home, he was disconcerted to find that both of his female cousins (ages fifteen and thirteen) were active and enthusiastic members of the Hitler Youth, "complete with uniforms." After visiting them, Bergner planned to take the train to Bremen to see his grandmother. His fifteen-year-old cousin wanted to go with him, and her mother agreed as long as he paid for the ticket, which he did, though it cut severely into his available spending money. When the cousins got to Bremen, their cab driver turned out to be an old friend of the family, so when they all arrived at their grandmother's house, her first hug was not for them, but for the cabbie.[10]

The next day, Bergner bought a train ticket to Berlin. Though he could afford only a third-class ticket, he stretched out in a first-class car, hoping to get some sleep. The conductor found him there, checked his ticket, and, unimpressed by his US Navy uniform, put him off the train at Potsdam. He bought a roll and some milk for breakfast, but when he sat down on the curb to eat it, the woman who had sold it to him came running out of the shop to tell him that he had to move—immediately. He retreated between two nearby buildings and almost at once a phalanx of motorcycles came roaring up the street to block off traffic, after which a long column of armored cars, towed artillery pieces, and other military vehicles rolled past at thirty miles an hour. Here was the New Germany flexing its muscles.[11]

He did eventually make it to Berlin, and on his second night there he went to a dance club. He was intrigued to find that the dance floor was surrounded by individual booths, each with a telephone. The idea was to spot someone interesting in another booth and call them, perhaps wave at them from across the room, and arrange an assignation. Bergner had no sooner sat down than his phone rang. It was two young couples in a booth across the dance floor who had seen him come in wearing his uniform and who invited him to join them. They were, as he discovered, Jewish. "They were determined to leave" Germany, Al remembered, "but they could not convince their parents" to go. Their parents insisted that Germany was a civilized country and no harm would come to them. Because their children were reluctant to leave without them, they all stayed. He never learned what became of them.[12]

Al Bergner was not the only one who made it to Berlin. In fact, the German government issued an invitation for a select group of midshipmen to make a formal call on the Führer himself. The sixty individuals chosen for this opportunity were carefully screened to ensure there were no Jews among them and that at least some of them could speak passable German. One of the Forties who was selected was Bruce Rohn, a lacrosse player from Ann Arbor, Michigan, whose paternal grandfather was German. He and the others, both firsties and youngsters, plus a few officers, loaded up at Kiel for the long bus ride to Berlin. There, before visiting the Reich Chancellery, they were joined by several diplomats from the US embassy.

When they disembarked, Rohn noted that the security was evident but discreet. They were escorted down a long corridor and into a high-ceilinged room that was both immense and nearly empty. It reminded Rohn of a gymnasium. "Just add the backboards," he wrote later, "and we could have had a basketball game." There were numerous flags around the edges—red flags with a white circle and a black swastika in the center—and a "very luxurious" rug. In almost the center of the room was a large, and nearly bare, wooden desk with Adolf Hitler sitting behind it. There were no filing cabinets, no chairs, no tables, nothing to indicate that any work got done there. Rohn mused to himself that "the dirty dictator business was done elsewhere."

The midshipmen entered in single file. Hitler got up from behind the desk and stood in front of it to greet them. It was like any other formal reception line, Bruce remembered, only faster and more pro forma. An unsmiling Hitler shook hands with each one, said a word or two in German, then turned to the next man. Rohn "got the impression that he was doing a necessary political chore," just as Rohn was.[13]

Afterward, the midshipmen were allowed to walk about the grounds. The Reichstag was not in session, so a group of mids looked into the empty chamber. One of them sat in the speaker's chair, playfully held his finger across his upper lip to simulate a mustache, and gave the Nazi salute. That night, they attended a reception where virtually everyone was in uniform. Nearly all of the men wore a red, white, and black armband with the swastika. That symbol had yet to assume the sinister implications it later acquired, and the midshipmen found the men themselves both friendly and personable—even charming. Bob Weatherup noted that although "there were swastikas everywhere," he saw nothing particularly threatening in it at the time. Neither did Ray Hundevadt, who noted that "although swastikas were very much in evidence, there were no political overtones." Perhaps not, though Bob Weatherup was perplexed when one of the German officers showed him the bomb shelters that had been built into the hotel "in case of an air raid," though just who might conduct such an air raid his host did not say.[14]

The next night, several of the mids found their way to a dance club, hoping to meet some fräuleins. Ed Rogers, a fun-loving practical joker from Fall River, Massachusetts, spied a table occupied by several unescorted young ladies and decided to try out one of his few words of German, *Tanz* (dance). After the dance, he escorted his partner back to her table, but, lacking any conversation skills, stood there awkwardly for a few moments before walking away. As he did so, a young German about his own age approached him and handed him a folded note. When Rogers got back to his table, he read it. It was in English: "To my american friend, if she says no, she means maybe, and if she says maybe, she means yes. . . . Ich liebe dich means I love you and the rest is international." With more enthusiasm than discretion, John Lacouture tried to cut in on a young Nazi officer who was dancing with a pretty girl. The German resented it and shouted, "I challenge you to a duel to the death. What do you want, swords or guns?" Before Lacouture could answer, several of his classmates hustled him out of the club.[15]

The midshipmen also visited the German Naval Academy at Flensburg, which at least one of them thought looked like "the feudal estate of some medieval lord." They were envious of the generous liberty policy there that allowed cadets to stay out until midnight on weekdays and 2:00 a.m. on weekends, and they appreciated the less formal relationship between officer faculty and students, noting that they mixed socially with an air of gemütlichkeit, cheerful friendliness. Overall, the American visitors were impressed by the "warm and cordial welcome" offered them by the German people, who seemed determined "to ensure that we had a good time." They noted that "everything was spic and span, people bustled with energy and apparent good humor." Periodically, though, something would happen to lift the veil of benign conviviality and expose a more sinister reality beneath. When John Lacouture and a few others were walking down a sidewalk in Berlin, a group of Nazi soldiers coming the other way made it clear they expected the Americans to step aside. That led to some unfriendly pushing and shoving "when they tried to elbow us into the gutter."[16]

Another eye-opener occurred on the last night of the visit. The Americans hosted a reception and dance on board the *Wyoming* to thank their German hosts for their hospitality. It was a fine July evening with sandwiches, punch, an orchestra, and, most important, a large number of pretty German girls who had been invited to provide dance partners for the midshipmen. Lacouture remained devoted to the girl he had met at Gunston Hall, but that didn't keep him from enjoying himself. Eventually, though, the *Wyoming*'s band signaled that the evening was coming to an end by striking up the German national anthem. With the first notes of "Deutschland über Alles," every German on board came to rigid attention, raised his arm in the Nazi salute, and began to sing. Lacouture was startled when "the sweet young thing" he had been dancing with came to stiff attention, flung her arm up in the Nazi salute, and shouted, "Sieg Heil!" Tom McGrath, a shot-putter and football player from Tucson, Arizona, was struck by "the fervor of the German people in their enthusiasm for the Nazi cause." Even years later, the memory of it made him shudder.[17]

Myers Montgomery almost missed the visit to Germany. Just before end of term, he had developed a cyst near his spine that had to be removed, and he was still in the hospital when the battleships departed. Academy authorities did not want him to miss his youngster cruise, so after he was cleared by the doctors, he got orders to catch up with his classmates. He spent a full day in Washington getting a passport and a ticket, then rushed back to the Academy, quickly packed, and headed for New York by train to catch the steamer *Manhattan*.

He had a far different transatlantic experience than his classmates. Instead of a hammock, he had a private cabin; instead of a 6:00 a.m. reveille for deck-scrubbing, he slept in as long as he wanted; instead of the enlisted men's mess, he ate in the *Manhattan*'s "magnificent dining room." If that were not enough, he encountered a woman from Dallas who was chaperoning a party of teenage girls from the Hockaday School in Dallas, Texas, on their European summer tour. Perhaps impressed by his uniform, she introduced him to the girls in her charge, and he developed a particular friendship with Cecelia Jane Metzger. "From then on," Montgomery wrote, "we had one swell time." The cruise was "a life of ease and merriment," with movies in the afternoon, dinner at the captain's table (complete with "balloons and noise makers"), and dancing with Cecelia in the evening. He even won the shipboard doubles Ping Pong tournament. After landing in Hamburg, he caught a train for Keil, where he reported aboard the *Wyoming*. It was a startling transition. As he noted laconically in his diary, "A battleship is quite different from being at sea on [the] Manhattan." Soon he was "standing 4-hour watches at nite [*sic*] in the hot smelly fire room and engine room."[18]

From Kiel, the American battleships steamed back around the Danish headland into the North Sea. The ships headed down the English Channel, rounded Ushant, and turned south toward Portuguese Madeira. They celebrated Independence Day at sea with "games and contests," though no fireworks. They gave the Iberian Peninsula a wide berth because the war in Spain had reached new levels of violence. In April, German warplanes, supporting Francisco Franco's Nationalists, had bombed the Basque town of Guernica (inspiring one of the most recognizable paintings in the Western canon), and Republican planes had retaliated by attacking the German pocket battleship *Deutschland* (sister ship of the *Graf Spee*), in the Mediterranean. In case one of the American battleships might be mistaken for a German warship, the captains on all three stretched enormous American flags over the top of the gun turrets.[19]

After five days at sea, the battleships dropped anchor in Funchal, the principal harbor of Portuguese Madeira. Disappointed because they were not to visit the historic sites of Italy and Greece, the midshipmen found the city charming, "a tapestry of red-shingled roofs dotting steep green hillsides sloping into clear blue waters." Most of them took full advantage of their three-day stop. Some rode "little ox carts" on a tour of the town; some bought Madeira linens as presents for their families. Warned that the water on the island might not be potable, they decided that was sufficient justification for sampling the famous Madeira wine, and several enjoyed dinners at the casino. All three battleships took on fresh stores at Funchal, but in the July heat, the food—and the vegetables in particular—spoiled quickly. Rotting cabbage gave off an especially pungent aroma. To improve their rations, several mids resorted to petty theft. When loading stores, they secreted some hen's eggs in their pockets and later cooked them by putting them in a bucket with a little water and holding them under a steam pipe.[20]

The most popular activity in Funchal was riding a wooden sled from the top of the mountain down into the city. A cog railroad carried them to the top, where they boarded specially designed wooden sleds that careened down the hill on a cobblestone path "with hairpin turns and many twistings and windings" all the way to the bottom. Some did it more than once.[21]

From Madeira, the battleships headed back north to the southern coast of England, dropping anchor in Torbay off the charming seaside town of Torquay (later the setting for the popular British comedy *Fawlty Towers*), only a few miles up the coast from the British Naval Academy at Dartmouth. Once again, the mids took full advantage of their shore liberty. Even riding the liberty boat ashore was an adventure. Waves sprayed them "as if it were raining," and one of the mids lost his hat overboard. Once ashore, they walked about Torquay, where several of them had their "first English tea and cakes." Almost inevitably, Myers Montgomery "met a nice girl from London," Daphne Webber, and he also got a letter from Cecelia Metzger, who was now in Rome.[22]

Several mids took the train to London, where they visited the Houses of Parliament, St. Paul's Cathedral, the Tate Art Gallery, and "The Old Curiosity Shop," made famous by Charles Dickens's novel and, though it was a fake, a popular tourist attraction. Some of them found England more foreign than either Germany or Madeira. It was a place, one recalled, "where the greatness of yesterday loomed up on every side and the pages of history seemed to come to life." The people, too, struck them as otherworldly, quietly complacent and surviving (as Bob Harris put it) on "tea, plum pudding, and pride."[23]

Some mids were more adventurous. After visiting London, Harris got off the train at Salisbury, rented a bicycle, and rode out to see Stonehenge. Ed Rogers and three others rented bicycles in Torquay and pedaled inland for seventeen miles to the little market town of Buckfastleigh at the edge of Dartmoor. There was a charming abbey there and a number of tea shops, but they bypassed those attractions and headed instead to the local pub. There the conversation focused almost exclusively on the decision of King Edward VIII to abdicate the throne to marry an American divorcee. Though it had happened six months before, it remained the hottest topic in town, with some residents finding it romantic and others insisting that it was a dereliction of duty.[24]

Asked what he wanted to drink, Rogers was reluctant to order a pint of ale, which seemed to be the default beverage, and, being fond of apple juice, he instead ordered a glass of cider, unaware that "Scrumpy Jack" cider was 7.5 percent alcohol. He had several glasses of it and became so disoriented his friends had to carry him back to their campsite. That night, as the others slept, he crawled out of the tent several times to throw up.[25]

One large group of midshipmen took a bus tour through the English Midlands. They visited Exeter Cathedral, the Roman ruins at Bath, Shakespeare sites in Stratford-upon-Avon, and Oxford. Then it was back to London for tours of Parliament, Westminster Abbey, Tower Bridge, and the crown jewels.

YOUNGSTER CRUISE 43

In London, Myers Montgomery somehow managed to meet up with Daphne Webber, and they visited the city by night. Montgomery was not impressed. "London," he wrote, "doesn't believe much in nite life."[26]

The visit to Torquay included a swimming competition between the midshipmen and the English Amateur Swimming Association. The midshipmen won the freestyle relay, but the teams battled to a dead heat in the medley, which featured a new stroke called the "butterfly." One of the most popular events as far as the midshipmen were concerned was a demonstration of "fancy swimming and diving" by the Western Counties Ladies and Girls champions. Afterward, there was a formal reception and a ball. According to the local paper, "The town was alive with sailors until a late hour." At the conclusion of the festivities, the mayor of Torquay announced that when the American ships departed the next morning, "there will be many aching hearts in Torquay," an apparent reference to budding romances, which elicited "great laughter" from the crowd. The mayor went on to wish them "a pleasant voyage home, and may you return again soon."[27]

The voyage home was largely uneventful. By now, the youngsters had grown accustomed to the ship's routines—including the hammocks—and found time to relax. "All thoughts are of home now," Montgomery wrote in his diary, "as the ship heads into the setting sun." There was, however, one more adventure. As if to remind them that the sea was a dangerous place, the battleships encountered a terrific storm west of the Azores. The hammocks swung like pendulums, mids were hurled to the deck, gear was thrown about, and water sloshed into the berthing spaces. No one was hurt, and in a few days the storm passed.[28]

When the squadron was only a few days out from Norfolk, members of the football team organized a few practice sessions aboard ship. They would all go on leave immediately after they landed and would have only a few days together before the first game after they returned in the fall. Indeed, on August 12, football team members were transferred off the battleships to the minesweeper *Owl* so they could get back to Annapolis a few days early for practice. Those who were left behind participated in "Short Range Battle Practice" off Norfolk, firing the ships' big guns at a towed target, after which the whole ship needed to be cleaned again before the trip up the Chesapeake Bay to Annapolis. There, on August 24, everyone disembarked, eager to begin a month's leave with home and family.[29]

4

Youngsters

Back in Annapolis after their leave, the Forties were feeling good about themselves. They were proud of the thin diagonal stripe on their sleeve that marked them as second-year midshipmen, and looked forward to the privileges it would bring. "Mighty nice being a youngster instead of a plebe," Montgomery wrote in his diary, and Bob Harris recalled, "We felt we were nautical at last and had acquired our sea legs." Joe Hanley remembered, "We liked the weight of that one stripe, and we liked the emancipation it stood for." For him, and for many of his classmates, "This was the fun year at the Academy."[1]

It is an old saw at the Naval Academy that the authorities take away all your rights when you arrive, then give them back to you, one at a time, as "privileges." One privilege that was returned to them now was permission to have a radio. Here was a vital connection to the outside world, and the youngsters took full advantage of it. To one member of the class, "It seemed like the radio was on during all of the waking hours." When Myers Montgomery and his roommate, Arthur Rhodes (inevitably nicknamed "Dusty"), got their radio, they spent an entire Sunday afternoon "seeing how many stations we could get." They listened to the big-band sounds of Tommy Dorsey, Fred Allen, and Kay Kyser. In the fall they got Redskins games, and in the spring they listened to Major League Baseball. Since the midshipmen were from all over the country, there were frequent arguments about the virtues or chances of various teams. One especially popular radio program was the *Lucky Strike Hit Parade*, which broadcast every Saturday night and featured a countdown of the top songs of the week.[2]

Another privilege extended to them was that they were now allowed to "drag," which was Academy slang for dating. Despite its connotations, "dragging" at the Academy was on the whole a decorous affair. It simply meant accompanying a girl or young lady—perhaps the sister of a roommate—to an

YOUNGSTERS

45

evening event. Because youngsters were paid a total of four dollars a month after deductions for expenses, the evening entertainments tended to be pretty modest: a movie and perhaps a Coke. In addition, periodic "hops" took place in Dahlgren Hall. For these, some mids "dragged" a local young woman or a girlfriend from home, who might stay overnight with a sponsor family. Less often, young women were bused into Annapolis from nearby schools and colleges. Sometimes midshipmen were paired up with these visitors by supervising matrons. Later, back in Bancroft Hall, irreverent mids discussed and disputed the dubious honor of having ended up with the most unattractive "drag"— unchivalrously dubbed a "brick."

The Academy encumbered dragging with all sorts of rules and restrictions. Physical contact was forbidden. Midshipmen greeted their dates with a salute, and they were not to hold hands or link arms, even when crossing a street. Midshipmen were not permitted to drive a car, so wherever they went on their date it had to be within walking distance. A particularly irksome rule was that midshipmen had to be back inside the wall by ten o'clock. For those who said goodnight at the train station or the bus station, that often required sprinting for the gate, "running full-tilt in a full dress uniform with a heavy overcoat." If, instead, the couple said goodnight at the gate, the mids were sometimes helpless witnesses when students from the nearby all-male St. John's College (then—and still—known as "Johnnies"), who did not have a curfew, would swoop in and offer to escort the young ladies somewhere for a late snack. John Lacouture's girl from Gunston Hall came to see him about once a month, which was about as often as he could get liberty outside the Yard, and his comment about this poaching by the Johnnies was "Grrrr."[3]

Some midshipmen developed reputations as "snakes," which had two meanings: It could be applied to a midshipman who managed to steal someone else's date, but more often it referred to individuals who were popular among young women. Snakes were generally admired for their social prowess, and because they had a large circle of female friends, they could sometimes provide blind dates for classmates. As Joe Hanley noted philosophically, blind dates could have "happy or disastrous consequences," though some led to long-term relationships. Bill Benbow's roommate fixed him up with a blind date for June week, and years later they married. Some members of the class did not drag because they had a steady girlfriend back home (an OAO, or "one-and-only"). Others dragged as often as they could. For many, it simply meant a fun evening out; for others, every encounter was a potential grand romance. Myers Montgomery seemed to fall more than half in love with every attractive girl he met. That fall, he dragged "Eleanor" to most Academy events, though when he was home in Missouri, he saw a lot of "Harriet," and, when neither was available, he dragged "Polly."[4]

Those who did not drag at all were known as "red mikes." The origin of the term is obscure. *Reef Points* defined it as "a dyed-in-the-wool misogynist." There was no suggestion at the time that a "red mike" might be gay. Statistically, it is almost certain that some of them were, though the mores of the 1930s were such that a gay midshipman remained thoroughly and determinedly closeted. Consequently, the accepted convention was that a "red mike" was either a "woman hater" or congenitally shy, though every now and then one would be swept off his feet by an especially charming drag.[5]

Another privilege that came with youngster status was the opportunity to check out one of the Academy's many sailboats—either a small single-masted knockabout or, if qualified and sanctioned by the sailing coach, a fifty-foot two-masted ketch. Checking out a sailboat for a weekend was an economical way to entertain a visiting "drag," as well as to escape the relentless pressures inside the Yard. As one member of the class recalled, lying on a wooden deck "listening to the soft slap of the waves against the hull and watching the white sail sweeping over a blue sky" made it possible to forget the difficulties and obligations of midshipman life. Alas, the weather did not always cooperate. One weekend when Myers Montgomery and two others checked out a ketch for themselves and their drags, a sudden gust of wind flipped the boat onto its side, pitching all six of them into the bay. Other mids came out in a whaleboat to rescue the girls; Montgomery and his two friends stayed with the boat as it was towed in. The mids suffered no consequences, other than wet clothes, but there was an interesting postscript. One of the drags was the daughter of recently retired Admiral Joseph M. Reeves, and she reported to her father that when she and the other girls came ashore dripping wet, the officer on the dock had treated them discourteously, or at least unsympathetically. That led Admiral Reeves to visit Captain Milo Draemel, the commandant of midshipmen, and lecture him on the importance of civility.[6]

By now, the members of the class of 1940 had developed an esprit de corps, and one manifestation of that was that most of them acquired nicknames that they carried for the rest of their lives. Some were simply contractions of their last names: Ray Hundevadt, for example, became "Hundy," Ernest Peterson became "Pete," and Paul Desmond was "Des." Other names derived from a prominent aspect of their physiognomy, such as Dolive Durant from Mobile, Alabama, who for reasons that were immediately evident became "Schnoz," or

YOUNGSTERS 47

William Keating from Baltimore, who was universally known as "Slim." Some nicknames presumably derived from an aspect of their personality. Warren Lowerre, for example, was "Sunshine"; James Farrior, who was on the sailing team, became "Sinbad"; and John Lacouture, described by his roommate as having "a philosophical nature looking for enjoyment," was nicknamed "Lover." Some nicknames were ironic, like that of Tom McGrath, the big football player and shot-putter from Arizona, who was dubbed "Tiny." Myers Montgomery was sometimes called "Monty," but since star football player Ulmont Whitehead had been "Monty" from the start, Montgomery generally used his middle name, Myers. More mysterious was the origin of the nickname imposed on Monty Whitehead's football teammate, Emmett Wood, who rather than, say, Woody, became "Punkin." It is also unclear why John Greenbacker became "Peck," Bob Weatherup "Doc," and R. R. Duyzyk "Pop" or "Pappy." Abraham Campo, the Filipino national, might have been "Abe" but instead became "Sparky." Among themselves these became lifelong monikers, and they referred to one another as "Pete," "Peck," or "Doc" for the rest of their lives, even if within the broader naval community they generally reverted to their Christian names.[7]

When classes began again in the fall, the youngsters took the same subjects they had in plebe year: math, steam, wires, bull, and Dago, though now at a more advanced level ("wires," for example, was now called "cables"). Many of the weaker students had been winnowed out, and those who remained had grown accustomed to class routines, so it was easier for them to "stay alive and prosper" (as Pete Peterson put it) or, more prosaically, to "plug and chug." As one member of the class put it, "The value of 'youngster' year was primarily learning to make the utmost of one's time."[8]

It was a tradition for each class to retain copies of old exams and pass them down to each succeeding class, and although the exams did change from year to year, they provided a reliable guide to the topics likely to be examined. Joe Hanley and others discovered that "if you studied these you would pass." If that meant there was little in the way of "intellectual discussion, stimulation, or individual research," the strict regimen at least encouraged habits of organization and personal discipline. Grades were important, but not predominant. Most concluded that it was not necessary to strive for a 4.0 as long as they were safely above the 2.5 threshold required to be "sat." To ensure that, when they marched past the bronze figurehead of "Tecumseh" (aka "the god of 2.5") on their way to final exams, they saluted the glowering icon with their left hand

48 ANNAPOLIS GOES TO WAR

and tossed him a coin to ensure a good result.* Myers Montgomery had academic problems in the fall when the spinal cyst that had delayed his participation in youngster cruise reappeared and he had to go back into the hospital. He missed two weeks of classes, and it took him more than a month to catch up. There were occasional moments of academic triumph. John Lacouture was astonished to receive a 4.0 mark from an English professor who was a notoriously tough grader. He acknowledged later that he had always been pretty good at "slinging the bull."[9]

Possessing copies of old exams was not an honor offense. Lying was. On one occasion, a midshipman who had been confined to his room for some minor transgression learned that his girlfriend had traveled to Annapolis to see him with a cake she had baked for his birthday. Eager to see her and get the cake, he signed out of his room to visit the head, then went down to a side door and got the cake. As he walked back, the duty officer asked him where he had been. "The head, sir." But with the cake in his hands, the jig was up. Had he confessed, he would have been punished with demerits and punitive marching, but lying was an honor offense. He was expelled that week.[10]

To fill the hours gained by their new academic confidence, some mids became avid readers, mostly of historical novels and biographies, which, in effect, constituted a kind of supplementary education. In addition, partly to compensate for the absence of courses in economics and literature, all midshipmen were required to select one book from a designated list and write a thousand-word essay about it before graduation. The essay was not graded, and most midshipmen saw it simply as one more hurdle to clear, though it may have exposed a few of them to topics they might otherwise have ignored.

There were also marathon bridge games in Bancroft Hall that went on until lights out, or even beyond. Sometimes, if a midshipman had to leave a game to study or sleep, another would simply slip into his place and the game continued. And there were lessons to be learned here, too. One inveterate bridge player was Edward "Fick" Fickenscher from Towson, Maryland, who was fond

---

* The bronze bust of "Tecumseh," which rests on a stone base in front of Bancroft Hall, is not, in fact, a depiction of the Shawnee chief Tecumseh, but of the Delaware chief Tamanend. The original was the figurehead of the old ship of the line *Delaware*, which was scuttled near Norfolk, Virginia, at the beginning of the Civil War to prevent her from falling into the hands of the rebels. The ship was raised in 1868, and the figurehead sent to the Naval Academy. The wooden original (now in the Visitor's Center) was replaced in 1930 by a bronze replica as a gift from the Naval Academy class of 1891. Despite its actual subject, it has been called "Tecumseh" for so many years that the name has become permanent. It has often been decorated with "war paint" before football games, and midshipmen walking (no longer marching) to their final exams still occasionally toss a coin to it for good luck.

of warning his partner that "there's many a man walking the street for not taking out all the trumps."[11]

One exciting event that fall of 1937 was the arrival of a motion picture crew from MGM studios that had come to film scenes for a new movie called *Navy Blue and Gold*. It was a drama about three midshipmen (played by Tom Brown, Jimmy Stewart, and Robert Young), and the plot concerned their development as friends and teammates on the football team. It also touched on hazing and the honor system with the plucky lads overcoming multiple challenges, including the determination by one of them (Jimmy Stewart) to clear his father's reputation as a disgraced naval officer. The film climaxes with all three of them on the football field as they win a hard-fought come-from-behind victory over Army. The filming took place during the fall semester, and many members of the class of 1940 got to be extras, walking (or marching) back and forth in front of Bancroft Hall for background shots. Alas, life did not imitate art that season, and there was no come-from-behind victory as Navy lost the big game 6–0. The film did well in the theaters, however, and brought the Naval Academy a lot of positive publicity.*

It was during their second year at the Academy that several members of the class began to develop eye trouble. Almost certainly it was the result of studying in the dark after lights out, though at least one was convinced that it was from standing in parade formation in the bright sunshine staring at a sea of white uniforms (sunglasses were not allowed). Diminishing eyesight was more than an inconvenience, for in the 1930s having twenty-twenty eyesight was a requirement for commissioning.[12]

Phil Glennon, the third-generation midshipman from Washington, DC, was one of many who was notified that his eyesight had deteriorated. A periodic medical exam revealed that his left eye was no longer 20/20. When his company officer saw that, he called Glennon into his office and showed him a typed letter of resignation. He told Glennon to sign it and said that if his vision did not improve by the end of the term, he would submit it. Glennon dutifully signed the letter and returned to his room, "crestfallen." He was determined, however, to beat it if he could, and the only remedy he could think of was to rest his eyes. In effect, he stopped reading. He relied on his roommate to tell

---

* *Navy Blue and Gold* was one of three Hollywood films that year that featured the Naval Academy. The others were *Annapolis Salute*, with Van Heflin, and *Hold 'Em Navy*, with Lew Ayres. The plot of all three centers on members of the Naval Academy football team. A fourth film that year, *Sweetheart of the Navy*, also included scenes filmed at the Academy.

him about assignments, listened carefully in class, and labored through his exams. Another victim of this draconian rule was Bob Harris, who adopted a similar solution, keeping his eyes closed during study hours and especially during the two weeks before each scheduled eye exam. One side benefit of this protocol was that he became an excellent touch typist.[13]

Desperate to pass his next eye exam, Glennon memorized the eye chart. On the day of the retest, however, he was horrified when, on entering a darkened room, he saw at once that it was a different chart. Even so, he was able to read most of the letters—all but one, which he couldn't make out at all. Believing he had to get all of them right or fail, he simply guessed—and guessed wrong. The doctor asked him to try again, and Glennon picked a different letter. Wrong again. The doctor told him to take one step forward and pointed again to the spot. "What do you see here?" Glennon decided to come clean and confess that he couldn't see anything there. "That's right," the doctor said. It was a blank space. He passed.[14]

Some who failed the eye test were simply dismissed. Sam Edelstein, for example, despite excellent marks, was dismissed from the Academy after two years for imperfect eyesight. He went to the University of Washington, joined the NROTC unit, and earned both a navy commission and a degree in electrical engineering. He and others who were compelled to leave joined the Navy Reserves, where perfect eyesight was not a requirement. Still others, including both Glennon and Harris, were allowed to remain at the Academy in a state of probation, required to pass a new eye exam every semester. At the end of term, these separations, plus a few more academic failures, reduced the size of the class again, from 616 down to 478. By now, a full third of those who had arrived the previous summer were gone.[15]

The news from overseas continued to be alarming. The Japanese army used the pretext of an arms clash near a bridge south of Peking (now Beijing) the previous July to initiate a full-scale invasion of China. Only in hindsight was it evident that this was the opening campaign of what would grow into World War II. Japanese armies penetrated deep into China, and the commander of Japanese forces declared that the war would continue until "the Chinese forces are completely annihilated." In December 1937, as members of the class of 1940 prepared to go home for Christmas break, two events in particular brought the war in Asia close to home.[16]

It was a symptom of the precarious nature of Chinese sovereignty that the US Navy conducted regular patrols on the rivers inside China, including the

YOUNGSTERS   51

Yangtze. The official explanation for this was that a naval presence was necessary to protect American citizens and American interests along the river. As Japanese armies neared Nanking (now Nanjing) on the Yangtze River in early December, most Americans fled the city, though a dozen journalists remained. The US Navy gunboat *Panay* evacuated them, including a Universal Newsreel cameraman named Norman Alley. He was still on board on December 12, 1937, as the *Panay* escorted three Standard Oil tankers upriver to get them beyond the range of the fighting. At about one-thirty that afternoon, a squadron of Japanese warplanes appeared overhead and attacked the *Panay* with bombs—even though two large American flags were conspicuously laid out on the deck. More planes arrived, attacking in groups of two or three until the *Panay* was sinking. A little after two o'clock, the wounded navy skipper of the *Panay* ordered abandon ship. Three Americans had been killed and another forty-five wounded; nearby British vessels rescued the survivors. Alley filmed it all, and his footage was later shown to the midshipmen in Mahan Hall auditorium.[17]

There was more. Well before the film reached the United States, the Japanese assaulted Nanking itself. In a confusing and chaotic battle and subsequent brutal occupation, the Japanese killed at least forty thousand people, though some accounts place the number as high as two hundred thousand. Soon afterward, graphic photographs of this "Rape of Nanking" made it into American newspapers and magazines.[18]

Both events outraged Americans. It is all but certain that the Japanese pilots who sank the *Panay* had acted under orders, yet the Japanese government quickly offered the "profoundest regret" for this "terrible mistake." Japanese officials organized a campaign of contrition that included letters of apology written by Japanese schoolchildren. It was not clear that would be enough, however, and the US relationship with Japan grew extremely tense. Roosevelt was as outraged as anyone, but, aware that American public opinion would not support more forceful measures, he accepted the Japanese apology and an indemnity of $2 million ($42 million in modern currency). Nevertheless, the incident marked a turning point in Japanese–American relations.[19]

When the midshipmen returned to the Academy after Christmas break, there was a lot of talk about exacting revenge. But nothing in their daily regimen hinted that anything in their world was about to change. Classes continued as before, with students drawing slips and manning the boards, and there was no serious discussion of the war in China, at least officially. If a professor mentioned Japan at all, it was usually disparagingly. As one member of the class recalled, "We were assured that they [the Japanese] were lousy aviators and that they could only copy the engineering achievements of others."[20]

The days gradually grew longer and the weather more benign. Spring fever arrived on May Day 1938, which was a beautiful Sunday. Inspired by the good weather, some of the Forties decided it would be a good idea to wake up the plebes, order them to don dress-blue uniform jackets and ties with swim trunks, and compel them to dance around a maypole. Everyone took it in good spirits, but several observers had cameras and, perhaps inevitably, a photograph of this unseemly carnival made its way into the newspapers. The authorities were not pleased. Lieutenant Ralph Waldo Christie, whom the midshipmen called "Snuffy," demanded to know who was behind this disgraceful performance. Myers Montgomery was one of those who was questioned forcefully about whose idea it was. He noted in his diary that "no one has owned up to having done it yet, but they have quite an investigation underway and are sure to find out soon." But they didn't. Instead, Lieutenant Christie ordered the whole class to double time around the track until he was satisfied. Most of the Forties decided it had been worth it.[21]

5

Beat Army

The class of 1938 graduated on June 2, with President Roosevelt giving what Montgomery, at least, considered "a clever talk." He congratulated them on their accomplishment, then cautioned them to widen their field of thought beyond the merely professional. Once the graduates tossed their hats, the youngsters in the class of 1940 became second classmen, authorized to wear *two* diagonal stripes on their uniforms. After the new graduates left, followed a day later by the rising firsties and new youngsters, who departed for their summer cruise, the Yard seemed strangely quiet. It was "a nice feeling to be a 2nd classman," Montgomery wrote in his diary, though Bancroft Hall felt "pretty bare and lonesome."[1]

There was no European cruise for the new second classmen. Instead, they were divided into groups to expose them to the various branches of naval service that would be available to them after their own graduation two years hence. One group set off to spend a month on board destroyers, old "four-pipers" that had been built for service in World War I. Displacing only about twelve hundred tons each, these "greyhounds of the sea" were vastly different from the lumbering battleships they had sailed on the previous summer. More important, the duties assigned to them were more like those of junior officers than deckhands.

Joe Hanley was among those assigned to the destroyer *Fairfax* (DD-93). The menial tasks he had performed the previous summer on a battleship had led him to doubt his decision to attend the Academy, but his cruise on the *Fairfax* convinced him that he had made the right decision after all.* On the *Fairfax*, he and ten of his classmates headed up the East Coast to New York City, making

---

* The *Fairfax* had an especially colorful history. She was one of the fifty destroyers given to Britain in 1940 as part of the "bases for destroyers" deal and re-christened HMS *Richmond*. Then in 1944 she was transferred again from the Royal Navy to the Soviet navy under Lend-Lease and became the *Zhivichy*.

several stops along the way. At each stop, they were entertained—even lionized—during receptions ashore. In New York they toured the site of the still-unfinished world's fair, then headed upriver to Poughkeepsie, where they cheered on the Navy boat in the national crew championship. In what Joe Hanley described as a "thrilling race," Navy led most of the way before ending up second to perennial champion Washington, winners of the Olympic Gold medal in Berlin the year before.[2]

While Hanley's *Fairfax* went north, John Lacouture and a dozen others headed south on a different destroyer to Norfolk and Virginia Beach. They, too, enjoyed receptions ashore. For the rest of his life, Lacouture remembered a party on the oceanside deck of the Dunes Club in Virginia Beach. To signal the end of the evening, the band members stood up, began a rollicking version of "When the Saints Go Marching In," and then paraded right off the deck, over the sand, and into the water, still playing.[3]

Those members of the class who remained in Annapolis took classes on communication, ordnance, and gunnery, though they had afternoons off for tennis, sailing, or golf. Perhaps the only arduous aspect of their program was at the rifle range, where the supervising marines treated them like boot recruits, requiring them to double-time from place to place. Under their direction, the mids learned to fire the Browning Automatic Rifle (BAR) and the Lewis Machine Gun. They also learned to use a gas mask, wearing one into a chamber filled with tear gas, and then, on command, removing it until their eyes watered before being allowed to leave the chamber.[4]

Much more exciting and enjoyable was their introduction to naval aviation. It was the prospect of flying that had convinced Doc Weatherup to apply to the Naval Academy in the first place, and he was overjoyed to sit in the copilot's seat of a big navy flying boat as it took off from the Severn River. He was both shocked and thrilled when, after the plane reached cruising altitude, the pilot turned to him and said, "Take it." Myers Montgomery was gratified that he "managed to keep from getting airsick," though he had to acknowledge that "the section of the country is beautiful from the air."[5]

It was more than just sightseeing. They learned to taxi the plane in the water, to use the radio, to fire the machine guns, and even to drop a few bombs on uninhabited Snake Island in the Susquehanna River, fifty miles north of Annapolis. Montgomery was pleased with himself when the flight instructor told him he "made good hits" on his bombing run. As a capstone to their aviation training, they had to calculate a flight path to the mouth of the Chesapeake, and then fly it. It was as wonderful as Weatherup had imagined.[6]

Weatherup and many others were less enthralled by their introduction to submarines. The R-class sub that visited Annapolis that summer was only 175 feet long and displaced a mere six hundred tons. Joe Hanley thought it "hot and smelly," and at six foot two, he spent much of the time on board stooped over. When the sub's skipper took them to the bottom of the Chesapeake Bay for fifteen minutes, he had to suppress a panicky claustrophobia. He resolved never to go voluntarily into a submarine again. Phil Glennon, on the other hand, found it fascinating, and years later he would opt for the submarine service.[7]

Hanley, Lacouture, and the others who rode destroyers for the first month of the summer all returned to Annapolis on July 1. For the next month, they and most members of the class were responsible for "running" (as it was called) the new plebes of the class of 1942. The first of the new entries arrived on June 10 and more trickled in throughout the summer. Only two years away from the plebe experience themselves, the Forties sought to combine a confident authoritarianism with a helpful introduction to Academy life. It was a nuanced task, and their success varied from individual to individual. Many sought to model the behavior they had encountered themselves two years before, either despotic or benign. Montgomery admitted in his diary that he got "a big kick out of running the plebes." As a platoon commander for twenty of them, he not only marched them from place to place, he presided over their meals, quizzed them on their rates, and inspected their uniforms and rooms. He developed an almost paternal relationship with them, reporting to his diary that they all performed well.[8]

It was not all marching and quizzing plebes. The schedule for the Forties allowed leisure time for tennis, Ping Pong, and pickup basketball games. They could go into town for a snack, a movie, or simply to wander around. Montgomery often dropped in on Mrs. Franklin D. Karns, the widow of a navy captain, who lived in town and welcomed him and other midshipmen graciously. On June 18, Mrs. Karns arranged for Montgomery and his roommate, Dusty Rhodes, to drag two girls who were visiting from Washington. Both were ambivalent about it—blind dates, after all, were something of a risk. But, as Montgomery noted in his diary, this time "they sure turned out swell." Indeed, he had such a good time with "Joann" that he and Rhodes missed curfew and had to sneak back into Bancroft Hall by climbing through an open window in the tailor shop.[9]

At the end of the month, those members of the class who had remained in Annapolis during June boarded destroyers for their own cruise. Montgomery was on the USS *Herbert* (DD-160), a smaller but newer destroyer than the *Fairfax*. The cruise began with the *Herbert* heading up the Potomac River to the Washington Navy Yard in DC. While passing Mount Vernon, the officer of the deck rang twenty-one bells in honor of the first president. Like Hanley and Lacouture, Montgomery found some aspects of the trip to be much like a yachting party. When the *Herbert* docked in Washington, for example, the two young women who had been introduced to him by Mrs. Karns—Joann and her friend Barbara—were waiting for them. Four couples crammed themselves into one car and headed off for a homemade spaghetti dinner at Joann's house, followed by a night of dancing. Montgomery was once again well and truly smitten, and found it "really hard to tell her goodbye."[10]

The next phase of the cruise was less charming. Once the *Herbert* passed down the Potomac and entered the open ocean, Montgomery noted that "most of the midshipmen soon got sick, with myself at the head of the list." After losing his breakfast over the side, he claimed he "never went through more suffering in all my life." The work assignments did not help, especially when he was ordered to scrape out a boiler, which he described as "the dirtiest job I've ever tackled."[11]

It got better. Before heading into the Hudson, the *Herbert* passed Coney Island, the Statue of Liberty, and "the beautiful Manhattan skyline," then proceeded upriver to the Military Academy at West Point. There, after hosting a group of second-year army cadets (called "yearlings") on the ship, the midshipmen went ashore to watch a parade, have dinner, and attend a hop. After that, the *Herbert* headed back down the river to New York to tie up at the Fifty-Ninth Street Pier off Manhattan. Most of the midshipmen headed into the city to visit the usual tourist attractions, including Times Square and Broadway. By prearrangement, Montgomery met up with Connie Chalkey, the only child of Otway Hebron Chalkey, president of the Philip Morris Tobacco Company. That connection gave her—and Montgomery—access to all sorts of opportunities, including a private table on the roof garden of the Astor Hotel, where they listened to Hal Kemp and his orchestra. Myers reported to his diary that he had "a glorious time."[12]

After New York, the *Herbert* headed back south, making several more stops along the way. At most of them, the mids were entertained at formal receptions ashore, which they referred to sardonically as "tea fights."[13]

At the end of August, everyone got two weeks' leave, and most of them immediately caught trains or buses for home. John Lacouture went first to his girlfriend's house outside Chicago, which meant he missed the hurricane that slammed into his family's home in Hyannisport that week. After a happy week in Chicago with his girlfriend and her family, Lacouture went to Hyannisport, where he competed in the afternoon sailboat races at the yacht club, often against the Kennedy boys, Joe and Jack. ("Bobby and Ted," he remembered, "were too young."). Other mids returned to more modest, but nonetheless welcome, environments, from Mount Lebanon, Pennsylvania, to Malden, Missouri, to Sacramento, California. In almost every case, their families urged them to wear their navy uniforms everywhere, especially to church, though most of them simply wanted to get into more comfortable civilian clothes.[14]

World events followed them home. They had barely said hello to their families before a major crisis erupted in Europe over Czechoslovakia. For years, a noisy minority of German-speaking Czechs in a border region known as the Sudetenland had lobbied for autonomy, and by September, violence had broken out between pro- and anti-Nazi elements there. Hitler insisted that the Sudetenland was historically German and that if it were not transferred to Germany, he would seize it by force. German troops mobilized near the border. Montgomery and his family were among the many who "listened to frequent radio reports of war crisis in Europe." It seemed possible—maybe even likely— that war could break out at any moment.[15]

Then, as the midshipmen packed for their return to Annapolis, they learned that a deal had been struck in Munich. The British and French pressured the Czechs into acceding to Hitler's demands, and in exchange Hitler pledged that he would have no more territorial demands in Europe. Later, after it became clear that Hitler had no intention of living up to that pledge, the very word "Munich" acquired an aura of infamy, and "appeasement" became a synonym for cravenness. At the time, however, most Europeans and Americans welcomed the news with "universal relief and thankfulness that war had been averted," as Montgomery wrote in his diary. Still, he spoke for many when he expressed disgust that "France and England backed down on [their] promise."[16]

The mids, now second classmen, arrived back in Annapolis on September 23 and hit the ground running. The twenty-third was a Friday, and there was a home football game the next day, with classes beginning on Monday. Coming off a leisurely month, the adjustment was jarring. "Sure hated to be back," Montgomery wrote, "everyone in very low spirits." Once again, they all took the same classes, though a few of the subjects changed: Math gave way to what was called "Skinny," a combination of physics and chemistry. There were also new courses called Seamanship & Navigation and Ordnance & Gunnery. The plebes in the class of 1942, whom they had indoctrinated that summer, also started classes, and "running" them remained another responsibility. When he quizzed his plebes at the dinner table, Montgomery was disappointed with their level of knowledge, and issued a number of "Come Arounds" that first week, ordering them to find the answers and report to his room. Like virtually every class in the long history of the Naval Academy, the members of the class of 1940 shook their heads at the sad performance of the new plebes and complained to one another that this new crop simply wasn't as "squared away" as they had been when they were plebes—though that is exactly what the members of the class of 1938 had said about them.[17]

On Halloween night, many of them were listening to the radio when the program was suddenly interrupted by a newsflash. A meteor had struck New Jersey, and creatures from Mars were invading the country! It was, of course, the famous Orson Welles dramatization of *War of the Worlds*, but it sounded so real that the duty midshipman threw on his uniform and rushed to inform the officer of the watch, only to return sheepishly a few hours later. The next night at dinner, his company mates presented him with a Buck Rogers pistol so that he could defend Bancroft Hall from the Martians.[18]

The football season started out well, with victories over William & Mary, the Virginia Military Institute, and the University of Virginia. In the Virginia game, Punkin Wood returned a punt ninety-five yards for a touchdown as Navy romped, 33–0. Yale handed Navy its first loss, and then—improbably— the next two games, against Princeton and Penn, both ended in ties. With a record of 3-1-2, the team went up to Baltimore to play Notre Dame. There was no magic this time, and Notre Dame dominated, winning 15–0 in front of a crowd of 58,271. In the next game, Navy's defense managed to stifle Columbia's all-American Sid Luckman, a future NFL Hall of Fame quarterback, and won 13–6. That sent Navy into the Army game with a record of 4-2-2.

It was cold in Philadelphia on November 26, 1938; heavy snow had blanketed the area, and a gusting wind made it feel even colder. The conditions intimidated a few potential attendees. Scalpers who had been charging fifteen dollars a ticket in the morning dropped their price to two dollars by game time. Even so, 102,000 people filled the stands by kickoff. Though six hundred men had spent the morning clearing snow from the playing field, the march-on by the Corps of Cadets and the Regiment of Midshipman left the field a muddy slough. In front of a largely pro-Navy crowd, the midshipmen jumped out to an early 7–0 lead, and hopes were high. Then Army took control in the second half to grind out a 14–7 win. After the final gun, the Army team charged across the field and serenaded the downcast Navy fans with a chorus of "Good Night, Ladies," followed by taps.[19]

BEAT ARMY 59

The news from Europe was as chilling as the weather. The *New York Times* reported that Hitler's government was now fully in the grip of extremists, including Field Marshal Hermann Goering, Dr. Joseph Goebbels, and Henrich Himmler. Not only was Germany pledging to punish German Jews for any antigovernment statements or behavior, it would also punish them for anything said or done by Jews *outside* Germany, including in the United States. "How the Jews are treated in Germany," Goebbels said in a statement, "will depend on their own good behavior and above all on the good behavior of Jews abroad." In response to that, Roosevelt recalled the American ambassador. "Don't know what will come of it," Montgomery wrote in his diary, "but world conditions are terribly strained."[20]

At Christmas, most members of the class headed home. This time John Lacouture did not stop in Chicago and headed directly to Boston. Given his family's prominence in Boston society, he received a number of invitations to "coming out" parties that season. It probably did not hurt that his navy dress-blue uniform with its gold buttons provided some relief to the black-and-white palate of such events. One of the balls he attended was in honor of the roommate of his Gunston Hall girlfriend in Norfolk; another, held two days after Christmas, was for President Roosevelt's eighteen-year-old niece, Eleanor Roosevelt, called Ellie, daughter of the First Lady's brother Hall. Lacouture had known Ellie Roosevelt as a child and was therefore one of "hundreds of young guests" who arrived in the East Room of the White House on December 27, to be received by the First Lady and her namesake niece. The *Washington Star* reported that the president and his eighty-four-year-old mother Sara "also received" the guests, though Lacouture had no memory of meeting the president. He did, however, remember meeting, and dancing with, the First Lady, describing her as "the belle of the ball," though her niece was the ostensible star of the evening.[21]

Lacouture was dancing and chatting with Mrs. Roosevelt when—disaster!— she suddenly slipped and fell to the floor. Mortified, he bent down to help her up, mumbling apologies and concern. Mrs. Roosevelt laughed it off, "smiled graciously," and insisted that they finish the dance, which they did.[22]*

---

* Though it was the first coming-out party held in the White House in twenty-eight years, accounts of the event were pushed to the bottom of the social pages by another party held that same night at the Ritz-Carlton Hotel in New York in honor of Diana Duff Frazier, hailed by the press as "America's Number 1 glamour girl of 1938."

Everyone was back in Annapolis on New Year's Day, on which day basketball practice began. Hanley was thrilled to make the starting five as a guard. Though he had been called "Joe" (his middle name) all his life to distinguish him from his father, he was now more often called "Mike," which is how his name appeared in the sports pages, and because of that, he came to be known as "Mike" to his classmates as well. The sports writers described him as "a lanky veteran," who was especially effective on defense but who could also hit the outside shot.[23]

The late return from Christmas break allowed only five days of practice before the first game against Gettysburg College, which may be one reason Navy lost 37–33 in spite of Hanley's eight points. Navy lost again at Syracuse a week later despite jumping out to a 12–1 lead. For the next game, the coach shifted Hanley from guard to center, and he scored a team-high eleven points as Navy beat Loyola. He stayed at center for the game against North Carolina, whose center was a prospective all-American, and Hanley's job was to contain him. It was a tough, physical game, and Hanley remembered having "a very rough time" of it. But he kept his man in check, and Navy won 46–38.[24]

The next day, a lieutenant commander approached Hanley in the Yard. Hanley thought he was coming to congratulate him. Instead, Hanley recalled, "He gave me hell for not having a proper haircut when so many people observed me at the game." As Hanley put it, "Athletes were not coddled."[25]

The big game, of course, was against Army. Each team had compiled an identical record of 11-2 and was ranked in the top ten in the country. The game was played at home in Dahlgren Hall, and there was a lot of extra attention paid to the contest because of the increasingly tense circumstances in Europe. In addition to print reporters, film crews from Pathé and Movietone News crowded into the hall. Extra stands were erected to hold the entire regiment, and hundreds more crammed into the balcony that encircled the playing court; the crowd was estimated to exceed seven thousand, with thousands more unable to get in. Hanley was convinced that "midshipmen are the greatest rooters and cheerers in the country. The noise level in Dahlgren Hall," he recalled, "would start your adrenalin [sic] pumping."[26]

That pumping adrenaline was evident in the first minutes. Hanley was fouled going in for a shot and scored the first points of the game when he made both free throws. Then he scored another basket, stole a pass, and went the length of the floor for a layup. Suddenly, Navy had a 12–5 lead. As the *Baltimore Sun* reporter put it, "For a few fleeting exuberant minutes, Navy had a chance." It did not last. Army ran off ten straight points and took command of the

BEAT ARMY

game. In the second half, Hanley scored three in a row to cut Army's lead to 36–28, but he got into foul trouble, and the rest of game was, as the *Sun* reporter put it, "a hopeless stern chase." Army won 46–32. At least Hanley was able to watch himself in the newsreel that was shown at the downtown theater the next week.[27]

Hanley was gratified a few days later when, during a bridge game in the Hall after class, the midshipman on duty, called the "Mate of the Deck," stuck his head in the door to tell him, "Mike, you have been elected captain of the basketball team." At that moment, Hanley remembered thinking, "Life was sweet."[28]

Other members of the class also had their moments in the athletic spotlight. The Navy lacrosse team was the defending national champion and seemed to be headed to another title before losing to the eventual champion Maryland. In track, Leon Chabot, known as "Chab," who had been the Massachusetts State sprint champion in high school, was all but unbeatable, winning both the 100 and the 220 in virtually every meet, and setting an Academy record of 9.6 seconds in the 100, only two-tenths of a second off Jesse Owens's world record. And "Sparky" Campo, the Filipino national, was equally dominant in fencing, becoming the national intercollegiate saber champion.

There was a lighter moment near the end of the academic year when the commandant of midshipmen, Captain Milo Draemel, the craggy-faced officer in charge of discipline, was shocked to see a newspaper photograph of a midshipman who had just returned from his destroyer cruise kissing a young woman who had come to meet him. Draemel was "a straitlaced and puritanical gentleman," according to Hanley, and he immediately declared that there was to be no more "public osculation" by midshipmen in uniform.[29]

It was not an official order, but the word was passed in the Hall. In addition to generating widespread mockery about Draemel's use of the term "osculation," it provoked speculation and concern within the class of 1940 about the forthcoming Ring Dance. As rising firsties, they were scheduled to receive their class rings on the Monday before the class of 1939 graduated. It was a milestone in midshipman life. The rings, which a committee of midshipmen that included Myers Montgomery had designed, were anointed in a silver bowl filled with water from the Atlantic, the Pacific, and the Gulf of Mexico, then as each rising firstie and his drag passed through a huge papier mâché replica of the ring, she would slip the ring on his finger and they would kiss. Was this now banned? And how would the new rule affect the "passing out" parade a few days later? It was a long-standing tradition for the company that won what was called the "color competition" to formally pass the national flag—the colors—on to the succeeding class, in this case, of course, the class of 1940. After the regiment paraded on Worden Field, the "color girl" (usually the girlfriend of the color company commander) made the symbolic presentation, and since 1924 that had been followed by a kiss from her boyfriend. Was that now banned as well?

The *Baltimore Sun* reported the widespread apprehension. "Midshipmen are in a lather," it divulged breathlessly: "Not about exams. Not about the next war. But about whether the color girl will give and receive the customary osculatory salute at the presentation of the colors." Reporters pestered Naval Academy officials about it. The Academy spokesman denied that there was any "official order" against kissing. The reporters persisted: "Will the color girl be kissed?" The spokesman avoided a direct answer: "We don't know. Maybe she won't want to be."[30]

The Ring Dance came first. Captain Draemel may have been especially sensitive to public scrutiny because Eleanor Roosevelt had accepted an invitation from the class to be their special guest. Several mids danced with her that night and later pronounced her to be "a most charming, gracious, and graceful First Lady." Whether or not her presence was a factor, Draemel announced that the format for the presentation of rings would be changed. As the *Sun* explained it, "Instead of each girl separately placing a ring on the finger of her midshipman as they go through a giant ring, the ceremony will take place simultaneously, as the band plays the Navy Blue and Gold." And that is what happened, except that, when the first notes of "Navy Blue and Gold" sounded, all the lights in Dahlgren Hall went out, and it was completely dark when the rings were presented. Under that veil of darkness there was a great deal of clandestine osculation. The lights came back on five minutes later. Someone in the class of 1940 had found a practical use for all those courses in electrical engineering. When the mids subsequently passed through the oversized ring, they primly shook hands with their drags, though as one recalled, they did not bother to wipe the grins, or the lipstick, off their faces.[31]

By then, the mercurial Montgomery had experienced another romantic conversion. He and Joann had a spat in October when Montgomery asked her to break a date she had made with another mid in order to be with him, and she had refused. Myers spent most of the next night "composing a good letter . . . trying to fix things up." It didn't work. His heart quickly mended, though, and he took "Nancy" to the Ring Dance, pleased to see how wonderful she looked in her "beautiful pink formal."[32]

BEAT ARMY

The most downcast member of the class that night was John Lacouture, who had received a literal "Dear John" letter the week before from his girlfriend in Chicago. She had fallen in love with another man, she wrote, and would not be able to see him anymore. Even fifty years later, Lacouture still felt the sting. It was, he said, a blow from which he never fully recovered. He went to the Ring Dance anyway, but "alas for me" he wrote, "with the wrong girl."[33]

The next day, there was a rehearsal of the color ceremony on Worden Field. The new superintendent, Rear Admiral Wilson Brown, escorted the "color girl," Francis "Minnie Mae" Moses of Little Rock, Arkansas, to the center of the field, and the colors were passed to the class of 1940 by the commander of the First Company, Benjamin Jarvis of Ferda, Arkansas. There was no kissing. But this, after all, was only a rehearsal.[34]

The next day was the real thing. The regiment paraded, Admiral Brown escorted Miss Moses onto the field, and she placed her hand on the flagstaff in the ceremonial passing of the colors. Here was the moment. According to the *Sun*, the crowd literally held its breath. Would they kiss?

No. As the paper put it, Francis Moses "became the first color girl in five years who didn't receive her reward in front of her company." The headline read: "Romance in Navy Succumbs Before Dictates of Dignity."[35]

There was, however, a good deal of kissing later that week after the graduation ceremony on Thompson Field. Now that they were commissioned officers, the members of the class of 1939 were no longer subject to Captain Draemel's edicts as commandant. After their girlfriends pinned their officer's shoulder boards on their uniforms, there was quite a lot of public osculation, and photos of embracing couples appeared in newspapers all over the country.

That graduation made the members of the class of 1940 firsties. And, as it turned out, Milo Draemel also got a promotion—to rear admiral.

6

Firsties

Their first class cruise was a bust—or, as one described it, "a disaster." The continuing war in Spain, plus concern over what could become an even wider war in central Europe, convinced the Navy Department to cancel the planned trip to Europe altogether, in favor of a cruise up and down the Eastern Seaboard. One class member described it as "sailing in circles around the Atlantic." After the change of plans was made public, a newspaper wondered mockingly whether the navy should change its recruiting slogan from "Join the Navy and see the world" to "Join the Navy and see the Atlantic Ocean." Pete Peterson's reaction to the news was, "Phooey," though, as it turned out, he would have occasion to reconsider that verdict.[1]

In an echo of their departure for youngster cruise two years earlier, class members either hoisted their seabags onto their shoulders or used one of the big laundry carts to trundle their belongings down to the *Reina Mercedes* dock, where they boarded whaleboats that carried them four miles out to the waiting battleships. Besides the 450 or so members of the class of 1940, another 650 new youngsters from the class of 1942 also boarded, making the battleships, once again, quite crowded. Two of the battleships were the same vessels they had ridden in 1937—the *New York* and the *Arkansas*. With the *Wyoming* in refit, the USS *Texas* became the third vessel of what was dubbed the Training Squadron. It was as chaotic a departure as it had been two years earlier, as eleven hundred mids got themselves and their seabags on board.[2]

This time, at least, the Forties got actual bunks instead of hammocks. This time, too, they had junior officer jobs rather than scut work. They even had tables and chairs in their staterooms so they could write letters in relative comfort. Pete Peterson, who kept a diary during the cruise, thought it was "pretty nice" not to have to get up at reveille. There were the usual daily drills: fire and rescue, collision, abandon ship, and periodic calls to general quarters, and though they each had a specific job, they also had five or six youngsters working

FIRSTIES

under them to do the actual work. As a result, they spent a lot of time supervising the youngsters, playing bridge, and, as one confessed, "loafing."[3]

There was little that was entirely unfamiliar, though Doc Weatherup found the engineering plant in the *New York* fascinating. The *New York* had been laid down in 1911 and was the last big US Navy ship to have a triple-expansion reciprocating engine rather than turbines. That meant that as the superheated steam passed through a series of chambers, giant steel pistons twenty feet long plunged up and down to turn an enormous crankshaft. To Weatherup, the moving parts were "so large as to be almost beyond belief."[4]

Steaming north along the Atlantic coast, the ships encountered a heavy fog, which entirely wrecked their planned star sight navigation practical. There were also icebergs. That was enough of a novelty that the battleships lowered boats so the mids could motor out to them and examine them close up. In New York, they enjoyed a tour of the world's fair, where the hopeful theme was "The World of Tomorrow." They contributed to the festivities by staging a formal parade through the center of the fair. The Canadian port visits were anticlimactic; Halifax and Quebec were poor substitutes for Rome and Athens. In his diary, Peterson wrote, "From all the dope about Halifax, I certainly didn't expect much of it, and that's what I got."[5]

Quebec was a little better. The Americans received a formal visit from the governor general of Canada, Lord Tweedmuir, better known to readers as John Buchan, author of *The Thirty-Nine Steps*, among other novels. The mids also had an opportunity to explore inland. John Lacouture and several others headed into the Canadian forests, where they encountered "deer, moose, and bear." They caught, cooked, and ate trout for dinner while camping. Back on the ship, however, Lacouture was devastated to receive a formal invitation to his former girlfriend's wedding. "Needless to say," he wrote later, "I was in the doldrums for the rest of the cruise."[6]

Members of the football team, including Monty Whitehead and Punkin Wood, were determined to find a way to practice some plays, especially since the cruise cut severely into their preseason practice time. Before leaving Annapolis, they had "liberated" several footballs from the team equipment locker (listing them as "lost at sea") in the hope of finding an opportunity to hold at least a few practices. So when their ship dropped anchor off Quebec, they went ashore in their gym gear and gathered on a broad swath of grass outside the old Citadel. It was, of course, the storied "Plains of Abraham" where General James Wolfe had defeated General Louis-Joseph, Marquis de Montcalm, in 1759 and won Canada for Britain. It was a hot day, and the mids soon stripped down to their shorts and shoes to run through some plays.

Then the police arrived. It turned out that there was a city ordinance against "people exhibiting their upper bodies without covering." The police explained this to the mids, who dutifully donned their jerseys. As soon as the police left, however, the jerseys came off again. The police returned, as did the jerseys. This went on for several iterations, much to the amusement of the handful of spectators.[7]

On Independence Day, the mids staged a skit they called *Jesse James Rides Again*, in which they satirized several of the ship's officers, including the captain. Most of the gibes were gentle and provoked appreciative laughter, though one self-important lieutenant recognized himself in the character of Count Vronsky in the skit, and through he laughed (a bit self-consciously) at the appropriate moments, Pete Peterson noted that he "shrank down a little in his chair" each time.[8]

After Quebec, the ships of the Training Squadron headed back down the St. Lawrence River. The mids caught several glimpses of the Northern Lights before the ships turned south through another dense fog, to Provincetown, Gloucester, and Marblehead on the Massachusetts coast. At Marblehead there was another reception ashore. As at most such events, the mids sought to ingratiate themselves with the local females. Pete Peterson, who had taken to rendering his diary in verse, found many of the young women charming, but he was utterly smitten by one in particular:

> There's Dolly, Irene, Bonnie, and Jane,
> But there's one meets my eye, who, like a chain,
> Grips my heart in a way I've not known before,
> For Lynn is beautiful, delightful and more.

If the cruise marked the termination of John Lacouture's romance, it marked the beginning of Pete Peterson's. Nevertheless, at midnight on July 27, he and everyone else were back on board the battleships waving goodbye. Philosophically, Peterson wrote, "Such is life in the Navy."[9]

He did not pine away. When the ships dropped anchor in Portsmouth, just up the coast in New Hampshire, he was pleased to find "three or four hundred cuties" available for dancing to the sounds of Ozzie Nelson and his orchestra.* They enjoyed another stop in New York, where they took in Broadway shows,

---

* Oswald "Ozzie" Nelson led a popular orchestra in the 1930s and had several hit songs. He married the band's vocalist, Harriet Hilliard, and after the war they developed a popular TV series, *The Adventures of Ozzie and Harriet*. Their younger son, Ricky Nelson, later became a successful singer in his own right.

FIRSTIES

67

including *Hellzapoppin*, and the stage version of *The Wizard of Oz*, with Judy Garland and Micky Rooney. Most of them made it to Times Square, where they "walked around for an hour seeing the sights."[10]

John Lacouture had lost his love, Pete Peterson had found one, and unsurprisingly Myers Montgomery fell back in love. He had invited Harriet June, whom he had known back in Malden, to meet him in New York. And sure enough, when the battleships arrived at the Fifty-Ninth Street Pier, she was there waiting for him. They had a wonderful time: dinner at a country club on Long Island, listening to the Glenn Miller Band at the Glen Island Casino, and just being together in New York. At the end of the evening, Montgomery noted that it was "certainly hard to say goodbye to Harriet at [the] station."[11]

Five days later, on the last day of August, they were all back at the Naval Academy. They did not tarry. Granted a month's leave, they clambered ashore, grabbed what they needed from their rooms in Bancroft Hall, and headed for the gate. Montgomery and five others crowded into a car and drove west through the mountains of Virginia, taking turns at the wheel in two-hour shifts. Others used public transportation. The *Baltimore Sun* noted that "the midshipmen wasted no time getting out of the city" and reported that "the busses to Washington, and trains to Baltimore were crowded."[12]

Not everyone headed home. Ever ready for the next adventure, John Lacouture and three others had been invited to a party in Toronto by "a really cute girl we had met in Halifax." They rented a Lincoln convertible (or was it a Packard, he couldn't remember) and "zoomed off to Toronto." The party was to take place on September 3, and to make it in time, they drove nonstop except for a quick look at Niagara Falls. They got to her house on the afternoon of the third, where instead of a party they encountered doleful expressions. They learned that only hours before Britain and France—and Canada, too—had declared war on Germany. They decided "we had better head home to await developments."[13]

While they had cruised up and down the Atlantic coast attending "tea fights" and receptions, listening to Glenn Miller, and falling in and out of love, Europe was edging closer and closer to the brink of war. Despite Hitler's promise at Munich that he had no more territorial ambitions in Europe, he had waited only six months before gobbling up the remnant of Czechoslovakia in March 1939. Then, as Punkin and Monty practiced football bare-chested on the Plains of Abraham, Hitler demanded that the "Free City" of Danzig, established by the Treaty of Versailles to give Poland an outlet to the sea, be returned to Germany. A spokesman for the German government insisted that Germany did not seek "a war like solution," but he also made it clear that the "problem" must be solved—and soon. Having been burned by the Munich fiasco, Chamberlain's government now pledged to support and defend Poland if Hitler attacked. It was also ominous that, as Montgomery noted in his diary, "Russia and Germany signed a 10-year non-aggression pact." He noted, too, that "Germany made definite demands on Poland, and England and France vowed to fight for Poland," adding, somewhat unnecessarily, "situation very serious." On the other hand, most Americans—and most midshipmen, too— saw it as a strictly European issue. The *New York Daily News* spoke for most when it editorialized that there was no reason why "any American should lose a wink of sleep over Danzig."[14]

On September 1, 1939, most members of the class who were not "zooming" to Toronto for a party were either home or en route there. Mike Hanley, who lived in DC, took a date to the movies that night. When they exited the theater, paper boys on the sidewalk were hawking "extra" editions of the *Evening Star* with the headline: "POLAND INVADED; CITIES BOMBED." Hanley remembered that "a chill went up my back." Montgomery was in Knoxville, Tennessee, packing the car for the last leg of his trip home to Missouri, when he heard the news on the radio. "The war," he noted, "had come at last."[15]

As promised, Britain mobilized its armed forces and sent an ultimatum to Berlin declaring that if Germany did not withdraw its troops at once, Britain would "fulfill its obligations to Poland." Germany ignored the ultimatum, and so, on September 3, 1939, Chamberlain went on the radio to announce, in a solemn tone, "This country is now at war with Germany."[16]

President Roosevelt ordered that the news be sent immediately to "all Navy ships and Army commands by radio." He did not, however, announce a mobilization or even recall servicemen from leave. Instead, he pledged that the United States would remain strictly neutral. Given popular sentiment, it was the only position he could take. Even after the Soviet Union stabbed Poland in the back by invading from the east on September 17, Americans' determination to stay out of it was unaffected. Astute politician that he was, Roosevelt knew he could not get ahead of public opinion. Consequently, while German planes bombed Polish cities and German ground units closed in on Warsaw, the midshipmen of the Naval Academy class of 1940 remained at home, visiting family, "dragging" local girls to movies, sleeping late, and generally enjoying themselves. The diary entry of Myers Montgomery for that

FIRSTIES

historic September 3 is revealing: "Jim and I went out to tennis courts and played a while. I won the set 6–4.... France and England dramatically declared war on Germany....Bud and I lost a doubles set to Laverne and Jim 12–10.... Went to the movies."[17]

The Poles fought hard, and the garrison of Warsaw held out for weeks against long odds, pummeled every day from the air and pressed from all sides on the ground. Finally, on September 28, Warsaw surrendered. Some 140,000 Poles were taken prisoner, most of them never to be heard from again. Poland itself virtually ceased to exist as Hitler and Stalin divided it between them.

That same day—September 28—the members of the class of 1940 headed back to Annapolis—however reluctantly. It was a sober group that reported to Bancroft Hall, and their collective mood was further depressed by news that four midshipmen, driving back to Annapolis from Texas, had been killed in a car accident in Tennessee. Suddenly, issues of life and death were all around them.

The next day, a headline in the *Baltimore Sun* read: "Academy Routine Unchanged by War." The *Sun* reporter wrote that it was "business as usual" in Annapolis. That was certainly true on the surface. The Academy administration and faculty made no effort to suggest that the European war offered any useful lessons. "We were not advised," one midshipman recalled, "on the trials and tribulations...being suffered by the British." As Bill Lanier put it, "Things continued as before, in the same familiar established routine": marching to class, drawing slips and manning the board, practicing with their athletic teams, and asking the new plebes, "How's the Cow?" Even so, there was a difference, if a subliminal one. Mike Hanley remembered that "the atmosphere at the Academy [had] changed." There was a new seriousness of purpose. With war raging in Europe, no one, he remembered, wanted to bilge out now. "We had lots of things on our minds."[18]

There were a number of privileges that came with being firsties. They could walk in any of the passageways in Bancroft Hall and use all of the ladders (stairways), while plebes and others gave way to them. It was also fairly common for firsties to hire one of the African American janitors (known as "corridor boys," regardless of their age) to make up their beds for them each morning and sweep out their rooms for a quarter a week. Such was the culture of the United States in 1939 that no one saw a problem with this practice or with the designation of those so employed as "mokes," an obviously derogatory term derived from "smokes." Indeed, "moke" was one of the words listed in *Reef Points* as traditional Naval Academy slang, defining it as a "colored corridor boy or mess attendant." The word "moke" continued to appear in the Glossary of Naval Terms until 1942, after which it quietly disappeared. Even then, the term was used colloquially in Bancroft Hall well into the 1950s.

There were also obligations that came with being firsties. Organizationally, the student body was designated as a "regiment" composed of four battalions, each with three companies.* All of the firsties got a leadership assignment within that structure, with responsibilities and perks depending on the number of stripes they were allotted. Tom "Tiny" McGrath from Tucson became regimental commander and wore five stripes on his sleeve. Al Bergner, who had made the train trip to Berlin back during youngster cruise, was a battalion commander with four stripes. Mike Hanley who was on battalion staff, wore three stripes; Bruce Rohn, who had shaken hands with Hitler, was a two-striper, as were Bob Harris, Peck Greenbacker, and Doc Weatherup. Myers Montgomery and John Lacouture each wore only a single stripe as squad leaders. Lacouture was not surprised. He acknowledged later that he "never did well in either conduct or grease," and he was not terribly disappointed. Having few responsibilities allowed him to kick back and "enjoy life at the Academy." Besides, even with a single stripe, both he and Montgomery stood in the front rank at parades and led their platoons.[19]

Once again, football dominated the fall schedule. The season started out well enough, with Navy notching victories over William & Mary and the University of Virginia, the latter win sparked by a trick play when quarterback Punkin Wood faked a punt and ran forty-seven yards to set up the go-ahead touchdown. Wood also kicked the extra point, which proved crucial in a 14–12 victory. Alas, Wood wrenched his knee in the second half and was lost for the season.

More than eighty thousand packed the stands in Cleveland for the game against Notre Dame. With Punkin out, backup quarterback Lou Leonard threw a long pass to Monty Whitehead for an early touchdown, though Navy lost the game 14–7. In the next game against Columbia, Whitehead scored again on a sixty-five-yard touchdown run, but the Navy defense proved vulnerable to the pass, something opponents soon discovered, and Navy lost to both Columbia and Princeton. Of course, none of that would matter if they could

---

* The designation of the student body as a "regiment" dated from 1914 and remained in place through World War II. With the enlargement of the Academy after the war, the student body was redesignated a "brigade" with two regiments. Today, the top midshipman is the brigade commander, who wears six stripes on his or her uniform.

FIRSTIES 71

beat Army, a confrontation the entire regiment had anticipated since the beginning of the year.

Neither Army nor Navy had a particularly good team that year. The week before the game, the *Washington Post* ran a scathing editorial about the disappointing Navy football team, and John Lardner, in the *Evening Star*, sarcastically offered free tickets to anyone who could name a worse team than either Army or Navy. "Everyone," Montgomery wrote in his diary, was "mad about it." There was a huge pep rally with two bonfires, and spirits were high. Almost as an afterthought, Montgomery added: "Russia attacked Finland."[20]

More than one hundred thousand people, including President Roosevelt, crowded into Philadelphia's Municipal Stadium for the game. Scalpers were charging so much that both schools announced that anyone who paid more than the official price of $4.40 for a ticket would not be allowed in the gate, though how they planned to enforce that was unclear.[21]

The day opened with gray skies and what the *Baltimore Sun* described as a "clammy mist that hung over the greatest crowd of American sport." With both sides keyed up, the game was a defensive struggle, and Navy clung to a 3–0 lead at halftime. In the second half, Monty Whitehead was the difference, repeatedly smashing into Army's line for three or four yards at a time as Navy muscled its way down the field for an insurance touchdown and a final score of 10–0. The midshipmen were elated. "Will we ever forget how proud and happy we were?" one asked rhetorically. According to the *Lucky Bag*—the Navy yearbook—it was an indescribable feeling "when the final gun barked and we knew we had done it." It was a "happy ride back from the victory."[22]

World events did not stop for football. On the day of the game, President Roosevelt declared a "moral embargo" on the Soviet Union for its invasion of Finland even as the Finns fought back with unexpected resilience. The war was coming closer to American shores, too. German U-boats were savaging British trade in the North Atlantic, and Roosevelt declared a neutrality zone around the Americas. Officially and publicly, his goal was to keep the war away from the Western Hemisphere, but by asking navy warships to enforce the neutrality zone, he increased the likelihood of a confrontation with German U-boats. Still, Roosevelt was determined to do whatever he could, within the limits of public support, to aid the Anglo-French allies. He was convinced that America's own national security depended on an Allied victory, and he was buoyed by a national poll showing that nine in ten Americans declared themselves willing to pay higher taxes to beef up the country's military, which was exactly what FDR planned to do.

Preparedness was one thing, but sending military arms to an active belligerent like Britain was another. Many Americans worried that aid to Britain was a slippery slope that would drag the United States into the war. The depth of such suspicions became evident to the members of the class of 1940 a few days before Christmas break. It was a tradition at the Academy for firsties to invite the congressman or senator who had appointed them to the Academy to Christmas dinner in Bancroft Hall. One of those who accepted the invitation that year was Senator Ernest Lundeen of Minnesota, officially a member of the Farmer-Labor Party but notorious for his fierce opposition to Roosevelt and the president's pro-British policy. Lundeen was more than an isolationist: He was an apologist for the Nazi regime and considered Britain, more than Germany, to be America's true foe. At dinner, he sat at the end of the table "flanked by four or five midshipman each to his left and right" to discuss events in Europe. As he talked, he "pounded his fist on the table" and proclaimed: "As long as I am in the Senate, you young men will not have to fight 'their' war. We bailed them out of World War I and we will not do it again."[23*]

In mid-December, most mids focused as much on the forthcoming Christmas leave as they did their studies. Myers Montgomery was now besotted with Harriet June, who had met him in New York during the first-class cruise, and whom he saw again when he returned to Malden for Christmas. This time, he sounded serious. "My heart was for only one girl," he told his diary, "and what a girl!" He solemnly concluded that it was "the first time I'm really in love." Yet when she revealed to him that she already had a date for New Year's Eve, instead of lapsing into despair, he made a date with Joann. He also found time to date "Rosie," and on his last night before returning to Annapolis, he confessed that he "sure hated to tell Rosie goodbye."[24]

Back in Annapolis after Christmas it was basketball season. Mike Hanley, now team captain, was excited about it, though it was not clear that Navy had the manpower to produce a winning season. The *Sun* sports reporter noted that the team had plenty of enthusiasm, but he introduced a note of caution in writing that there were "things that are difficult to teach." He offered what amounted to a tutorial on how to play the game: "feinting one way and cutting another; shooting passes instantly through openings you sense but do not see...when to switch, when to hold, when to give ground." By implication, at

---

* Lundeen was so adamant about halting aid to Britain that he became a paid propagandist for the Nazi government. At the time of his death in a plane crash in August 1940, he was under investigation by the FBI.

FIRSTIES

least, he suggested that these were things the Navy team could *not* do, or at least could not do well.[25]

He was right. Navy won only two games that year while losing eleven. In the final regular season game, Hanley scored twenty points, but Navy lost again, 52–46. Hanley was determined to salvage the season with a win over Army. Wanting it badly was not enough. Indeed, it may have been a weakness, for Hanley was whistled for three fouls in the first seven minutes and spent much of the game on the bench. Navy lost again.

There were other athletic disappointments that spring. Chab Chabot, who had been all but unbeatable in the sprints the year before, was hobbled by a pulled hamstring and missed several meets. Sparky Campo, the defending national champion in saber, was upset by fencers from Cornell and Columbia, and Navy lost the national fencing team title to NYU when Campo was upset again for the individual saber title.[26]

Final grades were posted at the end of term. John Lacouture was gratified to finish in the top 10 percent, ranking forty-fifth out of 456, in large part due to an excellent performance in English and history, where he ranked fifth overall. As he had admitted, he could "sling the bull" pretty well. On the other hand, his flexible approach to rules and regulations was evident in his ranking 340th in conduct.

Both Connie Carlson and Bob Harris ranked comfortably near the top: Carlson at 74th, and Harris at 89th (and 26th in "bull"). Mike Hanley, despite a busy basketball season, finished in the top third at 149th. Hundy Hundevadt graduated at 164th, Myers Montgomery at 181st, and Doc Weatherup, who had been 164th at the beginning of the year, coasted to 222nd. Others were bunched comfortably in the middle: Sparky Campo at 203rd, Des Desmond at 204th, and Chab Chabot at 208th. Others were happy to make it at all, including Monty Whitehead, who graduated 409th, only forty-seven from the bottom.[27]

The honor man in the class—the individual with the highest academic standing—was Joe D'Arezzo of Los Angeles. He got his picture in the paper and a nice round of applause at graduation, but he did *not* get a commission. D'Arezzo was one of thirty graduates who, despite trying multiple times, never managed to get his eye exam results to the required 20/20. Despite a stellar academic performance, he was declared "not physically qualified," handed his diploma, and sent on his way. Hugely disappointed, he went to the army, which, as it turned out, was less fastidious about eyesight, and within weeks, he had secured a direct commission as an army second lieutenant. Eventually he became a brigadier general. Another member of the class denied a commission for imperfect eyesight was John F. Freund, known as "Fritz," a quiet and studious midshipman described by his roommate as "outwardly jovial but inwardly serious." Though he graduated near the top of the class, Freund was also declared NPQ for imperfect eyesight, and, like D'Arezzo, he turned to the army. During the ensuing three decades, he earned the Distinguished Service Medal, Silver Star, two Bronze Stars, a Purple Heart, and twelve air medals, and retired as a major general, suggesting that perfect eyesight was not an especially accurate predictor of effective performance.[28]

The anchor man in the class, the one with the lowest academic standing, who by tradition got a dollar from every other member of the class, was Harold "Swede" Hansen, a "good natured and easy-going" football player and shot-putter from Philadelphia and a popular teller of amusing stories.

More important on a practical level than their class standing was the number they drew in the lottery for service assignments. Everyone, even those who had come to the Academy to fly, had to pick a ship for his first assignment because everyone had to serve two years at sea before he could begin specialized training. Getting a particular ship was quite literally the luck of the draw, because regardless of class standing, each graduating midshipman drew a number out of a hat. Warren Smalzel, who was the class photographer, drew number one and, in the conviction that the battleship remained the queen of naval warfare, chose the recently modernized USS *Idaho* (BB-42). John D. "Charley" Chase, though he ranked fourteenth academically, drew the last number—456—and discovered that there was still one junior officer billet left on the aircraft carrier *Saratoga* (CV-3), which he took. Their selections reflected the presumed hierarchy of combat ships at the time. Indeed, *Reef Points* was quite specific about it. In a naval engagement, it explained, the carriers would be "far behind the battle-line," and their mission was "to launch scouting planes to locate the enemy." Clearly the real fighting was to be done by the battleships with the carriers metaphorically holding their coats. That pecking order would soon be turned upside down.[29]

Excited as they were about graduation, by now nearly everyone in the class was keeping one eye on events in Europe. Though war had been declared in September, neither side had made a move, and the newspapers began calling the ensuing stalemate "the phony war." There was a brief flurry of activity in April when Germany, seeking a safe route for its ore shipments from Norway and Sweden, launched an audacious campaign into Denmark and Norway.

The Kriegsmarine used destroyers as troop transports to deposit soldiers at a half dozen sites along the lengthy Norwegian coast. The British counterattacked, and both sides suffered heavy losses, especially around Narvik, where each side lost several destroyers, though in the end Germany remained in firm control of both Norway and Denmark. Even then, however, things remained quiet along the Franco-German border.[30]

Then suddenly, with their graduation only days away, the phony war exploded into furious violence. After the long period of inaction, it was almost breathtaking. In May, spearheaded by tanks and with Luftwaffe planes flying cover, the German army sliced through the Ardennes Forest north of the supposedly impregnable Maginot Line and sped for the Channel ports. The onslaught was so swift, news reports could not keep up: Antwerp, Ostend, and other key Channel ports were in German hands; the British Expeditionary Force, which had occupied the lowlands upon the declaration of war, was cut off; other German forces were "lancing straight toward Paris."[31]

After only five days, French prime minister Paul Reynaud woke Winston Churchill, who had succeeded Neville Chamberlain as prime minister, with an early-morning phone call to tell him plaintively, "We have been defeated." Churchill tried to encourage him, but it was no use. We must have an armistice, Reynaud told him. The British army, trapped against the coast at Dunkirk, began evacuating forces on May 26. That same day in Annapolis, companies began the annual drill competition to determine which of them would win the right to name the "color girl" in the graduation parade.[32]

Two days later, Belgium surrendered. With the Belgians no longer holding their portion of the line, the British and French contracted their defenses around a shrinking beachhead at Dunkirk. British Admiral Bertram Ramsay, coordinating the evacuation, called for civilian volunteers to help, and hundreds of small boats, even sailing yachts, answered the call. Complaints from the French that their soldiers were being left behind led Churchill to order them to be rescued as well, and by June 1, British and French warships, plus the flotilla of volunteers, were rescuing fifty thousand men a day from the beaches.[33]

That day also marked the beginning of "June week" in Annapolis, a celebratory week of parades, balls, and athletic contests, including an Army-Navy baseball game and track meet. Navy won the baseball game 4–2 and won the track meet, too, thanks in part to Chab Chabot, who had recovered enough from his pulled hamstring to win the 100, and held on long enough in the 220 to place third and complete a Navy sweep of that event.[34]

The next day, as the evacuations off Dunkirk continued, members of the class of 1940 attended Baccalaureate Services in the Academy Chapel. The chaplain, Commander William Thomas, told them, "The test of a man's philosophy of life is what he does in a crisis." And here, without question, was a crisis.[35]

On June 3, a large and happy crowd gathered to watch the last formal parade of the year on Worden Field. For the members of the class of 1940, it was their last parade ever. After they passed in review and executed the manual of arms, they stood at parade rest while the commandant of midshipman, Captain F. A. L. Vossler, escorted the color girl, nineteen-year-old Helen Barbara "Bobbie" Engh of Sweet Briar College and the girlfriend of Second Company Commander William Croft, to the center of the field. There she assisted Croft in symbolically transferring the colors to the class of 1941. They did not kiss. As the *Sun* reported, "Academy officials have ruled that kissing was not the custom at the color presentation."[36]

By the time the parade ended, it was twilight in Annapolis, and happy family members wandered down out of the stands to talk with their midshipmen as fireflies blinked among the trees. Five time zones to the east in the English Channel, it was midnight, and under the cover of darkness, the last elements of the British rear guard at Dunkirk quietly slipped into small boats that took them through the surf to destroyers waiting offshore. Some 265 British soldiers, too badly wounded to move, remained behind, along with forty thousand French soldiers, all of whom were made prisoner by the Nazis.[37]

The next day was graduation day. It was held outdoors in Thompson Stadium behind Bancroft Hall. Until the last minute there was hope that the president would deliver the address. He had spoken at West Point the year before, and it was the Naval Academy's turn. But due to the ongoing crisis in Europe the president stayed in Washington and sent the colorless secretary of the navy, Charles Edison, son of the inventor, to give the address. Edison told the 456 graduates and nearly ten thousand spectators that, whatever happened, "the navy must be ready." Such anodyne advice made little impact on the grads; later, John Lacouture could not even remember who the speaker was.

After the graduates received their diplomas, 401 of them stood to take the oath as ensigns in the US Navy. Then twenty-five others, including John "Jocko" Antonelli and Fred Karch, both of whom subsequently became generals, as well as the sprinter Chab Chabot, were sworn in as second lieutenants in the Marine Corps. Thirty others, including valedictorian Joe D'Arezzo, got no

FIRSTIES

commission at all. Most of those who were not commissioned had failed the eye test, but one of them, Gaylord "Buck" Buchanan of Claysville, Pennsylvania, was NPQ because of an accident during his second-class year that had claimed much of his right leg below the knee. Though a prosthetic device allowed him to continue with his studies and graduate, he could not be commissioned. There was one more who remained seated. It was Abraham "Sparky" Campo, the Philippine national, who successfully graduated but got no commission. Instead, he returned to the Philippines, where he received a commission as a lieutenant in the Philippine army and was eventually assigned to the command of a torpedo boat.[38]*

In accordance with tradition, after the swearing in, the members of the class of 1940 offered three cheers to those they would leave behind, threw their midshipmen caps into the air, and dispersed to find family and friends. The new officers accepted kisses on the cheek from misty-eyed mothers, and firm handshakes from proud fathers. They stood still while mothers, sisters, and girlfriends affixed new shoulder boards (or second lieutenant's bars) to their uniforms. There were goodbyes, promises to stay in touch, even a few parties that evening. But soon enough, they parted to begin new lives as officers.

Theirs was the last Naval Academy class to complete a full four-year program for some time. Prompted by events in Europe and Asia, Roosevelt continued to urge military preparations, one of which was that the next Naval Academy class—the class of 1941—would graduate four months early, in February rather than in June, and that the next two classes (1942 and 1943) would graduate after only three years. He also announced an initiative to add five thousand Naval Reserve officers to the fleet after only four months of training.[39]

In that same press conference, Roosevelt revealed that the Pacific battleship fleet, to which more than 150 members of the class of 1940 had been assigned, instead of being homeported at San Pedro or Long Beach in California, would now be stationed in Hawaii, at a place called Pearl Harbor.

---

* Of the thirty NPQ graduates in the class of 1940, twenty-three eventually served on active duty: four were retained at the Naval Academy as instructors; two became army officers (both rising to general's rank), and seventeen were recalled to active service in the navy as war loomed. Of those seventeen, six became commanders and five became captains.

PART II

Junior Officers

It is on the battle forces . . . that a final decision of a large naval engagement must depend, because the basis of these forces, and in fact, of the entire Navy, is the powerful battleship.

—Reef Points, 1941

7

The Real Navy

On June 10, 1940, one month to the day after the Germans began their thrust into the Ardennes (*Fall Gelb*), and one week after the class of 1940 graduated, Italy declared war on France. Just as Stalin had waited to make sure Germany would defeat Poland before he joined the attack, Mussolini waited until it seemed certain France would fall before he piled on. The next day, a visibly angry FDR told the audience at the University of Virginia graduation ceremony: "The hand that held the dagger has struck it into the back of its neighbor."[1]

Two weeks later, on June 22, representatives of the French army met with a German delegation in a railway car near Compiegne in France. It was the same railroad car in which German representatives had signed the armistice ending World War I, and it had remained there as a historical monument ever since. Hitler chose the site deliberately, and he made a point of sitting in the same chair French General Ferdinand Foch had used in November 1918. Like Foch, Hitler did not stay for the actual signing. After listening to the preamble of the surrender agreement, he stood up and walked out to show his contempt for the French.

If the terms that France and her allies had imposed on Germany in 1919 had been harsh, those Germany now imposed on France were draconian. Germany would physically occupy nearly two-thirds of France, including all of its coastline along both the English Channel and the Atlantic Ocean, plus—the ultimate insult—Paris itself. France retained sovereignty over only a small area in the south with a "capital" in the spa town of Vichy. When the surrender ceremony was over, Hitler ordered the site destroyed, symbolically wiping away the stain of the earlier defeat. Now, only Britain remained to carry on the war against Hitler's triumphant empire.

While that staged drama played out, the 426 brand-new junior officers of the US Navy and Marine Corps were enjoying what they considered a well-earned respite before reporting to their initial duty stations. Most of them went home, though Pete Peterson went first to Marblehead, Massachusetts, to visit the girl he had met on first-class cruise and had praised as "beautiful, delightful, and more." That postgraduation visit only reinforced his initial assessment. "It was a wonderful weekend," he confided to his diary. "She's certainly one swell girl, and if possible, I'm going to marry her."[2]

But not yet. One more restriction the navy placed on Academy grads was that they were not allowed to marry until after they had served two full years at sea as commissioned officers. Many resented that as an unwarranted intrusion into their private lives. Ed Donley of Buchanan, Michigan, defiantly married anyway and had his commission revoked. Donley claimed that was fine with him, and, like Joe D'Arezzo and Fritz Freund, he went to the army, retiring forty years later as a major general. Others in the class of 1940 married secretly or tried to. The Academy roommate of Myers Montgomery, Dusty Rhodes, married Tippy Ross a year after graduation, though when navy officials found out about it, his commission was also revoked.

Others were more circumspect. William Croft who went by his middle name Crosswell, or Cros, had commanded the color company at graduation. He married Barbara "Bobbie" Engh, who had been the color girl at that ceremony, in March 1942, three months before the restriction was due to expire, though only a few family members and close friends knew about it. He remained on active service.[3]

While many found the rule against marriage annoying, even tyrannical, some were subsequently grateful for it. Bob Harris was utterly smitten by the girl he was dating first-class year and would have married her but for the navy's rule. Years later, he was thankful: "Looking back," he wrote, "the rule made a lot of sense." The three years he and his classmates had spent "dragging" young women to hops under restricted and artificial circumstances (no hand-holding, no osculating) had left them naive about relationships. Thinking about it years later, Harris acknowledged that the navy's proscription against marriage meant that he "had a better chance to find and marry the right girl—and I did."[4]

It was probably good news for the romantically inclined Myers Montgomery, too, who during his Academy years had carried the torch for a startling number of young women, including Cecelia, Daphne, Karolyn, Connie, Eleanor, Harriet, Polly, Joann, and Nancy. He fancied himself in love more than once and wrote "sweet" letters to each of them, but in the end he married none of them.

THE REAL NAVY

John Lacouture's girl had already married someone else, yet, disappointed as he was, he did not mope. After graduation, he went to his family's summer home in Hyannisport and threw himself into what he described as "the pleasant life of sailing, tennis, and parties." The two middle Kennedy boys, Jack and Bobby, were home from England, where their father was the US ambassador.* Kennedy had sent his sons back to America to get them away from German bombs, which is why they were in Hyannisport that summer to compete with John Lacouture in the afternoon sailboat races.[5]

Soon enough, though, it was time for everyone to report to their assigned duty stations, which in Lacouture's case was the aircraft carrier *Saratoga* (CV-2). Like Doc Weatherup, Lacouture had decided that he wanted to be a navy pilot, though that, too, was delayed by yet another navy regulation that Academy grads had to wait two years before they could begin specialty training, including flight school. At least on the *Saratoga*, Lacouture calculated, he could become acclimated to the naval aviation community. It was, he recalled, "as near as I could get to actually flying and still put in my two (ugh) years as a black shoe," that is, a surface warfare officer.† The *Sara*, as she was commonly known, operated out of San Diego, which was about as far from Hyannisport as it was possible to get, so Lacouture decided to fly there in a twin-engine DC-2, which carried fourteen passengers in relative discomfort in a cabin only six feet wide. It was a long flight with several stops, and instead of seats, there were bunks along the sides of the plane for the passengers to sleep.[6]

Doc Weatherup also got orders to the *Saratoga*. In fact, a total of fifteen members of the class reported to the *Sara* that summer of 1940, yet when they arrived in San Diego, they discovered that the ship was not there. She was off participating in the navy's annual fleet exercise (Fleet Problem XXI) in the Pacific Ocean west of Hawaii. Though no one knew it at the time, it would be the last fleet exercise of the prewar era. Rather than send the young officers out to Hawaii to catch up with the fleet, the navy ordered the fifteen new ensigns to check into the Bachelor Officer's Quarters (BOQ) on Coronado Island and wait there until she came back.

---

* It was already evident that Joseph P. Kennedy's days as ambassador to the Court of St. James were numbered. While Roosevelt was doing all he could to supply beleaguered Britain with whatever it needed to defy the Nazis, Kennedy was publicly expressing doubts that Britain could survive at all. Consequently, Roosevelt cut him out of most of the important negotiations with Britain, including the transfer of fifty older destroyers to Britain in exchange for long-term leases on naval bases in the Western Hemisphere.

† Because naval aviators in the 1930s wore forest-green uniforms and brown shoes, surface warfare officers called them brown-shoe officers, or simply "brown shoes." The aviators commonly referred to surface warfare officers as "black shoes."

84 ANNAPOLIS GOES TO WAR

It was not a hardship. "We had a super time," Lacouture remembered. They were being paid $125 a month as ensigns, and while that was not a munificent sum even then, it was a fortune compared with the eight dollars a month they had received as midshipmen. Besides, the BOQ was free and food was cheap. The jitney ride into the city cost ten cents, which was also the price of cocktails at the Officers Club. Connie Carlson recalled that "it was a delightful week," with "tennis, volleyball, surfing, [and] partying."[7]

The *Saratoga* returned to San Diego at the end of July, her appearance foreshadowed by the arrival of her embarked air group. Because a carrier had to be underway, steaming into the wind, to launch planes, the air group always flew off the ship while it was still well out to sea, and landed on an airfield ashore before the carrier came into port. Once the big flattop eased into her berth at North Island, the fifteen members of the class of 1940 reported aboard and were assigned various jobs and battle stations. Lacouture was detailed to the gunnery department with a battle station in the forward fire control director; Weatherup went to the communications division and became the communications watch officer and signal officer. Weatherup later wrote, "I would have preferred Gunnery," and Lacouture, who had earned a 4.0 in bull at the Academy, probably would have preferred Communications. But no one asked them what duty they preferred, or examined their record to see where their natural talents lay; they were simply expected to fill in as needed. Bill Braybrook, who was one of several Forties assigned to the heavy cruiser *Tuscaloosa* (CA-37), saw that as an indictment of the Naval Academy curriculum. When he arrived on the *Tuscaloosa* in the Brooklyn Navy Yard, he was named the assistant navigation officer, but he was also given "a host of collateral duties that I'd never heard of before." He was disappointed and a little annoyed that "the Academy program did not do much to prepare me for what was ahead." Lacouture was even more disparaging, insisting that "all the engineering courses I took at the Naval Academy [were] of absolutely no value whatsoever." In his view, the Academy should have taught them "strategy, tactics, naval warfare history, writing ability, imagination, [and] leadership."[8]

On the other hand, whatever duties they were assigned, virtually every member of the class learned (some sooner than others) that their success depended heavily—if not entirely—on the petty officers in their division, and especially on the chiefs. In a moment of honest self-reflection, Lacouture acknowledged that "in spite of my lack of attention and predilection for liberty, I did learn who really ran the navy—the chief petty officers." Though the newly commissioned ensigns were technically senior, the chiefs were older—often by a decade or more—and with years of practical experience. The chiefs saluted the new ensigns and called them "sir," but they were more mentors than subordinates.[9]

While Lacouture, Weatherup, and the others underwent patient instruction at the hands of navy chiefs, they also discovered that life in the peacetime navy was "a rather relaxed operation." It was certainly a far cry from the strict routine at the Academy, and not significantly different from their leisurely days in the Coronado BOQ. Their workday began at 8:00; there was a midday break for lunch in the Junior Officers' Mess; and by four in the afternoon they were done. Most of them caught the 4:30 liberty boat ashore, changed into bathing trunks, and spent long afternoons bodysurfing, playing volleyball on the beach, or enjoying a game of squash. In the evening, "It was out with the girls," for drinks, dinner, and dancing. After that, some headed back to the ship, while others (usually including Lacouture) continued to party. After the Pacific Coast Club closed at midnight, they sometimes went skinny-dipping in the Pacific Ocean. The stragglers caught the 4:00 a.m. boat back to the ship, got three hours of sleep, and started all over again the next morning.[10]

By far the largest cohort from the Academy got orders to battleships—still considered the sine qua non of naval warfare. And while some of them went to battleships in the Atlantic, the vast majority were assigned to the Pacific fleet, which was homeported on the West Coast. To get there, John Lacouture had flown, but most of the new ensigns took a train or a bus. Some drove. One group consisting of Ben Hall, Tom Nicholson, Dick Champion, and Cary Hall (who was no relation to Ben, though they were both from Macon, Georgia) pooled their money and bought a secondhand 1938 Ford V-8 in which they set out across the country. That was a more daunting experience in 1940 than it became in later years. The Pennsylvania Turnpike would not open to cars until October, and the new ensigns had to use mostly two-lane roads with a speed limit of forty-five miles per hour. That may have been just as well since the Ford, despite its V-8 engine, produced only eighty-five horsepower. The road seemed to lead unerringly through every small town on the map, each with its own speed limit, often twenty-five miles an hour. Since the car did not have air conditioning, they left the windows open, and when it was not their turn to drive tried to sleep while sweating into the upholstery.

Another group that included Crosswell Croft made the drive in a secondhand Packard, stopping at Yellowstone National Park and the Grand Coulee

86 ANNAPOLIS GOES TO WAR

Dam (still under construction in 1940) on the way. All of them made it safely to California, where, like John Lacouture and Doc Weatherup, they found that the ships to which they had been assigned were not there. Indeed, when Bob Harris, who had orders to the USS *Pennsylvania* (BB-38), reported to the Navy Yard at San Pedro, he was told not only that his ship wasn't there but that nobody knew where it was—at least not officially.

The confusion and uncertainty were a product of President Roosevelt's effort to forestall further Japanese aggression in Asia. Even as he kept one eye on the war in Europe and the Atlantic, he kept his other eye on Japan's ongoing war in China. After the fall of France, the Japanese moved into orphaned French Indochina, and to signal American disapproval of that, and in the hope that it might restrain further Japanese aggression, FDR ordered the Pacific fleet commander, Admiral James O. Richardson, to keep the fleet in Pearl Harbor after the summer exercises concluded. Richardson was annoyed by that. Keeping the fleet in Hawaii would complicate both his logistics and his training plans. He flew to Washington to protest. It was to no avail. Indeed, his complaints very likely shortened his tenure as fleet commander. Six months later, in February 1941, the president replaced him with Husband Kimmel. The fleet stayed in Hawaii.[11]

One result of those decisions was that there were more than a hundred new ensigns from the class of 1940 cooling their heels in San Pedro or Long Beach that summer while the navy tried to round up transportation to get them out to Hawaii. Some took passage on the battleship *Maryland,* which was so crowded with "boot ensigns" that, reminiscent of their youngster cruise, a number of them had to sleep on transoms. Others embarked on the *Saratoga*. One of them was Bob Harris, who learned that "bunks in bow staterooms of a carrier go up and down precipitously, even in calm seas." A handful of others rode destroyers and had to take their turn standing watch all the way. The luckiest were those—ninety-seven in all—who rode the Matson passenger liner *Monterey*, which proved even more luxurious than the Coronado BOQ. There were even flowers and fruit bowls in each of the staterooms. Others, arriving later, rode the fleet oiler *Cimmaron,* which, though relatively new, was encumbered with all the tanks and pipelines inherent to her service, and not nearly as comfortable as a Matson cruise ship.[12]

Once all the new officers arrived in Hawaii and joined their assigned ships, they, too, were allocated to various jobs and departments. There were a dozen or more members of the class on each of the eight battleships in Pearl Harbor, and many of them, including Bob Harris on the *Pennsylvania,* were assigned

THE REAL NAVY   87

to engineering departments. The battleships were older vessels, nearly as old as the ships of the Training Squadron they had ridden during their summer cruises, though some had been modernized. At least the *Pennsylvania* had turbines rather than a reciprocating engine like the *New York*. Still, her age was evident: she was steered by a huge spoked wooden wheel that took several men to turn, and one of her eight boilers was a Normand boiler that dated from the nineteenth century. Harris found that despite all the courses in marine engineering he had taken at the Academy, getting a feel for the *Pennsylvania*'s engineering plant was a challenge. To aid him, he, like all the other new officers, was ordered to keep a notebook in which they were to "sketch and describe" various elements of the engineering plant. Charles "Chick" Obrist remembered having "to trace all the pipes and conduits to the bitter end and back, a very complicated and dirty business." In effect, the young officers discovered that their service in "the real Navy" was more like a postgrad program that emphasized practical application rather than theory. Like "Chick" Obrist, Bob Harris recalled spending many hours "following piping through compartments and tanks, and then describing what you had learned in the notebook." As he put it, "When you have followed a drain line through a lube oil tank on your hands and knees, you remember it pretty well."[13]

Of course, it was not all crawling around engine spaces. Though Roosevelt had ordered the fleet to remain in Pearl Harbor as a deterrent to the Japanese, peacetime traditions and protocols continued, especially on the battleships. This was evident in the fact that the prescribed uniform for most onboard activities was service dress white: a formal uniform with white shoes, creased white trousers, a white tunic with gold buttons, and a high tight collar (then, and still, called a "choker"). It was mandated for morning colors and wardroom meals, even for morning exercises. The only concession to the circumstances was that the individual leading the morning calisthenics from atop a gun turret was allowed to unfasten "the top two hooks on the standing collar." There were also periodic formal inspections where, in a tableau that could have come from a Gilbert and Sullivan operetta, the officers wore fore-and-aft cocked hats, oversize gold epaulets, and dress swords. When John "Peck" Greenbacker, who was on the carrier *Yorktown* (CV-5), visited his classmate Jesse Worley on the battleship *Colorado* (BB-45), he was astonished by the "entirely different atmosphere" on the battleships, where, it seemed to him, appearance mattered more than function. Even worse, he sensed "a smugness" on the *Colorado* about the central role battleships were believed to hold in the navy hierarchy. Even Worley embraced the prevailing view. Showing Greenbacker around the

88 ANNAPOLIS GOES TO WAR

ship, he claimed that while "duty on an aircraft carrier might be interesting . . . this was the real Navy."[14]

Yet Worley, too, worried quietly about the absence of a clear sense of purpose or urgency on the *Colorado*. By his own description, Worley was "a rebellious guy" who at the Academy had more than once gone over the wall to spend evenings drinking "at a secret pub in Eastport." Though he defended his ship against Greenbacker's criticism, he could not dispute that there was probably too much emphasis on "spit and polish" and not enough on "vigor and enthusiasm." And while Worley himself was "far from being a teetotaler," he also thought "there was too much liquor consumption amongst the senior officers." On the other hand, like all the junior officers, Worley thanked God for the leading petty officers, who were, in his view, "true professionals." The engineering department, he believed, "survived mainly by the effort of the Petty Officers."[15]

The presence of a dozen or more Forties on each battleship facilitated ready-made social groups for adventures ashore. There was a lot of free time, which usually included Wednesday afternoons as well as weekends, and groups of classmates often got together to enjoy it. There were fourteen members of the class on the *California* (BB-44), including Ben Hall, who had made the drive across the country in the Ford V-8, and Crosswell Croft, who had done so in the Packard. Both of them, and indeed all the ensigns on the *California*, were impressed by the ship's executive officer, Commander Robert B. Carney (later chief of staff to Admiral William "Bull" Halsey), who in testimony to his Irish heritage had been called "Mick" since his Academy days. Soon after they arrived, Carney called the fourteen new ensigns together and told them, "When you work, you work hard. When you play, you play hard. If you don't know how to do either, watch me."[16]

So they did. By day, they took their jobs seriously: Croft as the assistant turret officer in Turret One of the main battery, and Hall as supervisor of the ship's Mark 58 rangefinder at the top of its 124-foot main mast. At the end of the workday, however, they, and most of the other junior officers, went ashore for swimming, golf, drinking, and dancing. As one of them put it, "Every night was fun night at Waikiki Beach." One annoying aspect of their trips ashore was that Admiral Kimmel, the new CinCPac (Commander-in-Chief, Pacific), mandated that every officer going ashore in civilian clothes must wear a hat— and not a baseball cap, but a serious fedora or Panama hat. "So, we all bought a hat," Pat Clancy recalled, "and we would go ashore and go to the O Club and hang the hat on a peg." Then, when they returned, "we'd pick up our hat,

THE REAL NAVY   89

or somebody else's that would fit, and go back aboard." The junior officers mockingly labeled their hats "Kimmels," as in "Don't forget to wear your Kimmel."[17]

Though the war news from Europe remained disquieting, most of the Forties were not unduly concerned. As one recalled, "most of us ensigns, busy with our daily tasks, didn't think" too much about the war: "Europe seemed so far away from Hawaii." Warren "Hooky" Walker, who had come west in the Packard with Croft, recalled that they all "carried on as through there was not a care in the world."[18]

In addition to the 50 members of the class assigned to carriers, and the 167 sent to battleships, another 101 of them got orders to cruisers, which, by tradition, were named for American cities. Those assigned to cruisers included Mike Hanley on the *Northampton*, Connie Carlson on the *Astoria*, Ray Hundevadt on the *Vincennes*, and George Kittredge on the *Chicago*. They discovered that, as on the battleships, peacetime traditions and protocols prevailed. Kittredge, who was one of six Forties on the *Chicago* (CA-29), described it as "a nice country club life." He was especially impressed each evening when the ship's fife-and-drum corps paraded through Officer's Country playing "Roast Beef of Old England" to announce dinner. In the wardroom, heavy silver cutlery (a gift from the citizens of Chicago to their namesake cruiser) was laid out on white tablecloths, and there was impeccable service from "attentive mess boys." After dinner there were movies on the well deck "with chairs set out for the officers and 'Attention on Deck!' called out when the captain appeared."[19]

On some of the cruisers there was less elegance and more training. Such was the case, for example, on the heavy cruiser *Astoria* (CA-34) where Connie Carlson reported. Carlson's friends thought he looked like a choirboy with his trusting expression and serene blue eyes. That was fair enough since he had, in fact, sung in the Naval Academy choir all four years. On board the *Astoria*, Carlson was impressed by the conscientiousness of the training regimen. For the first six months, he rotated among the several departments: Engineering, Gunnery, Communications, and Navigation, plus deck duties. He was required not only to keep a notebook but to show it to the XO each day before he was allowed to go ashore.[20]

Mike Hanley had a similar experience on the cruiser *Northampton* (CA-26). Right up to his first-class year, Hanley had assumed that because he had been a Marine Corps reservist he would go back into the Corps after graduation. But there were more members of the class who wanted to be marines than the

90 ANNAPOLIS GOES TO WAR

Corps could accommodate. As a result, only those who had served in the regular Marine Corps (as opposed to the reserves) were assured a spot. The rest drew lots, and Hanley drew a high number. So, like Kittredge and Carlson, he opted for a heavy cruiser, in his case the *Northampton*, which was the flagship of the Scouting Force. As the flagship, it hosted the scouting force commander, Rear Admiral Raymond Spruance, a quiet and somewhat enigmatic officer who was almost religiously devoted to exercise—especially walking. When the ship was in port, he would disembark for long walks, usually alone, returning incognito after several hours. The duty officer generally stationed a sailor at the brow as a lookout so he could report when the admiral was returning to ensure that he was received with proper ceremony. At sea, Spruance paced the deck briskly, repeatedly circumnavigating the ship. When he strode past work parties of sailors engaged in their duties, they leaped to their feet to salute him. After a few such episodes, Spruance called Hanley aside and told him that "he did not want my troops jumping to attention every time we saw him." He told Hanley that he, or whoever was supervising the work, could salute, but only the first time each day. After that, no salute was necessary or expected; the men should just ignore him and continue with their work.[21]

Hanley's initial assignment on the *Northampton* was as the second in command of Turret One, where he served under a lieutenant junior grade (j.g.) who put him through a rigorous training schedule. The turret crew on a heavy cruiser consisted of fifty to sixty men who performed a complex mechanical ballet, every part of which had to be carefully coordinated: hoisting the heavy projectiles from the magazine, inserting them into the breech, loading the premeasured silk bags of powder, sighting, aiming, and firing the guns, a routine that had to be repeated flawlessly every twenty seconds. It was all new to Hanley, and yet such was the intensive training he received that, within a few weeks, he could boast, "I knew every nook and cranny and every man in the turret." The turret officer also regularly invited Hanley home to dinner with his family.

Hanley soon realized why he had been singled out for such special attention. The lieutenant jaygee was expecting orders to a new-construction battleship back in the States, and to ensure that he could accept those orders, he wanted Hanley ready to take over as the senior turret officer. When the expected orders came in, however, the gunnery officer on the *Northampton* rejected the idea. Hanley, he said, was simply too junior and too inexperienced to be the senior turret officer. The jaygee pushed back, insisting that Hanley was "fully qualified to take over the turret both technically and as a leader." The gunnery officer grudgingly agreed to allow it on a probationary basis. Consequently, while Lacouture and Weatherup on the *Saratoga* and Croft and Ben Hall on the *California* all remembered their first year after graduation as a pleasant interlude of tennis, golf, and beach volleyball, Hanley remembered it as a period of hard work and "very little sleep." Later, during a fleet battle practice, Hanley was gratified when his turret was the only one on the *Northampton* to win a coveted "E" for excellence.[22]

It was not long before Kittredge, Carlson, Hanley, and the other Forties sensed an acceleration in both the pace of training and the operational tempo. When they first reported aboard, the usual protocol was for the ships to spend one week at sea followed by three weeks in port. After six months, that changed to two weeks out and two weeks in. By the summer of 1941, it was three weeks out and one week in, and by the fall, most of the battleships and cruisers were going out every day—or at least every weekday. In addition, the ships adopted wartime protocols: zigzagging during the day and steaming blacked out at night. Pete Peterson, on the light cruiser *Philadelphia* (CL-41), bemoaned the fact that with the ship blacked out, it was no longer possible to show movies. Far more serious was the fact that nighttime steaming was actively dangerous. In 1941, only a handful of US Navy ships had radar, which was still a new and experimental technology, and operating blacked out at night in close company with other ships, was (as Hanley put it) "hairy." More than once, ships came close enough to one another to sound the collision alarm; in one case, the battleship *Oklahoma* actually collided with the *Arizona*, and though it was only a glancing blow, both ships had to go into drydock for repairs.[23]

In addition to accelerated training, Roosevelt's efforts to improve and enlarge the navy were evident in the arrival of more men reporting for duty, not only enlisted sailors from boot camp but also reserve officers, some of them veterans recalled to active service. To the young ensigns in the class of 1940 they seemed pretty long in the tooth. "Pop" Dupyzk and his shipmates on the *West Virginia* (BB-48) referred to them as "metal men" because they had "silver in their hair, gold in their teeth, and lead in their ass."[24]

If the new protocols made maneuvering "hairy" in the Pacific, it was much more so in the Atlantic, where the shooting had already started. There German submarines (*Untersee*-boats or U-boats) were engaged in a determined campaign to sink as many British ships as possible and cut the island nation off from imports. Though the United States was officially neutral in that struggle,

92   ANNAPOLIS GOES TO WAR

the North Atlantic was still a dangerous environment. To ready the US Navy to deal with that environment, Roosevelt appointed a new commander of the Atlantic Fleet in December 1940: the hard-nosed, no-nonsense Rear Admiral Ernest J. King, who had orders to "lick things into shape."[25]

And he did. Phil Glennon, the third-generation Academy grad from Washington, DC, was on the light cruiser *Cincinnati* (CL-6). He noted that while the ship was in Pearl Harbor there was a "relaxed atmosphere that pervaded every phase of our operations and training." Like the other Forties, he often went ashore to swim at Waikiki Beach or dine at various restaurants in Honolulu. Then in December 1940, the *Cincinnati* was transferred to the Atlantic, and Glennon felt the change almost instantly. "As soon as we entered the Atlantic," he wrote, "it was entirely different. The tempo of operations increased, the readiness preparations on the ship were improved, and the physical readiness was enhanced." The new protocols not only required the *Cincinnati* to darken ship at night and zigzag while underway, the crew went to general quarters every morning at first light. It became clear to Glennon that "we were in the war zone even though we were not officially at war."[26]

That same December, Roosevelt decided that he needed a break from Washington and arranged a ten-day fishing trip in the Caribbean, the ostensible purpose of which was to inspect the naval bases the United States had obtained from Britain in September in exchange for fifty old four-stack US destroyers. The president took a train from Washington to Miami and, along with "Pa" Watson, Harry Hopkins, and his Scottish terrier Fala, boarded the heavy cruiser *Tuscaloosa* on December 3. Alerted to the president's imminent arrival, the crew modified the ship to accommodate his disability, including the addition of an elevator. The president did do some fishing during the cruise, often sitting quietly near the rail with a line over the side, and occasionally fishing from the ship's fifty-foot whaleboat. There was a standing order directing the *Tuscaloosa*'s officer of the deck to "maneuver the main engines in response to the President in the event he gets a strike."[27]

FDR was not just fishing; he was thinking. In particular, he was thinking about how he could continue to sustain Britain in its unequal war with Nazi Germany without triggering outrage from an isolationist public or a suspicious Congress. By the time the cruise was over, he had worked out the details of what would come to be known as the Lend-Lease program.

During the cruise, Bill Braybrook noted that Roosevelt developed a bantering relationship with Boatswain's Mate Second Class Bjork, who everyone—including the president—called "Swede." Braybrook never saw Swede without "a wad of tobacco in his cheek, a pinch of snuff in his lower lip, and a burning cigarette in his hand." Bjork also hated to wear shoes, and on most days he worked barefoot. One day when Swede was assigned as boatswain's mate of the watch on the quarterdeck, he showed up in uniform but without shoes, and the officer of the deck told him in no uncertain terms to go put his shoes on. As the lieutenant was issuing that order, a familiar voice with an unmistakable Hudson Valley patois came through the open porthole, "What's the matter Swede?"

"Well, you know me, Mr. President," Swede responded. "Shoes hurt my feet."

The president, laughing, then issued a directive: "OK, Swede," he said, "you now have presidential permission to go without shoes any time you please," adding: "Mr. Officer of the Deck, log that!"[28]

After the president returned to Washington, he laid out the particulars of the program he had formulated on the cruise. Shrewdly named an "Act to Further Promote the Defense of the United States," the president characterized it in a White House press conference as akin to lending a garden hose to a neighbor whose house was on fire. You don't charge him fifteen dollars for the hose, the president said, you lend him the hose and he gives it back after the fire is out. Despite criticism from isolationists, the Lend-Lease Act, as it was more popularly known, passed Congress comfortably on March 11, 1941.[29]

To protect all the new material being sent to Britain, as well as the ships that carried it, Roosevelt also expanded the navy's role in the Atlantic. In the spring of 1941, he ordered the *Yorktown* battle group, plus a cruiser division and a destroyer division, to leave Hawaii and join the Atlantic fleet. It was all done clandestinely. After leaving Pearl Harbor, the ships steamed west toward the mid-Pacific. Speculation among the crew, including the junior officers, was that they were headed for Singapore. Then, once all the ships were beyond sight of land, they turned around and headed east toward California. Pete Peterson was "happily contemplating leave and liberty in the States" until, only a day out of San Diego, the whole task force turned south for the Panama Canal. The ships passed through the canal secretly, at night, their hull numbers painted over, and with crewmen under orders "not to talk to anyone on shore."[30]

Once in the Atlantic, peacetime protocols "abruptly ended." Like Glennon, Peterson felt a new rigor in the exercises, and in particular an emphasis on sonar sweeps and antisubmarine training, some of it supervised by Royal Navy officers who had been hunting U-boats since 1939. By the mid-summer of 1941, the

94 ANNAPOLIS GOES TO WAR

Yorktown and the ships of her task force were conducting "search patrols in the central Atlantic as far east as the Azores." Peck Greenbacker and everyone else on board the *Yorktown* "became increasingly aware that we were engaged in an undeclared war."[31]

Roosevelt kept it all as secret as possible. On April 25, during a White House press conference, a reporter asked him if US Navy ships were engaged in escorting Allied convoys to England. Nonsense, the president replied. The US Navy was engaged in patrolling, that's all. A patrol, he insisted, is not an escort. "If by calling a cow a horse . . . you think that makes the cow a horse? I don't think so." The reporter persisted: "Mr. President, can you tell [us] the difference between a patrol and a convoy?" FDR shot back: "You know the difference between a cow and a horse?"[32]

June 22, 1941, was the one-year anniversary of the French capitulation, and a year and three weeks after the class of 1940 had graduated. On that date, the war in Europe got more much more complicated when three million German soldiers, bolstered by several divisions of Romanians, surged eastward into the Soviet Union across an eighteen-hundred-mile front in what the Germans called Operation Barbarosa. Hitler had concluded that even though Britain remined defiant in its island bastion, it no longer posed a meaningful threat. That allowed him to turn the full fury of the Wehrmacht on his one-time ally. Initially, at least, it was a powerful blow. The Luftwaffe destroyed more than a thousand Soviet airplanes on the first day of the war, and German armored columns thrust deep into Russian territory. For several weeks, it appeared that Russia would fall to the German steamroller as swiftly as France had done.

Churchill and Roosevelt had no love for Stalin, who was not only a communist and had partnered with Hitler in the destruction of Poland, but had also, in a blatant land grab, invaded Finland. Yet as long as the Russians held, their efforts would drain German resources that could otherwise be directed at Britain and its Commonwealth partners. The Lend-Lease bill authorized the president to extend aid to any nation that was "vital to the defense of the United States." As Roosevelt saw it, that meant he could now send material support to Russia as well as to Britain.

But should he? There was considerable concern in both Washington and London that any aid sent to Russia would only end up in the hands of the Nazis when the Red Army collapsed. Roosevelt dispatched his trusted aide Harry Hopkins to Moscow to assess the likelihood of that happening. Hopkins returned to report that the Russians would hold, and in October FDR offered

Stalin the first shipments of what would eventually become a flood of US aid. Of course, that also meant more transatlantic convoys and more escorts.

By now, the distinction Roosevelt had tried to draw between "patrolling" the North Atlantic and "escorting" British convoys—between a cow and a horse—had virtually disappeared. US Navy warships were openly and actively escorting Allied convoys. Hitler was infuriated, and his U-boat commanders were frustrated. Admiral Erich Raeder, head of the German navy—the Kriegsmarine—urged Hitler to allow his U-boats to attack the American meddlers. Hitler wouldn't do it; he was determined to finish off the Soviet Union first, and he ordered the U-boats to "avoid any possibility of incidents with the U.S.A."[33]

That, however, proved impossible.

8

The Cusp of War

On September 4, 1941, the old four-stack destroyer USS *Greer* (DD-145) was in the mid-Atlantic headed to Iceland with mail and supplies for the US Marines that Roosevelt had sent there—another expansion of American involvement—when a patrolling British aircraft blinkered her a signal that a surfaced U-boat had made an emergency dive ten miles ahead. The *Greer*'s captain, Lieutenant Commander Laurence Frost, changed course to close it. Arriving at the designated coordinates, Frost began an active sonar search, maneuvering over the area and sending out repeated pings. Almost certainly unaware of the source of that relentless pinging, the U-boat skipper fired two torpedoes at his tormentor. Both missed, but they led Frost to respond with a dozen depth charges, which also missed. Though no damage was done on either side, it was the first exchange of ordnance between the US Navy and the Kriegsmarine. President Roosevelt affected outrage and insisted that "the German submarine fired first upon this American destroyer without warning." He proclaimed that from now on, instead of waiting to be targeted, ships of the US Navy would shoot first.[1]

One day later, the battleship *Idaho* (BB-42) got underway from Casco, Maine, with a five-destroyer escort. Thirteen members of the class of 1940 were on board, including Warren Smalzel, who had picked the *Idaho* with his number-one draw in the lottery, as well as L. Patrick Gray, who three decades later would play a key role in the Watergate scandal as acting director of the FBI. Another was Donald Banker, the class practical joker, notorious for putting Grape Nuts in the bunks of his classmates. Myers Montgomery was also on board, and he noted in his diary that all the US warships sailed under strict wartime conditions: steaming under radio silence, darkening ship at night, going to general quarters every morning, and zigzagging during the day.

On the second day out, the *Idaho* and her escorts rendezvoused with a convoy from Canada consisting of one tanker, one transport, and eight freighters,

THE CUSP OF WAR   97

all bound for Iceland. Whether it was called a cow or a horse, there was no question now about the role the US Navy was playing in the Atlantic: It was escorting Allied convoys. Montgomery took note of the president's remarks after the attack on the *Greer*. "As the President says," he wrote in his diary, "if they approach us, it's at their own risk."[2]

A week later, there was what Montgomery called "a little excitement" when lookouts reported the track of a torpedo that had apparently been aimed at the *Idaho*. Montgomery recalled that "it crossed our bow and missed by twenty yards," which he decided was "good as a mile." The escorting destroyers swarmed to the attack, dropping twenty-three depth charges in the general area where the torpedo had originated, though with no visible effect. Three miles ahead of the convoy, another US destroyer dropped seventeen more depth charges on another suspicious contact. Whether these were actual U-boats or only phantoms, Montgomery concluded, "We're veterans of the Battle of the Atlantic now."[3]

The convoy arrived in Reykjavik, Iceland, on September 15. The harbor was crowded with "a steady procession of ships and boats of all kinds," Montgomery wrote, "mostly British, steaming in and out." The *Idaho* remained there for three months, and for the Forties it was a vastly different experience from that of their classmates in Hawaii. The weather was horrible. Day after day, the temperature hovered near freezing during nearly constant fog, lashing rain, sleet, and high winds. Nor was there much satisfaction in shore visits. Just getting into Reykjavik from the ship required two hours' transit time in a small boat with icy spray coming in over the thwarts. And Reykjavik itself offered few amenities. US Navy Seabees were building a recreation center there, but it was still under construction in 1941. As Montgomery wrote his family: "There isn't a lot to do; we don't go ashore much." On the few occasions when they did go ashore, they found that "everywhere we go there are men in uniform, soldiers, sailors, and marines." Obviously, there was no bodysurfing, beach volleyball, or hula dancers.[4]

There was, however, a lot of visiting between ships. The Forties on the *Idaho* all visited the British battleship *King George V* and the carrier HMS *Victorious*, which five months earlier had teamed up to sink the German battleship *Bismarck*. And British junior officers reciprocated by visiting both the *Idaho* and the other US battleship in the harbor, USS *Mississippi* (BB-41). The Americans discovered that unlike "dry" American ships, the British served wine at meals in their wardrooms. For their part, the British were amazed by both the quality and quantity of food on the American ships, and they were delighted, too, by the band concerts and nightly movies, usually held on the open deck even when it rained, which was most of the time. On September 26, hundreds sat on the deck of the *Idaho* to watch *His Girl Friday* with Cary Grant and Rosalind Russell. Montgomery reported that "the Englishmen got quite a kick out of it"—probably more due to Rosalind Russell than Cary Grant.[5]

The Forties also visited the other American ships in the harbor. The *Mississippi* had a Catholic chaplain who conducted mass every Sunday, attracting Catholics (including Montgomery) from all the American ships. Montgomery also visited the cruiser *Tuscaloosa*, which had recently hosted the president on his Caribbean fishing trip, in order to visit classmates Bill Braybrook and John Wright.[6]

With fifteen months of naval service under their belts, the Forties were no longer boot ensigns. Several of them, asserting their independence, began to grow mustaches. They also acted as instructors for members of the Naval Academy class of 1941 who, in the accelerated timetable, had graduated in February. And they served as role models for the newly commissioned reserve ensigns—so-called 90-day wonders—who showed up. Montgomery was assigned to teach them navigation and gunnery. It seemed odd to be assigning marks to others in courses he had completed so recently, though he found he enjoyed it. "My navigation course is still coming along very nicely," he wrote his sister. "I feel more and more like an instructor." He feared, though, that he wasn't tough enough. "I'm kinda soft hearted," he wrote. "I hate to give unsat marks."[7]

In mid-October, the destroyer USS *Kearney* (DD-432) limped into Reykjavik Harbor at three knots with a nine-foot hole in her starboard side. She had been escorting an east-bound convoy when a German torpedo struck her amidships. Though the *Kearny* had managed to stay afloat, eleven Americans had been killed and another twenty-two wounded. Roosevelt again put the blame squarely on the Germans, declaring bluntly that "America has been attacked!" The American chief of naval operations, Admiral Harold Stark, suggested that the president could ask for a declaration of war, but the politically savvy Roosevelt knew Congress would not support it. Hitler also held back, determined to finish off the Russians before taking on the Americans. The Forties took it in stride. Montgomery assured his parents, "We were very calm after the Kearney incident," concluding that "it was just one of those things."[8]

Less than two weeks later, however, another American destroyer, the USS *Reuben James* (DD-245), was victimized by a different U-boat, and this time

THE CUSP OF WAR   99

the destroyer sank. Nearly a hundred US Navy personnel were killed. The survivors—forty-five of them—were rescued from the frigid sea and taken to Reykjavik, where they were placed on board the *Idaho*. Montgomery was delegated to take charge of them. He quartered them in the crew's reception room, issued them new uniforms, bedding, toothbrushes, soap, and towels, and saw to it that they got hot meals. He was pleased and a bit surprised to find them "getting along fine and in good spirits." A few weeks later, he had to appear before a board of investigation to account for the large ships services bill he had run up in providing them with so much material. It was largely proforma, and he was both exonerated and commended.[9]

In just a few months, US Navy warships in the Atlantic had escalated from conducting "neutrality patrols" to engaging in active combat—and taking losses. In his press release about the *Reuben James* incident, Roosevelt openly acknowledged that she had been on "convoy duty" and that her loss was "an inevitable incident in the Navy's task of safeguarding war-supplies shipments to Britain." An administration spokesman insisted that changes to the Neutrality Laws were needed "so that the United States sailors who are being attacked will know that *the United States is not neutral in this struggle*" (italics added.) That was a statement no administration official would have made six months earlier.[10]

As an undeclared naval war raged in the North Atlantic, the operational tempo in the Pacific also increased, though more gradually. The accelerated training did not inhibit the social lives of the young ensigns, including (maybe especially) John Lacouture, though he was soon separated from the temptations of Oahu when the *Saratoga* left Hawaii for a lengthy refit on the West Coast. When the *Saratoga* arrived in San Francisco, Lacouture somehow managed to resume his social activities, meeting up with a female friend who took him to many of the iconic sights of the city, including the Top of the Mark—the glass-walled bar on the nineteenth floor of the Mark Hopkins Hotel on Nob Hill. After five days in San Francisco, the *Saratoga* headed down the coast to Long Beach. There Lacouture was surprised to get orders transferring him off the *Saratoga* and onto the destroyer USS *Blue* (DD-387), which was back in Pearl Harbor. Whether it was his irreverent demeanor, his high-wire social life, or simply circumstance, he suspected that he and the others that were transferred at the same time were "the ones they wanted to get rid of."[11]

Whatever the reason, Lacouture headed up to Bremerton, Washington, where the *Blue* was undergoing a refit before heading back to Pearl Harbor. He missed watching carrier ops, but he was happy to be back in Hawaii: "The spectacular mountains and beaches plus the cane fields and pineapple fields thrilled me as much as ever." He found that the training schedule on the *Blue* allowed him to resume his active social life. The *Blue* and the other ships in the destroyer squadron (or DesRon) generally went to sea on Monday or Tuesday, practiced formation steaming and maneuvers for three or four days, and then came back into port on Friday for the weekend. Lacouture's favorite part of these maneuvers was when the *Blue* acted as plane guard for a carrier so he could watch the landings. It made him more determined than ever to get to flight school as soon as he was eligible.[12]

Ashore, he and the other junior officers on the *Blue* all chipped in to buy a used car, and they rented a suite (which they called "The Blue Room") at the Moana Hotel. There were not quite enough beds for all of them, so they agreed that the last one in at night would sleep in the bathtub. Often that was Lacouture.

In August 1941, while perusing the society pages of the *Honolulu Star Bulletin*, Lacouture saw that the daughter of the late Lawrence Sperry (of Sperry Instruments), whose first name was Winifred but everyone called "Bam," was hosting a party for navy aviators. The purpose, according to the article, was to provide a social outlet for "the young ensigns . . . just arrived from the mainland with no dates, no friends, no place to go." Lacouture wondered why the aviators had been singled out for such consideration. He looked up Bam's number and invited her for a drink at the Royal Hawaiian. There he asked her why she didn't host a party for the "hard-working young destroyer officers." She agreed to do so at once.[13]

The party was held October 11 on the outdoor lighted tennis courts at the home of Sperry's mother, the former movie actress Winifred Allen, now called Mrs. Tenney after her second husband, Edward Davies Tenney, who had died in 1934. It included dinner, drinks, dancing, and a demonstration of Samoan sword dancing. According to the local papers, it was a grand success. By way of comparison, that same night in Reykjavik, the evening entertainment was the movie *Lady from Cheyenne*, starring Loretta Young, which the crew watched sitting outdoors under an awning on the deck of the *Idaho* in a misting rain.[14]

In planning the party, Lacouture worked closely with Mrs. Tenney, and during their collaboration, she took a shine to him, subsequently inviting him to several of her social events. The result was that he frequently found himself hobnobbing with the navy's top brass, including Admirals Kimmel, Halsey, Pye, Fletcher, and Draemel—the one-time Academy commandant who had

THE CUSP OF WAR 101

banned "public osculation." When Lacouture was hospitalized after a hernia operation, the result of overdoing a workout at the gym, Mrs. Tenney insisted that he recuperate in her home. By his own admission, he "lived there like a king." Eventually he was cleared to return to duty. By then, however, the *Blue* had left on a fleet exercise. No one was certain when she was likely to return, so he took a room in the Royal Hawaiian and waited, checking in periodically with the district commandant. Since the *Blue* was gone for three weeks, he had another luxurious vacation. As he put it, "Life in the Navy was never so good."[15]

But things were changing. In an effort to discourage further Japanese advances into South Asia, the Roosevelt administration had begun to apply economic sanctions, freezing Japanese assets in US banks in July and announcing an embargo of American oil and scrap iron exports in August. When an American reporter asked a Japanese official about Japan's attitude toward the sinking of the *Reuben James*, he replied that it was premature to comment, though he volunteered that "an armed clash in the Pacific could be averted only if the United States eased economic pressure against Japan." There was a limit, he declared, to Japan's patience with "America's adherence to an arbitrary, dogmatic attitude." The Japanese insisted that the United States must agree to a long list of specific demands at once "or face the alternatives." It was evident now that an armed attack by the Japanese was a very real possibility.[16]

If war did come, American planners assumed that it would begin with a Japanese attack on the Philippines. Concerned about that, the Roosevelt administration dispatched reinforcements to the Philippines throughout the fall. In October, as John Lacouture helped plan the party at Mrs. Tenney's and Myers Montgomery nursed the survivors of the *Reuben James* on the *Idaho*, Connie Carlson's cruiser *Astoria* (CA-34) escorted a convoy of transports filled with "troops, tanks, and other military equipment" to the Philippines. After the ships tied up to the dock in Manila, Carlson remembered hearing the tanks "clanking down the pier night and day for about four days." Even stronger in his memory, though, was the night he played bar dice at the Officer's Club and rolled five aces. He had to buy a round of drinks for the bar, though he also had his name inscribed on the dice cup. When the ships of the convoy left Manila, they carried away hundreds of dependents from what now seemed likely to become a war zone.[17]

In fact, on November 27, the administration sent an urgent message to all army and navy Pacific commands, including the Philippines. The message was blunt: "This dispatch is to be considered a war warning. Negotiations with

Japan . . . have ceased and an aggressive move is expected within the next few days." It mentioned possible Japanese attacks on the Philippines, Thailand, the Kra Peninsula, and possibly Borneo. It urged local commanders to "execute an appropriate defensive deployment."[18]

The message was addressed to senior commanders, which meant that members of the class of 1940 were not privy to its contents. Besides, the Forties were focused on their own immediate circumstances. In addition to pursuing social opportunities ashore, the Forties worked hard to qualify as officer of the deck (OOD) on their various ships. Doing so was a significant milestone in a young officer's professional advancement. The OOD wore a set of binoculars around his neck as a symbol of his authority, and he presided over the ship from the bridge (at sea) or the quarterdeck (in port) for a four-hour watch period, during which he was in de facto command of the ship. Of course, if anything important came up, he would call the captain, but for all the quotidian activities that filled the four-hour time slot of his watch he was effectively in charge. When the ship was underway, the OOD was usually a seasoned lieutenant or even a lieutenant commander. In port, however, and especially on weekends, OOD duty was less demanding and could be safely entrusted to a qualified ensign, which allowed most of the senior officers to go ashore. By the fall of 1941, several of the Forties had qualified as OOD on their ships, including redheaded Archibald "Nick" Nicholson of Tarboro, North Carolina, on the battleship *California*, Irving J. Davenport, from Pawnee, Illinois, on the *Oklahoma*, and Henry "Dave" Davison of Little Rock, Arkansas, on the *Arizona*.

As it happened, all three of them were assigned OOD duty for Sunday morning, December 7, 1941.

9

Infamy

The eight battleships of the Pacific fleet had been out exercising the week of December 1, and, like the destroyers, they had come back into port at Pearl Harbor for the weekend. Most of them were moored in a long line along the southern rim of Ford Island, with the *California* at the head of the line by itself, followed by three pairs of ships, and then the *Nevada*, also by herself, at the rear. The *Pennsylvania*, the fleet flagship, was on the other side of the harbor in the enormous Ten-Ten drydock, so called because it was 1,010 feet long. The *Oklahoma* was the outboard ship in the first pair, about a quarter mile behind the *California* with the *Maryland* alongside; the *West Virginia* and the *Tennessee* were astern of them, followed by *Arizona*, which was inboard of the repair ship *Vestal*.*

The morning watch (4:00 a.m. to 8:00 a.m.) would give way to the forenoon watch at 8:00 a.m. (oh eight hundred), and by tradition the relieving officer always arrived fifteen minutes early so the officer going off duty could brief him about any ongoing issues. Consequently, Irving Davenport, variously called Irv or Davy, reported to the quarterdeck on the *Oklahoma* in his service dress whites at 7:45 sharp. The lieutenant junior grade he was relieving (Bill Ingraham, class of 1938) told him that his main job after morning colors would be to accommodate a group of Catholic clerics who were coming on board to hold mass at 9:00. Davenport listened, nodded, and then, at about 7:50, said the words that put him in charge of the ship: "I relieve you, sir."[1]

Davenport's first act as OOD was to send the quartermaster of the deck to the stern to be ready to hoist the colors at 8:00, and he ordered the boatswain's mate of the watch to stand by to strike eight bells. Before either of those things could happen, he noticed an airplane approaching low off the ship's port side.

---

* The *Utah* was also in Pearl Harbor that day, moored on the northern side of Ford Island, and adding her to the list of battleships makes a total of nine. The *Utah*, however, had been decommissioned as a battleship and was being used as a target vessel. The Japanese sank her anyway.

It was only a few hundred yards away when it dropped a torpedo. Before he even had a chance to process that, the plane pulled up, directly overhead, and Davenport saw the red "meatball" on its wing. In an intensely personal moment, he saw "the pilot and the gunner peering down" at him. He did several things at once: ordered the messenger of the watch to go find the XO since the captain was ashore, ran to the side of the ship to wave off the Catholic boarding party, and shouted: "Man your battle stations. This is an air raid. No shit!" As he pulled the alarm for general quarters, bullets were striking the deck next to him. It was 7:57 a.m.*

The torpedo struck the *Oklahoma* amidships, and the big battleship shook violently. Within seconds, two more torpedoes hit. In all, a total of at least six, and perhaps as many as eight, smashed into the *Oklahoma*'s exposed port side. It felt, Davenport remembered, like "the beating of a kettle drum at the crescendo of a symphony." Millions of gallons of seawater poured in through the giant holes in her port side, and the *Oklahoma* began to roll to port, slowly at first, then faster.

Another of the Forties, Sidney Sherwin of Batavia, New York, was also on duty that morning, and he ran forward the second he heard the alarm for general quarters. As he ran through the passageway, he nearly lost his footing when the ship "bucked and shuddered." With the *Oklahoma* rolling to port, he worked his way over to the starboard side, scrambling uphill on the slanting deck. He ended up in a compartment with some two dozen others, but the watertight door on the starboard side had been dogged shut from the outside, part of the protocol during general quarters. There was only one escape hatch above the rising water level, and it was another of Sherwin's classmates (he could not remember who) who squeezed through it, rounded up a couple of sailors, and managed to wrestle open the watertight door from the outside so those inside the compartment could escape. Sherwin was the last one out. By the time he reached the ladder, the ship had rolled past forty-five degrees, and he climbed out on his hands and knees. The ship continued to roll inexorably until she rolled over completely, stopping only when her superstructure hit the bottom of the harbor. She was now virtually upside down with only her rounded bottom showing above the water like a small metal island.[2]

Climbing up onto that metal island, Sherwin saw that "planes were flying overhead, anti-aircraft guns were firing, smoke was rising in all directions."

---

* In his memoir, Davenport rendered his comment as "No #*#*," but his actual language here can be safely inferred.

Looking down, he saw only "open water between our ship and the Maryland." There was nothing for it but to swim: "I peeled down to my underwear," he wrote later, "left my white service uniform, wallet, watch and ring in my white shoes, and went down one of the parted mooring lines into the water." He flailed his way through the thick oil that had spilled out onto the surface, until crewmen on the *Maryland*, who had climbed down onto the ship's projecting torpedo blister, pulled him and several others from the water. They sent him to the dispensary to "remove the fuel from our mouths and eyes." Glancing up at the clock on the bulkhead, he noted that it was 8:15.[3]

By then Davenport was no longer on the quarterdeck. When the *Oklahoma* rolled past ninety degrees, he was thrown into the sea, and, like Sherwin, he was pulled from the water by friendly hands. Many others on the *Oklahoma*, however, did not get out. Asleep below deck, they awoke to jarring explosions that knocked out the power on the ship, so there were no lights. Trapped in a stygian darkness in which up became down as the ship rolled over and the compartments and passageways quickly filled with water, they found themselves in a real-life nightmare.

There were a few pockets of trapped air, and several dozen men crowded into them. Hours later, long after the attack was over, rescuers atop the *Oklahoma*'s rounded hull discerned a faint tapping from inside, and teams of men with acetylene torches cut through the *Oklahoma*'s exposed bottom to rescue thirty-two men from that aqueous hell. Another 429, however, never got out, and their bodies were not recovered until sixteen months later, in March 1943, when she was raised from the mud. Among those 429 were three members of the class of 1940: Joe Hittorf of Collingwood, New Jersey; Marshall Darby of Washington, DC, who was engaged to Phil Glennon's cousin Jeanne; and Irvin Thompson, who, though he had been born in New Jersey, claimed Alaska as his spiritual home and had universally been known as "Igloo."[4]

Directly behind the *Oklahoma* was the *West Virginia*. Harvey Jacob Smith, called "Snuffy" by his classmates, was asleep in his rack on the starboard (inboard) side of the ship and was jolted from his slumbers when a torpedo hit the port side. "I leaped out of bed," he remembered, "grabbed a pair of pants and a shirt and proceeded to the main deck." The ship had already begun to list to port. He made his way to his assigned battle station at the forward five-inch antiaircraft battery, though when he got there, all the ready ammunition had been expended, and because the power was out, the hydraulic lift needed to bring up more from the magazine was not working.

106   ANNAPOLIS GOES TO WAR

Lieutenant Commander Doir Johnson told Smith that the ship's captain, Mervyn Bennion, had been badly wounded, and ordered Smith to go to the bridge to move the captain to a safe place. When Smith got there, he found Bennion literally holding his guts in with his hands. Several men were trying to help him, including a Black mess attendant named Doris Miller, whom Johnson had also ordered there because he surmised that, with his powerful build, Miller could move a badly wounded man more easily. Miller and another sailor moved Bennion to a nearby cot, but the captain refused to leave the bridge. He told Smith and Miller to look after the ship and save themselves. Smith went down to the main deck to rescue wounded sailors from the rising waters. Miller, despite his rating as a mess attendant, took over an unattended Browning .50 caliber machine gun and opened fire on the swarming Japanese planes. Much later, Bennion was posthumously awarded the Medal of Honor; Miller received the Navy Cross.*

Smith had difficulty moving the wounded. The "Wee Vee" (as the *West Virginia* was called) was now listing alarmingly, and her decks were slick with oil. Eventually, Smith and others were able to move the more seriously wounded by wrapping them in bedsheets and dragging them uphill across the oily decks. The *West Virginia*, however, did not roll over. Though she was hit by seven torpedoes—as many as the *Oklahoma*—her damage-control officer, Lieutenant Commander John S. Harper, kept her stable by effective counterflooding. She did sink, however, settling slowly onto the bottom with the dying Captain Bennion still on the navigation bridge.[5]

The *Tennessee* was inboard of the *West Virginia* and though hit by several bombs, she was protected from Japanese torpedoes. Ben Frana was just finishing breakfast in her wardroom when he heard nearby explosions and machine gun fire followed by the announcement: "General quarters, general quarters! Man your battle stations!" He ran to his battle station in the Engine Control Room to find that he was the only officer there. The turbines were on line to run the electric generators, and Frana used emergency protocols to switch them to propulsion. He reported to the bridge that "Control was manned and ready to get underway." Up on the bridge, the *Tennessee's* gunnery officer was

---

* The midwife who delivered Miller was so certain he would be a girl, she filled out the birth certificate in advance. That was why Miller, though he was six feet tall and weighed two hundred pounds, was named Doris, and routinely called Dorrie. After news of his exploits with the machine gun that day appeared in several Black newspapers, public interest contributed to the navy's decision to award him the Navy Cross. The US Navy's newest aircraft carrier, scheduled to be commissioned in 2032, is to be called the USS *Doris Miller*.

the senior officer present, and he told Frana that "as soon as the *West Virginia* cleared, we were going out." Only minutes later, however, he called back to say that the *West Virginia* was on fire; the *Oklahoma* had capsized; and there had been a huge explosion on the *Arizona*. Forlornly, he told Frana: "It might be some time before we get underway." In fact, they never did.[6]

At the head of the line of battleships was the *California*. Anchored by herself, she was fully exposed to the torpedo bombers. Another of the Forties, Nick Nicholson, was OOD that morning, and his dominant memory was that it was "the busiest watch of his career." When he sounded the alarm for general quarters, classmate Crosswell Croft was still asleep in his rack and assumed it was another drill. He looked out the porthole, and "not 100 yards away" he saw a Japanese fighter plane strafing small boats in the channel. He threw on his clothes and ran to his battle station in Turret One, even though it was pretty evident that the ship's big guns would be of little use in an air attack. As he ran, he nearly lost his footing when the ship was convulsed by a violent explosion. He remembered thinking that it felt much as it did when they fired a salvo of all the big guns, but he knew at once that the *California* had been torpedoed. There was another explosion soon afterward from a second torpedo. As on the *Oklahoma*, the big ship began to list to port, though more slowly and, thanks to effective counterflooding, she stopped at eight degrees.[7]

Ben Hall was also in his rack when the alarm sounded, and like Croft, he threw on his clothes and ran to his battle station, which in his case was the rangefinder at the top of the ship's mainmast. Despite the organized pandemonium, Hall reached the base of the mast and began to climb, hand over hand. In his peripheral vision, he sensed rather than saw the aerial chaos. When he reached the fire director's platform, he looked around. From that elevated perch, he had what may have been the best view any American officer had of what was happening that morning: The sky was filled with airplanes, all of them emblazoned with the bright orange sphere of the Imperial Japanese Navy. They seemed to come from all directions at once: High-level bombers dropped heavy ordnance from twenty thousand feet; "Val" dive bombers screamed down to release their smaller 250-kilogram bombs from fifteen hundred feet; and low-flying "Kate" torpedo planes skimmed the surface to release their deadly weapons barely a hundred feet off the water. Over on Ford Island, Hall saw Japanese fighters strafing American planes that were parked in rows on the tarmac. He felt, rather than saw, the first torpedo hit the *California*, followed only seconds later by a second. The big ship shook so violently he had to grab the safety rail to keep his feet.[8]

In Turret One, Croft quickly realized that although he was at his designated battle station there was nothing he or his men could contribute from there. The two torpedo strikes had ignited fires that were burning out of control, so Croft made the practical decision to send his men to fight the fires, though that, too, proved difficult when the sailors discovered that the nozzles and adapters did not fit the hoses.

With the fires burning out of control, orders came down from the bridge to flood the forward magazine. Another of the Forties, Robert Kirkpatrick, a former track star from Dothan, Alabama, ran to do it. He found the passageway blocked with watertight doors that were dogged shut and "oil oozing out from around the doors." He wrestled the doors open and found twenty-five men trapped in the passageway, many of them dead or unconscious from oil fumes. Unable to flood the forward magazine because there was no water pressure, Kirkpatrick carried five of the unconscious men to safety.[9]

Croft was desperate to fight back against the attackers, but the loss of power not only shut down the water mains but also meant the ammunition hoists weren't working, so he organized a human chain of sailors to pass five-inch ammunition from the magazine to the guns. Each shell weighed fifty-five pounds, and passing them hand to hand up several ladders was cumbersome. Glancing skyward, Croft saw what looked like a dozen dive bombers all apparently lining up on the *California*. When they released their bombs, he instinctively stepped under the overhang of the big turret. Almost at once, a bomb struck the spot where he had been standing, passed through the deck, and exploded among the sailors who were passing up the ammunition.*

In his eyrie atop Sky Two, Ben Hall felt helpless. Clearly, there was no need for the rangefinder, which was his primary job, so he drew the only weapon he had to hand: his .45 caliber pistol. With only seven bullets and an effective range of about fifty yards, he knew it was unlikely that he could do any damage with it. Nevertheless, whenever a Japanese plane came close, he took careful aim and squeezed off a round. It was a gesture of defiance. Still, when one of the dive bombers he shot at subsequently crashed into the destroyer *Curtis* on

---

* One of those killed in the explosion was Ensign Herbert C. Jones. Not an Academy grad, Jones had received his reserve commission the previous November. When the bomb exploded, he was so badly wounded he could not be moved. Several sailors tried to carry him to safety, but he waved them off: "Leave me alone," he ordered. "I am done for. Get out of here before the magazines go off." He was posthumously awarded the Medal of Honor.

the other side of Ford Island, Hall told himself that maybe he had contributed to its destruction.[10]

Down on the main deck, the fires continued to spread. Another of the Forties, Dick Champion, from Tate, Georgia, was in charge of the Engineering Repair Party, but it was far too late for any repairs. The bulkheads were bulging from the flooding, the beams supporting the overheads were beginning to buckle, and a sea of burning oil from the capsized *Oklahoma* was steadily drifting toward the *California*. It was time to go, and an order came down from the bridge to abandon ship. "There was no rush or hurry," Warren Walker remembered. "Everyone was calm and obeyed orders implicitly." Unlike the *Oklahoma*, the *California* did not roll over. She settled steadily, but upright, with her superstructure above the waterline and Hall still clinging to his post in Sky Two. By then, Croft was in the water. He climbed on board the Ford Island ferry, and ignoring her protesting crew, directed it alongside the *California* to pick up other crewmen who were following the order to abandon ship.[11]

Nicholson, Croft, Hall, Kirkpatrick, Champion, and Walker all survived the attack, but they never forgot what they saw that day. Walker recalled that by the end of the day, he was "walking around like a zombie, more or less completely out of my head." Others were so badly burned, their flesh hung off them like peeling wallpaper. Croft was helping load wounded men into a boat when one of them said, "You don't know me, do you, Mr. Croft?" It was his own division boatswain's mate, burned so badly he was unrecognizable. Another man simply stood there silently, his flesh dropping off him in pieces. He wouldn't let anyone touch him. He just sat down and quietly died.[12]

Like many others that morning, Raymond "Ted" Hill on the *Nevada* was asleep at 8:00 a.m., and his first awareness of the attack was "the general quarters call to battle stations." Hill's battle station was in one of the gun turrets, and though he knew the big guns would be "totally useless" in an air attack, he ran there at once. Learning of heavy casualties in the antiaircraft crews, though, he ordered some members of his gun crew to replace them and sent the rest to assist the men who were making frantic efforts to get underway.

One of the casualties in the *Nevada*'s antiair battery was Hill's classmate, Tommy Taylor, a three-sport athlete whose battle station was as the AA fire director. Severely wounded early when a torpedo ripped a forty-foot hole in the *Nevada*'s side, he remained at his post, directing the gunfire against the attacking planes. His actions that day made him the first in the class to be awarded the Navy Cross.

The *Nevada*, with no ship alongside, was the only battleship to get underway that day. As she eased slowly past the other battleships and headed for the entrance channel, it seemed to Hill that "the dive bombers immediately concentrated their attacks on us." For the rest of his life, he remembered the "huge geysers of water from bombs exploding all around the ship." He felt the *Nevada* "shudder" whenever one of the bombs struck home. Even before the *Nevada* got underway, Hill both saw and felt "a massive explosion" on board the *Arizona*, which was moored just ahead of her.[13]

Dave Davison was the OOD on the *Arizona* that morning. When he had first checked the watch bill, he was not excited about it. He knew that being the OOD on a Sunday morning "meant looking smart and efficient as one paced the quarterdeck wishing the four hours of monotony would pass quickly." His only responsibility was to see that the crew rigged the ship for religious services on the fantail. Nevertheless, he reported to the quarterdeck in his service dress whites at 7:40, and after a short turnover, assumed the duty at 7:45. His predecessor had already arranged for morning colors, so there was really nothing for him to do.

Then he heard "the sound of aircraft." That in itself was not unusual in Pearl Harbor, though it was not common on a Sunday morning. He saw an airplane going into a dive. Now that *was* unusual. He looked closer and saw "red meatballs on the wing tips." His first thought was that the army was being "ultra realistic" in its maneuvers. Then, as he watched, "a bomb detached itself and headed for the California moored ahead," and he knew: "This was no exercise. We were under attack!"[14]

Like Davenport on the *Oklahoma*, Davison acted quickly, sending the boatswain's mate of the watch to sound general quarters and dispatching a messenger to notify the captain. Yet it was almost dreamlike. He recalled later that "while the naval officer in me was reacting as training dictated, the individual in me wanted to reject what his senses were telling him." Even as he gave the orders, he thought: "This isn't really happening . . . that rear seat gunner isn't actually shooting real bullets." It was, he realized later, "the paralyzing effect of surprise."[15]

The destroyer *Chew* (DD-106) was moored forty yards astern of the *Arizona*, and on board her that morning was another member of the class of 1940, Virgil Gex, who pronounced his last name "Zhey" in the French manner. During all four years at the Academy, on the first day of class when the instructor called roll, he invariably pronounced Virgil's name as "Gecks." Each time it happened,

Gex would politely respond, "It's Zhey, sir," after which he would be called "Mr. Jay." It became something of a class joke, so much so that at graduation, when the public address announcer called out his name, pronouncing it "Gecks," the entire class shouted back, nearly in unison, "It's Jay, sir!" Among his classmates, however, he, like several others, was known as "Doc."

Gex was one of the thirty in the class who, having failed the eye test, was denied a commission at graduation. He enrolled in the Navy Reserves and got a job working for Proctor & Gamble. Yet only five months later, in November 1940, despite his eyesight, he was recalled to active duty and commissioned an ensign as part of the national buildup. Now, on board the *Chew* in Pearl Harbor, he was shaken awake by fellow ensign, Bill Hartz.

"Hey, Doc," Hartz yelled at him, "Get up. It's started."

"What's started?"

"The war. The Japs are bombing Pearl Harbor."

Rolling away from this annoying shipmate, Gex mumbled, "What kind of a gag is this?"

Out of patience, Hartz grabbed his shoulder and shook him: "No bull. Get out of your damn sack!"[16]

Gex made it topside to see "smoke and flames from battleship row." He watched Japanese bombers pulling out of their dives, crisscrossing over the battleships, and then "jinking away over the northeast harbor." Having been told that Japanese pilots were mere amateurs, he remembered thinking, "Jesus, these guys are *good*!" He noticed one bomber in particular that was lining up on the *Arizona*. When the pilot released the bomb, Gex remembered, "The plane seemed to leap from its trajectory," which suggested that it was a particularly heavy bomb. Gex followed it with his eye until it hit the *Arizona*. He remembered the moment in vivid detail: "There was a small explosion as the bomb hit, followed 1–2 seconds later by a much larger explosion, and a split second later by a *tremendous* explosion in which a ball of flame seemed not to rise from the Arizona, but to materialize instantaneously to a height of 200′ above the ship." It was obvious to him that no one in the forward part of the ship could have survived.[17]

At the epicenter of that violence, on the quarterdeck of the *Arizona*, Davison had difficulty remembering the precise sequence of events amid "the kaleidoscope of activity: planes diving, planes strafing, bombs detonating, our own guns firing." He did remember that he was reaching for the sound-powered telephone to ask the engine room for more pressure on the fire mains, when there was "a tremendous explosion and a sudden rush of flame and heat." The quarterdeck became like an oven; he felt he was "being roasted in the most intense and painful heat." He couldn't stay where he was, and he couldn't go forward into the flames, so he and the boatswain's mate of the watch leaped over the rail and into the water. Davison's notion was that he could swim past the fire to the forward accommodation ladder and re-board the ship from there.

But when Davison looked back at the ship from the water, he saw that not only was there no forward accommodation ladder, the whole forward part of the ship was simply gone. Black smoke poured out of the twisted and collapsing wreckage of her superstructure, which careened forward drunkenly. It was obvious that the ship was beyond saving. When a small patrol boat came by, Davison and the boatswain's mate both climbed aboard. They spent the next hour picking up survivors until another officer, looking closely at him, ordered him to the hospital.[18]

There were few survivors from the *Arizona*. Whether it was the bomb that Virgil Gex had watched or (as most experts believe) one of the modified sixteen-inch shells dropped by a high-flying Kate, some piece of Japanese ordnance had pierced through the *Arizona*'s armored deck and exploded in her magazine. The detonation of all that stored ordnance had ripped the heart out of the ship, killing more than a thousand men. Mercifully, most of them probably died instantly.

Among them were seven members of the class of 1940. They included Ed Cloues, a slow-talking flute player from New Hampshire. Cloues had been scheduled for liberty on December 7 but had traded duty with another officer who had a date. Another was Carl Weeden, whose ironic nickname was "Dynamite," and who had found sailing at the Academy a marginally acceptable substitute for his beloved trout fishing in Colorado. There was Orville "Smitty" Smith, who was generally serious, though, according to his roommate, "not too serious to appreciate even the worst joke." Others were Howard Merrill, a confirmed "red mike" who was called "Ute" in testament to his Utah birthplace; Frank Lomax from Broken Bow, Nebraska, who had been the head cheerleader at the Academy; "Sam" Young, whose laugh was so contagious that when he laughed in a theater, the whole audience spontaneously joined in; and Ulmont "Monty" Whitehead, the indomitable and seemingly indestructible football player who had won the Army game almost single-handed two years earlier by crashing repeatedly and relentlessly into the Army line until he secured the winning touchdown.

Along with more than a thousand others, all seven of them are there still.

INFAMY 113

Mike Hanley was not in Pearl Harbor that morning. The *Northampton*, on which he was now the first turret officer, was one of three heavy cruisers, plus nine destroyers, escorting the aircraft carrier *Enterprise* to Wake Island. Following the "war warning" message of November 27, Husband Kimmel decided that the best way to "execute an appropriate defensive deployment" was to reinforce two vulnerable US outposts: Wake Island, twenty-four hundred miles to the west, and Midway, thirteen hundred miles to the northwest. To do that, he ordered his two carriers to deliver a squadron of fighter planes to each: *Enterprise* to Wake and *Lexington* to Midway.

The sense of impending conflict was palpable. As the *Enterprise* group steamed west, Admiral Halsey directed all the ships to enforce wartime protocols, put live ammunition in the guns, and to "strip ship," which meant throwing all nonessential material over the side. That last order was subject to interpretation; just exactly what was nonessential? Hanley remembered a long discussion in the *Northampton*'s wardroom before the officers decided that the wardroom piano would stay.[19]

After successfully delivering a dozen Wildcat fighters to Wake, the *Enterprise* group headed back toward Pearl Harbor. The high-speed run had left the gas-guzzling destroyers short on fuel, so they would have to refuel underway during the return trip, with the bigger ships refueling the smaller ones. Refueling underway—"unrep" in Navy lingo—was no longer experimental, but neither was it yet routine. Hanley was watching the *Northampton* refuel a destroyer alongside when suddenly "the destroyer veered out radically," snapping both the fuel line and the cables holding it. Worse, one of the broken cables then "wrapped around a shaft on the Northampton." All the ships had to stop, while divers went over the side to untangle the mess. It took all day, as, in Hanley's words, the other ships "steamed in circles around us." The *Enterprise* group had been scheduled to arrive back in Pearl on December 6, but thanks to this accident, it did not return until the eighth. Though the American carriers had been a principal objective of the Japanese strike, there were no carriers in Pearl Harbor on the Day of Infamy.*

With the tangled cable finally removed, the *Enterprise* group got underway again, though the ships were all still two hundred miles out to sea at 7:45 when Mike Hanley reported to the bridge to assume the duty as officer of the deck. Just ten minutes into his watch, he got a call from the ship's communications

---

* The *Lexington* was still five hundred miles south of Midway when her crew learned of the Japanese attack. The mission to deliver planes to Midway was canceled, and the *Lexington* returned immediately to Pearl.

officer, who told him that he was getting a lot of radio traffic suggesting that Pearl Harbor was under attack. Thinking it might be a drill, Hanley asked him if the messages had been authenticated. Instead of answering, the communication officer came up to the bridge with copies of the messages and told Hanley he should call the captain, which he did. When the captain arrived on the bridge, he looked at the messages and told Hanley to sound general quarters and run up the biggest American flag on the ship.[20]

John Lacouture very nearly missed the attack altogether. He did not have the duty on Saturday or Sunday, so he attended yet another party on Saturday night, this one in the Regency Room of the Royal Hawaiian Hotel, which, he recalled, had been "ornately decorated for the occasion." Admiral Halsey had been among the invited guests, and some were disappointed that he had not shown, though his absence did not dampen the festivities. Lacouture remembered that "Harry Owens and his Royal Hawaiian band were at their finest," and that "Hilo Hattie performed several hulas in her own inimitable style." At midnight, the band played the national anthem, and everyone headed home. Lacouture had escorted an old friend, Shada Pfleuger, to the dance, and since it was late, her parents invited him to spend the night in their guest room rather than go back to the ship.[21]

At eight the next morning, Shada rushed into his room shouting, "The Japs are attacking Pearl Harbor!" Like Virgil Gex on the *Chew*, Lacouture's first reaction was to tell her to stop joking. When, eventually, she convinced him it was true, he jumped into his car and drove back toward the base as fast as he could. As he got closer, he could see smoke rising from the anchorage. He arrived at the boat landing just as the last Japanese planes were leaving. "What a sorry sight met my eyes," he recalled later. "All the battleships were sunk and burning, as were the seaplanes and hangers at Ford Island." All he could think of, he noted later, "was all my classmates." He saw "a few lone destroyers" heading out to sea, among them his own ship, the *Blue*. Though there were only four officers on the *Blue* that morning—all of them ensigns—they got the ship underway and headed out with a few other destroyers to look for the enemy. As Lacouture watched them go, the captain of one of the other destroyers arrived at the boat landing and urgently called for his gig, the small boat that had brought him to shore. As the boat crew tossed off the lines, Lacouture jumped in, too, and they set off at full speed to try to catch the departing destroyers. They never caught the *Blue*, so Lacouture joined the crew of the nearest destroyer. Since he was a communications officer, he monitored the avalanche of radio messages coming in, many of them urgent but false reports about Japanese landings on the island.[22]

At sea, they looked for the enemy and conducted anti-submarine searches all day and into the night. Lacouture had the watch at 5:00 in the morning when, just as dawn was breaking, he saw a large aircraft carrier emerge out of the darkness. He immediately sounded general quarters and prepared for combat when the big ship blinkered out the correct code for the day. With the growing dawn it became possible to discern the oversize American battle flag it was flying. It was the *Enterprise*, returning at last. "Never," Lacouture recalled, "was I so glad to see an American flag."[23]

10

Retribution

Virtually overnight, the attack on Pearl Harbor erased Americans' commitment to isolationism and pacifism. The transformation was so sudden it was as if someone flipped a switch; even Charles Lindbergh and Henry Ford abandoned their flirtation with fascism and called for retaliation. At the same time, however, it triggered another reaction. Given the dismissive views most Americans held about the Japanese, it struck many that it was simply not possible for them to have carried out such an effective and devastating attack on their own. Surely there was more here than met the eye. In Congress and elsewhere, there was talk of negligence—even treachery. Both Admiral Kimmel and Lieutenant General Walter Short, who was the army commander on the island, lost their jobs. Eventually, a committee headed by Supreme Court Justice Owen Roberts interviewed officers and civilians to seek an explanation for how the disaster had been allowed to happen. Conspiracy theories reached all the way to the White House.

Few members of the Naval Academy class of 1940 gave credence to such rumors, but what had happened was nevertheless profoundly disorienting. Pete Peterson, who had recently transferred into the new destroyer *Bristol* at Norfolk, "found it difficult to believe that such an attack really happened," and on the cruiser *Pensacola* (CA-24), Jack Hardy and his shipmates found the initial reports scarcely credible. Indeed, a common reaction to the news was puzzlement as well as distress. Some struggled to assimilate it. An extreme example was Connie Carlson's skipper on the *Astoria*, Captain Preston Haines. When the *Astoria* entered Pearl Harbor on December 13 amid the visible devastation, it so horrified Haines that he literally broke down and had to be relieved of command by the captain of the *Nevada*, who was available because the *Nevada* was aground off Hospital Point. Two days later, Haines left to take over the NROTC program at Tufts University, near Boston.[1]

The news was also a shock to the Forties serving in the Atlantic. In Reykjavik, Myers Montgomery and his shipmates had spent the day cleaning up from a ferocious storm that had battered the *Idaho* for days. They were at dinner that night when the announcement came: The Japanese had attacked American forces in both Hawaii and the Philippines. "Everyone is so amazed," Montgomery wrote in his diary. "It's hard to believe." Even once it sunk in, it was widely assumed that the Japanese had been driven back with heavy losses. "Our Fleet steamed out to sea," Montgomery wrote in his diary that night, and "a naval battle was reported, but no confirmation has been received." One news story insisted that US submarines and airplanes had "surprised the Japs, sinking their aircraft carrier."[2]

Surprise, bewilderment, and confusion were common responses, but Mike Hanley put his finger on the dominant emotion: "It made us angry." Having lost ten of their own in what they saw as a deceitful and unprovoked Sunday morning attack, members of the class of 1940 burned for revenge. "Our class was blooded at Pearl," Hanley wrote, "more than any other class," and it provoked a fierce determination to strike back. As Bill Lanier put it, "What they have started, we will finish." In the aftermath of the attack, many volunteered for immediate combat duty. Others put in for specialized training in airplanes, submarines, or PT boats. Anywhere the navy asked for volunteers, members of the class of 1940 "responded in droves."[3]

The Japanese, meanwhile, were gobbling up new territory at an alarming pace. They had gone to war with the United States in the first place not expecting to "win" it in any conventional sense, but to neutralize the US fleet while they conquered the resource-rich islands of the South Pacific, especially the Dutch East Indies. That would give them unfettered access to the raw materials they needed to sustain their war in China so they would no longer be dependent on the United States. The Japanese assumption was that once they had consolidated their Asian maritime empire, the United States would agree to negotiate a settlement. That betrayed a fatal misunderstanding of the American temperament.

First, however, the Japanese had to complete their conquest of South Asia, including the American-held Philippines. They also seized a number of outlying islands to serve as early warning outposts for a likely American counterattack. One of them was tiny Wake Island, twenty-four hundred miles west of Hawaii. As we have seen, Kimmel had sent the *Enterprise* there to deliver a dozen Marine Corps fighter planes, and those planes proved invaluable when

ANNAPOLIS GOES TO WAR

the marines on Wake successfully fought off the initial Japanese assault on December 8, sinking two enemy destroyers. After that, Kimmel decided to send the *Saratoga* battle group under Rear Admiral Frank Jack Fletcher to Wake with more reinforcements, including a second squadron of Marine Corps fighter planes.*

Doc Weatherup was the communications watch officer on the *Saratoga*, and like everyone else on board, he was eager to get to Wake and exact some revenge. John Lacouture was no longer on the *Saratoga*, but the *Blue* was one of eight destroyers, along with three cruisers, that made up her escort as she set out on the rescue mission. He remembered that "everyone was keyed up hoping at long last to get some retribution for the thousands of Americans killed and wounded that Sunday morning, and to get there before the gallant marine defenders were overwhelmed." It was a race against time, and to Lacouture, the "days seemed like weeks." It was clear to him and almost everyone else that "the marines couldn't hold out much longer."[4]

In an incident that subsequently became controversial, Fletcher ordered the task force to refuel while it was still several hundred miles east of Wake. Some of the destroyers were down to less than half of their fuel capacity, and Fletcher wanted to top them off now instead of waiting until they were inside Wake's defensive perimeter. In order to execute the maneuver, the whole task force had to slow to about five knots, at which speed the *Saratoga* could not launch or recover planes. Acutely aware of that and determined to go into action with his ships topped off, Fletcher ordered the refueling to begin on December 22.

It did not go well. As Mike Hanley had witnessed on the *Northampton*, accidents were not unusual when ships steamed side by side only yards apart, connected by cables and hoses, and on December 22, long cross swells made coming alongside dangerous as well as difficult. More than once, fuel hoses and supporting cables parted, and despite furious efforts, by nightfall only four of the nine destroyers had been refueled. Back in Pearl Harbor, Vice Admiral William S. Pye, who had assumed command after Kimmel resigned on December 16, decided that the whole mission had become too risky. When he learned that the Japanese had committed two carriers to a renewed attack on Wake, Pye was unwilling to risk the *Saratoga* against a superior force. He ordered all the ships to return. Virtually everyone in the task force, from

---

* Fletcher was routinely called by all three of his names to distinguish him from his uncle, Admiral Frank Friday Fletcher, who died in 1928, and after whom the *Fletcher*-class destroyers were named.

Fletcher on down, was frustrated and angered by the order. When he read it, Fletcher threw his service cap onto the deck.[5]

John Lacouture believed that, like Nelson at Copenhagen in 1801, Fletcher should have metaphorically put a telescope to his blind eye and continued with the mission. After all, he reasoned, the Japanese had not yet discovered their approach, and "It should have been possible to launch a very effective 'hit and run' raid on the Japanese amphibious ships." He remembered that "many pilots and officers considered disobeying the order and launching anyway." Weatherup sympathized with such views, but, as he noted philosophically, "it is initiative when it ends well, otherwise it is unwarranted assumption of authority." Despite the collective frustration and disappointment, the *Saratoga* and her escorts, including the *Blue*, turned around and headed back to Pearl, having accomplished nothing. The marine garrison on Wake surrendered the next day. It was, Lacouture recalled, "a crushing disappointment for all hands."[6]

One reason Pye decided on the recall was that the United States had only three large-deck aircraft carriers in the whole of the Pacific Ocean. Back in April, Roosevelt had ordered the *Yorktown* to the Atlantic to support the undeclared war against German U-boats. Now, in the aftermath of the Pearl Harbor attack, he ordered her back, which would give the United States four carrier groups in the Pacific. The *Yorktown* loaded up with ammunition at Norfolk before heading south toward the Panama Canal. During that transit, one of the Forties, Ensign Harvey Vogel, was the underway officer of the deck. He remembered that everyone was jumpy. Though no U-boats were sighted, suspicious sonar returns led the *Yorktown*'s escorting destroyers to drop dozens of depth charges at regular intervals. Vogel noted that most of these attacks took place after the *Yorktown* completed a zig or a zag, and he was convinced that the destroyers were reacting to sonar pings bouncing off the wake of the "knuckle swirl" in the water that maneuver left behind. Unmolested by U-boats, real or imaginary, the *Yorktown* passed back through the Panama Canal—with no secrecy this time—and up to San Diego, where she got a new commanding officer.[7]

That new commander was Frank Jack Fletcher. After turning the *Saratoga* over to Rear Admiral Herbert Leary, Fletcher flew from Hawaii to San Diego on New Year's Day to take over the *Yorktown* group, which was designated Task Force 17 (TF 17). John "Peck" Greenbacker was the *Yorktown*'s secretary, and he was kept busy all day with the paperwork associated with the change in command. He had a scary moment, though, when he was ordered to the hospital in San Diego for yet another eye exam to determine whether he would be

120   ANNAPOLIS GOES TO WAR

allowed to remain in the navy. He was annoyed that the doctor expressed skepticism about his honesty when he read the eye chart, but he passed the test and was back on the *Yorktown* when she put to sea again on January 6. She was the centerpiece of a large escort for three Matson passenger liners repurposed as troop transports to carry five thousand US Marines to another vulnerable South Pacific outpost at Samoa, twenty-five hundred miles southwest of Hawaii.[8]

Other capital ships were also recalled from the Atlantic. After topping off their fuel tanks, the battleships *Idaho* and *Mississippi* left Reykjavik on December 9. Myers Montgomery and the other Forties were at high alert throughout the crossing, fearing a possible U-boat attack—though, in fact, the United States was not yet officially at war with Germany. Hitler had been as surprised by the Japanese attack on Pearl Harbor as the Americans, and for a few days Germany remained technically neutral in the Pacific War. After thinking it over, however, Hitler took the plunge. In a rambling presentation to the Reichstag on December 11, he announced that Germany was at war with the United States. The delegates cheered. It was as foolish and self-destructive a decision as the one Hitler had made the previous June to launch an invasion of the Soviet Union. Indeed, that invasion was beginning to flag. Outside Moscow, Hitler's previously triumphant ground forces were encountering stiff resistance.[9]

By then the *Idaho, Mississippi*, and their escorts were "steaming at full speed and headed home." There was gunnery practice almost every day, Montgomery noted: "Our guns are loaded and ready to shoot," though as yet there was nothing to shoot at. Five days out, lookouts reported seeing periscopes in the water, and the *Idaho* fired its first shot of the war, using the shell splashes from her big guns to point out to the destroyers the location of the sub—if there was a sub. The battleships did not wait to find out, steaming ahead at eighteen knots, faster than a submerged U-boat could go, and they arrived safely in Norfolk two days after Christmas. After another refueling, they headed south, passed through the Panama Canal (following the *Yorktown*, if they had known it), then up the West Coast to San Francisco, where they arrived on the last day of January.[10]

While the big ships were recalled to the Pacific, most of the destroyers remained in the Atlantic, where the U-boat peril continued to be an existential threat. Indeed, with the German declaration of war, that threat now extended all the way to the East Coast of the United States, where, in January 1942, U-boats began to attack shipping off the Carolina capes. Despite enormous pressure to organize coastal convoys, Admiral King, still in command of the Atlantic Fleet, simply lacked enough destroyers to do it. Indeed, the navy's supply of destroyers was so depleted that it caused concern when orders from Washington sent several of them out to escort a British battleship, the *Duke of York*, which was arriving from Britain with a VIP on board.

Winston Churchill had learned about the Pearl Harbor attack while he was having dinner with the new American ambassador, Gil Winant, who had replaced Joe Kennedy in March. Churchill immediately phoned Roosevelt, who confirmed the news: "Yes, it's true," Roosevelt told him. "We are all in the same boat now." Though Churchill expressed sincere sympathy for the losses the United States had suffered, he was hugely relieved—almost giddy. With American resources and Soviet manpower, he now believed, as he put it later, "Our history would not come to an end." That night he went to bed and "slept the sleep of the saved and thankful." Three days later he was on board the *Duke of York* headed for a meeting with the American president.[11]

The USS *Bristol*, with Pete Peterson on board, was one of three American destroyers assigned to escort the *Duke of York* into Norfolk. The weather was miserable, as it often was in the North Atlantic in winter, and Peterson was so seasick while standing watch he kept a bucket over his arm, which he was forced to use periodically. Even after the *Bristol* successfully rendezvoused with the *Duke of York*, she and the other American destroyers had a terrible time holding station. While the big battleship sliced through the heavy seas at twenty-eight knots, the small destroyers were knocked about like so much flotsam. Trying to sustain twenty-eight knots under such conditions put such a strain on the *Bristol*'s engines that the instruments on the bridge vibrated violently. One large wave carried away the ship's port side whaleboat; another claimed the *Bristol*'s anchor chain as "105 fathoms of anchor chain went roaring out the hawse pipe along with the anchor." Seeing her escorts falling behind, the *Duke* slowed to twenty-three knots so they could catch up. Once all the ships arrived in Norfolk, Churchill went ashore and caught a train to Washington. There, in what was dubbed the Arcadia Conference (December 22–January 14), Anglo-American planners committed themselves to defeating Germany first before focusing on the war in the Pacific.[12]

The *Bristol*, meanwhile, required a weeklong repair at the Brooklyn Navy Yard before she was dispatched to Portland, Maine, presumably to escort one of the North Atlantic convoys to Britain. Instead, she was ordered to the Caribbean to take over a coastal convoy. Peterson remembered vividly how the weather changed dramatically as the *Bristol* headed south. After a few days, he

122 ANNAPOLIS GOES TO WAR

began removing layers of his seagoing uniform: first his muffler and sweater, then his bridge coat, and eventually his winter underwear, "until within a week we were wearing only shoes, shirts, pants, and tans." The *Bristol* picked up the convoy at Trinidad and headed back north. As it did, on again came the coats, sweaters, and mufflers. After dropping the convoy off in New York, it was back to Portland to await the next assignment.[13]

In Hawaii, the Pacific fleet got a new commander. It was Admiral Chester Nimitz (Naval Academy class of 1905), who relieved Pye on the last day of 1941. Nimitz was as eager as anyone to strike back at the Japanese, but his options were limited by a scarcity of tools. Still, in January, as the *Bristol* worked its way up and down the Atlantic coast, Nimitz organized a carrier raid against Japanese positions in the Marshall and Gilbert Islands, more than two thousand miles west of Hawaii in the central Pacific. The *Saratoga* was no longer available since she had been torpedoed by a Japanese sub on January 11 and had to return to the States for repairs. But with the arrival of the *Yorktown*, Nimitz would have three carriers, and he decided to commit two of them to his planned strike: He ordered Halsey's *Enterprise* task force to attack Japanese bases in the Marshalls, and the *Yorktown*, once it delivered the troop convoy to Samoa, to attack Japanese bases in the Gilberts. Finally, members of the class of 1940 would have an opportunity for revenge.[14]

The *Northampton* was one of the three cruisers assigned to Halsey's *Enterprise* Task Force 8 (TF 8). Despite the earlier wrangling about whether Mike Hanley, as a mere ensign, was qualified to command a turret, once the war began, there were a great many rapid promotions, and Hanley left Turret One for the more important job of main battery director for Turret Three on the ship's stern. His new battle station was Sky Two, a small, enclosed platform high atop the ship's secondary mast. It was an early example of how the onset of war acted to accelerate both promotion and responsibility. It would not be the last.

The American plan was for planes from the *Enterprise* to bomb selected targets in the Marshall Islands while the cruisers, including the *Northampton*, used their main battery guns to find targets of opportunity, especially shipping.

Just before daybreak on February 1, Hanley was in his elevated perch at Sky Two when the *Northampton* arrived off tiny Wotje Atoll, where the Japanese had both an airfield and a seaplane base. Hanley counted ten Japanese merchant ships in the harbor, including one that was so close he could see it without his binoculars. He ordered the ship's stern battery to fire some ranging shots, and when they achieved a "straddle," with some shells landing long and others short, he ordered the guns to fire for effect. The three eight-inch guns in Turret Three banged out half a dozen rapid-fire salvos, and huge shell splashes erupted all around the targeted vessel, all but obscuring it. Hanley ordered the guns to keep firing as he waited for the telltale explosion that would indicate the ship was destroyed. In the midst of it, he got a sound-powered phone call from his counterpart at Sky One in the forward mast: "Mike, what the hell are you doing? Shift targets! That one is sinking." The *Northampton* was using armor-piercing shells that were going right through the thin hull of the merchantman without exploding. Hanley concluded later that he had seen "too many movies" where enemy ships blew up when they were hit. He quickly shifted targets, and the *Northampton*'s guns worked their way around the harbor, blasting, by his count, "about seven" Japanese transport and cargo ships. Officially, one transport was sunk and six others damaged.[15]

Meanwhile, the Japanese were shooting back. It was Hanley's first experience of being under fire. He noted that the three-inch shells made a whistling sound; the five-inch shells "whined," and what he assumed were eight-inch shells "sounded like a freight train." Fortunately, none of them struck the *Northampton*, and after about an hour—an hour that seemed much longer— the *Northampton* disengaged and rejoined the strike force. Hanley noted that there were "no casualties except [to my] nervous system."[16]

There was some excitement as the task force withdrew. A squadron of big two-engine Japanese bombers, dubbed "Bettys" by the Americans, flew out from the Marshalls to attack the Americans. Hanley confessed that "the *Northampton* did not distinguish itself" in the engagement that followed. Her 1.1-inch antiaircraft guns opened fire, but hitting fast-moving airplanes at altitude proved far more difficult than hitting anchored merchant ships. Hanley's post-battle comment was that it was "a fiasco!" Fortunately, despite a near-miss when a crippled and smoking Japanese plane tried to crash land into the *Enterprise*, there was no significant damage to the task force.[17]

While Halsey's task force hit the Marshalls, Fletcher's *Yorktown* group attacked the Gilberts. On the *Yorktown*, "Peck" Greenbacker candidly acknowledged that the "raid was not particularly effective." The Japanese had only been in the Gilberts for a few weeks, having seized it from the British, and as a result there were fewer worthwhile targets. In addition, bad weather closed in, obscuring even those few. About the best that could be said for it was that it gave the aviators some practice.[18]

When Halsey's *Enterprise* group, including the *Northampton*, returned to Pearl Harbor a week later, on February 5, it met a rapturous reception. Small and indecisive as the attack on the Marshalls had been, it was the first American counteroffensive of the Pacific War, and the sailors at Pearl were positively giddy about it. Hanley was "amazed to see that every ship we passed had turned out all hands, and they were cheering like mad even on the grounded battleships." He decided that it was better than the crowd at a Navy basketball game.[19]

It was quite different when the *Yorktown* arrived a day later; this time, the general reaction was a collective shrug. In part that was simply because the fleet had already spent itself in celebration. In part, too, it was a perception that the *Yorktown*'s performance was less worth celebrating. That annoyed the men on the *Yorktown*, who had spent six months on war patrols in the Atlantic before war even began in the Pacific. "We considered ourselves veterans of war," Greenbacker recalled, "and far more combat ready" than the crew on the *Enterprise*. When his classmate, Jack Holmes, who was on the *Enterprise*, visited him and made a disparaging remark about the *Yorktown*, Greenbacker was annoyed, even angry. His reaction suggested that loyalty to one's ship and shipmates was beginning to eclipse loyalty to one's classmates.[20]

A few months later, the *Enterprise*, again accompanied by the *Northampton*, raided Marcus Island, even further to the west and only a thousand miles from the Japanese homeland. While returning to Pearl Harbor from that raid, Admiral Halsey sent the *Northampton* and another cruiser off to bombard Wake Island, now in the hands of the Japanese. Hanley's specific assignment was to destroy a big dredger that the Japanese were using to improve the harbor at Wake. This time, the *Northampton* employed high-explosive ammunition instead of armor-piercing shells. As a result, Hanley got to see the spectacular explosion he had looked for in vain at Wotje. When the fourth salvo struck the target, he was gratified when "pieces of the dredge flew up into the air" and the target all but disappeared.[21]

Despite these successes, Hanley remembered those first weeks of war as an exhausting blur. For one thing, he was on watch almost all the time. As the squadron flagship, the *Northampton* had been one of the first to get a rudimentary CXAM radar unit, but radar technology was so new that many veteran officers did not yet trust it. That meant someone had to be on watch in Sky One or Sky Two twenty-four hours a day. Since there were only two officers trained in that job, Hanley and his counterpart in Sky One took turns: one took the watch from 8:00 p.m. to midnight, the other from midnight to 4:00 a.m., and then the first one came back on duty again at 4:00 a.m. The next night, they switched. As a result, neither of them ever got a full night's sleep. "To add to the problem," Hanley recalled, "on moonlight nights we had to put the windows down so the moon would not reflect off the windows. In our northern ops we damn near froze to death."[22]

In these early months of the war, the Japanese focused their main effort on the South Pacific, where no one worried about freezing to death. The desperate Allies, in full reaction mode, sought to slow them down by combining their forces to create what was called ABDA: an acronym for American, British, Dutch, and Australian forces. The naval component of ABDA was initially under the command of an American, Admiral Thomas Hart, who had preceded David Sellars as superintendent at the Naval Academy. To gratify the Dutch, however, he was replaced by a Dutch admiral, Conrad Helfrich, a move that Hart resented both then and later. Helfrich had no carriers and no battleships, though he did have two heavy cruisers, one of which was the USS *Houston* (CA-30), which had six members of the class of 1940 in her wardroom.

One of the many weaknesses of the ABDA command was that it had virtually no air cover, and on February 4, 1942, a lone Japanese bomber landed a five-hundred-pound bomb on the *Houston*'s stern near her aft eight-inch gun turret. The explosion started a number of fires that came perilously close to the ship's magazine, though alert crewmen successfully dogged down the fireproof doors to save the ship. Afterward, the charred bodies of the dead were laid out side by side on the fantail, and the job of identifying their remains fell to Ensign John B. "Nelly" Nelson, a hefty football player from the class of 1940 who had spent a lot of his spare time at the Academy lifting weights in the gym. A witness recalled seeing Nelly's eyes fill with tears as he examined the bodies of his shipmates. He was able to identify some, but given the condition of the remains, he simply had to guess at the others.[23]

Three weeks later, Helfrich sent the ships of what was optimistically called the ABDA Naval Strike Force under another Dutch admiral, Karel Doorman, to intercept a Japanese invasion force headed for Java. In the Battle of the Java Sea (February 27, 1942), the ABDA forces were badly mauled, and the surviving Allied ships, including the *Houston*, sought to escape around the western tip of Java. There they blundered into another Japanese surface force, and in the Battle of the Sunda Strait (February 28), the *Houston* was overwhelmed by superior forces, struck repeatedly by both shells and torpedoes. Her skipper, Captain Albert Rooks, turned her toward Java, perhaps hoping to get closer to shore so his crewmen would have a better chance to survive after the ship sank.

126   ANNAPOLIS GOES TO WAR

Whatever his plan, the *Houston* was too crippled to get very far, and Rooks himself soon became a mortal casualty. His executive officer, Commander David W. Roberts, tried to carry on the fight, but he was forced to order abandon ship. By then, it was already too late for many.

A total of 721 men went down with the *Houston*, including three members of the class of 1940. One was Alva Nethken, who was so short that the medical board at the Academy had repeatedly measured him to ensure that he met the minimum height requirement for commissioning. Another was the "congenial and care free" Fred Mallory from Georgia, who affected a good old boy manner with his southern drawl. The third was Coleman Sellers, called Jim, who, despite being a champion swimmer at Annapolis, never made it off the ship.*

Three other Forties got over the side and into the water. One was John "Ham" Hamill of Tulsa, Oklahoma, who spent the night wondering whether he "would be bitten first by a shark or one of the big crocodiles that inhabit the narrow passage." Instead, he was one of about 350 pulled from the water by the Japanese, who took him first to a temporary holding pen, then to Singapore, and eventually to Burma. There he was set to work on the Bangkok to Maulmein Railroad (the setting for the movie *Bridge on the River Kwai*). Hamill and the others "dug and carried dirt, cracked rocks, built bridges, and cut firewood for the wood burning locomotives." He spent the rest of the war—more than three years—a prisoner of the Japanese.[24]

Nelly Nelson avoided being picked up by the Japanese. Swimming doggedly through the dark toward Java, he was nearing exhaustion when he encountered a native in an outrigger canoe and gratefully climbed on board. He was able to convince its owner to help him rescue other survivors by offering him the only thing of value he had with him: his Naval Academy class ring. While it remained dark, Nelly picked up more of the *Houston* survivors, some of whom stayed with the boat as it headed to shore, while others decided to swim for it as it passed an offshore island.[25]

Charles D. Smith, known as "CD," also made it ashore. Another member of the Academy swim team, he swam to an offshore island and crawled up under some foliage, sleeping through the daylight hours of March 1. A passing rain squall the next day gave him and a few others concealment to swim from there to the main island of Java. They dashed across the narrow coastal road and up through thick foliage into the hills. From there, they looked down to see Japanese

---

* That same day, entirely by coincidence, Burton Hanson, known as Ollie, was killed off the coast of New Jersey when a German U-boat (U-578) torpedoed and sank the USS *Jacob Jones* (DD-130). His death raised the number of Forties killed in the war to fourteen.

RETRIBUTION 127

ships unloading troops and equipment. They headed inland, hoping to find a Dutch military unit. For three days they walked without any food until they encountered a native islander who offered them rice and fish. While they ate, however, he left to inform the Japanese, who soon arrived to take them prisoner.[26]

They were taken to a different prison facility than Hamill's, one known as "Bicycle Camp" since it had once been the headquarters of the Tenth Battalion of the Dutch army, which was a bicycle unit. There they lived in concrete block barracks with tile floors, sleeping in small cubicles that held four or five men each. They were segregated by nationality, so at least the Forties were together. Having come ashore with only what they had on, an Australian POW who was imprisoned at the same time thought they "looked like they had been through a shower, and somebody stole their clothes."[27]

Japanese military culture held that any warrior who allowed himself to be captured lost his honor and was thereby undeserving of honorable treatment. One consequence of that attitude was that the Americans and the Australians, too, had to salute every Japanese soldier they saw regardless of rank. If the prisoner was unable to salute because he was not wearing a hat, he had to bow deeply from the waist. Failure to do so resulted in immediate physical punishment. Even so, their treatment at Bicycle Camp was more annoying than brutal, especially compared with Japanese POW camps elsewhere, including in Burma and the Philippines, some of which were little more than death camps.

A month later, another of the Forties arrived at Bicycle Camp. It was Gaylord "Buck" Buchanan, the class member who had lost most of his lower leg in an accident during second class year. After extensive surgery, he had been fitted with a prosthetic, which allowed him to walk, to march, and even to play tennis. He was allowed to continue his studies at the Academy and graduate with his class, but he was not offered a commission. After graduation, therefore, he went to work for Sperry Instruments testing bombsights, and in that capacity he was a passenger in a Dutch B-18 bomber headed for Australia when it ran out of gas and crash landed in Java, where he, too, was taken prisoner and interred at Bicycle Camp. At the Academy, Buchanan had been an active member of the Radio Club, and now as a POW he scrounged enough parts to build a small short-wave radio receiver that he kept concealed inside his prosthetic foot. As a result, not only did prisoners at Camp Bicycle keep track of the war news, but one of them claimed that he could listen to Frank Sinatra on a San Francisco radio station.[28]

In addition to Java, the Japanese also landed soldiers on the Kra Peninsula in both Siam (Thailand) and British Malaya, and on the islands of Borneo and

Sumatra in the Dutch East Indies. The greatest shock to the Allies—and especially to the British—was the fall of Singapore, the British stronghold at the tip of the Malay Peninsula. Often referred to as the Gibraltar of the Pacific, its capitulation on February 15 was a terrible blow to British prestige and a signal victory for the Japanese. All these Japanese triumphs triggered enthusiastic celebrations in the home islands. The biggest prize, however, was the American-held Philippines. Indeed, the fact that those islands lay athwart the maritime supply lines from South Asia to Japan had been a major factor in convincing the Japanese that they had to go to war with the United States in the first place.

Though the Philippines were largely self-governing, they remained a US commonwealth. Consequently, while the Philippine government had its own army, that army was under the command of an American general, Douglas MacArthur, who had arrived there in 1935. Two years after that, MacArthur resigned from the US Army to accept a position as field marshal (the title was his idea) in the Philippine army. Then in July 1941, with Japanese-American relations deteriorating, Roosevelt recalled him to active duty, so that, in effect, he commanded both US and Filipino forces. At the same time, the United States began sending additional equipment and supplies to the Philippines, including thirty-five valuable B-17 bombers. Even so, given its location, the Philippines remained vulnerable to a large-scale Japanese attack.

In recognition of that, the American strategy to defend the islands did not call for an all-out defense of the beaches. The plan was for all the forces there—both American and Filipino—to withdraw into the Bataan Peninsula across the bay from Manila and hold out there in prepared defenses for six months or so, until the navy battlefleet steamed to the rescue. To execute that plan, MacArthur had a cadre of just over ten thousand well-trained Filipino soldiers (called the Philippine Scouts) and about sixty thousand Philippine militia. They were bolstered by twenty thousand US National Guard troops, recently reinforced by two battalions of M-3 "Lee" tanks. (Connie Carlson remembered hearing those tanks being unloaded in Manila on the night he rolled five aces at the Army-Navy Club.) MacArthur also had 250 airplanes and fifty small-motor torpedo boats, one of which—the Q-113—was commanded by "Sparky" Campo, now a lieutenant in the Philippine navy. And finally, there was a contingent of US Marines in the Philippines, including Company E, Second Battalion, of the Fourth Marine Regiment, commanded by the Massachusetts-born track sprinter "Chab" Chabot.[29]

Chabot was one of the twenty-five graduates of the class of 1940 who had selected the Marine Corps. At the time, the Corps was still relatively small, with a total of only about twenty thousand men worldwide. (Over the next three years, it would expand to ten times that number.) The notion that the US Marine Corps should constitute the spearpoint of an American transpacific offensive was already being discussed in Marine Corps circles, but in 1940 its principal duty remained the protection of navy bases, including the base at Olongapo on Subic Bay, which is where Chabot was stationed.

Despite the official plan to withdraw into the Bataan Peninsula in case of invasion, MacArthur worried that building defenses and stockpiling food in Bataan might look defeatist, so he convinced Washington to allow him to defend all of Luzon, including Manila. That turned out to be a mistake. The Japanese landed on Luzon on December 22 (the same day Fletcher refueled his task force enroute to Wake), and, unable to prevent the landing, the Allied forces fell back. The next night—Christmas Eve—MacArthur moved his headquarters from Bataan to the small, fortified island of Corregidor. Chabot's battalion (and Campo's torpedo boat) fell back from Subic Bay to the navy base at Mariveles River at the southern tip of Bataan, across from Corregidor. Because MacArthur had declined to stockpile supplies for fear of looking weak, the prospects for holding out very long were slim from the start. As the historian Richard Frank has noted, "The fate of besieged Bataan was determined not by Japanese arms but by malaria and malnutrition." The Allies went on half rations on January 5, and their supply of quinine ran out on February 15 (the day Singapore fell). All the while, the marines and US Army soldiers at Mariveles endured nearly continuous bombing and artillery fire.[30]

Tracking all this and unwilling to have MacArthur end up a Japanese prisoner of war, Roosevelt ordered him to leave the Philippines and make his way to Australia, which MacArthur did on March 11, leaving Major General Jonathan Wainwright to contend with a near-impossible situation. After holding out for another month, Allied forces on Bataan surrendered on April 7. That night, Chabot's Marine Corps unit crossed over to Corregidor, and "Sparky" Campo managed to escape as well by executing a bold torpedo attack against Japanese destroyers.*

---

* Years later, in 1961, Campo, by then a captain in the Philippine navy, was a student at the US Naval War College in Newport, Rhode Island. There he encountered Captain Kiniori Kunishima of the Japanese Maritime Self Defense Force, who was also a student there and who had commanded a destroyer off Mariveles in 1942. Kunishima told Campo that when he took his ship back to Okinawa for repair after the fall of Corregidor, yard workers discovered an unexploded torpedo sticking out of the ship's side. Campo was convinced it was one that he had fired.

130   ANNAPOLIS GOES TO WAR

Cut off from support or supplies, the defenders of Corregidor were bombed and shelled relentlessly. Under pressure from Tokyo to finish off the campaign, the Japanese commander launched an amphibious invasion of the island in May, and though they took heavy losses, the Japanese captured it on May 6, at which point Chabot became a prisoner of war. His experience was far more agonizing than that of his classmates in Camp Bicycle on Java. Though he did not participate in the notorious "Bataan Death March," Chabot's odyssey was nearly as traumatic. He and the other Americans were transported across the bay to Manila, where, in their own personal Gethsemane, they were paraded through the streets of the city, escorted by mounted Japanese soldiers who prodded them with swords and whips. The point was to demonstrate to the local population the utter subjugation and humiliation of the Americans. From there, the prisoners were packed into crowded boxcars and transported to a fenced-in schoolyard in Cabanatuan City, and from there they walked nine miles on a gravel road, many of them without shoes, to Bilibid Prison Camp, which was soon overcrowded with some ten thousand men. Like Hamill in Burma, Chabot remained a prisoner of the Japanese for the next two years.[31]

There was some good news. As a gesture of defiance, President Roosevelt okayed a carrier-based bombing attack on a handful of Japanese cities, including Tokyo. To do it, the navy had to commit two of its four Pacific carriers: the brand-new *Hornet*, encumbered with sixteen two-engine Army B-25 bombers, and the *Enterprise*, which had to accompany her since the *Hornet* could not provide her own combat air patrol. They had a substantial escort, including the cruiser USS *Vincennes*. One of the officers on the *Vincennes* was Hundy Hundevadt, who fifteen years earlier, as a ten-year-old, had sat on the New Jersey Palisades, entranced by the spectacle of battleships anchored in the Hudson River. Hundevadt was realistic enough to appreciate that the mission to bomb Tokyo was, as he put it, little more than "a morale booster for the American public." Still, it cheered him and everyone else on board to know that "we were finally doing something rather than defending against Japanese initiatives."[32]

It was an uncomfortable crossing. In order to meet the timetable and to minimize the time spent in Japanese waters, the task group maintained a speed of sixteen to eighteen knots despite unusually rough weather that severely tested both the ships and the men. Hundevadt remembered the voyage vividly: The *Vincennes*, he wrote,

RETRIBUTION

would slam into the heavy rollers in a violent and alarming fashion. She would ride her bow high up onto one swell and then fall into the next one with a tremendous crash, almost as if she had run into a solid object. Water would be thrown as high as the ship's mast as the bow buried itself deeply into the sea; the forecastle would then be submerged in green water while the thrown water would practically inundate the rest of the ship. Then the ship would shudder heavily as it struggled to bring its bow up from beneath the surface.

It was even more dramatic at night because the water was highly phosphorescent, and "the tremendous inundation from the bow spray was made pyrotechnic in appearance." It was, Hundevadt recalled, "quite an experience."

The bombers, commanded by Army Brigadier General James "Jimmy" Doolittle, launched earlier than planned after the task force was sighted by Japanese picket boats. As soon as the planes flew off to the west, the ships turned south to get as far away as possible before the Japanese could react. Only later did Hundevadt and the others learn that the Doolittle bombers successfully attacked several cities before flying on to crash land in China or elsewhere. Though the damage inflicted was minimal, Hundevadt noted that "the effect on national and shipboard morale was electric."[33]

Those Forties who were imprisoned at Bicycle Camp in Java learned about the raid on Buchanan's illicit radio. Indeed, Nelly Nelson almost gave the secret away when, during a work party soon afterward, a Japanese guard was taunting him by claiming that the Japanese were destroying American cities. "San Francisco," he said, "boom, boom, boom. New York: boom, boom, boom." Nelson looked at the guard and said, "Tokyo: boom, boom, boom." Suspicious, the guards conducted a search of their cells looking for a radio. They found nothing.[34]

11

U-Boats, Convoys, and Matrimony

The Doolittle raid notwithstanding, the Allies remained in a reactive and defensive mode all that spring. That was true not only in the Pacific, where the Japanese continued their rampage, seizing new acquisitions almost effortlessly, but also in the Atlantic, where German U-boats continued their effort to cut the maritime supply lines to Britain. The head of the German U-boat force, Admiral Karl Dönitz, was convinced that a "tonnage strategy"—sinking as many transport and cargo ships as possible, laden or empty—would deprive Britain of the shipping needed not only to sustain the war effort but even to feed her population. He might have been right if he had possessed the three hundred U-boats he told Hitler he needed. Instead, when the war began, he had only fifty-two, half of them small coastal boats. The number would grow, especially during 1942, though Allied resources would grow, too. Because of the need to rotate U-boats in and out of port for refueling and supplies, Dönitz could put only about thirty U-boats on patrol at any given moment. By the fall, though, there were more than one hundred. And with Germany in control of the French coast, those U-boats had relatively short passages out to their prime hunting grounds. In those circumstances, Dönitz's ambition to starve Britain into submission was a literal and proximate threat.

The counterstrategy to U-boat warfare was convoys: assembling the transports into groups of thirty or forty ships, protected by armed escorts. The Allied effort to get those convoys through the challenging weather of the North Atlantic and past the lurking U-boats was a constant struggle that has gone down in history as the Battle of the Atlantic.*

---

* Dönitz coordinated his U-boats by radio from a shore base near Kerneval on the Bay of Biscay. That allowed codebreakers at Bletchley Park north of London access to Dönitz's messages, parts of which they were able to decode, enabling them to reroute the convoys to avoid the wolfpacks. This aspect of the war, however, was a tightly held secret, and none of the members of the class of 1940 knew anything about it until much later.

The British had established regular convoy routes even before the war began, though they never had quite enough escorts to protect them; some convoys in 1940 had sailed with only a single escort. That was why Roosevelt had engineered the bases-for-destroyers agreement with Churchill in September 1940, and why he had allowed US Navy ships to act as de facto escorts for convoys in 1941, disguising the fact from the public for months until it became impossible to do so. After Pearl Harbor, pretense was no longer necessary, and over time convoy escort became the primary function of the US Navy's Atlantic Fleet. Members of the class of 1940 were in the thick of it.

By then, the British had built a network of convoy routes all over the globe, though the most frequently traveled—and the most strategically consequential—were those across the North Atlantic. The eastbound convoys, filled with Lend-Lease goods from the United States, were designated "HX" convoys since they departed initially from Halifax, and they retained that designation even after they began departing instead from New York. The westbound (empty) convoys from Britain back to the United States were designated "ON" (outbound, North America) convoys. Throughout 1942, the losses were horrific. In January, the U-boats sank 50 ships, a number that rose to a startling 124 in June. Two factors kept those losses from being strategically decisive. One was the American ability to build new ships in unprecedented numbers, and the other was the construction of more escort ships so that by late 1942, instead of only two or perhaps three escorts per convoy, which had been the norm, it was now possible to assign six or seven. By 1943 some of the larger convoys might have as many as a dozen escorts.[1]

To staff the new ships, US Navy officers were elevated to positions of increased responsibility. Division officers became executive officers; executive officers became commanding officers. And younger men, including ensigns from the class of 1940, moved up, too, becoming engineering officers, torpedo officers, gunnery officers, even, on some smaller ships, executive officers. For many, it was an abrupt adjustment. Serving as a turret officer on a battleship or assistant engineer on a cruiser did not necessarily prepare them for shepherding dozens—or scores—of merchant ships across an ocean infested with U-boats. On the other hand, it was expected in the navy that a good officer could move from job to job with seamless efficiency even if some of them faced a steep learning curve in doing so.

A typical North Atlantic convoy contained between thirty and fifty ships, generally organized into seven to ten columns of four or five ships each following each other at thousand-yard intervals. As a result, a single convoy might cover an area of ten or fifteen square miles. Moreover, each transport

134 ANNAPOLIS GOES TO WAR

was under the command of a civilian skipper who was not accustomed to steaming in company. The U-boat threat mandated that the whole convoy zig and zag in unison most of the way across, and getting forty or fifty civilian skippers to put their helm over simultaneously in the middle of the night with no running lights, without any of the ships colliding with one another, was daunting.

Then, too, the entire convoy necessarily had to proceed at the speed of the slowest ship. The goal for most convoys was to maintain a speed of six knots, though it was a goal seldom met. The slow speed, the bad weather, and the zigzagging meant that a transatlantic crossing could take between two to three weeks. In short, shepherding a large convoy across the Atlantic was a difficult, wearisome, time-consuming, and stressful undertaking. It was, nevertheless, absolutely critical to eventual Allied success.[2]

On March 11, 1942, two American destroyers, *Buck* (DD-420) and *Bristol* (DD-453), got underway from Argentia in Newfoundland with four British corvettes (small open-bridge escorts) to shepherd an HX convoy to Londonderry at the tip of Northern Ireland. It was, coincidentally, the same day that General Douglas MacArthur boarded a PT boat on Corregidor to begin his journey to Australia, where he would deliver his speech pledging to return to the Philippines. Unlike MacArthur's famous odyssey, the departure of two American destroyers from Newfoundland was entirely unremarkable since by then convoys from Canada or the United States to Britain had become routine. More than a dozen HX convoys left for British waters that month—four of them that week.

Pete Peterson was the torpedo officer on the *Bristol*, and he tracked the convoy's progress—or lack thereof—in his diary. It was typical March weather in the North Atlantic, which meant strong winds, high waves, and cold temperatures. The weather was so bitter that Peterson found it a challenge just to carry out his daily duties. There is an old navy proverb that a sailor should always have one hand for himself and one hand for the ship. That was almost literally true during particularly violent movements of the *Bristol* in the North Atlantic when Peterson often used one hand to take a bearing or use the sound-powered telephone, while he gripped the rail with his other hand just to stay on his feet. It was also true when he sat down to a meal. Metal poles had been installed in the *Bristol*'s wardroom next to the tables, and Peterson noted, "If it were not for the vertical poles secured between the chairs, there would be no way of staying at the table."[3]

The British novelist Nicholas Monserrat, who served on a corvette in the North Atlantic during the war, described what it was like to eat a meal in rough seas: "When you drink, the liquid rises toward you and slops over; at meals the food spills off your plate, the cutlery will not stay in place. Things roll about and bang, and slide away crazily." Peterson experienced all of that, noting stoically, "We manage the best we can, using cold food, when we feel like eating."[4]

Even sleeping was a trial. As Jack Wright, another of the Forties, described it: "Between the pitching and the rolling, with the ship's motion giving its best possible imitation of a giant corkscrew, and the pounding of the waves, the groaning of the ship itself [and] the ever-present threat of a submarine attack, who slept?" On the *Bristol*, Peterson found that he could remain in his bunk only if he crammed himself against the bulkhead and used the covers to wedge himself into place. Even then, unpredictable movements of the ship sometimes compelled him to make "frantic grabs" for the side of his bunk to keep from falling out onto the deck. Somewhat resignedly, he noted, "That gets awfully tiresome after a couple of days." And when he did get to sleep, it was regularly interrupted when duty called. He wrote that "struggling out of your bunk and into some clothes to go on watch is an ordeal." Again, Monserrat: "You're woken up at ten to four by the bosun's mate, and you stare at the deck-head and think: My God, I can't go up there again in the dark and filthy rain, and stand another four hours of it. But you can of course."[5]

After the *Bristol* and *Buck* met up with the convoy, the first task was organizing the merchant ships into files and columns and positioning the escorts around them. That proved more time-consuming than Peterson expected. It was, he noted, "something of a mess." It took most of the remaining daylight hours to herd all the ships into place, and even after the convoy got underway, confusion and uncertainty dominated. The *Bristol*'s assigned position in the convoy was on the port quarter, but after full dark, with all the ships steaming blacked out, it was difficult to determine exactly where that was. The *Bristol* had a brand-new radar set (still rare in 1942), though no one on board had any operational experience with it. Besides, with so many ships in company, and radar returns coming off the towering waves as well as the nearby ships, the radar screen was a confusion of illuminations. Peterson recalled that only one ship in the convoy "came in bright and clear amongst all the clutter." Consequently, all through the night, each officer of the deck on the *Bristol* sought to maintain a constant bearing and range to that one ship.[6]

With the coming of dawn, it became instantly obvious that that had been a mistake. The ship they had used as a guide was still there, but it was the only ship in sight. The convoy was simply gone. Perceiving that they had been left behind, the *Bristol* abandoned the straggler and raced ahead to find the rest of the convoy. After a few tension-filled hours, there it was. At 8:00 a.m., with a collective sigh of relief on the bridge, the *Bristol* took up its assigned position on the port side of the convoy. Only minutes later, a call came in on the short-range TBS (talk between ships) radio: It was the escort commodore in the *Buck*. He wanted to know how the convoy was doing because he had become separated from it during the night and had not seen another ship for hours. On the one hand, it was a consolation to Peterson and his skipper to know they were not the only ones who had fallen out of position; on the other hand, it was disconcerting that the convoy had plodded eastward throughout the night without either of its escorting destroyers. At least the four British corvettes, experienced at this sort of thing, had been there all the time.

Once reunited, the convoy plowed on, zigging and zagging periodically, inviting chaos among the ships in the columns each time. The weather not only made sleeping and eating difficult but also played havoc with the convoy's speed. The goal for this particular convoy was to maintain an average speed of three knots, which is about the speed of a strolling pedestrian, yet even that proved impossible amid the strong seas and headwinds. Indeed, the navigation officer on the *Bristol* calculated that during one twenty-four-hour period, they actually regressed several miles.[7]

After six days, the weather abruptly moderated. The North Atlantic became "duck pond smooth," as Peterson put it, and he felt the "decrease in tension and worry" as an almost physical sensation. Still, he and everyone else on board knew that "with the better weather the more chance there was of running into submarines." And the closer they got to British waters, the more likely that was. "We haven't heard much about submarines in this area yet," Peterson wrote on March 18, "but when we do, it will probably be first hand," adding philosophically: "Well, come what may!"[8]

The encounter—if it was an encounter—took place only two days out from Londonderry. The *Buck*'s sonar detected a submerged U-boat, and her skipper immediately began dropping depth charges. The *Bristol* raced to the scene of action and activated her own sonar search. Picking up a contact, she, too, began dropping depth charges. While there was always a possibility of damaging or even sinking a U-boat with a depth charge attack, the more immediate objective was to keep it submerged and maneuvering radically to avoid the depth charges so that it could not get into position to fire torpedoes. As the two American destroyers churned up the sea with explosives, the convoy chugged onward. None of the depth charges revealed any visible damage—no oil slick or wreckage—so after a while, the destroyers discontinued the action and "proceeded to catch up with the convoy."[9]

Two days later, on March 22, after more than two weeks at sea, the ships all arrived safely in Londonderry. Aside from that one flurry against a foe that may or may not have existed, the ships of the Allied escort had seen no combat—or even an enemy, and the successful crossing would not command so much as a footnote in the long history of the naval war.

Those convoys that did claim a spot in the historical record were the ones that suffered the most. One was Convoy HX-299, which left Newfoundland three days before the *Bristol* and followed virtually the same route. Dönitz sent no fewer than thirty-seven U-boats against it, and in a four-day running battle that began on March 16, the U-boats sank twenty-two Allied ships while losing only one submarine. Dönitz called it "the greatest success we had so far scored against a convoy." That confrontation made the history books; the uneventful journey of Peterson's convoy did not. Yet it was the convoys where little happened (apart from discomfort and sleeplessness) that allowed the British people and nation to stay in the war. The arrival of Peterson's convoy in Londonderry was a quiet victory, hardly noticed at the time or afterward, but a victory nonetheless.[10]

Peterson and his shipmates had a chance to look around Londonderry for a day, and they had two days leave in Belfast while the *Bristol* refueled and resupplied. After that, it was back the other way with a smaller ON convoy of thirteen transports and a robust escort of eight warships, including a Canadian destroyer and a British-built corvette manned by a crew of Free French. The westward crossing took only ten days, and after dropping off the transports in Halifax on April 10, the *Bristol* went into the yards for another refit. A week later, she was underway again escorting a different convoy. Now a salty veteran of the Battle of the Atlantic, Peterson wrote laconically, "Weather calm, no submarine contacts."[11]

Peterson's experience on the *Bristol* was typical. Ben Frana, who was on the *Baldwin* (DD-624), noted that in making three consecutive runs across the Atlantic escorting convoys, they "did not meet any hostile submarines." Even so, Frana observed, "Our strong Merchant Marine service was a vital factor in the winning of the war." And it was.[12]

In April 1942 the Forties all got promoted. Their elevation from ensign to lieutenant junior grade ("jaygee")—or in the case of the marines, from second

138   ANNAPOLIS GOES TO WAR

lieutenant to first lieutenant—had been scheduled for June, two years after their graduation, but with the onset of war, that schedule was accelerated. By then most of them were already doing jobs well above their putative rank anyway due to the demands of wartime operations. That same month, the navy also annulled the provisions of General Order No. 117, Paragraph 1B, that prohibited them from getting married until they had served two full years as officers. The revocation of that requirement was not only gratifying but for many also financially remunerative. The pay for an unmarried ensign was $125 a month, and for a jaygee it was $166 per month, but for a *married* lieutenant (j.g.) it was $225 a month.

In addition to whatever financial incentive there may have been, the men from the class of 1940 embraced the institution of marriage as a signifier of adulthood. It was an aspect of American culture they had unconsciously embraced by choosing the Naval Academy in the first place, and it had been reinforced by their four years there. Just as they believed in duty, responsibility, and hard work, they also believed in family, fidelity, and, in due time, fatherhood. Though the number of marriages in the United States had dropped during the Great Depression, hitting a low of 7.9 per 1,000 in 1932, the number jumped to 13.2 per 1,000 in 1942. Moreover, the average age at which American men married in the United States dropped from almost thirty in 1932 to twenty-four in 1942, which is how old most of the Forties were that year. Their eagerness to be married was due not only to a natural desire to be with their loved ones but also to a view of marriage as a marker of responsibility.[13]

Of course, a number of Forties had married secretly, and a few of them, as we've seen, had been caught and dismissed because of it. Now the lifting of the ban allowed those who had secretly married to come into the open. "Hundy" Hundevadt had married his longtime girlfriend, Del Kronmeyer, the previous November. The *Vincennes* had been in Portland, Maine, that month, and Hundevadt was assigned to command the sailors on shore patrol, working closely with the local police. In casual conversation with them, he mentioned how frustrating it was that several of the brand-new ensigns—90-day wonders—who had shown up to join the ship's company had brought along their wives, who set up housekeeping ashore. How fair was it, he asked rhetorically, that these instant ensigns were allowed to be married, whereas he, who had earned his commission after four years at the Academy, was not? The policemen were sympathetic and told him they could fix it. Thus encouraged, Hundy wrote Del to ask her to travel up to Portland, and when she arrived, the police escorted them both into the office of the city mayor, who, by prearrangement, quietly performed a marriage ceremony. No one in the navy was any the wiser.

Now, five months later, as the *Vincennes* returned from the Doolittle raid, Hundevadt saw the All-Navy (ALNAV) message announcing that the restriction against marriage had been lifted. He and two other married members of the wardroom went to see the ship's paymaster to apply for an increase in benefits. They did not expect any back pay, they said, only that their future pay should reflect their married status. The paymaster was dubious. After all, they had married in defiance of regulations; why should they benefit now? The paymaster went to the ship's captain, Frederick Riefkohl, to ask if he should endorse their request. Riefkohl waved off the paymaster's scruples as "petty nonsense" and told him to approve it. Hundevadt immediately wrote to Del to tell her that, if she wanted, she could quit her nursing job.[14]

Some who had married secretly before the ban was lifted got married again. One of them was Crosswell Croft, who married Bobbie Engh a second time, this time in a public ceremony. (In later years, he liked to get a rise out of people by introducing her as his second wife, a joke that usually fell flat with Bobbie.) Another was Allen Cook, who had married Velda Craven nine days after the Pearl Harbor attack and had kept the marriage secret. Four months later, on April 4, 1942, he and Velda went to see Episcopal Bishop Samuel H. Littell, who had married them back in December, to ask if he would perform the ceremony again, for the record this time. Littell was offended. As Cook remembered it, he told them, "If the first marriage ceremony was not enough, we had been living in sin and in either case he wanted nothing more to do with us!" Crestfallen, they went to see a justice of the peace, who claimed to be very busy but agreed to perform the ceremony if they were willing to do it immediately. They had not been prepared for that. Cook was wearing old khakis and Velda's hair was in curlers. Still, this might be their only chance, so they agreed. It was pretty pro forma. The JP read off the ceremony, got a phone call in the middle of it, then, without changing tone or expression, held out his hand and said, "That will be ten dollars."[15]

There were literally hundreds of weddings that spring, and even more in the summer after class members who had been at sea in April returned to port. One of those who had to wait was Bob Harris, who was on the brand-new battleship *Washington* (BB-56), which left Casco Bay, Maine, five days before the ban was lifted. His ship was bound for Scapa Flow in the far north of Scotland. In addition to the *Washington*, the task force there (designated Task Force 39) included the heavy cruisers *Tuscaloosa* and *Wichita*. The task force commander was Rear Admiral John W. Wilcox, a 1905 Academy classmate of Chester Nimitz. On the second day out, March 27, 1942, officers on the bridge looked about and noted that Wilcox was no longer present. A quick search topside elevated the alarm, and soon a cry of "man overboard" galvanized everyone into action. Despite frantic efforts, it was several hours before Wilcox's lifeless body was seen floating face down. The seas were so rough no vessel could get close enough to recover the body before it disappeared under the waves. The cause of the mishap was never resolved, and the task force continued on its way with Rear Admiral Robert Giffen assuming command.

The *Washington*'s journey to the isolated Royal Navy base at Scapa Flow was another element of Allied convoy defense. With the Red Army bearing the brunt of the ground war in Europe, it made sense to keep that army supplied and fighting, and that meant convoys filled with Lend-Lease goods had to steam through the Arctic Ocean and around the North Cape of Norway to Russian ports in the Barents Sea. Designated as PQ convoys (the routing orders were written by Royal Navy Commander P. Q. Richards), the conditions were even more challenging than those in the North Atlantic. On the *Tuscaloosa*, Jack Wright recalled what it was like. "The ship's bow would float upward creating a sensation of weightlessness and then plunge hard and deep enough to plow green water over the bow. As often as not the water would freeze on contact with any and all severely sub-cooled metal." Even in relatively calm seas, he noted, "You had to hold on day and night."[16]

Because the Germans had airfields in northern Norway, the convoys gave the Norwegian headland a wide berth, skirting the polar ice cap. Though many of the Forties who served in the Pacific became "Shellbacks" for crossing the equator, Harris, Braybrook, and Wright were among those who earned the honorific title of "Polar Bear" or "Bluenose" for crossing the Arctic Circle. Fog and intermittent snow, often a nuisance to sailors, were welcomed because they kept the Luftwaffe planes grounded. Bill Braybrook on the *Tuscaloosa* recalled that "bad weather was a friend in the Norwegian Sea."[17]

In addition to German airplanes and U-boats, another threat to the PQ convoys were German heavy surface warships, and in particular, the battleship *Tirpitz*, sister ship of the *Bismarck*. The *Tirpitz* was in an anchorage near Narvik in northern Norway, which was one reason why the *Washington* had been sent to Scapa Flow. The *Washington* had nine sixteen-inch guns, making her a presumed match for the *Tirpitz*, which carried eight fifteen-inch guns. In the spring and summer of 1942, therefore, the *Washington*, *Tuscaloosa*, and

U-BOATS, CONVOYS, AND MATRIMONY

Wichita, along with Royal Navy battleships and cruisers, sortied periodically from Scapa Flow to provide distant cover for the PQ convoys.

At Scapa Flow, Bob Harris (like Myers Montgomery in Reykjavik) enjoyed visiting the British ships to take advantage of the "traditional Wine Messes and liquor rations" on board. The American officers reciprocated, and friendships bloomed between the English-speaking allies. Harris also noted visits to the *Washington* by a few famous guests. One was the movie star Douglas Fairbanks Jr., who had volunteered for the navy immediately after Pearl Harbor and had been commissioned a lieutenant, junior grade—the same rank as Harris. Though Fairbanks didn't stay long, Harris found him "easy talk to and well liked in the officer's mess." Another celebrity guest was King George VI, and in preparation for that visit, the whole ship was cleaned and polished. When the king boarded, the flag of Great Britain was raised at the main truck, above the US flag, which flew at the gaff. The sailors in Harris's engineering division were not happy about that, and they came to him to complain about it. This was an *American* ship, they insisted, why was it flying the *British* flag—and *above* the American flag? Harris explained to them that the flag was the king's personal flag, not the British national flag, and it simply indicated that the king was on board. They heard him out, but not all of them were satisfied.[18]

The *Tirpitz* did sortie from its lair, twice. Each time, the battleships at Scapa Flow headed out to intercept her, and each time, the *Tirpitz* turned back. Despite regular, almost routine, bombing of the *Tirpitz* by planes of the Royal Air Force, she remained a looming potential threat to any PQ convoy.[19]

The *Washington* never came to grips with the *Tirpitz*, though there were moments of excitement. On one occasion, when the *Washington* was following the British battleship *King George V* in formation, the ubiquitous fog suddenly closed in so thick that visibility fell to near zero. In the midst of it, a British destroyer, the *Punjabi*, cut across the track of the *George V*, which was unable to avoid her and literally cut her in half. The bow section of the *Punjabi* remained afloat, but her stern, including the depth charges in their racks, sank. The charges were preset to detonate at specific depths, and as the two battleships passed over the *Punjabi*'s sinking stern, the depth charges began to explode. Harris was in the *Washington*'s engineering spaces below decks when he heard "a faint explosion," followed a few seconds later by another, much closer, explosion. Then, almost directly under the ship, there was a third "tremendous explosion." Harris felt the forty-five-thousand-ton *Washington* lift "straight up about a foot!!" Deck plates flew into the air, unsecured items careened about the engine room, steam lines and oil lines burst, and the bilge filled with oil. Somewhat to his surprise, Harris found that he was terrified. Yet he was pleased with himself that despite a powerful instinct to "get out of the engine room fast, my feet stayed put and my training took over." He directed crewmen as they corralled unsecured equipment, supervised the cleanup and repairs, and was soon able to report to the bridge that the engines were operational and on line.[20]

In the last week of June, the Allied fleet at Scapa Flow, including the *Washington*, put to sea again, this time to provide distant cover for another PQ convoy, designated as PQ-17. Originating in Iceland, it was bound to Archangel in the Kola Inlet because the nearer harbor at Murmansk had been damaged by a German air raid. The convoy consisted of thirty-four ships loaded with trucks, tanks, crated airplanes, and other military supplies, and it had a substantial escort of more than a dozen warships in close support, plus a shadowing cruiser force that included the *Tuscaloosa*, with Bill Braybrook and Hatchie Wright on board. The big ships of the British Home Fleet, including the *Washington*, hovered over the horizon.

There were problems from the start. One of the transports had engine trouble and had to turn back. Two more hit floating ice in the Denmark Strait and also turned back. Then, several days later, on July 4, German scouting aircraft spotted the convoy north of Norway. Within hours twenty-six German bombers attacked. Despite heavy AA fire from the escorts, including the *Tuscaloosa*, which earned a battle star, three ships of the convoy were hit and had to be abandoned. The surviving ships, now numbering twenty-eight, continued eastward. At that point, the Allied big ships, including the *Washington*, were recalled, leaving the convoy to the care of the close escort ships plus the cruisers.

Throughout the Battle of the Atlantic, the Allies had benefited from the fact that they were able to read portions of the German naval code thanks to the codebreakers at Bletchley Park, an unassuming town sixty miles north of London. On this occasion, however, that presumed advantage proved a liability. The codebreakers intercepted a series of German radio messages that suggested the *Tirpitz* and other heavy German ships were getting underway. If they did, the ships of the escort force, even the cruisers, would be all but helpless. It was too late to recall the big ships from Scapa Flow, so, in something of a panic, the British High Command issued orders for the cruisers accompanying the convoy to withdraw "at high speed" to prevent their annihilation by the *Tirpitz*. Braybrook, on the *Tuscaloosa*, was unhappy with those orders and even a bit ashamed: "We hated the feeling of running away." Worse yet, the orders from Whitehall called for the transports to "scatter."[21]

U-BOATS, CONVOYS, AND MATRIMONY

It was a mistake. The *Tirpitz* did not sortie, and over the next several days, the transports, proceeding independently, were picked off one at a time by German airplanes and U-boats. Twenty-three Allied ships were sunk—one more than in the slaughter of HX-229 back in March. Along with the lost ships went 430 tanks, 210 bombers, and 3,550 other vehicles, plus one hundred thousand tons of munitions.[22]

Stalin was understandably upset, and his disappointment turned to rage when, in the wake of this disaster, the Allies told him that they were canceling the next several PQ convoys. To the paranoid Stalin, it was yet another example of the continuing iniquity of the Anglo-Americans. After all, the Americans sent dozens of convoys to Britain every month, and when a disaster occurred in the Atlantic, as in the massacre of HX-229, they did not suspend shipments. Stalin suspected the Anglo-Americans were sending him only enough material to keep the Russians in the war, and not enough to win it.

Hoping to assuage his fury, the Allies did organize one more, much smaller, resupply effort in August. The *Tuscaloosa*, reconfigured with heavy-lift cranes and crammed with military stores plus a "complete hospital unit, including medical personnel," joined two other cruisers for a high-speed run into Archangel. The only US Navy cruiser with an elevator (installed when she had hosted the president the previous year), the *Tuscaloosa* now became the only cruiser with heavy-lift cranes. Accompanied by three destroyers (two British and one Russian), she made it safely through to Archangel. Braybrook remembered that, with a German airbase only twenty-five miles away, "off-loading was an all-hands evolution and was accomplished in record time." On the return trip, the *Tuscaloosa* carried 243 passengers, many of them survivors from the slaughter of PQ-17.[23]

By then the *Washington* had left Scapa Flow to return to the United States. Eventually, she would be routed to the war in the Pacific, but for Bob Harris and many others on board, the good news was that she would spend two weeks in the New York Navy Yard undergoing repairs from the depth charge accident. That meant Harris could meet up with his fiancé, Joanne Smullin, and marry her.

There was one problem: Smullin did not know her fiancé's ship was coming—information concerning the movement of ships was classified. Only after the *Washington* dropped anchor in New York Harbor was Harris able to get a friend to send her a telegram. And even after Smullin arrived in New York, Harris could not immediately get off the ship because as acting chief engineer he had to shut down the engines before the *Washington* could go into the yards. That required him to crawl through all eight boilers personally to ensure that they were secure, a task that not surprisingly left him filthy dirty. He went ashore, cleaned himself up, and, a few days later, he and Joanne were married in a double ceremony with her sister and her beau. Theirs was one of twenty-six weddings that week involving officers from the *Washington*. In acknowledgment of it, the officers on the *Washington* reached deep into their pockets to present each couple with a silver bowl "appropriately engraved."[24]

Not everyone in the class rushed to the altar. Myers Montgomery, who had fancied himself in love at least a half dozen times, remained single, as did Pete Peterson, despite carrying the torch for the "delightful, beautiful" Lynn Stolstrom. Surprisingly, perhaps, one of the Forties who did become engaged that summer was the social butterfly John Lacouture. The lifting of the ban on marriage had hardly been made public before newspapers in California and New Mexico ran stories announcing the engagement of Amelia Ames Stembel of Pasadena, California, and Santa Fe, New Mexico, to Ensign John E. Lacouture of Boston and Cape Cod.[25] The wedding, the papers proclaimed, would be a small affair, after which the couple would honeymoon in Santa Fe. Before any of that could happen, however, the prospective groom had to return to sea, and the war, on the USS *Blue*. The wedding—and the honeymoon—would have to wait.

12

The Coral Sea and Midway

If listening in on the enemy's communications occasionally led to a snafu, as it did in the Barents Sea, it more often created strategic opportunities. During those desperate early months of the war in the Pacific, one of the few tangible advantages Admiral Nimitz enjoyed was provided by a group of dedicated cryptanalysts in an organization colloquially known as Hypo, the phonetic representation of the letter H, which stood for He'eia, the navy's radio receiving station on the north coast of Oahu. Led by Lieutenant Commander Joseph Rochefort, who was not an Academy grad, the group put in long hours in two basement rooms at the Fourteenth Naval District headquarters at Pearl Harbor, where, with hard work, they managed to read just enough of the intercepted Japanese radio messages to predict where they might strike next. On April 5, 1942, Nimitz's intelligence officer, Lieutenant Commander Edwin Layton, came into Nimitz's office to tell him that Rochefort's team had found sufficient hints in the radio traffic to conclude that the Japanese planned to attack Port Moresby, a small but strategically significant harbor on the south coast of New Guinea. They would do so, Layton told him, by making an amphibious end run through the Coral Sea sometime in the first week of May, only a month away.[1]

The news came at a precarious moment. Though Nimitz had four carriers again, thanks to the arrival of the brand-new *Hornet*, two of those four—including the *Hornet*—were thousands of miles away with Jimmy Doolittle's army bombers. That left Nimitz with only two carriers to try to block the Japanese move through the Coral Sea. And if he accepted the challenge, those two carriers would almost certainly confront a superior force. Was the possession of advanced knowledge a sufficient advantage to justify risking them? Nimitz decided that it was.[2]

None of the newly promoted officers from the class of 1940 knew any of this, of course. The kind of intelligence the Hypo team passed on to Nimitz was tightly controlled and did not filter down to junior officers. Peck Greenbacker and the other Forties on the *Yorktown* were already in the Coral Sea under the command of Frank Jack Fletcher, and they had no conception that, as Greenbacker wrote later, "our situation was close to being desperate." In fact, their confidence was sky high, and not just because of their recent promotions. In addition to the *Yorktown*'s embarked air group of more than eighty bombers, torpedo planes, and fighters, Greenbacker could scan the horizon and see three heavy cruisers and four destroyers plus support ships, literally surrounding them. Whatever concerns the admirals might have about a possible engagement in the Coral Sea, Greenbacker and his classmates metaphorically snapped their fingers at any possible danger. "We junior officers were entirely carefree in the good weather of the South Pacific," he wrote. Long afterward, when the Battle of the Coral Sea had become history, he appreciated that "we were not smart enough to realize how precarious a situation we were in."[3]

The campaign began well enough, with the *Lexington* conducting a high-speed run from Pearl Harbor to join the *Yorktown* in the Coral Sea on the first of May. One of the two heavy cruisers in her escort was the *New Orleans* (CA-32). She was literally the last of the so-called treaty cruisers, built to the specifications of the 1922 Washington Treaty, which had limited cruisers to ten thousand tons and eight-inch guns. Four members of the class of 1940 were on board, including Louis "Sandy" Saunders, who kept a diary (despite regulations against doing so). As much in the dark as anyone else about why the *Lexington* and her escorts had been suddenly rushed into the Coral Sea, Saunders echoed the scuttlebutt on board when he wrote, "It appears that we will attempt to stop anything that comes south."[4]

Three days after the two American carriers rendezvoused, Fletcher learned that the Japanese were unloading men and supplies onto the tiny island of Tulagi in the Solomon Islands, three hundred miles to the north. Leaving the *Lexington* behind to refuel, he sped north with the *Yorktown* to attack them. In three consecutive air strikes on May 5, planes from the *Yorktown* sank two Japanese minesweepers and damaged several other ships. Though it was a mere skirmish in the long history of the war, it added to the confidence and sense of well-being within the task force. The Japanese had been surprised; they had suffered losses. The Americans had lost three planes and one air crew, but that did little to dampen the high morale on the *Yorktown* as it rejoined the *Lexington*, after which both carriers, plus their escorts, headed west into the Coral Sea to look for the main Japanese fleet.

THE CORAL SEA AND MIDWAY   147

That same day, three thousand miles to the west, Jonathan Wainwright surrendered Corregidor to the Japanese, and "Chab" Chabot became a prisoner of war.

The Battle of the Coral Sea (May 7–8, 1942) became famous as the first naval battle in history in which neither fleet ever sighted the other. All of the combat was conducted by carrier-based airplanes. Since none of the members of the class of 1940 had yet been to flight school, their perception of the battle was limited to what they could see from the task force. Naturally, their perspectives differed depending on their assigned duty stations. As the assistant engineering officer on the *New Orleans*, Saunders remembered that while the ship was buttoned up during general quarters, the ventilation in the engineering spaces was "terrible," and working in the engine room was "just like standing in a furnace." As the assistant navigation officer on the *Lexington*, Joe Weber remembered monitoring the many course changes as the carriers turned into the wind to launch or recover planes. Connie Carlson in Sky Two on the cruiser *Astoria* (the same job Mike Hanley had on the *Northampton*) scanned the skies for bogeys (unidentified aircraft) and calculated gun ranges. Peck Greenbacker, the communications officer on the *Yorktown*, monitored and forwarded the signals received from the radio room. Because all the ships were operating under strict radio silence, neither he nor anyone else sent any radio messages until the battle was over. Whatever their onboard duties, their most vivid memory of the Battle of the Coral Sea concerned those crowded moments when they all came under Japanese air attack.[5]

The first day of the battle was May 7, and on that day the American scout planes failed to locate the main Japanese carrier force, though American bombers did find and sink the light carrier *Shōhō*, which was accompanying the enemy transport fleet. When Lieutenant Commander Robert Dixon, who led the scout bombers from *Lexington*, broke radio silence to report, "Scratch one flattop!" it sent a thrill throughout the task force. The Japanese also failed to find the American carriers that day, sending their bombers and torpedo planes against the American oiler *Neosho* and her accompanying destroyer *Sims*, sinking both of them. One of the mortal casualties on the *Neosho* was Bob Allsopp, described by his Academy roommate as "navy through and through," who became the fifteenth member of the class of 1940 to die in the war. The loss of the big oiler was a blow to Fletcher's logistics, but, painful as it was, the fact that the Japanese had expended their fury on the *Neosho* meant that they had not yet found the *Yorktown* or *Lexington*.

An especially suggestive example of the kind of confusion and chaos that characterized the fighting on May 7 occurred a few hours after sunset. Connie Carlson on the *Astoria*, which was screening the *Yorktown*, watched as planes circled overhead in preparation for landing. Suddenly, his enlisted spotter, standing next to him, pointed to one of the circling planes and cried out, "Jesus, they got wheels!" Unlike American planes, Japanese dive bombers did not have retractable landing gear. Clearly—and shockingly—there were at least some Japanese planes mixed in with the American planes circling over the *Yorktown*. It was not a sneak attack; several Japanese pilots, attempting to return to their own carriers, had seen planes in a landing pattern, and in the gathering darkness had assumed the *Yorktown* was one of their own. Carlson directed the *Astoria*'s five-inch antiaircraft guns to open up, and the .50 caliber gun crews on the *Yorktown* sent a curtain of red tracer fire snaking skyward. It was, he recalled, "quite a fireworks display." Like quail flushed from cover, Japanese and American planes scattered in all directions. One Japanese plane was shot down; the others fled. One American pilot, speeding off into the darkness, got disoriented after twilight turned to full dark and was unable to relocate the task force. He was never found.[6]

The main battle took place the next morning (May 8, 1942). Fletcher sent full deckloads from both *Yorktown* and *Lexington* toward the reported location of the enemy carriers, and the Japanese did the same. The opposing air armadas actually passed each other en route. Alerted by their radar (which the Japanese did not have), the American ships went to general quarters around ten o'clock, and the Japanese planes arrived an hour later. Brushing aside the small American combat air patrol, the superbly trained Japanese pilots came in both high and low: the dive bombers screaming down from fifteen thousand feet, and the torpedo bombers coming in barely above wave height. To those on the targeted ships, the sky seemed full of airplanes. Joe Weber on the *Lexington* thought there were "about 125" Japanese planes, though Saunders more accurately estimated their number at "about forty torpedo planes and dive bombers."[7]

Gunners on all the American ships opened fire; black puffs from exploding five-inch shells punctuated the clear sky, and red tracers from the machine guns weaved and danced skyward. Later in the war, American scientists developed a proximity fuse for the five-inch shells, so they exploded when they came near an enemy plane, but in the Coral Sea the gunners actually had to hit the attacking planes, and difficult as that was when it came to the slow and low-flying torpedo planes, it was all but impossible against the faster, high-flying dive bombers. The determined Japanese pilots simply ignored the AA fire and pressed on toward the big flattops. The American carriers maneuvered frantically, throwing the helm right and left as the big flattops sought to avoid the torpedoes streaking toward them. Neither of the big carriers was especially nimble, but the newer and smaller *Yorktown* managed to twist and turn quickly enough to dodge several torpedoes, though she was hit by an eight-hundred-pound bomb that landed almost in the middle of her flight deck, penetrated deep into the ship, and exploded, killing or badly injuring sixty-six men.[8]

The *Lexington*, which had been built on the hull of an unfinished battlecruiser, was a hundred feet longer than the *Yorktown* and much slower to respond to the helm. Japanese torpedo planes executed a textbook "anvil attack" against her, coming in from both sides so that no matter how the *Lexington* turned, she could not escape. Several of the Japanese torpedoes missed, but two smashed into her port side in quick succession. Joe Weber felt the big carrier convulse, noting that the torpedoes "ruptured the ship's gasoline and oil tanks," triggering several fires.[9]

Though it seemed much longer, the air attack lasted barely an hour. A quick assessment afterward showed that although both of the American carriers had suffered damage, neither appeared to be in serious difficulty. Damage-control teams on the *Yorktown* patched the hole in her flight deck so quickly she was able to recover the planes returning from their own strike against the Japanese. The two torpedoes that hit the *Lexington* were more serious; seawater rushed in though the gaping holes in her side and she took on a seven-degree list. Her crew corrected that by counterflooding and by shifting fuel in her oil tanks, and she, too, was able to recover the returning planes. After landing, the almost giddy American pilots reported that they had hit one of the two enemy carriers with several thousand-pound bombs, leaving her in a sinking condition, though in fact the *Shōkaku* survived to fight another day. Still, by noon on May 8, with both American carriers operational and reports of serious damage to the enemy, it looked and felt a lot like a victory.[10]

The feeling was premature. Watching from the *New Orleans*, Sandy Saunders noted that fires were still burning on the *Lexington*, and at 12:47 they ignited seeping gas fumes and triggered a massive explosion. The forward elevator platform, weighing several tons, flew up into the air and crashed down onto the flight deck. Less than an hour later, there was another explosion that destroyed the ship's ventilation system. That meant her engines had to be shut down. It was clear the ship had been mortally wounded. Reluctantly, Captain Frederick "Ted" Sherman ordered abandon ship. There was no panic; the crew conducted an orderly evacuation, and the escorting cruisers and destroyers closed in to pick up the survivors. Joe Weber climbed down one of the dangling ropes into the water and swam away from the ship. Looking back, he saw that she was burning from stem to stern with smoke almost completely enveloping her. To him, she seemed almost to glow. "When last seen by me," he recalled, "she was incandescent." Fletcher, unwilling that the Japanese should find her and tow her off as a trophy, ordered US destroyers to finish her off with torpedoes. She sank into water so deep her wreckage was not discovered until 2018.[11]

Even after that, Peck Greenbacker, for one, considered the battle "a great success." While critical of the fighter direction from the *Lexington*, which he thought was poorly executed, he was proud of the gunners on *Yorktown*, who had been, in his view, "outstanding." Afterward, he insisted that "we had shot down 14 planes," while *Lexington*'s fire was "ineffective." If that was an exaggeration, it reflected the continuing high morale on the *Yorktown*, a product, in Greenbacker's view, of "the long months the ship had spent in the South Pacific," which "had welded the ship and the air group into a single unit."[12]

Fletcher decided to discontinue the action and ordered the task force to turn south. The *Yorktown* was still operational thanks to the damage-control teams, but the Americans had lost one of their two carriers and more than half of their airplanes—including thirty-six that had gone down with the *Lexington*. In addition, the American escort ships were now crowded with survivors who had been rescued from the sea when the *Lexington* sank. Each of the two heavy cruisers (*Minneapolis* and *New Orleans*) had more than three hundred *Lexington* survivors on board. "Too many," Saunders wrote in his diary, "for us to fight our ships." Most importantly, reports indicated that the Japanese invasion force for Port Moresby had turned back. Since preventing the enemy from seizing Port Moresby had been the objective from the start, there seemed little reason to press the issue further. In fact, the Japanese never did get Port Moresby, and the Battle of the Coral Sea marked the furthest extent of their southward conquests.[13]

Even so, Admiral King, who was by now chief of naval operations, was disappointed. He wondered why Fletcher did not continue the fight, and in particular why he had not sent his destroyers speeding north to attack the Japanese carriers in a night torpedo attack. Such a move might have looked reasonable from Washington, but given the fuel situation and the distances involved it was entirely impractical. Unaware of the disappointment in Washington, Greenbacker and the other Forties in the *Yorktown* task force felt like winners. And their morale was further enhanced by their expectation that after a lengthy

THE CORAL SEA AND MIDWAY

deployment and a major battle, they were due for "a long period in the Puget Sound Navy Yard at Bremerton, Washington," where the ship would get a thorough overhaul. There would be shore liberty and reunions with wives and sweethearts.[14]

The war had other plans for them.

Only two days after Fletcher began his withdrawal from the Coral Sea, on May 10, Commander Layton came into Nimitz's office again to report that Hypo had achieved another intelligence breakthrough. Rochefort now predicted that the Japanese, with at least four carriers plus some battleships, planned to attack the tiny two-island atoll of Midway, thirteen hundred miles northeast of Pearl Harbor. Rochefort estimated the attack would come in the first week of June—again, only a month away. Nimitz considered his options. The *Lexington* was gone of course, but the two carriers that had taken Jimmy Doolittle's bombers to Japan would be back by then. Still, if Rochefort was right, the Japanese were coming with twice that number. It was obvious that if Nimitz accepted this challenge, the *Yorktown* could not go back to the West Coast for a refit. She would have to be repaired locally—and quickly. Even if that were possible, Nimitz could put only three carriers to sea, though the airstrip on Midway would give him a fourth airplane platform. The way he saw it, that was four against four. And, thanks to Rochefort and his team, he knew the Japanese were coming. Once again, Nimitz decided to exploit the advantage handed him by the codebreakers. He would lay a trap for the Japanese and pounce on them as they approached.[15]

None of the junior officers from the class of 1940 were aware of this, of course. Nonetheless, it became evident to them almost at once that something was up. When Halsey's two carriers returned from the South Pacific, everyone could see that the whole task force "commenced fueling at once." Saunders noted that scores of electricians came on board "to work on [the] turrets and cranes," and the ship "started loading all sorts of stocks." The same thing happened a few days later when the *Yorktown* limped into Pearl Harbor. She went immediately into the large drydock without discharging her aviation fuel, a serious violation of standard safety protocols. Yard workers swarmed over her to effect what Greenbacker called "hasty and partial repairs to our battle damage." To him and the other Forties, it was evidence "of preparation for further action." Clearly, something big was in the offing.[16]

As the *Yorktown*'s secretary and communications officer, it was Greenbacker's job to receive and route incoming messages. Consequently, he was among the first to see the operational order for the upcoming battle. As he scanned it, he was initially surprised, then suspicious, and finally incredulous. The intelligence summary concerning enemy plans and their order of battle was so complete, he wondered how it was possible for the high command to know so much. When he asked the *Yorktown*'s captain, Elliott Buckmaster, about it, Buckmaster told him, "Don't even talk about it."[17]

The *Hornet* and *Enterprise* went to sea first, leaving Pearl Harbor on May 28. Admiral Halsey did not go with them. He had contracted a painful rash (very likely shingles), and Nimitz ordered him to the hospital. To take his place, Nimitz accepted Halsey's recommendation to appoint Raymond Spruance, Mike Hanley's former boss on the *Northampton*. Fletcher remained in command of the *Yorktown* group, and he would be the senior officer overall if the patched-up *Yorktown* were able to join Spruance's two carriers at a designated position 325 miles north of Midway, optimistically labeled "Point Luck." Two days later, the *Yorktown* eased out of the drydock, took on fuel and stores, and put to sea, heading north. The trap was set.[18]

The *New Orleans* was one of the six cruisers escorting Spruance's two carriers, and Saunders summarized what the junior officers in the class of 1940 knew—or thought they knew—about what was going on. "Dope as follows," he wrote on May 31 after all the ships were at sea and headed north: "Large Jap force coming up on Midway; four carriers, two battleships, and transports. An attack on Midway is expected. Also, a Jap force is up north (near Aleutians) with four carriers. We will stay around Midway to wait for the Jap attack and then try to make a flank attack on them. It appears that we are rather badly outnumbered, but we will have some air support from Midway, and it is rumored that the Saratoga, Long Island, and Yorktown are on their way to support us." Most of that was remarkably accurate. The *Saratoga* was indeed en route from the West Coast, though she would not arrive in time; the *Yorktown* showed up the next morning.[19]

June 4, 1942, was a milestone day in the Pacific War and in the lives of many of the Forties. The Japanese struck first, hitting Midway Atoll with an air strike from their four carriers. Though all US Navy ships were operating under radio silence, they could still receive messages from Midway, and the news was disseminated throughout the ships. "Japs hit Midway about nine this morning," Saunders wrote in his diary. "Damaged runway and power plant." Soon afterward came a report that "two Jap carriers and two BBs [battleships] had been sighted north and west of Midway (175 miles). Hornet, Enterprise, and

THE CORAL SEA AND MIDWAY   153

Yorktown launched everything they could." Like all of the Forties, Saunders was unaware of disputes within the American high command about the timing and direction of the air strikes. He merely noted that the three American carriers were well separated from one another. "We are with the Hornet," he wrote, "the other two [carriers] being on either side of us, practically hull down over the horizon. Each carrier had cruisers and destroyers protecting it. We have a large fighter patrol up waiting for a Jap attack." It was not long in coming.[20]

Given their positions at the lower end of the command pyramid, Saunders and the other Forties were entirely unaware of the intense drama that played out over the Japanese carrier force that morning. They did not know about the confusion and misunderstanding of the American search, or the sacrifice and martyrdom of the US torpedo planes that found the enemy first and were nearly annihilated. Not until later did they learn of the miraculous arrival of the US dive bombers that mortally wounded three of the four Japanese carriers in a history-changing five-minute onslaught. Knowledge of all that came later. What they were very much aware of at the time was spending thirteen consecutive hours at general quarters surviving on coffee and sandwiches during which the American carriers engaged in "launching and recovering planes [the] entire day." In fact, the Forties who served with Spruance's task force never saw the enemy at all, because the Japanese scout planes never found either the *Hornet* or the *Enterprise*. They did, however, find the *Yorktown*, which was operating separately, and they concentrated everything they had on her.[21]

By chance, the officer of the deck on the *Yorktown* that fateful day, the man wearing the Bausch & Lomb binoculars around his neck as a symbol of that responsibility, was Lieutenant (junior grade) Peck Greenbacker. Though the ship's captain, Elliott Buckmaster, made the key tactical decisions, and the task force commander, Frank Jack Fletcher, made the strategic decisions from the flag bridge, Greenbacker was at the center of the storm throughout the day. He was on the bridge when the Japanese bombers arrived.[22]

Thanks to radar, the Americans on the *Yorktown* knew they were coming. Even without radar, Greenbacker could see them from quite a distance because the skies were unusually clear, with nearly unlimited visibility. The Japanese sent only eighteen dive bombers, all they could muster quickly given the devastation inflicted on three of their carriers that morning. Greenbacker watched as the Wildcat fighters flew out to intercept them. The enemy bombers lacked fighter protection, and the Wildcats tore into them unmolested. It seemed to Greenbacker "that the burning [Japanese] planes were falling like leaves." He remembered thinking that "surely none would get through." Seven of them did. When they were within five miles of the task force, the Wildcats were supposed to peel off and leave them to the gunners on the escorts. But several of the Wildcat pilots, in hot pursuit, stayed on them anyway, firing in short bursts and making it difficult for the gunners to pick their targets. Despite that, the escorts opened up with what one witness described as "a fireworks display at the Fourth of July."[23]

Not all of the escorts had radar, but by listening in on the fighter director radio net and calculating the trajectory of the approaching bogies, Connie Carlson on the *Astoria* figured out how to "set up a barrage between the Yorktown and the dive bombers," essentially a curtain of exploding ordnance, "through which they had to fly." He was satisfied that "our shooting was quite effective." Similarly, Herschel "Hershey" Sellers, on the destroyer *Hughes* (DD-410), remembered, "We shot at them with everything we had from 5-inch guns to 0.45 caliber pistols." Black puffs of smoke from five-inch guns and tracers from the machine guns filled the blue sky. The resolute Japanese pilots pressed through that curtain of fire with what Greenbacker called "the determination and recklessness of desperation." He was convinced that "those pilots knew that they would never return to Japan." Two more bombers were shot down by AA fire, but five of them got close enough to drop their bombs, and three of them hit the *Yorktown*.[24]

Greenbacker watched one bomb, tumbling as it fell, land square on the *Yorktown*'s flight deck, "creating a large hole in it and ripping to pieces the crews of our 1.1-inch machine gun mounts." Almost immediately, a second bomb penetrated the deck to a flag locker and started fires that compelled Buckmaster to flood the forward magazine. It was the third bomb, though, that was most serious. It passed through the flight deck and the hanger deck and exploded among the ship's engine uptakes. Instead of fresh air being drawn into the engine spaces, stack gas filled the area, forcing the men to evacuate the boiler rooms. Buckmaster had to shut down the engines. The big ship slowed, lost momentum, and stopped. She was dead in the water, with black smoke pouring out of her. It was, Greenbacker recalled, "a helpless feeling knowing that we were a sitting target." He was standing next to Buckmaster on the bridge when Dixie Kiefer, the ship's executive officer, reported the obvious: "The situation was quite grim."[25]

It was actually not as bad as it looked. Greenbacker was impressed that, as in the Coral Sea, the hole in the flight deck was repaired "rather rapidly . . . by covering it with long metal planks carried expressly for that purpose." Fixing the damaged engine uptakes took longer. As progress reports came up from the engine room, however, the mood on the bridge lifted dramatically. Soon, almost imperceptibly, the big ship began to move, slowly and ponderously at first, then more obviously, gradually building up speed to twenty knots, almost fast enough to launch planes. At that moment, another group of Japanese planes arrived—ten torpedo planes, coming in low. Employing another anvil attack, the Japanese split their planes into two groups of five and came in from both sides at once. Greenbacker remembered the moment vividly: "In they came through the furious crescendo of AA fire from both our own guns and those of the support ships. They seemed to keep coming in, miraculously untouched. Their determination was impressive (and frightening), but equally impressive was the performance of our fighter aircraft." There were only a few Wildcat fighters left on the *Yorktown*, and none of them had been refueled; some had only enough gas for two or three minutes of flight. They launched anyway and headed straight into the fight. As Greenbacker recalled it, "They courageously banked sharply to the left immediately upon being airborne and flew directly down our own line of fire making head-on passes against the incoming torpedo planes."[26]

Several of the Japanese planes were shot down by the determined Wildcat pilots; others got through. Greenbacker watched one of them drop its torpedo and then continue on across the *Yorktown*'s flight deck at low altitude. As it did, the rear seat gunner leaned out of the canopy and shook his fist at the Americans who responded with gestures of their own and by screaming obscenities. The torpedo hit the *Yorktown* fifteen feet below the waterline and knocked out six of the ship's nine boilers. Only seconds later, another torpedo hit so close to the first that together they created a single large hole, sixty feet wide, below the waterline. Power went out all over the ship, and the compartments below went dark. The *Yorktown* began to slow and eventually she was once again immobile. Worse, as millions of gallons of seawater rushed in through the gaping hole in her side, she began to list steadily to port. The big ship rolled to ten degrees, then fifteen, twenty, and finally to twenty-six degrees, where it stabilized, though Greenbacker was not sure "that it had gone as far as it would go."[27]

Greenbacker noted that "there was no sense of panic" on the bridge. The *Yorktown*'s first lieutenant, Commander Clarence Aldrich, who was responsible for the physical condition of the ship, arrived on the bridge to tell Buckmaster "with impressive calm" that "there was simply nothing he could do to take the list off the ship." Greenbacker stood by in silence, as befitted a mere lieutenant (j.g.), as "The Captain paced up and down the starboard catwalk in agony for several minutes, saying he didn't want to abandon ship." Then, coming to a decision, he issued the order to do so. Thinking about it later, Greenbacker concluded that Buckmaster could not have made any other decision. If he had delayed and the ship capsized, hundreds would have died.[28]

Buckmaster had not emphasized abandon-ship drills in training because he believed it hurt morale. Nevertheless, the crew carried out the order with no apparent panic. They even lined up their shoes in a neat row on the flight deck as if they expected to reclaim them later. There was some confusion: A few of the rafts became overcrowded and lost their buoyancy so that the men had to cling to its edges, while others held onto their pant legs. The result was a series of concentric circles of men in the water. "It was an odd sight," Greenbacker recalled. "They reminded me of pond lilies floating in an immense pool."[29]

Before he left the bridge, Greenbacker ensured that all the confidential publications, which were encased in lead covers, were thrown over the side. He did not know if down in the radio room, all of the "coding machines, code lists, code books and secret message files" were similarly disposed of. As the ship's communications officer, making sure that was done was his responsibility, but he was also officer of the deck and could not go down to check. He simply had to hope that those who were on duty there did their jobs.

Greenbacker made his way off the bridge and down to the flight deck; it was hard to walk with the ship at a twenty-six-degree angle. He thought about shimmying down from the flight deck on one of the dangling ropes, though he decided instead to descend to the hanger deck and climb down from there. On the hanger deck, he joined a small group of officers who lingered there, reluctant to leave. "We were more deliberate and calm than we might have been," Greenbacker recalled. Aldrich found a one-man life raft in one of the spare planes that were suspended from the overhead, threw the raft over the side, and then lowered himself into it. He didn't even get wet! That looked like a good idea, so Greenbacker did the same, though when his little raft hit the water, swimming crewmen grabbed it and paddled away. There was nothing for it but to climb down into the water and swim for it, which he did. At least he was wearing his kapok life vest, which was a good thing since he still had both his .45 caliber pistol and the binoculars around his neck. Even so, he was pleasantly surprised to find that the life vest kept him "quite high out of the water." Eventually, he climbed aboard a motorized whaleboat that took him to one of the destroyers, where he spent the night "making out muster lists of all the refugees we had on board." The next day, the destroyer transferred him to the cruiser *Astoria,* where he and several other Forties—eight in all—had what Connie Carlson called "an impressive class reunion."[30]

The *Yorktown* did not sink. Instead, it hung there motionless all night, holding steady at a twenty-six-degree angle. The destroyer *Hughes,* with Hershey Sellers on board, was detailed to watch over her, and he remembered it as "a scary night" as the *Hughes* repeatedly circled the wounded flattop. At dawn, Sellers heard a 20 mm machine gun, and, looking over to the *Yorktown,* saw a sailor who had been left behind trying to call attention to that fact. The officer of the deck on the *Hughes* told Sellers to go pick him up and make sure that no one else had been overlooked. Sellers took a ship's boat over to the crippled flattop and pulled himself up onto the deck with guy ropes. A grim sight met him. "There were bodies stacked high on the flight deck in many places," he remembered, "some still harnessed in the 40 mm straps." Sellers found the man who had fired the machine gun and sent him back to the *Hughes,* then began a search for others. He found one more in the sick bay who was still alive, and sent him back, too. The man from sick bay survived; the other man did not. As Sellers explored the ship, he remembered for the rest of his life the eerie feeling "of being alone in a dead ship at sea." He fully expected that the enemy would be back any minute to finish her off.[31]

But no planes came, and on the *Astoria,* Captain Buckmaster put out a call for volunteers to go back and see if the *Yorktown* could be salvaged. There were more volunteers than were needed—so many, in fact, that the *Astoria* had to put an armed guard at the rail to prevent men from overfilling the whaleboats. Greenbacker was one of those who went. He remained concerned about the code lists, message files, and coding machines in the radio room.

Rather than climb up to the flight deck, as Sellers had done, Greenbacker boarded on the hangar deck, which was so close to sea level he could simply step aboard. He headed straight for the radio room and, as he had feared, found the codebooks and coding machines open and the safe unlocked. He secured all the confidential materials, made sure nothing was left behind, then started back to the hangar deck to board the destroyer *Hammann* (DD-412), which had come alongside to provide electrical power and water pressure for the fire-fighters. En route he passed a crate of Coca-Cola bottles and stopped to drink one. It very likely saved his life, for just as he was finishing it, he heard sustained 20 mm gunfire as an alarm, and the cry went up, "Torpedoes in the water!"

A Japanese sub had worked its way through the screen to launch one of its deadly fish at the *Yorktown*.*

The torpedo struck the *Hammann* directly amidships and went all the way through her and into the *Yorktown*, where it exploded. The *Hammann* sank almost immediately. "She sank smoothly," Greenbacker remembered, "submerging rather evenly and plunging forward with her fantail disappearing last." As she went down, the depth charges on her stern began to detonate when they reached the preset depth settings, and the explosions in the water killed many of the men from both the *Hammann* and the *Yorktown* who had been hurled into the sea by the initial explosion.[32]

That last blow proved the coup de grâce for the battered *Yorktown*. It was evident now that she could not be saved, and there was a second evacuation. Determined to be the last one off the ship, Buckmaster stood on the lip of the hangar deck for a long moment, waiting. Satisfied there was no one else left on board, he stepped off the *Yorktown* into the tug alongside. At that moment, the ship's chief engineer and two of his men appeared from below where they had been looking at the engines. Buckmaster was so upset not to have been the last one off the ship, he tried to reboard. The captain of the tug was having none of that. Unimpressed with Buckmaster's reverence for navy tradition, he pulled away. Buckmaster never forgave him.

The *Yorktown* sank the next morning. Greenbacker watched from the destroyer *Porter* as "the Old Lady" slowly rolled over and disappeared. It was a hard blow. Most of the members of the class of 1940 did not yet know the full details of what had happened two hundred miles to the west three days before. Pete Peterson heard a rumor that "our attack force hit the enemy and probably got three Jap carriers," though he added that there were so many rumors coming in "we can't be sure."[33]

The rumors were true. In fact, the Japanese lost all four of their large-deck carriers—the *Kaga*, *Akagi*, *Soryu*, and *Hiryu*—though the fact that all four had gone down did not become clear for several more days. One or more of them were thought to be badly crippled but still afloat, and Nimitz ordered submarines and PT boats in the area to find the cripples and finish them off. One of the PT boats in receipt of that message was PT-30, under the command of Ensign R. R. "Pop" Dupzyk. Along with another PT boat (PT-29), Dupzyk set a course for the probable coordinates. It was a dark night and they were

---

* Many years later, long after the war was over, Greenbacker wondered if he had missed "a great opportunity to profit from a testimonial for a Coca-Cola ad" by asserting that drinking a Coke had saved his life.

operating without radar, so Dupzyk was startled about an hour later when he suddenly realized that "we were in the middle of a retiring Jap formation, ships on all sides of us." He told the skipper of the other PT boat, who as a lieutenant jaygee was senior to him, that they should attack at once and "use our torpedoes to good advantage." The jaygee said no. Their orders, he insisted, were "to sink the disabled carrier and that was what we were going to do." Dupzyk pressed his case. "I pleaded, urged, begged, that we use at least two of our four torpedoes here." The answer was still no. When, in due course, the PT boats arrived at the coordinates where the crippled carrier was supposed to be, there was nothing there, for it had already succumbed. After searching for several hours, the two PT boats returned to base with all their torpedoes still on board. Dupzyk regretted the lost opportunity for the rest of his life.[34]

Even so, the Battle of Midway was nothing short of a catastrophe for the Japanese. It marked a tipping point in the Pacific War and opened a new chapter in the global struggle against the Axis.

PART III

On the Offensive

A very important development of this, the Second World War, is the recognition of Air Power as one of the most important factors in any military operation, whether ashore or afloat. With this recognition, Naval Aviation has come of age.

—Reef Points, 1943

Operations in the current war are conducted by task forces rather than by fleets. A naval task force is a group of vessels organized for a specific task. It usually consists of several types, and may be composed of ships from different fleets.

—Reef Points, 1944

13

Savo Island

A pilot flying over the Coral Sea during the first week of August 1942 might have spotted an armada of more than forty ships steaming in formation to the northwest. A score of them were warships, including six heavy cruisers, and they were escorting twenty-six troop transports filled with US Marines who were en route to an island in the Solomons called Guadalcanal. They were there because, after the astonishing and improbable American success in the Battle of Midway, the American chief of naval operations, Admiral Ernest J. King, decided that it was time for the United States to take the offensive in the Pacific.*

Doing so was contrary to the overall Allied war strategy to defeat Germany first, but while King officially accepted that strategy, he was ready—even eager—to regain the initiative against the Japanese by conducting an offensive in the Pacific as well. He saw his opportunity when he learned that the Japanese were building an airfield on Guadalcanal. Once it was finished, it would give them the ability to overfly the Allied lines of communication between Hawaii and Australia. It was evident to King that it was necessary to seize that airfield as an essential defensive move before the Japanese could finish it.[1]

One difficulty with that ambition was that the island and its nascent airfield were inside the theater of operations assigned to General Douglas MacArthur. Determined that the seizure of Guadalcanal should be conducted by the Navy–Marine Corps team, King prevailed on the Joint Chiefs to move the administrative dividing line between the theaters by one degree, which put Guadalcanal just inside Admiral Chester Nimitz's command area. King's other

---

* King wore two hats. He was both the operational commander of the navy as "Commander in Chief of the US Fleet" with the acronym Cominch, and also the administrative head of the navy as "Chief of Naval Operations," or CNO. King used the title Cominch rather than CNO throughout the war, even though according to the Constitution the president was the actual commander in chief.

problem—one not so easily resolved—was that in order to take the island, and do so quickly, the United States would need to scrape together just about every maritime asset it had in the Pacific. Nimitz sounded a cautionary note, telling King that while he was confident that the marines could *take* the airfield if they achieved surprise, he was less certain they had the necessary sealift to *hold* it against a serious Japanese counterattack. Whatever the merits of those concerns, King directed that the invasion—officially Operation Watchtower—take place in the first week of August, just two months after Midway.[2]

That decision set in train a six-month-long battle ashore for control of the island, as well as a series of fierce naval engagements in the waters around Guadalcanal, most of them fought in the dark of night in near-zero visibility and characterized by uncertainty, even chaos. In those battles, it helped that a few of the American ships had radar, though that technology, still new in 1942, was both rudimentary and not fully trusted by the senior American commanders. Doc Weatherup, who participated in three of those engagements, wrote later, "I don't recall any [training] session in which an attempt was made to explain the concept [of radar] or its operational use." The Japanese did not have radar, at least not yet, but they did have superior optics, including giant low-light binoculars, called "Big Eyes," that gave them an edge in night fighting.

These were the circumstances from August to November 1942, when more than two dozen members of the Naval Academy class of 1940 played key roles in this shadowy maritime vortex of confusion and violence that one scholar has labeled "Neptune's Inferno."[3]

Though three US Navy aircraft carriers under Frank Jack Fletcher would provide daytime air cover for the landings from south of the island, direct support of the invasion itself was entrusted to six heavy cruisers—four American and two Australian—plus eighteen smaller ships. There were multiple members of the class of 1940 on each of the American cruisers. Among them were George Kittredge, who commanded Turret Three on the cruiser *Chicago*; Hundy Hundevadt, who was the machine gun control officer on the *Vincennes*; Connie Carlson, who remained at Sky Two on *Astoria*; and Dick "Moon" McElligott, who was gunnery division officer on the *Quincy*. Those four cruisers, each with an impressive battery of nine eight-inch guns, had three missions: to escort the transports to the targeted beach, provide gunfire support for the landings, then guard the beachhead from any attempted Japanese counterattack. For several of the Forties it was their first trial by fire; for some it was also their last.

Luck was with them as they approached Guadalcanal. A heavy cloud cover concealed the convoy from Japanese scout planes, and when the Allied ships rounded Cape Esperance at the western end of Guadalcanal with everyone at their battle stations, George Kittredge was hugely relieved to see that there were no Japanese warships in the anchorage. As the *Chicago* passed Savo Island in the predawn darkness, Kittredge thought it looked like "a purple lump in a pool of oil." John Lacouture, who was the gunnery officer on the destroyer *Blue*, noted that it was "a hot, muggy morning" and, perhaps with hindsight, decided that Savo Island had a sinister aspect: "an ominous specter of things to come."[4]

The initial Allied target was Tulagi, a tiny island on the north side of Sealark Channel opposite Guadalcanal. Despite its small size, Tulagi hosted a seaplane base and was the Japanese headquarters in the Solomons. It was also where their best combat troops were quartered. Two hours prior to the landing, which was scheduled for 8:00, the heavy cruisers prepared to open fire. Kittredge remembered it vividly. His gunners in the Turret Two flung open the breech of the big guns as a hydraulic lift brought the shells up from the magazine. There was "a rumbling as the rammermen sent the ugly, black, pointed projectiles home into the open mouth of the gun.... Powder bags shot into the gun room from powder boxes.... The breech plugs flew closed.... The lights flashed on simultaneously." Kittredge glanced at his watch: It was ten minutes to six, and he used the sound-powered telephone to report to the bridge: "Turret Two ready." After a tension-filled wait, the order to fire came promptly at 6:00. Flame erupted from the muzzles, and each gun sent a 335-pound shell filled with high explosives toward the targeted island. "All morning," Kittredge wrote later, "we steamed back and forth about 2,000 yards from the beach and fired salvo after salvo" into the Japanese defenses.[5]

At 8:00, the marines went ashore. Two members of the class of 1940 were among them: John "Jocko" Antonelli and George Herring, each leading a company of the First Marine Raider Battalion. Kittredge watched it through a periscope mounted in his turret. He took particular note of a lone American tank crawling up a slope that had pushed ahead of its infantry support. Suddenly, "Half a hundred Japanese Special Naval Infantry came out of nowhere and swarmed all over the tank." They poured gasoline on it and set it on fire. When the tank lid popped open and an American Marine scrambled out, the Japanese grabbed him, threw him to the ground, and beat him with their rifle butts until he stopped moving. Infuriated, Kittredge was happy to get an order to shift targets. Within seconds, "The ship shook as nine eight-inch

166   ANNAPOLIS GOES TO WAR

guns recoiled in unison." That salvo sent more than three thousand pounds of high explosives onto the targeted area. When Kittredge looked again through the periscope, "There was no charred tank. There were no Japanese Special Naval Infantry.... There was just a pall of white smoke and a very large hole in the ground."[6]

In the midst of the fighting ashore, about forty Japanese two-engine "Betty" bombers appeared overhead. Their objective was to destroy the Allied transports that were supporting the invasion. Forewarned by Australian coast watchers, the transports got underway to make themselves difficult targets, and the escorting warships formed an antiaircraft screen around them. The Bettys carried torpedoes, which the Japanese believed was their most effective antiship weapon, and they came in low to drop them. That made them vulnerable to the gunners on the escorts. John Lacouture found it "fairly easy to shoot at someone when he is aiming at someone else." He was confident that his gunners on the *Blue* got at least one, and possibly two, of the Bettys. There was another air attack that afternoon, though neither of the air assaults was especially effective. The Japanese sank the transport *George F. Elliott*, and a torpedo struck the destroyer *Jarvis* (DD-393), killing fourteen members of her crew, one of whom was William F. Greene of Whitestone, New York, the first of the Forties to be lost in the campaign.[7]

Meanwhile, the fighting on Tulagi continued. For fourteen hours, the cruisers pounded away at enemy targets until the marines declared the island secure at eight o'clock that night. The marines had lost 122 killed; the Japanese defenders had been virtually annihilated. Of a garrison of nearly a thousand men, only five were taken alive.[8]

There was less resistance on the much larger Guadalcanal Island. There the marines splashed ashore, chased off the Japanese construction crews, and set up a defense perimeter around the unfinished airfield. With the objective secured, the mission of the cruisers changed from gunfire support to protecting the beachhead from a possible enemy counterattack. There were two possible lines of approach the Japanese could use, one on either side of Savo Island. To guard both routes, Royal Navy Rear Admiral Victor Crutchley, who had been seconded to the Royal Australian Navy and commanded all six of the Allied cruisers, divided his assets. He put three of them, including both of the Australian ships plus the *Chicago*, south of Savo Island, and the other three— *Vincennes*, *Quincy*, and *Astoria*—north of it. Twenty-five miles west of each group, he stationed a picket destroyer to provide an early warning of any

SAVO ISLAND

approaching Japanese threat. The ship assigned to watch the southern pass was John Lacouture's USS *Blue*.[9]

On the afternoon of August 8, with the situation ashore apparently under control, Crutchley steamed off in his flagship to discuss future plans with the Allied amphibious commander, US Navy Rear Admiral Richmond Kelly Turner. That left two cruisers instead of three to guard the passage south of Savo Island. Most of the men in the cruisers had not slept for at least forty-eight hours, so the skippers set Condition II, which meant that only half of the guns were fully manned. Those not on duty collapsed into their racks. One of those who had to remain on duty was Ray Hundevadt, who had the 8:00 p.m. to midnight watch on the *Vincennes*. Hundevadt was exhausted, but whenever he felt his eyelids drooping, a rain squall jolted him awake. Just before he was due to be relieved, at about 11:45, he noticed a "slow-flying and low-flying airplane [that] came weaving its way around the ships." It was displaying all its running lights, so naturally Hundevadt assumed it was friendly. In fact, he found it "a comforting sight."[10]

On the *Astoria*, Connie Carlson had been one of the lucky ones who was able to get some rest. He got three hours of uninterrupted sleep and went back on duty at 11:45 for the midwatch just as Hundevadt on the *Vincennes* was going below. Coincidentally, as Carlson settled in at Sky Two, another of their classmates, Carl "Sandy" Sander, was in Sky One. With a heavy cloud cover and no moon, and with all the ships steaming blacked out, it was dark as pitch, though an occasional flash of light from the distant shore showed where pockets of enemy resistance were still being eliminated. The man Carlson relieved when he came on watch told him there had been reports of planes flying overhead, but "nothing to get excited about."[11]

Though no one in the Allied ships knew it, that wandering airplane was a Japanese scout, boldly burning his running lights as he flew over the Allied warships and reporting their location and disposition back to Rear Admiral Gunichi Mikawa, who was approaching swiftly through the dark with seven cruisers of his own.

The first indication the Americans had that something was amiss came at 1:30 a.m., when the destroyer *Patterson* (DD-392) sent out a message: "Warning, warning. Strange ships entering harbor." Fifteen minutes later, the general alarm sounded on the *Chicago*: "Bong, bong, bong..." Kittredge had been asleep for less than an hour and had to shake himself awake before he rushed back to his post. The crew was fully alert now, though it was unclear exactly what was happening. A rumor ran through the ship that the *Blue* had been hit and was sinking. Then, suddenly, the Australian cruiser *Canberra*, which was directly ahead of the *Chicago*, burst into bright yellow flames. "My God," Kittredge cried out, "the Canberra's on fire. She's blazing from stem to stern." Even in the reflected light of that blaze, however, he could see nothing of the enemy. Where were they? *What* were they? Submarines? Aircraft? Looking over the side, he saw the phosphorescent tracks of torpedoes in the water headed their way. The *Chicago* lurched hard to port as Captain Howard Bode up on the bridge sought to avoid them. A few of them missed, but one didn't. As Kittredge remembered it, "The deck beneath me came up under my feet," the turret door flew open, and "the pungent smell of exploded TNT" met his nostrils. A torpedo had blown the bow of the *Chicago* right off the ship. Had Kittredge been in Turret One rather than Turret Three, he would surely have been killed.[12]

Even with her bow missing, the *Chicago* remained afloat, though uncertainty and confusion persisted. As perplexed as Kittredge was, Captain Bode seemed equally mystified. A member of the crew recalled later that "there was mass confusion on the bridge as nobody had any idea what was happening." The *Chicago* maneuvered off to the south and out of the fight, stricken, though still afloat.[13]

Obviously, the *Blue* had failed in its primary mission of providing an early warning for the rest of the fleet. Steaming back and forth across the passage between Cape Esperance and Savo Island, the *Blue* had its radar in active mode, but it was an SC radar designed primarily for air searches, and the returns from the land on both sides of the channel rendered the readings all but useless. When, at about 12:40 a.m., at the end of its eastward run, the *Blue* made its U-turn to recross the passage, no one on board noticed the seven blacked-out Japanese cruisers slipping past them in the dark. "The fact is," Lacouture wrote later, "we did not see the Japs either visually or on radar." Speculating about it later, he decided that the Japanese must have had "much better binoculars and telescopes than we did, enabling them to see us although we couldn't see them." Which was, in fact, the case.[14]

The *Blue* did have a chance to redeem itself. Mikawa, the Japanese admiral, left a destroyer behind to guard his rear, and lookouts on the *Blue* spotted it at about 2:15. Lacouture got it in his crosshairs and told the gunners to stand by. The ship's captain, Commander Harold Williams, unsure of who was who on that confusing night, refused to give permission to open fire. Lacouture pleaded with him to no avail. Years later, he was furious when he read Williams's official report, which stated that the *Blue* did not engage because "no enemy ships or planes" came "within effective striking distance." Lacouture knew this was manifestly untrue.[15]

With both the *Chicago* and the *Canberra* out of the fight, the Japanese cruisers turned north toward the other three Allied ships, which were maneuvering in a box pattern north of Savo Island. *Quincy* led the column with the *Vincennes* behind her and the *Astoria* third in line and therefore nearest to the approaching Japanese. Four members of the class of 1940 were on the *Astoria* that night: Carlson was in Sky Two after his three-hour nap; Carl Sander was atop the forward mast in Sky One; Ike Blough, who had been the class vice president, was in charge of Turret Three; and Vince Healey, a curly-haired New Yorker with an "Irish smile" who had been captain of the track team at Annapolis, was the port battery officer of the deck.[16]

At 2:00 a.m., Carlson both saw and heard gunfire coming from the south, near where the *Chicago* and *Canberra* were patrolling, but a rain squall dampened the sound and obscured what he could see. Only minutes later, he was nearly blinded when a powerful searchlight suddenly bathed the *Astoria* in white light, followed immediately by incoming tracer fire. The duty officer on the bridge ordered Carlson to open fire, which he did, directing the ship's main batteries to aim for the source of that searchlight. Only seconds later, however, the ship's skipper, William Greenman, countermanded the order. He had rushed up to the bridge when the alarm sounded, and fearing they were shooting at friendly ships, shouted: "Cease fire! Cease fire!" Quickly reassessing the situation as enemy shells struck the ship, he ordered the guns to resume firing. That short delay allowed the Japanese to pound the *Astoria* unmolested for one or two crucial minutes. One shell struck her hull at the waterline, causing flooding below; another hit Turret Two, killing everyone inside it; and a third exploded in the number 4 fireroom, rupturing the steam lines. Scores were killed outright; others were badly wounded. When the electrical system failed, Carlson shifted the guns under his command to local control and continued to fire, though as he confessed later, he had no idea if he hit anything.[17]

With no power, the *Astoria* lost headway. Fires burned out of control, and enemy shells pounded the ship. When one of them struck the ship's "Seagull" floatplane amidships, it touched off the plane's aviation fuel and generated a massive fireball. Carlson's phone talker, who was standing on the exposed platform, literally burst into flames. Carlson grabbed him and "beat out the flames" with his hands. Only after that did he discover that his own right eyebrow and half of his mustache were burned off.[18]

Those not killed or wounded fought the spreading fires, but with no hydraulics or electrical power, the pumps did not work. Carlson and Healy joined others who, in desperation, used empty five-inch shell casings as buckets, lowering them over the side to collect seawater and then throwing the water into the flames. It was like trying to put out a forest fire with a thimble.

The Japanese ships sped past, seeking other targets. Carlson and Healy went below to try to plug the holes in the hull using mattresses while bodies of their shipmates drifted past them. It was no use. The waters continued to rise, and the *Astoria* continued to list, until it was evident she was doomed. Before she rolled over completely, Captain Greenman ordered abandon ship, and Carlson "climbed over the rail, slid down the side of the ship, and gently entered the water." He swam about fifty yards, then turned back to look. As he watched, "The ship kept rolling and quietly slipped under the waves with scarcely a ripple." A total of 219 crewmen went with her.[19]

The next ship in line was the *Vincennes.* Her alarm sounded at 1:45, dragging Hundy Hundevadt out of the first sleep he had had in two days. Muzzy-headed, he was initially confused about what was happening until "the sound of the ship firing its main battery was a quick cure." He rushed back to his battle station: four quad-mounted 1.1-inch machine guns. "The noise," he recalled, "was indescribable. It was one continuous succession of explosions." When an eight-inch shell struck the five-inch gun mount directly above his position, it caused "a shower of metal and human parts [to] rain down on the platform on which I stood." He got orders from the gunnery officer "to fire on any appropriate targets," but there was no way to determine which targets were "appropriate." Before he could ask, phone communications went out.[20]

As on the other Allied cruisers, there was confusion about where the fire was coming from. Captain Frederick Riefkohl believed that at least some of the gunfire—perhaps all of it—was coming from friendly ships. He repeatedly blinkered out messages to cease fire to the ships that were firing, messages that, of course, were ignored. The pounding was relentless; by one estimate, the *Vincennes* was struck eighty-five times in less than twenty minutes. Hundevadt remembered "a bitter metallic odor" that "permeated everything." As on the *Astoria*, one of the enemy shells hit the gasoline-filled seaplane amidships and triggered a fire that was soon burning out of control. With the American cruisers burning brightly, it was no longer necessary for the Japanese to use their searchlights. Despite the pounding she took from Japanese gunfire, the fatal blow to the *Vincennes* came from two torpedoes that smashed into her hull and opened huge holes in her side.[21]

Adrift and powerless, relentlessly pounded by enemy shells, the *Vincennes* listed dramatically, and at 2:35, only forty-five minutes after the initial alarm, Riefkohl ordered abandon ship. With the communications out, Hundevadt didn't get the order for ten more minutes. He had hung his life vest on the railing, and as he reached for it now, he saw that it had been cut to pieces by flying shrapnel. He made his way down to the port railing, grabbed a kapok vest from a whaleboat, and jumped. He swam away from the *Vincennes*, and then (as Connie Carlson had done) he turned to look back. He watched as the big cruiser "rolled over to port and sank."[22]

The loss of life on the *Vincennes* was even worse than on the *Astoria*: a total of 322 men died, including two from the class of 1940: John Spears, who was in command of Turret Two when it suffered a direct hit from an eight-inch shell and who probably died instantly; and Ray Murray, who was the Plotting Room officer and below deck when the *Vincennes* sank. Both went down with the ship.

The *Quincy*'s fate was similar. With his ship caught in a vicious crossfire between multiple Japanese cruisers, Captain Samuel Moore directed her toward Savo Island, four miles away, in the hope of running her aground before she sank. Even as he gave the order, two torpedoes smashed into her hull, and only minutes later, a third. By then, Moore was dead, as was every other person on the bridge except the signalman, who took the wheel and, in obedience to Moore's last order, tried to steer the ship toward Savo Island. He didn't make it, and the *Quincy* sank only eight minutes after the *Vincennes*. The death toll was even higher, with 370 killed.[23]

The morning sun on August 9 revealed a crippled *Chicago*, missing its bow and barely able to maneuver, two burning and sinking Allied cruisers—*Canberra* and *Astoria*, and where the *Vincennes* and *Quincy* had been, only empty ocean dotted by wreckage and small clusters of survivors struggling to stay afloat. Ray Hundevadt was one of them. Bobbing on the surface in his kapok life vest, he initially found himself entirely alone, though after daylight he connected up with a few others and they grouped together for mutual support. The water was relatively warm, and though several of the men had been wounded and were bleeding—including Hundevadt—there were thankfully no sharks. Some of the men did not have life vests, so they worked out a protocol

172 ANNAPOLIS GOES TO WAR

where the men who did have vests flanked those who did not in order to keep them afloat.[24]

From sea level, Hundevadt could not see any other ships, and he wondered if he would ever see his wife again. Long afterward, he wrote, "One struggles to understand something of his life under such circumstances." He and Del had discussed starting a family before he left for the South Pacific, and they had decided that doing so in the midst of war might be irresponsible. Now, adrift in the warm water of the South Pacific, he changed his outlook. "I decided that night that if I survived, we should not hold off having a family." He and the others were picked up the next afternoon by a destroyer and taken to Nouméa in New Caledonia, and by the late fall he was in a hospital in Oakland, California. His first daughter, Linda Gail, was born nine months later, on August 5, 1943.[25]

The *Blue* was among the many destroyers engaged in rescuing survivors from the water. In the midst of it, John Lacouture witnessed an incident he remembered all his life. It concerned a Black "messboy" named Stillwell, who had already performed beyond expectations by manning one of the AA guns during the battle.* While the *Blue* was taking survivors off the wrecked and sinking *Canberra*, an internal explosion on the cruiser blew an Aussie sailor over the side. If he fell into the narrow gap between the two ships, he would almost certainly be ground to pulp. Stillwell ran to the rail, leaned out over the open space between the ships, and caught the sailor in midair, bringing him safely on board the *Blue*. Lacouture remembered that after that, no one ever again referred to Stillwell as a "messboy."[26]

The Battle of Savo Island was the worst defeat in the history of the US Navy. The disaster at Pearl Harbor had been the result of a surprise raid, or as Americans liked to call it, a sneak attack. By contrast, Savo Island was a battle between relatively equal forces during a campaign that the Americans had initiated. And yet the US Navy suffered three cruisers sunk and a fourth badly damaged, while the Japanese suffered only moderate damage to the cruiser *Chokai*. It could have been worse. Had Admiral Mikawa's cruisers continued eastward to target the scarce and valuable Allied transport ships, it could have forced the Americans to call off the invasion of Guadalcanal altogether. Instead, determined to get beyond range of the American carrier planes before daylight,

---

* As noted in chapter 8, Mess Attendant Second Class Doris "Dorrie" Miller, who had manned an antiaircraft battery during the attack on Pearl Harbor, received the Navy Cross for his actions that day. Stillwell did not get the same level of press coverage, and his deeds went largely unrecognized.

SAVO ISLAND

Mikawa headed back up "The Slot" toward his base at Rabaul. En route there, an American submarine exacted a modicum of revenge by sinking one of his seven cruisers.

In the aftermath of the battle, the Americans reacted in something of a panic, withdrawing the transports and most of the warships from the landing beach. The nineteen thousand marines who had gone ashore had only about thirty days of food, and limited ammunition. The transports also left with much of the barbed wire and nearly all of the heavy construction equipment still on board. The marines held the unfinished airfield, but they lacked equipment and robust naval support. It was a precarious moment.[27]

For John Lacouture, there was one more unhappy postscript. On August 22, two weeks after the battle, the *Blue* was patrolling the waters off Guadalcanal, and Lacouture, who had the midwatch, spied "two florescent torpedo wakes" headed directly for the *Blue*'s starboard quarter. He reacted quickly, shouting: "Torpedoes starboard quarter! Right full rudder! All ahead full!" The *Blue* lurched forward, but it was too late. Lacouture could only watch "spellbound" during the few seconds it took for the torpedoes to arrive. The first of them passed astern; the second hit the *Blue* about ten feet from her fantail "with a tremendous explosion." It killed nine men and wounded twenty others, destroyed the main shaft and rudder, and left "a big tail of twisted metal hanging down in the water."[28]

The *Blue* did not sink. Another destroyer, the *Henley*, took her in tow and headed for the anchorage at Tulagi. Alas, the twisted metal hanging down from the *Blue* acted as a drag in the water, and the towline repeatedly parted. The job of getting her to a safe anchorage was entrusted to ten landing boats, which pulled and nudged the crippled *Blue* to Tulagi. It was evident, however, that the kind of repairs she needed could not be done there, so there was another effort by the modified destroyer *Stringham* (with Pop Dupzyk on board) to tow her to Nouméa. After several attempts, however, it became evident that was not going to work. The commander of the destroyer division, Captain Leonard B. Austin, concluded that it would be better simply to scuttle her.

Lacouture and the rest of the crew on the *Blue* "opened control closures and magazine flood valves, secured all watches and engineering station personnel." The twelve officers and 123 enlisted men who remained, carrying only their personal possessions, transferred over to the *Henley*. Before he left, Lacouture walked all through the ship, making one last check to ensure that sure no one was left behind. Amazingly, he found one, "a sailor in the gyro compartment reading a comic magazine who had not heard the word to abandon ship."[29]

With everyone off the *Blue*, including the ship's mascot (a cat named Jarvis), the *Henley* backed away and fired a torpedo into the *Blue*. It missed. So gunners on the *Henley* fired round after round of five-inch shells into her until the *Blue* rolled over to starboard and sank stern first, her bow pointing straight up in the air. The *Henley* carried her crew first to Wellington, New Zealand, and then to Australia, where Lacouture received orders to fly back to the States and begin pilot training.

14

Ironbottom Sound

The American hold on Guadalcanal remained precarious. On the island itself, much of the fighting centered on Japanese efforts to break through the marines' defensive lines around the airstrip, which they had christened Henderson Field after Major Lofton "Joe" Henderson, who had been killed in the Battle of Midway. The Japanese repeatedly and recklessly hurled themselves at the marines' positions, accepting terrible casualties, but never quite managing to break through. Meanwhile at sea, the cruisers and destroyers of both sides engaged in a series of battles, most of them confused melees at night, with both sides enduring heavy losses. Indeed, so many ships were sunk in the waters off Guadalcanal that it soon earned the sobriquet "Ironbottom Sound."[1]

Both sides rushed reinforcements to the island. The Japanese, unwilling to expose their transports to American airplanes in daylight, sent their convoys through the passage between the Solomon Islands called The Slot almost exclusively at night. They did this with such regularity that the Americans dubbed these convoys the "Tokyo Express." The Americans sent their reinforcements and supplies to the island during the daylight hours. In September, a month after the disaster at Savo Island, they dispatched the Seventh Marine Regiment of just over four thousand men from Samoa to Guadalcanal, doing so in six transport ships protected by a powerful escort that included both of the available aircraft carriers (*Hornet* and *Wasp*) plus the new battleship *North Carolina*, along with several cruisers and destroyers. In spite of that powerful escort, on September 15 the Japanese submarine I-19 slipped inside the screen and fired a spread of six torpedoes. It was one of the deadliest torpedo spreads of the entire war. One torpedo hit the *North Carolina*, which slowed it down but did not sink it; one hit the destroyer *O'Brien*, which stayed afloat temporarily, but sank later; and three of them hit the carrier *Wasp*. Worse, all three struck the big flattop in the vicinity of her fuel tanks and stored ammunition, touching off a series of secondary explosions. In less than half an hour, it was evident that the *Wasp* was doomed, and her skipper ordered abandon ship.[2]

The *Wasp*'s escorts closed in to undertake rescue operations. One of them was the destroyer USS *Duncan* (DD-485), with Doc Weatherup on board. He had transferred from *Saratoga* to the brand-new *Duncan* that summer, becoming part of her initial crew, and thus what was known as a plank holder. After the *Wasp* went down, the *Duncan* was fully engaged in rescuing her crewmen from the sea when the sonarman on the *Duncan* reported a submarine contact. Apparently, the Japanese sub—or maybe a different sub—was still out there, perhaps preparing another attack. Weatherup believed that rescuing drowning sailors had a higher priority than going after the enemy sub—if, indeed, there was a sub. The captain of the *Duncan*, Edmund B. Taylor, told Weatherup to go down to the sonar room "and see if you think there is a valid submarine contact." In the sonar shack, Weatherup put on the earphones, listened to about five pings, and then went back up to the bridge and told Taylor that he didn't hear anything. The *Duncan* stayed by the *Wasp* and eventually picked up 660 of her nearly 2,000 survivors. In fact, there *was* a second sub—the I-15—but it did not attack. The loss of the *Wasp* was a heavy blow, though it could have been worse if a torpedo had hit one of the troop transports. In the end, all six of the transports made it to Guadalcanal, boosting the number of marines on the island to over thirty thousand.[3]

Only days afterward, Weatherup got new orders. He left the *Duncan* to become the staff communications officer for Destroyer Squadron (DesRon) 12, commanded by Captain Robert G. Tobin, who used the destroyer USS *Farenholt* (DD-491) as his flagship. The assignment was a kind of promotion since it demonstrated the navy's growing confidence in Weatherup's abilities. When Weatherup reported aboard, Tobin told him to stay close by him on the bridge when they were at general quarters, not only to send and receive messages, but also to act as Tobin's eyes and ears. "In those days," Weatherup recalled later, "my night vision was pretty good."[4]

In the second week of October 1942, almost exactly one month after the loss of the *Wasp*, and two months after the Battle of Savo Island, the *Farenholt* was leading a column of cruisers and destroyers under Rear Admiral Norman Scott in the passage between Cape Esperance and Savo Island. Aware that the Japanese were sending convoys of troops to Guadalcanal by night, Scott hoped to intercept one of them. The conditions were much the same as they had been two months before: overcast skies with no moon or stars—the only light coming from an occasional lightning flash so distant that it made no sound. That environment made radar, much improved since the Battle of Savo Island, particularly valuable.

Just past midnight on October 11–12, nearing the end of the column's eastward run, Scott issued orders for the ships to reverse course, with each ship following in the track of the ship ahead of it. With the order to "Execute," the *Farenholt* put her helm over, and she was followed in turn by the next two destroyers in line, which were Weatherup's former ship *Duncan* and the *Laffey* (DD-459). Further back in the column, however, Scott's flagship, the cruiser *San Francisco*, rather than follow in their track, put the helm over immediately, thus turning inside the destroyers. Now, instead of a single column, the US force was steaming in two columns side by side.[5]

Staring through the darkness with his binoculars, Weatherup saw that the *San Francisco* had turned, and he told Tobin that the next two ships in line had followed her. That gave Tobin two options: He could slow down and fall in behind the cruisers, or he could speed up and try to get back in front of them. Weatherup reported that the trailing destroyers were also following the cruisers, so Tobin decided to go to flank speed and get back to the front of the column to reestablish the original formation. Weatherup admired the way Tobin assessed the situation quickly, and it might have worked out exactly as he planned except that at exactly that moment the cruiser *Helena*, which had one of the new radar sets, reported enemy ships approaching from the west. It was, in fact, a column of Japanese cruisers intent on shelling the American positions on Guadalcanal. Tobin's three destroyers were now between the American cruisers and the approaching Japanese. When the two sides opened fire, Weatherup remembered, "All Hell broke loose." The *Farentholt* was hit by eight-inch shells from *both* the American and the Japanese cruisers. The cruiser *Boise* even illuminated the *Farenholt* with her searchlight, though after her crew read the *Farenholt*'s hull number, the searchlight quickly snapped off. Even that brief moment of illumination in the eight hundred million candlepower of a navy searchlight allowed the Japanese to target both the *Farenholt* and the *Boise*, each of which received severe punishment.[6]

At close range, in pitch darkness, confusion reigned. At one point, the *Farenholt* nearly collided with a Japanese destroyer. Too close to employ either torpedoes or even their five-inch guns, both sides fired their machine guns at one another. Weatherup, still on the bridge, remembered that "our 20 mm guns raked her topsides. There must have been many Japanese casualties even though the 20 mm guns could not do any structural damage." During that

178   ANNAPOLIS GOES TO WAR

wild exchange, Weatherup realized he had lost track of Captain Tobin. He took a "quick look about," but, not seeing him and already wounded himself, he decided to take cover behind a steel splinter shield. As he dove for cover, he nearly landed on top of Tobin, who had done the same thing.[7]

In the end, the superior firepower of the American cruisers, plus the advantage provided by radar, resulted in an American victory in what was called the Battle of Cape Esperance. The Japanese lost a cruiser and a destroyer; the Americans lost the destroyer *Duncan*, on which Weatherup had been serving just weeks before. It was not as one-sided a victory as the one the Japanese had achieved at Savo Island, yet it was enough of a victory to allow the Americans to assert that the earlier defeat had been avenged. In due time, Admiral Scott received the Medal of Honor; Tobin got the Navy Cross; Weatherup got a Purple Heart.[8]

Undeterred by this setback, the Japanese continued to run reinforcement and supply convoys down The Slot to Guadalcanal; American warships, mainly cruisers and destroyers, continued to try to stop them. Henderson Field was critical in the campaign, for it gave the Americans control of the air during the daylight. At night, however, the planes were grounded, and the warships on both sides groped uncertainly toward one another in the dark, the Japanese relying on their "Big Eyes," and the Americans on their rapidly improving radar.

The aircraft carriers of both sides operated at the periphery of these nighttime skirmishes. Due to losses in the Coral Sea and at Midway, as well as to Japanese submarines, the Americans had only two carriers left: the veteran *Enterprise* and the relatively new *Hornet*. Tom Wells, a lantern-jawed Texan from the class of 1940, was one of the original crew members (plank holders) on the *Hornet* and had sailed in her on the Doolittle raid back in April. In the third week of October, he found himself at the center of the fighting for Guadalcanal.

Only two weeks after the Battle of Cape Esperance, the Japanese decided to commit their fleet of aircraft carriers to yet another major attempt to reinforce Guadalcanal. The new US theater commander, Admiral "Bull" Halsey, sent both the *Hornet* and *Enterprise*, literally all he had left, to intercept it. The result was the Battle of the Santa Cruz Islands (October 25, 1942). This time, instead of a gun battle, it was an air battle, and the Japanese got much the better of it.

On the morning of October 25, twenty-one Japanese dive bombers successfully avoided the *Hornet*'s combat air patrol and landed three bombs on the

Hornet's deck. One of them landed only twenty feet from where Tom Wells was standing, knocking out the electricity and communications and forcing Wells to exercise local control over the guns, three of which got stuck in the vertical position. Another bomb punched through the flight deck and exploded almost directly below him, and only seconds after that, Wells watched as a third bomb "exploded on contact and slaughtered a large number of marines on the machine guns." Worse was to come. Within minutes, two torpedoes hit the *Hornet*'s starboard side, one forward and one aft. The concussion was so great that Wells was knocked about, in his words, "like a ball on a roulette wheel." With her main engines out, the *Hornet* slowed to a stop and began listing to starboard. It seemed to him that "the ship just seemed to die then," almost as if it had lost heart. "Burning planes littered the air and water about us," he recalled. Though the Japanese had not yet adopted kamikaze tactics, two pilots whose planes had been damaged decided to sacrifice themselves by deliberately crashing into the *Hornet*.[9]

By the time the attack ended, Wells surveyed a deck that was "littered with dead, and slippery with blood." In some places, the blood was half an inch thick. Several bodies of dead sailors were on fire and they burned "with a light blue flame," that gave off a sickly sweet smell. Wells felt helpless; all he could do was give the badly wounded a morphine syrette.[10]

The cruiser *Northampton* took the crippled *Hornet* under tow and headed south. The two ships had barely begun to make forward progress, however, when there was a new announcement: "Torpedo planes approaching." Wells looked up, which caused him to trip over dead bodies on the deck. He cheered when he saw several of the attacking planes shot down, spinning into the sea, though the cheers died in his throat when he saw one Japanese plane that seemed to be headed directly for him personally. He remembered thinking, "He might kill me." At the same time, however, he could not imagine how that was possible. "Death was not a thing that could affect me . . . I could not be standing there conscious and thinking, and then cease forever." He watched as the approaching plane dropped a torpedo that ran straight and true and hit the *Hornet* directly below him. The explosion knocked him down, but it did not kill him.[11]

It did, however, kill the *Hornet*. After the Japanese pilot dropped his torpedo, he executed a turn to deliberately crash into the *Hornet*. Hit by three bombs, three torpedoes, and three suicide planes, the big flattop, only one year after her commissioning, could not be saved. The crew, including Tom Wells, was taken off and carried by transports to New Caledonia. The *Hornet* was left

180 ANNAPOLIS GOES TO WAR

where it was, abandoned. The Japanese, arriving several hours later, finished her off with more torpedoes.[12]

The Japanese also attacked the other American carrier, *Enterprise*, hitting her with three bombs, but no torpedoes, which is probably why she did not share the fate of the *Hornet*. Badly crippled, she escaped southward under her own power. She was now the only American aircraft carrier left in the Pacific theater. Sailors on board made a banner and stretched it across the hangar deck: "Enterprise vs. Japan."

By then, Doc Weatherup was on his third destroyer in three months. The *Duncan* had sunk, and the *Farenholt* was undergoing repairs, so in early November Weatherup transferred to the *Aaron Ward* (DD-482). It would prove to be the proverbial leap from the frying pan into the fire, for instead of confronting Japanese cruisers, in his new ship he would confront Japanese battleships.

That is because in the second week of November 1942, the Japanese sent two battleships—*Hiei* and *Kirishima*—to shell Henderson Field. Their idea was to render the airstrip temporarily inoperable so that the Japanese could send another, larger, reinforcement convoy to the island. Like both Savo Island and Cape Esperance, the Naval Battle of Guadalcanal (November 13, 1942—Friday the thirteenth) took place in pitch darkness, and to add to the confusion, it also occurred amid a driving rainstorm. The two fleets approached each other head on, neither aware of the other. The lead American destroyer, the *Laffey*, nearly collided with an approaching Japanese battleship. After that, in Weatherup's words, the battle "broke down into a melee." Another participant likened it to "a barroom brawl with the lights out." Muzzle flashes, torpedo wakes, flares, searchlights, explosions—it was so confusing that participants on both sides, including on the *Aaron Ward*, simply fired at any vessel they saw, friend or foe. At least two torpedoes, their depth gauges set for battleships, passed under the shallow-draft *Aaron Ward* without exploding. Soon after that, she nearly collided with the American destroyer *Sterret*. She also received nine shell hits; whether they came from friend or foe was unclear.[13]

When dawn broke on November 14, crippled, burning, and sinking ships were scattered all over the horizon. Some, including the destroyer USS *Barton* (DD-599), had disappeared altogether. Cut in half by two Japanese torpedoes, the *Barton* sank in the middle of the chaotic violence, taking one of the Forties, Billy Guice of Biloxi, Mississippi, down with her. As daylight spread, several of the damaged American ships, including the heavy cruiser *San Francisco* and the light cruisers *Helena* and *Juneau*, limped away toward Espiritu Santo for repairs. As they were en route, a Japanese sub fired two torpedoes at the *San Francisco*. Both of them missed, streaking past the cruiser's bow, though one of them hit the light cruiser *Juneau* (CL-50) and literally broke her in half. Many of her crew were lost in the initial explosion or were unable to get off the ship as it sank; about a hundred others went into the water. Expecting that they would be rescued by others, the *San Francisco* and *Helena* continued on their way. That decision became controversial later because rescue efforts were delayed and all but ten of those who had survived the initial explosion subsequently drowned or were killed by sharks. Among them were five brothers named Sullivan. That tragedy led to a reconsideration of the policy that allowed brothers to serve together in a combat zone. Also among the killed were two members of the class of 1940: Tom Roddy and John Blodgett.[14]

As for the *Aaron Ward*, she remained at the scene of the battle, dead in the water and unable to move. One of the nearby ships was the Japanese battleship *Hiei*, so close that Weatherup could see her without his binoculars. Lookouts on the *Hiei* saw the *Aaron Ward*, too, and at first light, the Japanese fired a salvo of fourteen-inch shells in her direction. A single fourteen-inch shell, weighing fifteen hundred pounds, could break a destroyer in half. Weatherup saw the orange muzzle flashes and knew they had been targeted. Even with a muzzle velocity of twenty-six hundred feet per second, it took a full thirty seconds for the shells from the *Hiei* to reach the motionless *Aaron Ward*, and there was absolutely nothing Weatherup or anybody else could do besides hold his breath and wonder if it would be his last. "You have no way of knowing," Weatherup wrote later, "how long 30 seconds can be under such circumstances."[15]

The shells from that first salvo landed short. Over on the *Hiei*, the Japanese gunners made adjustments and fired again. Weatherup and his shipmates waited another tense thirty seconds. This time the towering shell splashes were much closer. The third salvo was likely to be decisive, and indeed, with the third salvo the Japanese gunners got a straddle, though none of the shells actually hit. The *Hiei* fired a fourth salvo, which also missed. By then, US Marine bombers and fighters from Henderson Field had arrived over the *Hiei*, and the Japanese were too busy fending them off to worry about the little *Aaron Ward*. In fact, the *Hiei* began to withdraw, though not fast enough to avoid the marine bombers, who pursued her and eventually sank her.

Towed into Tulagi, the *Aaron Ward* was patched up and in due time rejoined the fleet. Weatherup, though, did not stay with her, for at Tulagi he found new orders waiting for him—orders he had anticipated since he was

ANNAPOLIS GOES TO WAR

ten years old. Like John Lacouture, he was going to New Orleans for pilot training.

The savage fighting in the waters around Guadalcanal continued all that spring and into summer. American and Japanese surface ships clashed repeatedly in confusing night battles with exotic names like Kula Gulf (July 5–6, 1943) and Vella Gulf (August 6–7, 1943). In the former, the Japanese sunk the light cruiser *Helena* with both Dick Cochrane and another Forty with the Anglophilic name David Lloyd George King on board. Both survived. In the Battle of Vella Gulf, Hank Davison, who had been OOD on the *Arizona* at Pearl Harbor, was awarded the Silver Star for his actions aboard the destroyer *Craven* (DD-382). In these engagements and others, the Americans had the advantage of improved radar that negated Japanese superiority in night optics.*

The fighting in the Solomon Islands was still ongoing in the fall of 1943 when Connie Carlson returned to this vortex of maritime violence. After the loss of the *Astoria* back in August, the navy sent Carlson to Gunnery School for three months before appointing him gunnery officer on the brand-new USS *Foote* (DD-511). By now, navy recruits were being rushed out of boot camp and straight to the fleet. As the most senior of the department heads, Carlson got first pick of the 225 sailors assigned as the *Foote*'s initial crew. Carlson gathered them together and asked who among them had experience with five-inch guns. No one raised his hand. Well, Carlson continued, what about experience with machine guns? Again, no hands. Desperate now, Carlson asked, "Has anyone ever fired a rifle or a pistol?" A dozen raised their hands. Clearly, he had his work cut out for him.[16]

After escorting a convoy to the Mediterranean and back in the spring of 1943, the *Foote* steamed back across the Atlantic, through the Panama Canal, and out to the South Pacific and the Solomon Islands. The Japanese had evacuated Guadalcanal by then, and the ground combat had moved on to Rendova, New Georgia, and Bougainville. The naval confrontations continued. The American destroyers engaged in these battles, commanded by Captain Arleigh Burke, got the nickname "Little Beavers," for their nonstop activity. On a typical day, Carlson wrote later, the *Foote* got underway from Tulagi about four-thirty in the afternoon, intercepted "Jap traffic of all sorts" during the night, then hightailed it back to Tulagi in order to be under friendly air cover by

---

* Lieutenant David Lloyd George King wanted his wife to name their son Winston Churchill King, but he was at sea when the child arrived, and the mother decided he should instead be christened David Lloyd George King Jr.

daybreak. "We would arrive at Tulagi, load ammunition and supplies, take a short break in our bunks, and then get underway again. . . . I simply don't remember when we got any sleep."[17]

In addition to relying on destroyers like the "Little Beavers," the Americans also employed much smaller (eighty-foot) vessels known as patrol torpedo (or PT) boats. The most famous of these, at least subsequently, was PT-109, whose skipper was Lieutenant (j.g.) and future President John F. Kennedy, whom John Lacouture had occasionally competed against in the sailboat races off Hyannisport. Kennedy's boat was part of Motor Torpedo Boat Squadron No. 5, which also included PT-111, commanded by John Henry Clagett, a class of 1940 grad from Bowling Green, Kentucky. Like Connie Carlson, Clagett had sung in the Academy choir all four years, and also like Carlson, he had acted in the annual musicals. Because of his short stature and clear tenor, he was often assigned female roles in the all-male cast, including the title role in *Madame Butterfly.*[18]

On February 1, 1943, Clagett's PT-111 was patrolling The Slot with the rest of the squadron when a Japanese destroyer loomed up out of the fog. Clagett pushed the throttle forward, closed to within five hundred yards, and fired all four of his torpedoes. All four missed—or perhaps malfunctioned. As he turned away, the destroyer opened fire with its five-inch guns, and a direct hit on the 111 caused it to burst into flames. Clagett was severely wounded and badly burned. He crawled to the side of his sinking ship and flopped over into the water. Barely conscious, he was kept afloat by his crewmen until another PT boat arrived to rescue them. Years later, he described it as the night he was "blown up, burned up, chewed up." Miraculously, he survived, though he spent most of the next two years in navy hospitals undergoing skin grafts and plastic surgeries to reconstruct his body and his face. He tried to resume active service, reporting aboard the light cruiser *Fargo* in 1944, but the doctors refused to certify him as fit for service, and he was medically retired.[19]

Quite apart from those—like Clagett—who were badly wounded, seven members of the class of 1940 lost their lives in the fighting for the Solomon Islands: William F. Greene in *Jarvis,* John Hanna in *San Francisco,* Ray Murray and John Spears in *Vincennes,* William Guice in *Barton,* and Tom Roddy and John Blodgett in the *Juneau.* Their loss brought the number of class members killed in the war to thirty-six.

15

Flight Training

Back on May 16, 1940, eighteen days before the Forties graduated, Franklin Roosevelt appeared before Congress, his physical presence signaling the seriousness of the moment. Six days earlier, German armies had stormed into France and were driving toward the English Channel, and the president had come to urge Congress to support a historic escalation in military readiness. He was careful to couch his request in terms of defending the Western Hemisphere rather than intervening in the European war, though he made it clear that, as he put it, "the American people must recast their thinking about national protection." In addition to increases in both the army and the navy, he emphasized the need to expand military aviation. He noted that the production of military aircraft had increased recently, yet he insisted that Congress needed to do more. Much more. "I believe that this nation should plan at this time a program that will provide us with 50,000 military and naval planes."[1]

Fifty thousand airplanes! There were only 1,741 aircraft in the whole of the US Navy, and an equal number in the US Army Air Corps. Accustomed to thinking in terms of acquiring twenty or thirty planes a year, it led to what one navy authority called "a violent readjustment in thinking" about naval aviation. It had also provoked a lot of conversation among the Forties on the eve of their graduation. Many of them had already decided to seek flight training as soon as possible; some, like Doc Weatherup, had come to the Academy specifically for that purpose. Still, the numbers the president now projected were astonishing. Even if only a quarter of the 50,000 airplanes the president called for went to the navy, that was 12,500 airplanes, seven times the current number. And if the number of pilots increased proportionately, that meant more than twenty-one thousand pilots. And where were they to come from? Even if everyone in the class of 1940—and from every other class as well—opted for flight training, that would still fall thousands short of the number needed. The

FLIGHT TRAINING

unavoidable answer was that the vast majority of new pilots must come from outside the Naval Academy.[2]

Roosevelt got most of what he requested. In June, just a few days after the class of 1940 graduated, Congress raised the number of authorized navy aircraft to ten thousand, and a few weeks later, after the fall of France, raised it again to fifteen thousand. To produce the pilots needed to fly those planes, Congress established what was called the V-7 Program. It was supposed to produce an eventual total of thirty-six thousand naval aviators. That was an eye-popping number: double the total number of officers in the entire US Navy at the time. Under the new legislation, college graduates who signed up for the program would spend just thirty days studying gunnery, navigation, engineering, and seamanship. Then, after completing a three-month pilot-training program, they would emerge at the end of four months with both their gold wings and a commission as a navy ensign.*

Some in the class of 1940 thought those terms remarkably generous, especially since after spending four years at the Academy, they had been compelled to wait two more years before they could even apply to flight school. And when they did apply, their commanding officers were often reluctant to let them go, frequently adding an endorsement to their request stipulating that "a qualified relief will be required." That generally led to the request being shelved. One of the Forties, Ted Hill, of Cedarville, California, who had been on the *Nevada* during the Pearl Harbor attack, decided that he "preferred to deliver bombs rather than to receive them." When his application to flight school disappeared into the administrative morass with no response, he decided to do what they had all been told never to do: "I went around the system." Because he personally knew the officer in the Bureau of Navigation who supervised officer transfers, he wrote him to explain his conundrum. It worked. "In a couple of weeks, I received my orders to flight training."[3]

Those who opted for pilot training in 1942, including Ted Hill, John Lacouture, and Doc Weatherup, got orders to the Naval Air Base at New Orleans on the shore of Lake Pontchartrain. The first of the Forties to arrive, however, was a marine, Otis Calhoun, who reported there in the spring of 1942 and pinned on his wings in July while Lacouture and Weatherup were still

---

* In the US Navy, almost all pilots were commissioned officers. Though there were some warrant officer pilots, flying combat aircraft in the US Navy was considered an officer's assignment. That was not the case in the Imperial Japanese Navy. To the Japanese, flying a plane was like driving a truck or a tank—an assignment for an enlisted man. Japanese commissioned officers commanded squadrons, but most Japanese pilots were noncommissioned officers, or what the US Navy called petty officers.

186   ANNAPOLIS GOES TO WAR

fighting the Japanese in the dark waters off Guadalcanal. Another marine who went to flight training that summer was David Wolfe (nickname Lobo), who reported to New Orleans on Independence Day in 1942. Over the ensuing weeks and months other members of the class arrived, and soon there were more than thirty; by the fall there were more than fifty. One of them, Johnny Miller, wrote Myers Montgomery that there were so many of their classmates there "it almost looked like a class reunion."[4]

By then, they had all been promoted again. Having spent only six months as jaygees (or Marine Corps first lieutenants), they were advanced to the rank of navy full lieutenant (or marine captain) on October 1, 1942. Only a few years before, as midshipmen at the Academy, lieutenants, with two broad stripes on their sleeves, had seemed lofty and imposing individuals; it was almost disorienting now to find themselves advanced to such exalted heights so quickly.

The early arrivals in New Orleans found the facilities pretty rudimentary: an airstrip, a steel hangar, barracks for one hundred aviation cadets, a small repair shop, and storage for fifty thousand gallons of fuel. The base was expanding swiftly, however, and in November it was officially upgraded to a naval air station. Meanwhile, the authorities scrambled to keep the early arrivals occupied. Some of the Forties were assigned administrative duties: serving on courts martial, teaching classes on weapons, navigation, and other topics to the new aviation cadets, even exercising them in marching drills.[5]

Soon enough, though, all the aspiring pilots were immersed in a rigorous training program. They had ground school (classroom study) six days a week and flight training seven days a week. They were told at the outset that there would be no leave granted except for emergencies. As one of the Forties noted sarcastically, the schedule left "half a day on Sunday to do whatever we liked!" Classroom work focused on the theory of flight, aerial navigation, internal combustion engines, and the recognition of airplanes and ships.[6]

The actual flying was far more interesting. It took place every afternoon, Sundays and holidays included, in N2S Stearman biplanes. With their fixed landing gear and cloth-covered wings connected by struts and wires, the Stearmans looked like something left over from the last war. Painted a bright yellow, they were called by virtually everyone the "Yellow Peril." Yet the Stearman was a sturdy and forgiving airplane, ideal for flight training. Ted Hill always retained "a warm spot" in his heart "for these rugged, simple, and trustworthy flying machines."[7]

FLIGHT TRAINING 187

The Stearman had two open cockpits, one behind the other, with the student sitting in front and the instructor behind him. Though the Forties were now full lieutenants, some of the instructors were mere ensigns, aviation cadets who had completed their training only months before and who had been retained as instructors. Others were civilian pilots who had accumulated one hundred hours of flying time and been certified as flight instructors. Because many of the Forties were now decorated combat veterans, they were reluctant to defer to ensigns who had been in the navy for less than a year. As one example of that, though it had been a tradition for student trainees to carry the parachute of their instructor to the airplane, that protocol was discarded immediately. After a few months of flying, with the instructor observing and advising from the rear seat, the trainees were allowed to solo, which was an important milestone.[8]

Many of the Forties were married by then, and with their husbands fully occupied at the airfield, some of the new brides felt abandoned. Determined to provide their husbands with some R & R and inject a little merriment into their own lives, they organized a dinner dance for New Year's Eve, 1942. It was a great success—or so it seemed until the next morning. Despite being a holiday, New Year's Day was another fully scheduled workday. A number of the trainees were no-shows for ground school in the morning, and there was some "pretty sloppy flying" that afternoon. The authorities were annoyed and threatened punishment, though in the end, as one of the Forties recalled, "nothing ever came of it."[9]

John Lacouture arrived in New Orleans in September following the loss of the USS *Blue* off Guadalcanal; Doc Weatherup arrived three months later after the Naval Battle of Guadalcanal. For both men, their time in the Crescent City marked a decisive change in their lives, and not only because of their transition from the surface navy to aviation. The instructors had made it clear from the start that once they began training, no leave would be granted except for emergencies. Even so, Weatherup pleaded for an exception so he could marry Kathryn (Kay) Hesser, who had come from California for that purpose. Perhaps influenced by the row of medals on his uniform, including the Purple Heart, the authorities granted him a forty-eight-hour leave. He married Kay on January 27, 1943, and was back in training on the twenty-ninth.[10]

By then, Lacouture had completed his preliminary training in New Orleans and moved on to intermediate training in Pensacola, but the three months he spent in New Orleans had changed his life, too. Back in the spring, before he had deployed to the South Pacific in the *Blue*, newspapers had announced his engagement to Amelia Ames Stempel. That wedding never took place. Instead, eighteen months later, on October 26, 1943, he married the former Elizabeth "Betty" Monrose, whom he met while she was a student at Sophie Newcomb, the women's college of Tulane University. For all his openness about his experiences in the navy, Lacouture remained utterly silent about how this came to pass. Did he receive another "Dear John" letter from Amelia (who married Army Lieutenant Robert Andrae in February 1944), or did he break off his engagement to Amelia after falling hard for Betty while he was in New Orleans? Whatever the explanation, John and Betty remained married for thirty years and raised four children. In the meantime, he flew airplanes, starting with the Stearmans.*

After successfully soloing at New Orleans, the would-be pilots packed up and moved two hundred miles east to Pensacola for intermediate flight training. In place of the Stearman biplane, they now flew a low-wing metal monoplane, the Vultee BT-13 Valiant. Like the Stearman, the Valiant was a two-seater with the student in the front and the instructor behind him, but it was a far more sophisticated airplane. It had a closed cockpit, a more powerful engine, a mixture control for the fuel, and a variable speed propeller. The budding pilots called it the "Vultee Vibrator" for its tendency to shake violently at stall speeds.[11]

At Pensacola, the Forties had a lot more flying time, "putting in lots of hours in the air," as one reported home. They learned to do "snap rolls, loops, wingovers, the Immelmann, split-S, and falling leaf," along with other maneuvers. They practiced formation flying, learning to hold their position by maintaining a constant bearing and distance to the leader without coming so close that it affected the air flow around the plane. They learned to fly by instruments and to navigate across country. They practiced dive bombing and aerial target shooting. Some of the instructors at Pensacola had flown in the Coral Sea or at Midway, and they were both supportive and encouraging. Back at the Naval Academy some of the Forties had suspected that a few of the instructors had looked for reasons to wash out weak performers, but in 1943 so desperate was the need for more pilots that the instructors at Pensacola worked hard to qualify as many as possible.[12]

---

* Another curiosity is that John's younger brother Paul, who earned his navy commission as an NROTC student at Yale and was a submarine officer in 1943, married Jeanette Kittredge in New York City on October 23, three days before John's wedding in New Orleans.

FLIGHT TRAINING

The Forties who completed the program at Pensacola were designated naval aviators and awarded their gold wings. That was another significant milestone, though they were not finished with their training, for they were then assigned to one of a number of sub-specialties. The marines, like Otis Calhoun and Lobo Wolfe, went to Cherry Point, North Carolina, which Wolfe thought was "the best airfield I had ever seen," confirming his opinion that marines were innately superior to sailors. The navy pilots were sent to several locations. Before the war, the navy had insisted that to be a naval aviator, a pilot had to be able to fly every type of naval aircraft. Amid the crisis of 1943, that rule was jettisoned, and pilots were allowed—indeed required—to specialize. The navy asked each of them for their preference, though, as always, the needs of the navy came first, and not everyone got his first choice. Some were retained at Pensacola to serve as flight instructors for the next class. Those who got such orders were often disappointed not to be joining the fleet, though, in fact, keeping the pipeline filled with new pilots was a critical element of eventual Allied victory. Others were assigned to multiengine, land-based aircraft or seaplanes. But the most popular and desirable assignment, especially after the Battles of the Coral Sea and Midway, was to Opa-Locka, Florida, to become a carrier pilot.[13]

Opa-Locka was one of many new facilities set up quickly as war loomed and had been designated a naval air station in August 1940, just two months after the Forties graduated. To accustom the students to carrier operations, the instructors painted the outline of a carrier on the tarmac. A carrier flight deck was just over eight hundred feet long, and from five thousand feet, an eight-hundred-foot landing strip looked like a postage stamp. As they approached the painted outline, the student pilots learned to keep one eye on the landing signal officer (LSO), who held colored paddles the size of those used in pickleball. If the pilot came it too high, the LSO would hold the paddles out in a V, bringing them down slowly as the pilot leveled out. If the pilot came in too low, the LSO made an inverted V. If the approach looked good, the LSO gave him the cut sign, slashing the paddle across his throat to indicate that the pilot could land. Otherwise, the pilot got a wave-off and had to go around for another try.[14]

After Opa-Locka, there was another sorting. Those selected to become dive bomber pilots went to Daytona Beach; torpedo plane pilots went to Fort Lauderdale; and fighter pilots went to Melbourne, all located on Florida's east coast. Their wives went with them, and as always finding new housing was difficult, though Daytona was one of the few naval air stations where there was a surplus of affordable housing. Ted Hill was one of those sent to Daytona, and he noted that in addition to readily available housing, Daytona also served as a training center for thousands of young women in the Women's Auxiliary Army Corps (WAAC), though as a married man he professed to have no interest in that.[15]

Both Lacouture and Weatherup got their first choice and reported to Melbourne to become fighter pilots. There they flew F4F Wildcats, sturdy and resilient single-seat fighters, which, along with the Vought Corsair, remained the navy's front-line fighter until it was replaced late in 1943 by the faster and more maneuverable F6F Hellcat. The Wildcats had a few curious features. One was that the pilot had to use an oversize shotgun shell to kickstart the three-bladed propeller, and another was that although the Wildcat had retractable landing gear, the wheels had to be cranked up (and down) by hand, while the pilot continued to fly the airplane.

The most critical milestone for all carrier pilots was making an actual carrier landing. To qualify, an aviator had to complete two successful takeoffs and two landings on a carrier. Landing on a carrier that was underway—literally a moving target—was significantly more challenging than doing so on a painted outline on the runway. The problem was that there was a dearth of carriers on which the aspiring pilots could qualify. The new *Essex*-class carriers that Congress had authorized back in 1940 were mostly still on the building ways, and the few operational carriers in the Pacific could not be spared from the war. To enable the new aviators to qualify, the navy purchased two paddle-wheel passenger steamers on Lake Michigan, erected a flight deck on each of them, and commissioned them as the training ships *Wolverine* and *Sable*.[16]

That is why after completing their fighter pilot training in Melbourne, both Lacouture and Weatherup, as well as other aspiring carrier pilots, boarded trains to the Glenview Naval Air Station just north of Chicago. There they got a short briefing and a chance to make a few practice landings on the airfield before they flew off to land on one of the two ersatz carriers. Displacing only seven thousand tons each (barely a third the size of a fleet carrier), the *Wolverine* and *Sable* had flight decks that were 550 feet long. The flight decks on the *Yorktown* and *Enterprise* were longer, but pilots who operated from them almost never had the full deck run available. During takeoffs, aircraft waiting their turn to launch would be parked astern, thus shortening the amount of deck space. For landings, aircraft on the flight deck would be manhandled up to the bow, protected from arriving planes by a safety fence in case an arriving airplane missed the arresting wires. Thus a 550-foot deck was actually a suitable length for practice takeoffs and landings.

Eager to qualify as many pilots as fast as possible, the authorities ran the prospective aviators through the qualification process quickly. Lacouture left no record of his experience; Weatherup completed his two required take-offs and landings in a single day. As routine as that was for those running the program, it was a white-knuckle experience for him. "Every carrier pilot remembers his first carrier landing," he wrote later. "You cannot quite understand the apprehension, the thrill, and the relief until you have made a carrier landing."[17]

Weatherup had spent virtually his entire adult life looking forward to becoming a pilot. Thinking back on his flying experience later, he decided that it had lived up to his expectations. He was impressed with the planning, the seriousness, and especially the dedication of those who ran the program in 1942 and 1943. It was, he thought, "a tribute to a generation of Naval Aviators who were doing their active flying 10–15 years ahead of us." They were the ones who "provided the structure and direction for the expansion of Naval Aviation to meet the challenge of World War II."[18]

Both Lacouture and Weatherup, now fully qualified carrier pilots, were designated as pilot instructors: Lacouture at Melbourne, and Weatherup at Pensacola. That gave each of them a kind of honeymoon, and a chance, as Weatherup put it, "to improve my air-to-air gunnery score as well as to mature as a flight leader." In time, they joined fighting squadrons on carriers and participated in the drive across the Central Pacific in 1944, as we will see.[19]

In addition to the navy carrier pilots and marine pilots like Calhoun and Wolfe who flew ground support for their fellow marines, there was another, altogether separate and often overlooked, aspect of flight training in 1942–43. The same month Congress authorized an enormous expansion of military aircraft, it also approved the construction of two hundred lighter-than-air (LTA) ships for the navy.* Officially labeled "airships," virtually everyone called them blimps. K-class blimps were unwieldy at 450-feet long (nearly as long as the *Wolverine* or *Sable*), and they required enormous hangars to house them on shore. Beneath their huge bags of helium gas was the "car," a bus-sized compartment that held a crew of ten plus machine guns and depth charge racks. In 1942, the blimps were organized into two commands: Airship Wing 30 in the

---

* The designations for navy combat aircraft during World War II all included the letter "V" (for heaVier than air) to distinguish them from lighter-than-air craft. Thus, dive bombers were VB, torpedo planes VT, and fighters were VF. Similarly, aircraft carriers were designated CV (carriers of heavier-than-air planes).

Atlantic and Airship Wing 31 in the Pacific. It was a curious nomenclature since, of course, the blimps had no "wings" at all.[20]

A reliance on blimps for combat in World War II might strike the modern ear as archaic—like deploying cavalry against tanks—but they possessed several characteristics that made them particularly useful against submarines. For one thing they could remain in the air for long periods, well over twenty-four hours, flying almost silently at fifty miles an hour (about three times the speed of a surfaced U-boat) to scan a broad swath of ocean. Early in the war, when the US Navy lacked sufficient escorts to protect convoys along the East Coast, blimps sometimes filled that role, hovering over a convoy at 250 feet, and maneuvering back and forth over the transports to look for U-boats. Radar, already much improved from the rudimentary sets used early in 1942, could detect a surfaced submarine from miles away even at night, and, after 1943, the blimps were also equipped with what was called a magnetic anomaly detector (MAD), which could pick up a disruption (anomaly) in the earth's magnetic field that could indicate the presence of a submerged submarine. A hovering blimp equipped with both radar and MAD could find and attack a U-boat before the U-boat's crew even knew they were in jeopardy.[21]

Service on a blimp over the North Atlantic could be stomach-churning. The K-class airships rolled and pitched much like a ship at sea, and seasickness was as prevalent in the blimps as it was on the North Atlantic convoys. Nor was service in a blimp without risks. In July 1943, when the airship K-74 encountered a U-boat running on the surface in the Florida Straits, it immediately attacked. Firing continuously, its crew prepared to drop depth charges, but for whatever reason, the depth charges failed to release. The U-boat fired back, and several shots compromised the helium bags that kept the K-74 aloft. It descended alarmingly and crash-landed, its rubber-coated cotton bag puddling on the surface. The members of the blimp's crew were able to scramble out of the car and were subsequently rescued (though one was killed by sharks). The U-boat did not get away unscathed. Damaged by machine gun fire from the K-74, it had to abandon its patrol, and while returning to its base in the Bay of Biscay, it was sighted and sunk by planes of the Royal Navy.[22]

Nine members of the class of 1940 served in blimps during World War II. One of them was Mike Hanley, who reported to Lakehurst, New Jersey, in September, the same month John Lacouture reported to New Orleans. After three months there, Lieutenant Hanley assumed command of his own blimp at the Richmond Air Base in Florida. By then, the German U-boats had moved

FLIGHT TRAINING 193

south from their initial hunting grounds off the North Carolina capes and were stalking transports and especially tankers in the Caribbean.

In mid-June 1943, Hanley got a report that a U-boat had attacked and sunk an oil tanker fifty miles east of Key West. He and his ten-man crew lifted off and headed south in the gathering twilight to find it. Hanley calculated that the U-boat skipper would try to take advantage of the Gulf Stream and run north along the east coast of Florida, so he planned to follow that course. Beginning his patrol from the scene of the U-boat's attack on the tanker, he cruised north at forty miles an hour while darkness closed in and the glow of lights from Miami became visible to port. With the radar in active mode, Hanley urged the radar operator to stay alert. For two hours, there was nothing.[23]

Then, suddenly, eight miles behind them was a bright, clear, unmistakable contact on the surface. Hanley was watching the radar screen over the shoulder of the operator, and they "yelled at each other at the same time." The radarman insisted "the contact was too sharp to be a snorkel. It had to be the submarine we were looking for and it had surfaced." With his adrenaline pumping, Hanley ordered the crew to battle stations. He started a high-speed run (seventy miles per hour) toward the target and radioed the base that "we were attacking an unidentified contact, most probably a surfaced sub." He ordered the depth charges armed and set for twenty-five feet, and he instructed the gunner "to fire back without command if we were fired upon."

When they were within half a mile of the contact, the blip disappeared from the screen, which Hanley attributed to interference from sea return. He needed to make a visual sighting. He could take the blimp no lower than three hundred feet since below that, the exploding depth charges could damage the blimp. As they drew nearer, he remembered thinking how odd it was that the sub had not fired at them.[24]

And then, directly ahead, he saw it: a dark shape in the water. He told the bombardier to stand by. At that moment, the lookout yelled: "Red light at eleven o'clock!" Hanley saw it, too; it was dim but distinct. It struck him that a U-boat in enemy waters would not be showing a light of any kind. "By instinct, divine guidance, or whatever you wanted to call it, I decided not to drop." His crew, eagerly awaiting the order, was "amazed" when instead of attacking, he took the blimp up to three thousand feet. From there he dropped an illumination flare, and as it floated down in its parachute, casting a bright white light over the sea below, he saw a Pan American passenger seaplane that had made an emergency landing. In a release of tension, some in the crew got the giggles.

194 ANNAPOLIS GOES TO WAR

One of them looked over at Hanley. "Lieutenant, you almost became famous in the Navy as the only aviator to sink a Pan Am seaplane."[25]

For the next few hours, instead of the hunter, Hanley's blimp was the rescuer. He radioed the coordinates of the downed plane to the base and hovered overhead, dropping more flares to pinpoint the location of the downed plane until a tug and escort arrived. Once the Pan Am clipper was under tow to Miami, he headed back to base. For the rest of his life, he had occasional nightmares, waking up in a sweat thinking about how close he had come to dropping depth charges on a passenger plane.

That was not quite the strangest part of the tale. The next night Hanley had a date with Chris Nystie, who later became his wife. She told him she had received a phone call that afternoon from another of her suitors who told her that the Pan Am airplane he had been piloting had been forced to land in the Florida Straits and that the plane and its passengers had been rescued by a blimp hovering overhead.[26]

Navy blimps continued to operate until the end of the war, though the demand for airships eased as more conventional surface escorts became available. In fact, the unprecedented production of more conventional combat airplanes, and new models of airplanes, plus the efficiency of the pilot-training program, gave the United States overwhelming superiority in the air by 1944, both in the Pacific and in Europe. In the end, the Allies overwhelmed the Axis powers as much by industrial production—including airplane construction—as by strategy or military prowess. Indeed, by late 1944, so many new planes were being produced that rows of them were parked unused on remote airfields and the government began to cancel contracts for more airplane production; the contract for Corsair fighters, for example, was cut in half. And as the demand for new airplanes diminished, so did the demand for new pilots.[27]

Hanley was an unwitting victim of that decision. After a year in blimps, he applied for training as a fighter pilot in early 1944 just as the perceived need for more pilots was waning. From the moment of his arrival in New Orleans, he sensed that the navy was not as eager for his success as he had expected. One night, in the middle of his training, he got a call from Chris, now his wife, who told him she was about to deliver their first child. Jumping into his car, he got her to the hospital in time, but it was a long delivery, and their daughter did not arrive until 6:00 a.m. Mentally and physically worn down after his all-night vigil, he asked for the day off. The officer in charge "sharply" ordered Hanley to "carry out [his] flight schedule for the day." Hanley wondered if some of his evident animosity was a resentment of Academy grads. Whatever the reason, when he ground-looped his plane after landing that morning, he was dropped from training. He returned to the surface navy, eventually becoming the executive officer on the new-construction destroyer USS *Dashiel* (DD-659).[28]

Flying was dangerous, and not just because of enemy action. It had been only forty years since the Wright brothers had demonstrated the practicality of manned flight at Kitty Hawk. Leaving the ground in a metal airplane, flying in excess of three hundred miles per hour, and plunging almost straight down in a dive bomber or maneuvering radically in a fighter plane were intrinsically life-threatening activities. Weather and circumstance could by themselves prove fatal to an aviator or passenger. A total of 116 members of the class of 1940 opted for flight training during World War II, and 30 of them did not survive the war.* Some died in combat or during inherently dangerous carrier landings. Others were killed when the plane they were riding went down in bad weather. Fifteen of them—half the total—were killed in training accidents.

They included Donald "Joe" Bried, a basketball teammate of Mike Hanley, whose plane crashed on Cecil Field near Jacksonville, Florida, on February 24, 1943. He scrambled out of the wreckage, told everyone he was fine, and began to walk away until he suddenly collapsed and died, his spine having been severed in the crash. He never learned that on that same morning his wife had given birth to their son. Those killed also included Milton "Mo" Jarrett of Huntington, West Virginia, who reported for aviation duty in Palm Beach, Florida, on May 29, 1943, and died only eleven days later in another plane crash. And it included Ben Hall, who had defiantly fired his .45 caliber pistol at Japanese planes from the masthead of the battleship *California* on December 7, 1941. He was killed when his plane crashed into a pine forest near Lake City, Florida.[29]

---

* Of the thirty aviators from the class of 1940 who were killed in the war, eight were non-graduates who left the Academy before graduation either for academic reasons or for failing the eye exam. After the war began, they re-entered the Navy, some through the V-7 program, and became naval aviators. One, William H. Matthews, Jr., was killed flying for the Royal Canadian Air Force.

16

The Med

It is not clear how Warren "Hooky" Walker earned his Academy nickname. It may have derived from his excellence on the gymnastics team, of which he was captain and dominant on the rings. A native of Ardmore, Pennsylvania, "Hooky" was one of the four who drove out to California in the Packard with Crosswell Croft back in the summer of 1940, and he was one of the fourteen Forties on board the battleship *California* on the Day of Infamy. Even after the order to abandon ship came down from the bridge that day, Walker stayed on board to fight the fires. The *California* sank slowly but inexorably, and Walker was still on board four days later, on December 11, when she finally settled gently onto the bottom mud of Pearl Harbor with much of her superstructure still above the water. Even after that, Walker, along with a few others, stood watch on the sunken battleship until he left to supervise the placement of some of her five-inch guns ashore as antiaircraft batteries. Not until March 1942 did he get orders to report to Quincy, Massachusetts, to join the pre-commissioning crew of the brand-new battleship *Massachusetts* (BB-59). When Walker reported aboard the *Massachusetts*, she was still fitting out at the Boston Navy Yard, which meant that Walker became her assistant navigation officer even before she could navigate.[1]

Before reporting aboard, Walker had to undergo another physical, and during it, the navy dentist told him he had a "malocclusion" that made him ineligible for sea duty. Walker was incredulous. He told the dentist that he had already served two years at sea, including during the attack on Pearl Harbor, that he had passed the exacting physical exam for submarines, and in any case, he had no intention of using his misaligned teeth to *bite* any Japs! The dentist relented.[2]

Displacing thirty-eight thousand tons, the *Massachusetts*, like the *Washington*, carried nine massive sixteen-inch guns in three triple turrets. Though she had been launched two months before the Japanese attacked Pearl

THE MED   197

Harbor, she was not officially commissioned until May 12, 1942, while the *Yorktown* was returning from the Battle of the Coral Sea and Nimitz was contemplating what to do about the threat to Midway. At the commissioning ceremony, her initial commanding officer, Captain F. E. M. Whiting (a 1912 Academy grad), offered a stirring speech to the assembled crew. He told them that the *Massachusetts* "had built into her the intestinal fortitude of the Pilgrim fathers, the watchfulness of Paul Revere, the discipline of Bunker Hill, and the education of John Harvard." These traditions, he proclaimed, are "handed down to us who walk the deck of the Massachusetts: daring, fortitude, character, and a love of liberty so fierce that a man would rather give up his life than give up his freedom." Walker did not record his reaction to the captain's address, though he saved a copy of it.[3]

Over the next few months, the *Massachusetts* conducted several shakedown cruises between Boston and Casco Bay in Maine, and in August (as US Marines went ashore on Guadalcanal) Walker became the second division officer in charge of Turret Two. In the Chesapeake Bay, he experimented with new uses for the sixteen-inch guns, firing them on a flat trajectory to see if the towering shell splashes they created could deter or deflect attacking torpedo planes. He concluded afterward that it was "not an overly successful idea."[4]

Along with the other Forties, Walker was promoted to full lieutenant on October 1, 1942, and only a few weeks later it became evident that something big was up when Rear Admiral Robert C. Giffen, who had commanded the *Washington* at Scapa Flow, came on board with a large group of staff officers. Within the crew, "Scuttlebutt was flying fast," and in days, the *Massachusetts* and her escorts were at sea, headed, as Walker put it, "for parts unknown." Three days out, the battleship and her escorts joined an enormous convoy of troopships, supply ships, and warships of every type. Officially, it was Task Force 34, and it was under the overall command of another rear admiral, H. Kent Hewitt. In addition to the transports and escorts, there were two other (much older) battleships: the *New York* and *Texas*, both of which the Forties had ridden during their first class cruise. There were also seven cruisers, including the *Tuscaloosa*, back from the icy Barents Sea with Bill Braybrook still on board, plus thirty-eight destroyers, several of which carried other newly promoted lieutenants from the class of 1940. Air cover was provided by the carrier *Ranger* and four small auxiliary carriers that had been converted from oilers. It was a far greater invasion force than the one that had targeted Guadalcanal two months earlier. Once the whole force was organized into columns and files, it covered six hundred square miles of ocean. On October 26, it headed east, across the Atlantic, toward Africa.[5]

From the start, the Allied strategy for World War II had been to defeat Germany first and remain on the defensive in the Pacific until the Nazi regime was overthrown. It had not worked out that way, as we have seen, but politics as well as strategy kept the Allies faithful to the original notion, at least officially. Germany was a far greater economic powerhouse than Japan, and her armies occupied most of Europe. Churchill in particular was committed to the Germany-first strategy. The difficulty was that in 1942 the Allies simply lacked the resources to execute it. Though the United States had made impressive strides toward full mobilization since Pearl Harbor, it was evident to all that there was simply no way that, even in combination with the British and Canadians, it could effect a lodgment on the mainland of Europe and come to grips with the Wehrmacht in 1942. Despite that, Roosevelt, who feared that the Soviets might collapse or, worse, make another deal with Hitler, had assured Stalin's representative, Vyacheslav Molotov, that the western Allies would do something that year—1942—to take pressure off the Red Army. But what? Churchill insisted that the only place an Allied offensive was possible was North Africa.

The US Army chief of staff, George C. Marshall, thought that was a terrible idea. First of all, there were no Germans in French North Africa, so how was that supposed to relieve pressure on the Red Army? Second, Marshall also feared, with some justification, that once the Allies ventured into the Mediterranean, it would suck up reinforcements, supplies, equipment, and all the other things needed to build up Allied forces in England for an eventual cross-Channel invasion of occupied France in 1943.[6]

Marshall was not wrong. Yet Roosevelt knew that the American public, not to mention Stalin, would not tolerate doing nothing for a full year while forces were built up in England. Something had to be done against the European enemy, and it had to be done in 1942. In the end, therefore, he approved the decision of the Combined Chiefs to mount an amphibious assault into French North Africa in early November. It was designated Operation Torch.

The American invasion convoy, including the *Massachusetts*, arrived off the coast of French Morocco on November 7. Another convoy filled with British troops passed through the Strait of Gibraltar that same week and headed for French Algeria. The Allies nursed a faint hope that the French might accept them as liberators, but despite intense negotiations, the French saw the Americans—and especially the British—as invaders rather than liberators. As Pierre Laval, the pro-Nazi French prime minister put it, "We are attacked; we will defend ourselves."[7]

The French were not without resources. The forty-thousand-ton French battleship *Jean Bart* in Casablanca Harbor had eight fifteen-inch guns housed in two enormous quad turrets. Alas for the French, she was still unfinished, immobile in her drydock, and had only one working turret. Even so, the big guns of that turret posed the greatest threat to the American invasion. As the *Massachusetts* approached the shore after dark on November 7, Hooky Walker did not know what to expect. He noticed that the 167-foot El Hank lighthouse at Casablanca was still operating and hoped that meant the French were unaware of their arrival. Reveille on the *Massachusetts* sounded early at 3:40, breakfast was served at 4:00, and at 5:45 the entire crew was at battle stations. The big question was: Would the French fight?

The answer came at 7:05, when a French shore battery near the lighthouse opened fire. Admiral Giffen sent the prearranged message, "Play Ball," and the *Massachusetts* and the other American ships opened fire. The French gunners on the *Jean Bart* fired back, and their aim was distressingly accurate. Walker noted that they "managed to straddle us in four salvos." In order to identify the fall of shot and adjust their aim, the French, like everyone else, used different colored dye packets with their heavy shells to determine which shell splashes were from which battery so they could adjust fire as needed. The El Hank battery used a green dye, and the *Jean Bart* a yellow dye. Shells from the *Jean Bart* landed so close to the fantail of the *Massachusetts* that they covered the entire stern with yellow dye. The French also targeted the cruisers. Bill Braybrook noted that some of the *Jean Bart*'s salvos "landed within a few feet of the *Tuscaloosa*." Afterward, Braybrook decided that "the stubbornness and accuracy of the fire of this enemy, who later became our ally, far surpassed anything we later encountered from the Germans."[8]

Walker was proud of his turret crew, nearly all of them new recruits, and he reported afterward that "the conduct of the crew, both officers and enlisted, was superb." They managed to fire a salvo every sixty seconds, each salvo sending six tons of explosives toward the targets, and they maintained that rate of fire throughout the battle. He did note some issues with the guns themselves. The constant firing heated the gun barrels to such a degree that one of them jammed and would not return to the firing position. Another problem was that the ship had only armor-piercing shells, which were effective against the *Jean Bart*, though less so against the shore batteries. When the first salvos landed ashore, the French gunners headed into their bombproofs. Walker noted that "as soon as we stopped [firing] the enemy re-manned the gun and picked up their fire." The rate of fire also stressed the rifled sleeves inside the gun barrels, whose function was to put a spin on the projectiles to increase their accuracy. After a score of salvos, the sleeves began to work their way out of the barrels. By the end of the action, they protruded three-quarters of an inch from the muzzles, potentially reducing accuracy. Even so, observers reported smoke roiling out of the harbor, suggesting that the *Jean Bart* was on fire. A few minutes past 8:00, a sixteen-inch shell from the *Massachusetts* hit the base of the one operational turret on the *Jean Bart* and jammed it in place. Soon the *Jean Bart* herself was "a blazing wreck." Walker noted laconically that "we managed to score enough hits" to put the French battleship "out of action."[9]

After that, Walker and the other gun captains on the *Massachusetts* shifted their attention to the shore batteries, which were "causing problems with quite accurate fire." Indeed, three shells from shore actually struck the *Massachusetts*, though they did no serious damage. American marksmanship was aided by spotting reports from two American float planes, called Kingfishers. The Kingfishers were not combat aircraft, and French fighter planes quicky shot one of them down. The pilot of the other, with two French fighters on his tail, requested support from the *Massachusetts*: "Am coming in on starboard bow with a couple of hostile aircraft on my tail," he radioed. "Pick them off." He added, perhaps unnecessarily, "I am the one in front." The five-inch guns on the *Massachusetts* opened up, and with the arrival of American fighter planes from the *Ranger*, the French fighters fled.[10]

Heavy guns and French aircraft were not the only dangers. The French also had several submarines, and one of them fired a spread of four torpedoes at the *Massachusetts*. The big battleship turned into the approaching torpedoes and managed to comb them. Walker watched with some trepidation as three of them passed down one side, and one streaked past on the other.

While the *Massachusetts* dueled with the *Jean Bart* off Casablanca, American troops were going ashore at Fedala, a dozen miles to the north. There, despite the overwhelming odds against them, three French destroyers charged defiantly out of the harbor, behaving, as one British officer put it, "with a bravery worthy of a better cause." The American heavy cruisers, including the *Tuscaloosa*, took them under fire, sinking one and forcing the others to retire. After that, Walker noted, the shore batteries ceased fire.[11]

The entire sea battle had lasted only a few hours. Walker wondered if some of the big German warships might try to interfere, though in fact there were no German heavy ships in the area. That was just as well, for the *Massachusetts* had fired off 90 percent of its sixteen-inch ammunition and there was no resupply closer than Norfolk. That became moot in a few days when the Anglo-Americans reached an accommodation with the French, allowing the *Massachusetts* and the *Tuscaloosa* to return to the United States for resupply and refit.

Walker was happy to get several days of shore liberty in Boston. He was pleased when Navy beat Army 14–0 on Saturday, November 28, but his strongest memory of his visit was a fire at the Cocoanut Grove nightclub in Boston that same night. Rumored to be under mob protection, the nightclub was packed to twice its legal capacity and its exit doors had been chained shut to prevent more people from coming in. When an electrical short started a fire, there was a panic, and despite rescue efforts by US Navy sailors and others, the result was the death of nearly five hundred people. It was the worst nightclub disaster in history.[12]

Back in North Africa, the Allied theater commander, General Dwight Eisenhower, had hoped to rush swiftly eastward after the initial landings to secure Tunis, the principal port of Tunisia. Instead, the Allied advance was slowed by difficult logistics, bad weather, and the German decision to send forces under General Erwin Rommel into North Africa. A sharp American reverse in the Battle of Kasserine Pass in February slowed the advance further. As George Marshall had feared, the Allied foray into Africa required additional support, attracting supplies and material into the theater like a magnet. Instead of a quick success, the battle for North Africa turned into a months-long slog. Worse, from Marshall's point of view, after North Africa was pacified, the Allied high command decided to jump across the narrow waist of the Mediterranean to Sicily. By May 1943 the Allies had nearly eight hundred thousand men in North Africa, and it seemed logical to use them in the Mediterranean rather than try to transfer all or most of them to England for a cross-Channel invasion. As Marshall had predicted, the foray into North Africa effectively derailed any possible invasion of France in 1943.

Sam Edelstein's father had not wanted him to attend the Naval Academy. An attorney in Spokane, Washington, Edelstein Senior had hoped that his son would go to Gonzaga University, then to law school, and join him in his practice. Edelstein himself, however, never regretted his decision. "I loved our Naval Academy experiences," he wrote later, "even the trials of Plebe Year." His classroom performance was excellent, and he made a number of good friends.

In spite of his enthusiasm and his academic prowess, however, he did not graduate. He was one of many in the class dismissed for "defective vision." After failing several eye exams, he was invited to resign in June 1938 after his youngster year. Though he graduated from the University of Washington, he always considered himself a member of the Naval Academy class of 1940. At Washington, he joined the NROTC unit and majored in electrical engineering ("double E"). He was commissioned a navy ensign in May 1941, a year after his former classmates. That made him junior to them in rank, and yet his expertise in electrical engineering gave him a leg up, not only on his classmates, but on most naval officers in 1941. As a double-E major, he was one of a small number of naval officers who had the background needed to understand the complexities and capabilities of the still-emerging technology called Radio Detection and Ranging: radar.[13]

In 1941 only nineteen ships in the entire US Navy had radar sets, three of them battleships that were in Pearl Harbor on the Day of Infamy. Yet the technology was so new few officers knew what to do with it. When the USS *Pennsylvania* got a radar set, her executive officer chose one of the Forties, Frederick "Mike" Michaels, to be the radar officer, presumably because he was the junior man in the wardroom. Michaels was surprised since, as he put it later, neither the exec nor he even knew what a "radar" was.[14]

The initial CXAM radar sets, designed and built by RCA, were bulky and cumbersome: six feet high, five feet wide, and two feet deep, the equipment barely fit in a radio shack below the bridge. The telltale antenna, which many believed looked like a bedspring, was installed on the mast. Early radars were designed to detect incoming airplanes at a range of up to fifty miles, but they were unreliable and difficult to use. For one thing, they gave the bearing of the contact on one dial and the range on another. If the first dial indicated a possible contact, the radar operator had to hand crank the antenna around to that bearing, punch a button to indicate if it was inside the fifty-mile range, then confirm that on a second indicator. Only then could he report to the bridge that he had a possible contact.[15]

There were other types of radar. Two dozen longwave SC radar sets were installed on smaller ships, including, as we have seen, on John Lacouture's USS *Blue*. Like the CXAM units, SC radars were designed to detect incoming

---

* The *California* had a CXAM radar unit, which rather miraculously survived the Japanese attack unharmed. Afterward, it was removed from the ship and set up on a hill overlooking Honolulu.

THE MED   203

aircraft. For both types, detecting surface ships was more difficult. The horizontal radar beams did not follow the curvature of the earth and were therefore effective only out to about twelve miles, at which distance most approaching ships would be visible with binoculars. Another problem was that returns from nearby land masses confused the readings, as had been the case at Savo Island. Finally, the data had to be interpreted by inexperienced operators who often did not have their own ship's navigational data at hand to determine the relative bearing to a contact. It was cumbersome enough that most veteran officers remained skeptical of its value and tended to ignore it.[16]

By the end of 1942, however, a far more sophisticated radar system—the SG radar, built by Raytheon—began to arrive in the fleet. This system relied on a shorter wavelength and featured the now-familiar circular screen, called a planned position indicator (PPI), with its sweeping arm, like a high-speed second hand on a clock, that flashed brightly with each contact, providing both the range and the bearing to the contact. Commanding officers began to appreciate that this new technology could allow them to "see" in the dark—or in fog—giving them a tremendous advantage. At about the same time, another innovation was the establishment of what came to be called a "combat information center," or CIC, just below the command bridge. There input from all sources—including radar—could be collected and evaluated and could produce recommendations to send up to the bridge. After that, it became common for a ship's executive officer (XO) to position himself in the CIC from which he could coordinate the battle. It was a game changer. Doc Weatherup thought "it took the Navy a little time to really grasp the potential of radar and to evolve an organization to exploit it." And due to Sam Edelstein's double-E background, he was on the front edge of that effort.[17]

In June 1941, still six months before the Japanese attack on Pearl Harbor, Edelstein was one of thirteen ensigns sent to take a postgraduate training course at the Naval Reserve Radio School at Bowdoin College in Maine. There was one other Forty in the class: Paul Desmond, who had been plucked from the deck crew of the USS *Maryland* back in 1935 and ordered to the Naval Academy. After a series of technical (but unclassified) courses at Bowdoin, both Edelstein and Desmond moved on to the Naval Research Laboratory in Anacostia near Washington, DC. There about fifty ensigns received classified instruction from radio technician warrant officers. Afterward, Desmond returned to the aircraft carrier *Ranger*, where a CXAM radar had been installed in his absence and where he was immediately reassigned as the radar division officer. As for Edelstein, after a tour of staff duty with the Atlantic fleet's anti-submarine forces, he got orders to the Mediterranean.[18]

To get there, Edelstein rode an American-built but British-manned LST (Landing Ship, Tank) from New York. LSTs were extremely useful, even invaluable, in amphibious operations, but they were not comfortable ships for passengers. With a flat bottom and blunt bow, they pitched and rolled extravagantly even in a mild sea, and the one Edelstein rode had two US Navy Yard tugs as deck cargo, which made the ship top heavy and increased her tendency to roll. Worse, at least from Edelstein's point of view, the chow on board was prepared to the less discriminating (or more resigned) tastes of Royal Navy seamen. Edelstein was the senior US Navy officer on board, and he complained about the food repeatedly to the ship's commanding officer, a Royal Navy reserve lieutenant. The LST's skipper was very likely relieved when the pesky American transferred to a different ship in mid-ocean. That ship carried Edelstein to Oran on the coast of Algeria, where he arrived in May 1943. By then, preparations for the invasion of Sicily were well underway, and Edelstein noted that LSTs were conducting practice landings on the African coast night and day.[19]

From Oran, Edelstein caught a hop on a DC-3 to Algiers, where he reported to Rear Admiral Richard Connolly's staff headquarters, located in a former elementary school. (Among the many adjustments Edelstein had to make there was dealing with low, tiny urinals in the head.) There was no doubt he had arrived at the front line. German bombers attacked almost every night. It was Edelstein's first experience of being under fire, and when the air raid alarm sounded on his first night, he dashed out of his second-story room and took cover in a nearby culvert. Eventually, he grew accustomed to the nightly visits and came to ignore them.[20]

Edelstein had been sent to the Mediterranean on the virtual eve of the Allied invasion of Sicily to supervise the installation of an SG radar set in Admiral Connolly's flagship, the USS *Biscayne* (AVP-11). To get to the ship, Edelstein rode in a truck convoy to Bizerte, during which he saw "an almost endless column of German prisoners marching in the opposite direction."[21]

Edelstein and several enlisted electronics technicians uncrated the SG radar components on the *Biscayne* and began to install them. They laid the foundations for the radar shack in the chart house, and Edelstein set up the antenna on the *Biscayne*'s single mast. Fitting the new technology into a space not designed for it proved challenging. He had a number of "anxious moments" as he manipulated the radar components to fit the space. He knew that if the

THE MED 205

sensitive elements were bent or heated too much, they could malfunction. Yet by the first week of July, the radar was installed and working fine, and Edelstein returned to Algiers.[22]

Admiral Connolly was impressed, though he wanted someone on board who could monitor and repair the system if something went wrong, so he asked Admiral Hewitt if Lieutenant Edelstein could be assigned to the ship's company for the invasion of Sicily. Edelstein headed back to Bizerte, where he learned that in his absence a German bomb had landed close alongside the *Biscayne* and sent shards of shrapnel into the junior officer's stateroom he had occupied. Edelstein felt "truly lucky" not to have been there at the time.[23]

Within days, the *Biscayne* was at sea bound for Sicily, part of an invasion convoy even larger than the one that had targeted French North Africa. Edelstein was impressed by all the gold braid on board, and he took comfort from the fact that the ship had been built near his hometown of Spokane, Washington. The sea conditions were challenging. As Edelstein put it, "The wind came up and kicked the sea around quite a little bit." In fact, the waves crested at twelve feet, and green water crashed over the decks of some of the smaller ships, slowing them down and putting the invasion behind schedule. The *Biscayne* arrived off the south coast of Sicily in the Gulf of Gela on schedule in the early morning hours of July 9, 1943. Almost immediately, searchlights on shore snapped on, bathing the ships in a bright white light. Edelstein described the glare as "blinding," noting that "the whole ship seemed to bask in daylight." In a V-mail letter to his father, he wrote that it made him feel like "a gobbler at a Kentucky turkey shoot."[24]

Edelstein stood next to Admiral Connolly on the bridge of the *Biscayne* and was impressed that the admiral did not react to, or even seem to notice, the glare of the searchlights. "The Admiral was certainly a cool cucumber," Edelstein wrote. He believed that "most people would have had the impulse to start shooting out the searchlights," yet Connelly stuck to the timetable and waited for the rest of the fleet to catch up.[25]

At first light, the big ships in the invasion fleet opened fire, which made quite a display. Edelstein went down to the deck to watch the fall of shot, "blithely rubbernecking," as he put it. The *Biscayne* did not participate in the shelling, but the heavy gunships nearby sent salvo after salvo toward the shore. "All the shells had various colored tracers on them," he wrote his father, "and they would arc through the air for miles, their trajectories illuminated by their tracer lights." When they hit, Edelstein heard "a dull boom" from shore.

At once the searchlights all went dark. After that, the smaller vessels moved in and sprayed the beach with heavy machine gun fire. "As it was still quite dark, the beach seemed to have a lacework of colored streaks over it from the tracers of these smaller guns." Edelstein found the impact of naval guns truly awesome. "You simply can't realize the accuracy and devastation of naval gunfire until you've seen it."[26]

Small landing craft filled with soldiers had been circling for hours, and at about 4:30 they headed for the beach. The *Biscayne* remained close to the landing beach, only a few thousand yards offshore. Later in the war Connelly would be endowed with the moniker "Close-in Connelly" for his tendency to keep his command ship near the battle front. Edelstein noted that the *Biscayne* was "peacefully swinging around her anchor chain," sending off radio orders "right and left." Soon enough, however, shell splashes began landing nearby, reminding everyone that it was, indeed, a combat zone. Connolly ignored the fire for some time until "the tall splashes of the shells hitting the water grew uncomfortably near." Edelstein watched one of them land only a hundred yards off the ship's beam. Connolly decided that was too close and ordered the flagship to move away, or as Edelstein put it, "to get the hell out of there." At the same time, the *Biscayne* opened fire with her own five-inch guns. Edelstein did not know the *Biscayne* was about to open fire, and he was standing next to one of the gun mounts when the concussion of the opening salvo literally knocked him down. He thought the ship had been hit and quickly moved to the side away from the landing beach. When he realized that it was his own ship's guns shooting, he felt sheepish, though he remained a little deaf in one ear for the rest of his life.[27]

There was uncertainty within the Allied high command about how tenaciously the Italians would resist. Many Italians had never been enthusiastic about Mussolini's war. Eisenhower's official communiqué on the landings emphasized "fierce resistance," yet Edelstein was impressed by how quickly the American soldiers seized control of the beaches. He was not the only one. Another passenger on the *Biscayne* that day was the journalist Ernie Pyle, who wrote in his column that "we had expected a terrific slaughter on the beaches and there was none." He reported that "it gave you a jumpy, insecure feeling of something dreadfully wrong somewhere." For his part, Edelstein attributed it to "the combination of sea and air power, plus our well planned landings," though he might have added that another factor was a lack of Italian zeal. One US soldier recalled later that a group of Italians manning a machine gun position on the beach "simply refused to fire on us and allowed themselves to be captured."[28]

Edelstein decided that the *Biscayne* was a lucky ship, and wrote his father that "instead of carrying around lucky pennies or rabbit's feet for charms, I'm going to saw me off a section of its mast and hang it around my neck for future life insurance."[29]

Exactly as George Marshall had feared, the Allied foray into the Mediterranean had drawn off men, supplies, arms, and equipment that might otherwise have gone to England for a possible 1943 invasion of France. The conquest of Sicily, however, did undermine Italian support for the war, and on July 24, 1943, the Fascist Grand Council in Rome voted no confidence in Mussolini's government. Almost at once, a successor government began surreptitious negotiations for an Italian surrender.

17

Submarine Warfare

In the summer of 1938, when a small (175-foot) R-class submarine visited the Naval Academy to introduce the new second classmen to the Silent Service, Philip Thompson Glennon, often known as P.T., had been one of the few members of the class who thought the trip to the bottom of the Chesapeake Bay was interesting and exciting. Once he completed his two years aboard the light cruiser *Cincinnati*, rather than move up to, say, a heavy cruiser, he applied to the US Navy's Submarine School. His choice is noteworthy in light of the fact that his father, uncle, and grandfather had all commanded battleships. Perhaps he chose submarines as a modest rebellion against family tradition. Whatever his motivation, during the summer of 1942, when John Lacouture and Doc Weatherup headed to flight school in New Orleans, and Mike Hanley and George Kronmiller went to Lakehurst, New Jersey, to train on blimps, P. T. Glennon reported to the Submarine Base New London, which, despite its name, was located in Groton, Connecticut, across the river from New London.

The Sub School was a sprawling facility that included diesel laboratories, torpedo shops, periscope shops, and a one-hundred-foot-tall water tank whose purpose was to train submarine crews how to escape from a downed sub.* In the classroom, Glennon studied diesel engineering, subaqueous navigation, torpedo overhaul and repair, and the strategy and tactics of undersea warfare. Outside the classroom, there was hands-on training in actual submarines, though they were old, nearly obsolete models.

During World War I, Congress had approved the construction of several classes of American submarines, ranging from small O-class to midsize R-class and larger S-class boats. (Then, as now, submarines are referred to as "boats"

---

* A similar escape tower on Ford Island in Pearl Harbor was repurposed as an aircraft control tower after the Japanese attack, and a third such tower at the submarine base nearby was later converted into a cocktail bar, which offers a spectacular view of the naval base.

rather than ships.) Only seven of the R-class subs were still in service in 1942, and they had all been sent to Key West to operate against German U-boats in the Caribbean because submarines were one of the most effective weapons against other submarines. The S-class boats, along with the newer and larger fleet submarines, were all on active service in the Pacific, so Glennon and his fellow aspirants trained on the few remaining O-class boats. In effect, they were the submarine equivalent of the Stearman N2S biplanes used in flight training. Displacing only 520 tons, they had four torpedo tubes and a top speed of just 11.5 knots. Still, they allowed the students to grasp the fundamentals of submarine warfare.[1]

One daunting aspect of the training was the requirement to demonstrate mastery of what was called the Momsen Lung (invented by Navy Captain Charles Momsen): a primitive underwater breathing device that relied on soda lime to remove carbon dioxide from exhaled air so that it could be rebreathed—up to a point. It was supposed to allow crewmen escaping from a crippled submarine to survive an ascent from as much as 100 feet down. Every student in the program, including Glennon, had to demonstrate his ability to use a Momsen Lung and ascend from the bottom of the training tank to the top. Glennon successfully completed that and all the other elements of the program and graduated in mid-June, a few days after the Battle of Midway. He then headed west, first to California, then out to Pearl Harbor, to join the crew of the USS *Greenling* (SS-213).[2]

The *Greenling* was a *Gato*-class submarine, newer, larger, and faster than the boats Glennon had trained on at Groton. Only the second of an eventual seventy-seven of her type built during the war, the *Greenling* represented a huge technological advance over earlier versions. At 311 feet long and displacing fifteen hundred tons (twenty-five hundred tons submerged), she was roughly the size of a destroyer escort. Instead of four torpedo tubes, she had ten, six in the bow and four astern. With her four engines, she could make twenty-one knots surfaced and had more than twice the range of an O-class boat—more than eleven thousand miles—which meant she could operate in the western Pacific to threaten Japan's maritime traffic, which carried the raw materials, especially oil, from the newly conquered provinces in South Asia to the home islands. Glennon was no doubt gratified to discover that the *Greenling* was also far more habitable, with larger compartments and more headroom, plus air conditioning, refrigerated food storage ("reefers" in Navy lingo), coinless Coca-Cola machines, and a coffee urn that was kept filled round the clock. The *Greenling* even had freshwater showers, though they were seldom used when underway in order to preserve electricity. With sixty men living and working in a confined space for two or three months at a time, it was essential that every member of a sub's crew have an even disposition, and officers and men were tested for that before being assigned to submarine duty.[3]

Some considered the *Greenling* an unlucky boat. For one thing, she had nearly been sunk on her shakedown cruise off New London in February, when a patrolling US Navy Catalina mistook her for a U-boat and bombed her, though unsuccessfully. She also had little luck on her first war patrol before Glennon joined the crew. On April 20, 1942, her skipper, Henry Bruton, had fired six torpedoes at a large freighter, none of which had exploded. He tried two more, with one missing forward and the other exploding prematurely. So frustrated was Bruton that he surfaced and took the ship under fire with the *Greenling*'s three-inch deck gun. The target ship fired back, and when a shell flew directly over the conning tower, Bruton called off the attack and submerged. The ship escaped. On May 4 the *Greenling* sank a midsize Japanese cargo ship with a single torpedo. However, her great opportunity seemed to arrive a few days later, when lookouts spotted a Japanese convoy. As Bruton tracked it, he and everyone else on board suddenly heard "loud high speed screws" coming fast. Bruton raised the periscope and saw a destroyer "heading directly for us." He ordered a crash dive, and, as the boat descended, depth charges began exploding close alongside. The boat shook violently; ventilation valves sprang leaks; the periscope was jarred out of position. After enduring several hours of such punishment, the explosions finally ceased. The destroyers, satisfied that the American sub was no longer a threat, sped away to catch up with the convoy, which escaped.[4]

Glennon was not on board for any of that, but it affected him nonetheless, because the experience so rattled one of the boat's junior officers that when the *Greenling* returned to Pearl Harbor in July he asked to be relieved. That created a vacancy that was quickly filled by the newly arrived Lieutenant Glennon. Indeed, he barely had time to stow his seabag before the *Greenling* was underway again, heading for Truk Atoll, thirty-six hundred miles to the west in the mid-Pacific.[5]

It is noteworthy that the United States conducted a campaign of submarine warfare at all, since Germany's use of unrestricted submarine warfare in World War I had been the official justification for America's declaration of war in 1917. "Unrestricted" meant exactly that. Every ship proceeding to or from enemy ports was fair game: from aircraft carriers and battleships to cargo ships, transport ships, even fishing scows. They could be attacked without notice and without mercy. In his 1917 speech to Congress in which he called for a declaration of war against Germany, Woodrow Wilson affected incredulity when he noted that "vessels of every kind, whatever their flag, their character, their cargo, their destination, their errand, have been ruthlessly sent to the bottom without warning and without thought of help or mercy." The president could hardly imagine a government so callous as to sanction such inhumane acts. And yet the first order that came out of Washington after the Japanese attack on Pearl Harbor was to "execute unrestricted air and submarine warfare against Japan."[6]

Early on, US sub skippers were encouraged to seek out enemy warships, and while they remained valuable targets, by mid-1942, when Glennon joined the *Greenling*, strategists in Washington had changed their minds, or at least their focus. The new primary mission was economic warfare: to sever Japan's maritime lifeline by destroying the ships that kept Japan supplied with the raw materials she needed to sustain her economy. It was the same strategy employed by German Admiral Karl Dönitz against England in the Atlantic.

During the first year of the war, American efforts to implement that strategy against Japan were hampered by several factors. The first was that the US Navy simply did not have enough submarines to do it. The United States had fifty-one submarines in the Pacific in 1941—curiously, about the same number Dönitz had had in 1939. And since at any given moment a third of them might be in port for resupply and another third transiting to or from the western Pacific, the United States could have only about fifteen to eighteen subs on station at any given time.

A related factor was the long distances the subs had to travel. After the loss of the Philippines, American subs operated out of either Australia or Hawaii. From Hawaii in particular, it could take ten days to two weeks to get on station, and of course an equal number of days to get back. Since the amount of food and fuel they carried mandated that patrols last no more than fifty-six to sixty days, that gave them barely a month on station, or until they expended all their torpedoes.

Another weakness was that, initially at least, the United States did not develop a unified strategy for the use of submarines. Individual subs were sent out on "war patrols" to a designated geographical area with orders to do whatever damage they could to whatever they could find.

Yet the biggest factor limiting American submarine success in the early months of the war was the disappointing performance of the Mark XIV torpedo. Because an explosion under a ship's keel was far more lethal than the impact of a torpedo hitting its side, the Mark XIV had been designed to pass *under* the targeted ship and detonate when it recognized the magnetic anomaly of a ship above it. Unknown to the designers, however, the Mark XIV torpedo ran eleven feet deeper than the settings indicated, and therefore it often did not explode at all. Another problem was that torpedoes had to run four hundred yards toward the target before the warhead armed itself, and the Mark XIV was sufficiently delicate that it occasionally exploded at that point. That not only foiled the attack, it also revealed the presence of the submarine and generally provoked a furious counterattack. And finally, the navigational gyros in the torpedoes could malfunction and send a torpedo veering off unpredictably, or, worse, speeding back toward the sub that had fired it. When returning submarine skippers reported these problems, they encountered skepticism from their superiors, especially the engineers at the Bureau of Ordnance who had designed the torpedoes.[7] When Glennon joined the *Greenling* in July 1942, Henry Bruton had just received an earful about wasting eight torpedoes on a single ship and failing to hit it. Instead of seeking to discover why the torpedoes behaved as they did, Bruton's superiors attributed the results to inexperience, timidity, or both. Such attitudes explain why the torpedo problem went unresolved until late 1943. The most prominent historian of the submarine war, Clay Blair, concluded that "the torpedo scandal of the U.S. submarine force in World War II was one of the worst in the history of any kind of warfare."[8]

For Glennon, the ten-day passage from Pearl Harbor to Truk was essentially a shakedown cruise. With only six officers on board, he was immediately inserted into the watch rotation. Since the captain and the exec did not stand watch, that meant the rest of them had to stand watch two hours on and four hours off around the clock seven days a week, plus, of course, their regular duties. He easily adjusted to the markedly less formal environment in a wartime sub, where saluting was kept to a minimum, officers wore open-necked khaki shirts and slacks or even shorts, and sailors worked in T-shirts and dungarees. It was a far cry from the Naval Academy or even the protocols on the peacetime *Cincinnati*. In addition, the maritime geography was also new to him. Glennon confessed later that until that moment he "had never heard of Truk, nor of some of the places we passed enroute such as the island of Ponape and the atoll of Eniwetok."[9]

Truk (now called Chuuk) was the principal base of the Imperial Japanese Navy in the central Pacific. Like many of the islands in the Caroline archipelago, it

SUBMARINE WARFARE

was an atoll with a large central lagoon formed by a coral reef that had grown atop the rim of an extinct and submerged volcano. Given the maritime traffic in and out of that commodious harbor, there were abundant targets for a hunting submarine, most of them freighters, called "marus" due to the Japanese practice of adding *maru* to a ship's name for good luck.* But while the area around Truk offered good hunting, it was also dangerous, for in addition to Japanese destroyers and airplanes, there were other aspects of the marine environment that made it perilous.

A submarine's unique characteristic is its ability to hide. On the surface, a *Gato*-class sub was remarkably fragile. A single hit from a three- or four-inch gun could send it to the bottom. It was its near invisibility while submerged that made it a kind of stealth weapon. Consequently, once it was on station, the *Greenling*, like most other subs, generally remained submerged during the daylight hours, surfacing only at night. Yet submerging did not grant perfect invisibility. For one thing, the waters around Truk were isothermal, meaning that the water temperature did not change significantly with an increase in depth. That mattered because submarines would often position themselves below a thermal layer that could deflect or distort sonar returns. Absent such layers, the subs were more detectable. In addition, as Glennon noted, "The water [around Truk] was clear making aircraft detection of the silhouette of our hull more possible when we were submerged during daylight hours." As a result of these factors, the *Greenling* was never completely out of danger, as Glennon quickly learned when Japanese planes "dropped depth charges on us several times."[10]

At night, it was different. In the dark, the low profile of a submarine was difficult to spot, even with Japan's excellent optics, whereas a large transport, even one running blacked out, found it harder to hide. Consequently, like German U-boats in the Atlantic, American subs in the Pacific were night hunters. After full dark, the *Greenling* came up to periscope depth and, after the skipper took a quick look around the horizon through the periscope, surfaced. Lookouts scrambled out onto her small conning tower and peered out into the blackness with their binoculars, searching for a dim silhouette or a wisp of smoke between the dark sky and even darker sea. Though the *Greenling* would later be equipped with a surface-search radar, at this point, as Glennon put it, "We had to use 'seaman's eye' to estimate ranges and visual bearings to solve the

---

* *Maru* translates as beloved or perfection, and the symbol for it is a circle. That symbology also carries the implication that the ship will complete the perfect circle of a round trip and return safely to port.

night attack fire control problem." Those estimates were fed into what was called a torpedo data computer (TDC), which, despite its name was actually an electromechanical analog calculator that determined the proper settings for a shot. The TDC operator entered the bearing and range to the target, its estimated speed, the angle on the bow, and the speed of the torpedo (either thirty-three or forty-five knots, depending on the range), and crewmen in the torpedo room applied the settings.[11]

A lot of submarine service was tedious. As one sub veteran put it, "Continuing the vigilance hour after hour and on into days could be more wearing than when occasional [ship] tops came in view." Days, even weeks, might pass between ship sightings, and the crewmen played a lot of acey-deucy and cribbage, or they studied for their advancement exams. Then, suddenly, a trace of smoke on the horizon would provoke a frenzy of activity as the sub headed off at full speed toward a possible target. That, in turn, could be followed by a period of high tension as the sub tracked the target, carefully maneuvering for a shot. Whether the attack was successful or not, it could provoke a swift counterattack by an escorting destroyer that compelled the sub to dive and endure a barrage of depth charges that ratcheted tensions even higher.[12]

Glennon was excited when, on July 24, 1942, only the boat's second night on station, lookouts sighted a medium-sized trawler. Bruton ordered the torpedo tubes flooded with seawater, waited for the pressure to equalize, then ordered the outer torpedo doors opened. He maneuvered the *Greenling* into position while others called out the bearing, speed, and angle on the bow. When the numbers lined up, Bruton ordered "Fire!" and the torpedo officer hit the plunger. There was a slight shudder when the torpedo left the tube, and Glennon felt the pressure change in his ears as air from the torpedo tube was released back into the boat. Two more torpedoes followed at ten-second intervals. As the seconds ticked past, everyone waited for an explosion. It never came; all three torpedoes either missed or failed to explode. The results were the same two nights later, when the *Greenling* fired a four-torpedo spread at a large tanker. This time, Glennon "heard muffled explosions shortly after firing," suggesting that the torpedoes had detonated prematurely.[13]

There was some success. A week later, on August 4, a topside lookout spied another ship, and again the boat prepared to execute an attack. It was a large vessel, and Bruton initially thought it might be an aircraft carrier. Determined it would not get away, Bruton tracked it for four hours, sometimes hiding in rain squalls, and when the numbers lined up, he fired four torpedoes. All four missed. The target—whatever it was—increased speed and began zigzagging. Determined it would not escape, Bruton pursued. Several hours later, the *Greenling* fired three more torpedoes. This time, two of them exploded and, after twenty minutes, the ship went under.[14]

It was a troop transport. That became evident when the *Greenling* surfaced amid dozens of lifeboats filled with Japanese soldiers, as well as other survivors trying to stay afloat in the water. The sub's crew pulled one of them on board. Taking a prisoner was unusual. It had been hammered into every Japanese soldier and sailor that allowing yourself to be made a prisoner dishonored yourself, your family, and your emperor. Consequently, most Japanese fought off would-be rescuers, preferring to drown. A second reason was that there was simply no room for prisoners on a submarine. And finally, remaining in the vicinity of a sunken ship to collect survivors gave enemy ships or planes an opportunity to find and attack the sub. It was normal practice, therefore, to ignore survivors in the water.* This particular prisoner, however, was a Korean who had been conscripted by the Japanese as a laborer, which may explain why he did not rate a place in a lifeboat. He could speak a little English and was happy to supply whatever information he could, including the name of the ship: *Brazil Maru*.[15]

Service on a sub was dangerous. That became evident the next night, when an enemy aircraft suddenly appeared overhead and dropped two depth bombs that landed dangerously close alongside. Bruton ordered a crash dive, and as the *Greenling* descended everyone on board could hear approaching propellers in the water. Each type of ship made a distinct sound. Propellers on transports made a low-pitch throbbing sound; destroyers produced a high-frequency cavitation that was entirely different. It was evident that these were destroyers, and that there were three of them, one on each side and one astern. Soon, sharp pings from their sonars resonated against the hull. Bruton ordered, "Rig for depth charges. Rig for silent running." Watertight doors were closed; valves in the ventilation lines secured; machinery not required for maneuvering was

---

* Some skippers did more than that. Five months later, in January 1943, Commander Dudley "Mush" Morton in the sub *Wahoo* sank a troop transport in the Bismarck Sea, and after surfacing he ordered the sub's crew to machine gun the survivors. When his XO, Richard O'Kane, remonstrated with him, Morton told him that if those soldiers escaped to shore, they would kill Americans, so it was his duty to make sure that didn't happen. Far from being chastised, Morton was awarded the Navy Cross. Interestingly, at the postwar Nuremberg Trials, the Allies accused German Admiral Karl Dönitz of crimes against humanity for ordering his U-boat skippers not to rescue survivors. He was found not guilty of that charge in large part because Admiral Chester Nimitz confirmed that US submarine skippers were given the same instructions.

shut down, including the air conditioning, which meant the temperature rose dramatically and everyone began to sweat. Then came the explosions. Even when they did not hit the sub, the detonation of nearby depth charges created pressure waves that slammed into the sub's hull like a giant hammer. They broke lights, bent metal fittings, burst pipes, and dislodged cork from the bulkheads. The only defense was to run silent; Glennon and everyone else on board all but held their breath. After nearly three hours, the underwater concussions grew more distant. When the pinging resumed, it grew fainter as the destroyers moved away. When the *Greenling* eventually surfaced, no ships were in sight.[16]

Such experiences affected the crew. Sailors developed boils or ulcers on their legs, some so serious they had to be relieved from duty. One man broke down, becoming hysterical, though he "subsided" (Bruton's word) overnight. On August 21, after forty-five days at sea, Bruton wrote: "Limit of effective personnel endurance reached," though he didn't start back for Hawaii for three more days.[17]

En route there, the *Greenling* encountered a small wooden fishing vessel. Because such ships supplied food to the Japanese soldiers on Truk, they were considered legitimate targets, especially in the environment of unrestricted warfare. Bruton was unwilling to waste a valuable torpedo on it, however, so he ordered the *Greenling* to take it under fire. The sub's three-inch deck gun had been damaged during the depth charge attack, so the crew used the machine guns.

The description of it in the official report was terse: "Closed vessel and raked it several times with machine guns from close range. Small white flag finally displayed by target which then stopped. . . . Went alongside, saw four dead men topside, remainder of crew of six or eight undoubtedly dead below. Executive Officer boarded vessel and started fire using rag and oil. Vessel caught fire immediately." As the *Greenling* continued on its way, the fishing vessel "was dead in the water and burning fiercely."[18]

It left Glennon with a bad taste. Attacking an anonymous ship at night was like a math problem involving angles and ranges. "When you're looking at targets," he recalled years later, "it was a game. You looked at the ships you attacked as *things*." It was different when "there were actually people you could see that you were shooting at." "I had no liking for this type of combat, with blood and guts visible to us."[19]

When the *Greenling* returned to Pearl Harbor in September, it was officially credited with having sunk twenty-four thousand tons of enemy shipping. The

SUBMARINE WARFARE

authorities were pleased, and Bruton was complimented for "pressing home his attacks." The endorsement to Bruton's report especially praised the destruction of the fishing sampan, noting, "Dead men tell no tales."[20]

While the *Greenling* took on fresh supplies and more torpedoes, the crew, including Glennon, went to the Royal Hawaiian Hotel on Waikiki Beach. The navy had set aside "the pink palace of the Pacific" for submarine crews, officers and enlisted alike, who were returning from war patrols. Glennon and the rest of the *Greenling*'s crew spent as much time in the sun as possible to absorb vitamin D. They were also encouraged to eat fresh vegetables and butter and drink lots of milk. After a few weeks of that, it was back out for another patrol on September 22.[21]

This time, the *Greenling* bypassed Truk and took station off the Japanese home islands, where there were plenty of targets. There were also fewer problems with the torpedoes, mainly because the crews checked them over with great care. Nevertheless, they remained unpredictable. On October 18, the *Greenling* stalked a freighter that was steaming southward along the coast, and, after carefully setting up for a shot, Bruton fired three torpedoes. Two of them hit and exploded, but the big freighter remained stubbornly afloat. Bruton decided to finish her off with two more. This time, both torpedoes misbehaved, veering off course and circling back toward the *Greenling* to pass close alongside. Undeterred by that near-disaster, Bruton fired one more torpedo, which sent the ship to the bottom.[22]

Greenling's fourth patrol (Glennon's third) was even more productive. Now equipped with an SJ surface-search radar system, the *Greenling* patrolled the area north of Bougainville Strait in the Solomons. On December 22, under a bright full moon, she encountered a tanker escorted by two warships. Deciding that the larger of the two escorts was the most valuable target, Bruton fired four torpedoes in its direction, getting three hits, then swung around and fired another torpedo at the tanker. Both ships sank. The smaller escort ship conducted a halfhearted counterattack, dropping only two depth charges before it cleared the area. When the *Greenling* returned to periscope depth, there were no ships in sight.[23]

The *Greenling* put in at Brisbane, Australia, on January 30, 1943. Again, the high command was pleased. The *Greenling* was awarded a Presidential Unit Citation and Bruton himself received the Navy Cross—the first of three he earned during the war. Such success came at a cost. The lengthy patrols, cramped conditions, and high stress caused skin lesions and induced fevers of up to 105 degrees among many of the crew members. Bruton reported that "the

ANNAPOLIS GOES TO WAR

health of the crew was considerably worse than on any previous patrol," noting that most of the symptoms appeared after the fortieth day, which, apparently, was about the limit of what men could tolerate.[24]

This time, the *Greenling* underwent a full refit, and there was some turnover in personnel. Glennon himself was detached and told that he would be assigned to one of the new submarines under construction. While he waited, he was assigned temporary duty as executive officer of a different *Gato*-class sub, the *Guardfish*, which was also undergoing repairs in Brisbane. Almost at once, however, the skipper of the *Guardfish* fell ill and was transferred off the boat. That made Lieutenant Phil Glennon the commanding officer. He was twenty-three years old.[25]

Other Forties also served in submarines. Perhaps the most harrowing individual odyssey—at least of those who survived the war—involved Philip F. Eckert, a genial and easygoing native of Minnesota who had initially aspired to flight training, though after witnessing several air crashes, decided instead to go to Sub School. After a tour in the submarine *Argonaut*, Eckert became the dive officer on her sister ship, *Nautilus*.* Both were older and oversize V-class submarines built in the late 1920s as long-range scouts. In January 1943, after rescuing a group of priests, nuns, and civilians from Bougainville in the Solomons, the commander of the *Nautilus*, William H. Brockman, was eager to return there because coast watchers had reported heavy Japanese tanker traffic in the area. In a hurry, Brockman decided to keep the *Nautilus* on the surface, even in daylight, and dive only if an enemy aircraft appeared.[26]

On January 5, 1943, Eckert was the assistant officer of the deck. Brockman sent him topside to supervise the lookouts, telling him that if a plane appeared, he should try to identify it as friend or foe using a flashing light signal. If the plane failed to respond, the boat would conduct an emergency dive. The *Nautilus* had an SJ radar system, but it was unmanned that morning because the sailor whose job it was to watch the screen was up on the periscope cleaning the lens.

All the topside lookouts, including Eckert, wore inflatable life vests as a safety precaution. Brockman had made it a rule: "You either wear a life jacket

---

* The *Nautilus* is often best remembered for the role it played in the Battle of Midway, where it kept a Japanese destroyer occupied long enough to allow the dive-bombing group from *Enterprise* to spot the destroyer and use it as a guide to find and attack the Japanese carrier force. Along with another oversize submarine, the *Argonaut*, the *Nautilus* also carried the men of the Second Raider Battalion to Japanese-held Makin Island on August 17–18, 1943.

when you are on my bridge, or take some form of punishment." The inflatable life jackets were an improvement over the bulky kapok vests, though their utility was compromised by a modification that nearly every sailor made to them. The lanyard for the CO_2 cartridge that inflated the vest had a metal ball at the end of it so that the wearer could grasp it easily. In the tight confines of a submarine, however, that ball was continually getting caught on one or another piece of equipment and the vest would suddenly inflate. Consequently, almost everyone cut it off the lanyard.[27]

As the *Nautilus* plunged through a fairly heavy sea, visibility was obscured by intermittent rain squalls and a low cloud cover. Suddenly, one of the topside lookouts shouted a warning: An airplane had emerged out of the clouds. Eckert readied his flashlight to signal, but before he could, an order came: "Clear the bridge!" Eckert did not panic; he was, after all, the diving officer. Yet, after the forward lookouts clambered down the hatch, the ensign in the conning tower, assuming the bridge was clear, called out: "Dive! Dive! Dive!" Eckert and the stern lookout, Yeoman Second Class J. P. Rossi, were still topside. Eckert was twenty feet away from the hatch when it banged shut, and he watched as the hatch wheel turned clockwise, indicating that it had been dogged shut from the inside. He heard the hiss of air venting from the main ballast tanks as the submarine nosed downward.[28]

Eckert knew that he had to get off the bridge and away from the sub as quickly as possible lest the suction pull him under. Ordering Rossi to follow him, he climbed over the lifeline and jumped, landing well clear of the hull. Rossi hesitated, and when he jumped, he hit the side of the ballast tank, though he soon washed clear. Eckert was wearing his raincoat and had his binoculars around his neck, yet managed to swim away from the boat and the whirlpool it created as it descended. From twenty yards away, he looked back just in time to see the letters "USS NAUTILUS" on the boat's hull disappear under the surface.

Eckert discarded the binoculars but kept the flashlight, thinking he might need it to signal possible rescuers. He took off his raincoat and wrapped it around his exposed legs to discourage sharks. Swimming over to Rossi, he inflated the yeoman's life vest by blowing through the attached tube, then inflated his own. With the seas running at four to five feet, neither man could see more than a few dozen yards in any direction. It was a peculiar feeling to be bobbing around on an empty sea. Eckert remembered that he felt no sense of panic; he was confident that his absence would be noticed, and that the sub would come back for them.[29]

It was the skipper, Captain Brockman, who noticed. Brockman was having his breakfast when he heard the report of the airplane sighting. He abandoned his meal and made his way to the control room below the conning tower. By then, the *Nautilus* was well into its dive. Brockman looked about, noticed the absence of a full complement, and asked: "Where's the diving officer?" When no one answered, he shouted, "*Where's the goddam diving officer?*" Someone volunteered that he was probably in the conning tower and on his way down. But of course he wasn't. A quick headcount revealed that two men had been left topside. Brockman was livid and loudly threatened to court-martial everyone in the control room. He soon recovered his equanimity, however, and turned his attention to the immediate problem. Huddling with the boat's navigator, he asked how they were going to get them back. "Very simple, Captain," the navigator said calmly, consulting the dead-reckoning board. "We will turn around, blow all main ballast, battle surface near point X, and pick 'em up."[30]

Meanwhile, Eckert and Rossi were trying to stay afloat. Since Eckert had played water polo at the Academy, he had little difficulty in doing so. Ten minutes passed, then twenty, before Rossi, lifted up to the top of a wave, called out, "Mr. Eckert, they're coming back!" And when Eckert found himself at the top of a wave, he saw it, too. As he recalled it later, "The appearance of the *Nautilus* when the wave lifted me up was one of the most beautiful sights I ever saw."

By the time the two men were safely back aboard, Brockman had calmed down. He decided all's well that ends well, and despite his earlier threats, did not file any charges. In fact, he omitted the incident altogether from his official report. The entry in the log of the *Nautilus* that morning reads simply: "Sighted plane bearing 220 T, distance about 7 miles. Submerged."[31]

Another of the Forties who served in submarines was Tom "Tiny" McGrath, the strapping, square-jawed star athlete who had been universally admired by his classmates. At his high school in Tucson, Arizona, he had been named the "best all-around boy," and at the Academy he had been both regimental commander and the recipient of the silver sword presented by the class of 1891 to the best all-around leader in each class. Though his roommate described him as "gentle as a St. Bernard" most of the time, McGrath was ferocious on the football field, where he anchored the Navy line as a guard and was named a Second Team All American. His size alone made his decision to join the submarine service something of a puzzle.[32]

McGrath served in the USS *Pompano* (SS-181), a *Porpoise*-class sub, slightly older and smaller (and therefore more crowded) than the *Gato*-class boats.

When McGrath reported aboard the *Pompano* in July 1942 (the same month Glennon reported to the *Greenling*), it was preparing to depart on its third deployment. It was McGrath's first war patrol and very nearly his last.

On August 9 (the day of the Battle of Savo Island), the *Pompano* was off the coast of Japan when topside lookouts spotted a heavily laden transport on the horizon. The skipper of the *Pompano*, Lieutenant Commander Willis Thomas, ordered the boat to periscope depth and began maneuvering for a shot. As Thomas was looking through the periscope, McGrath heard him say quietly, "There's two of them, and one is a destroyer." That was both good news and bad news. It meant that the target was valuable enough to rate an escort, though it also meant that the *Pompano* could expect a swift counter-attack as soon as it attacked. Undeterred, Thomas maneuvered into position and fired a spread of torpedoes. At least one of them detonated. Thomas invited McGrath to have a quick peek through the periscope as the transport erupted in flames.[33]

The escorting Japanese destroyer did not linger to pick up survivors. Instead, it charged directly at the *Pompano*, fixing it in the glare of its searchlight. Thomas ordered an emergency dive, and as the boat descended, McGrath and everyone else could hear five-inch shells slamming into the water above them. The *Pompano* had underwater sound detectors that allowed everyone on board to hear the whine of the destroyer's screws as it closed; it reminded McGrath of "the sound of freight cars." Then came the depth charges. At least twice, canisters actually hit the *Pompano*—the clang clearly audible—but did not explode since they had not reached their preset depth for detonation. The depth charges that did explode broke lights, knocked the paint off bulkheads, and burst open pipes and tanks. The *Pompano* was one of the last American subs whose hull had been riveted rather than welded, and the explosions opened seams in her outer hull. Seawater poured in even as the *Pompano* continued her descent. Thomas took her down to what was supposed to be her maximum depth of 250 feet, then kept going, all the way down to 403 feet, as the hull plates groaned from the pressure. She touched bottom twice, shearing off her sonar receptors. Thomas hoped to "hide" silently on the bottom, but with water rising in the engine room, he had to engage the pumps, and the noise they made was detected by the destroyer, which delivered another barrage of depth charges, many of them much too close for comfort. After several hours, nearly out of battery power, and with water rising quickly, Thomas quietly told the officers to prepare to scuttle the boat. At that depth, it meant certain death for all of them. They convinced him to surface and, if necessary, fight it out with the destroyer on the surface. Thomas took the *Pompano* as close to the shore as he dared, touching ground twice, and then surfaced. Obscured by the shadow of the shoreline, he "set course to clear locality."[34]

The near-disaster left everyone exhausted. A number of the crew had severe cases of nausea and vomiting from the prolonged tension and extreme depth. Yet Thomas kept the *Pompano* on station. A week later, she attacked and sank another freighter. And as that ship went down, Thomas invited every crewman in the control room to take a quick look through the periscope.

There was another scare on August 12 when the *Pompano* was lining up on a freighter, and an escorting destroyer emerged from behind the target, heading directly for the sub. With no time to dive, Thomas fired two torpedoes at it in a low-percentage "down the throat" shot. This time the torpedoes behaved perfectly. The first exploded forty-five seconds after leaving the tube, and there was a second "very heavy" explosion immediately afterward. McGrath remembered that "both sets of enemy propellers stopped immediately." The freighter and the destroyer both sank.

By now the crew was (in Thomas's words) "tired and jittery." In the previous thirty-six hours, they had been on the receiving end of sixteen five-inch shells, two aerial bombs, and fifty-nine depth charges.[35]

Having expended all the *Pompano*'s sixteen torpedoes, Thomas headed back to Pearl Harbor, arriving in mid-September. After one look at her battered hull and wrecked sonar, the Yard supervisor concluded that the repairs could not be done locally. She would have to go to Mare Island Navy Yard in San Francisco Bay for a full refit. The extended stay in the Yards allowed members of the crew to take leave in groups, and McGrath headed south by train to Tucson to see his family.

He was celebrated as a war hero. His mother hosted a social evening in his honor, and the local newspaper carried several stories about him, most of which emphasized his starring role on the Tucson Badgers football team back in 1934. He even attended a practice session of his old high school team, offering the current players what the newspaper called "the finer points of grid play." He was invited to speak to both the American Legion and the Kiwanis Club, and while he was reluctant to discuss his own experiences, he wanted people to understand that the war would demand commitment and sacrifice. The Japanese, he told the Kiwanis Club, "are tough, and savage and hard hitting, and above all they are not afraid to be killed." Indeed, he said, "They want to be killed if they can no longer fight. I've seen them beg to be killed." The point was, no one should expect the victory to come soon or without sacrifice.

"The navy has no doubt that we will win," he told them, "but it is going to be a hard job."[36]

When a reporter urged him to describe the fighting, McGrath demurred, though he was willing, even eager, to talk about his shipmates. He emphasized the dedication and efficiency of the men he served with. He had heard some people speculate that men on a submarine would get on each other's nerves; he insisted that was not the case. The proximity and shared danger drew them closer together. "The discipline is strict," he acknowledged. "But those men have the best spirit I've ever seen."[37]

After his respite in the Arizona desert, McGrath rejoined the *Pompano* in San Francisco at the end of October 1942. The next two patrols proved somewhat frustrating due to continued torpedo failures. When the *Pompano* came across two of Japan's big fleet carriers, it seemed an astounding opportunity. McGrath, who was now the boat's assistant approach officer, worked with Thomas to find a way through the destroyer screen and get within four thousand yards. Then they fired six torpedoes at the nearest flattop. Four of them exploded prematurely, though Thomas thought he heard two others hit. Japanese records do not corroborate damage to any of its carriers that day, though US Navy authorities credited the *Pompano* with a "probable" hit.

Thomas put McGrath in for a Silver Star for his actions against a Japanese patrol boat when McGrath manned a machine gun and "maintained an accurate and effective fire" until the enemy ship sank. Then in August 1943 radio reports from the *Pompano* suddenly ceased. Months passed before the navy listed her as "missing, presumed lost." Speculation at the time was that she had fallen victim to a mine, though postwar Japanese records show an attack by both aircraft and multiple destroyers against an American sub off Honshu on September 17, 1943. Neither the boat nor any of her crew were ever found.[38]

The *Pompano* was one of fifty-two American submarines lost during the war. Some 375 officers—14 of them from the class of 1940—and more than three thousand enlisted men died in them. Two of the Forties, William "Salty" Burgan and Don Scheu, were killed when the near-legendary *Wahoo* (SS-238) was sunk in the Sea of Japan in October 1943. Ed O'Brien, who had spent three years at Boston College before coming to the Academy and was accused of having a "Havaad" accent, was killed when the *Seawolf* (SS-197) was lost a year later. A month after that, in November 1944, Richard Mason, called "Arky" in testimony to his Camden, Arkansas, birthplace, was on the *Growler* (SS-215) when it sank. And only a week after that, Walter Shaffer, a three-sport star at the Academy, went down with the *Scamp* (SS-277). Most tragic of all, perhaps, was the loss of the *Tullibee* in March 1944, with David Spencer Wilson on board. At the Academy, Wilson's roommate had insisted that Spence had "more than anyone's share of bad luck," and it apparently continued when during an attack on a Japanese convoy, one of the *Tullibee*'s faulty torpedoes circled back to sink it. Only one crewman survived. Altogether, the submarine service endured a loss rate of 22 percent, which is astonishing, considering that the percentage of those killed-in-action in the Marine Corps was 3.3 percent, and in the Army Air Force it was 7.4 percent.

The sacrifice of those submarine crews was not in vain. American subs sank 1,314 Japanese ships during the war, and if that was fewer than the number sunk by German U-boats in the Atlantic, it was more strategically meaningful because Japan could not replace such losses the way the Allies could—and did. With less than 2 percent of the navy's active-duty personnel, US submarines accounted for 55 percent of all Japanese shipping lost during the war. Such catastrophic losses made it increasingly difficult, and eventually impossible, for Japan to import the raw materials she had gone to war to secure. American Army Air Force bombers wrecked Japan's factories—especially in 1945—yet many of those factories had already ceased to function because American submarines had destroyed the ships that brought the raw materials they needed.[39]

18

"Moored as Before"

Not every member of the class of 1940 spent the first two years of the war in the vanguard of global violence. Most of them—indeed, most US servicemen worldwide—had no contact with the enemy at all. With more than ten million Americans in unform by 1943, there were far more personnel in rear areas serving the administrative and logistical functions of the service than there were confronting the enemy. That was certainly true of the several dozen Forties who were still serving on the older battleships of the prewar navy. Once considered incomparable engines of maritime violence, the battleships that had been commissioned during or just after World War I were virtual dinosaurs by 1942. With a top speed of only twenty-three knots, they were too slow to keep up with the carrier task forces, and without air cover they were sitting ducks. Then, too, because of their heavy armor, they burned up prodigious amounts of fuel, typically fifteen hundred barrels (sixty-three thousand gallons) of fuel oil per day. Their heavy guns could hurl enormous shells, weighing fifteen hundred pounds, fifteen or twenty miles, but only if they could get that close to the enemy, which without air cover was unlikely. Admiral King repeatedly urged Nimitz to find some way to make use of the old battlewagons in the Pacific War, and Nimitz challenged his staff to come up with some ideas. In the end, though, Nimitz concluded that it was best to keep them on the West Coast as training ships.[1]

Because of that, the majestic battleships of the prewar navy spent most of 1942 tied up to piers in San Francisco or San Pedro. Ed "Jug" Gillette, who was on the battleship *Mississippi*, ironically referred to this as "the Battle of San Francisco Bay." He and the other Forties had a lot of time ashore, and they were sensitive about how that looked. That was partly why in June 1942 (as Nimitz's carriers sortied for the Battle of Midway), the five battleships in San Francisco Bay got up steam, cast off, and went to sea—not to engage the enemy, but to avoid the inevitable questions about why they remained quietly tied up in the harbor while a fierce battle took place three thousand miles away in the mid-Pacific. They steamed out under the Golden Gate Bridge into an offshore fog and remained there for two weeks conducting battle maneuvers, returning only after news of the American victory at Midway had been disseminated.[2]

One of those five battleships was the *Idaho*. Most of the thirteen Forties who had initially been assigned to her had moved on to other duties, many of them to flight school or submarine school. Only Warren Smalzel and Myers Montgomery remained. Even without action against the enemy, their days were fully occupied with all the quotidian activities inherent to managing a warship with a crew of a thousand men. Montgomery, who was the Turret Two officer, wrote regularly to his family back in Malden, Missouri, and a central theme in those letters was how "terribly busy" he was with "ship's work." Even so, the long periods in port gave him and everyone else on the *Idaho* opportunities to go ashore, where the attractions of San Francisco Bay easily eclipsed those of Reykjavik. All summer, groups of sailors in whites roamed Chinatown and filled up the bars and movie theaters. Montgomery, too, got ashore fairly often to play golf or tennis or go to the movies. In July, he wrote his grandmother that he had just seen an unusual animated film called *Fantasia*. He enjoyed it, he told her, but "it was so different from anything [he'd seen] before that it takes a long time to really understand." A few days later, he reported to his sister, "We had a ship's dance last night and it turned out to be a huge success." He was both pleased and proud that "our ship's band is really swell."[3]

Montgomery knew how fortunate he was, especially when he heard from classmates who were differently situated. While on the one hand he bemoaned the fact that "when I finish my work it's either time to go on watch, or else I'm ready to turn in and catch what little sleep is available." On the other hand, he fully appreciated "hot showers, [a] bed to sleep on, and tablecloths with our meals." It was, he confessed to his father, "a pretty soft way of fighting the war."[4]

The *Idaho* spent July 1942 tied up at Alameda, across the bay from San Francisco, the tedium broken occasionally by battle practice offshore. Finally, on August 1 (as US Marines headed for Guadalcanal) the three battleships of Battleship Division 3 (BATDIV III)—*Idaho*, *Mississippi*, and *New Mexico*— cast off and headed out to sea, bound for Hawaii. En route, they joined up with the carrier *Hornet* (whose denouement in the Battle of the Santa Cruz Islands was still two months away) and her escorts. During the ten-day passage, the *Idaho* fulfilled the somewhat ignominious role of acting as a target for *Hornet* pilots who simulated dive bombing runs against her.[5]

"MOORED AS BEFORE"   227

On August 10, 1942 (the day after the Battle of Savo Island), the Hawaiian Islands came into view. The *Idaho* spent a week firing her main battery guns at Kahoolawe, an unoccupied island in the Hawaiian chain near Maui that was used by the navy as a gun range. Then on August 14 she and the other battleships entered Pearl Harbor. It was Montgomery's first visit there since the December 7 attack, and the consequences were still evident. In addition to the somber wreckage of the *Arizona* and *Oklahoma*, in which ten of his classmates remained entombed, black fuel oil still covered the shoreline. The *Idaho* tied up at Pier 19 on the south rim of Ford Island just behind the *California*, still aground on the bottom mud. The arrival of the carrier *Enterprise* a week later with visible battle damage all along her starboard side was another reminder that a shooting war was taking place three thousand miles to the southwest.[6]

Reminders of war notwithstanding, Hawaii was a popular liberty port for the sailors on the *Idaho*, who enjoyed both the beach at Waikiki and the bars in Honolulu. There was more battle practice, too, a lot of it involving firing at target sleeves towed by airplanes or, less often, remote-controlled planes. All that practice, however, did not presage immediate war service. Nimitz remained unwilling to employ the old and slow battleships in the fighting going on around Guadalcanal, and in late September, he sent the ships of BATDIV III back across the Pacific to California. They passed under the Golden Gate Bridge on October 4 and tied up once more at Alameda. There the entire crew was amused to read an Associated Press story reporting that the Italian government had announced the sinking of the American battleship *Idaho* off the coast of North Africa.[7]

This time, the *Idaho*'s stay was relatively short. After a week, she steamed up to Puget Sound in Washington State to enter the Bremerton Navy Yard. Her aging five-inch guns were removed and replaced, and even the gigantic gun barrels of her main battery, weighing thirty tons each, were exchanged for new ones. That took months, and the extended stay meant that most of the crew could take leave, one section at a time, for two weeks each.[8]

Montgomery headed home. He took the train from Seattle to St. Louis, where his family met him for the car ride down to Malden. Much of the talk on the way was about the army's plan to build an airfield near Malden, about the impact of sugar rationing on baking, and especially the burden of gas rationing, which dramatically limited driving. Of all the belligerent powers, the United States had by far the greatest oil reserves, more than enough to fuel the war and maintain a robust economy at home. What it did not have was rubber, access to which had been cut off by the Japanese occupation of South Asia. Therefore,

228 ANNAPOLIS GOES TO WAR

in order to minimize the use of rubber tires, the government rationed gasoline and set a nationwide mandatory speed limit (called the "Victory Speed") of thirty-five miles per hour.[9]

Montgomery had a delightful visit. Like most servicemen who returned to their hometowns on leave, he was treated as a war hero, though the *Idaho* had yet to fire a meaningful shot in the war. His family insisted that he wear his uniform to mass on Sunday, where everyone wanted to shake his hand, and he was invited to deliver a speech at his old high school. He returned to the ship on Friday, November 13, the day Doc Weatherup was wounded in the Naval Battle of Guadalcanal.[10]

As Montgomery had expected, a mound of routine paperwork had piled up on his desk during his absence. Writing to thank his family for the wonderful visit, he noted that there was so much work waiting for him that "I don't know when I'll ever struggle through." One of the pieces of mail was a wedding invitation from a former roommate at the Academy, Albert Street. Montgomery's first roommate, Dusty Rhodes, had married in violation of regulations and had been dismissed for it. Since then, the lifting of the restriction against marriage had led other of his former roommates to tie the knot. Now the last of them was getting married. As Montgomery wrote to his family, "I'm the only hold out." Who would have guessed?[11]

The *Idaho* remained in the Yards at Puget Sound for two and a half months, as workmen swarmed over the ship, installing the new guns and adding radar equipment. Throughout all that, the familiar routines of the service were maintained. Still in command of Turret Two, Montgomery, like every other qualified officer, also had to stand officer of the deck (OOD) duties: four-hour time blocks when he presided over the quarterdeck with the purely decorative binoculars around his neck, supervising the arrival and departure of workers, cataloging the receipt of supplies (seventy gallons of fresh milk every day), and checking off leave-takers and sailors returning from liberty. Inevitably, some of the returning sailors overstayed their authorized liberty, some by hours, others by days or even weeks. That meant they had to face what was called "Captain's Mast," summary punishment handed down by the ship's skipper, Roscoe Schuirmann, usually consisting of confinement for a specified number of days, or stoppage of pay, or both. As an example, one afternoon when Montgomery was OOD, the shore patrol delivered a drunken and belligerent sailor who had not only overstayed his liberty, he had refused to obey the orders of the shore patrol and had cursed at them. Schuirmann sentenced him to twelve days of solitary confinement on bread and water.[12]

"MOORED AS BEFORE" 229

When Montgomery wasn't on watch or catching up with paperwork, he often went ashore to eat a meal, see a movie, or play some tennis. He sometimes played tennis with opponents significantly senior to him. One of them was Rear Admiral William R. Munroe, the commander of BATDIV III, who used the *Idaho* as his flagship. Monroe was thirty years older than Montgomery, but he told the lieutenant not to go easy on him. So he didn't. In fact, as Montgomery confessed to his family, "I tried my darndest to win." Even so, the admiral won the first set, Montgomery battled back to win the second, and they were tied at 6–6 in the third when it got too dark to see the ball and they had to call it a draw. They played again on December 7, the one-year anniversary of the attack on Pearl Harbor, but as the days grew shorter and the weather became more problematic, there were fewer opportunities, and, just a few days later, Montgomery shipped his golf clubs and tennis racket home to Malden.[13]

As the renovations on the *Idaho* continued, time dragged for the officers and men. Day after day, Montgomery began his OOD watch by entering the same three words in the ship's log: "Moored as before." Only at the end of the year did the now-refurbished *Idaho* return to San Francisco to take part in practice amphibious landings. Even then, Montgomery found time to see a movie. He was especially impressed by *Mrs. Miniver*, a film about an English housewife, played by Greer Garson (who won an Oscar for the role), attempting to cope with the daily trauma of living with a war on her doorstep.[14]

Letters from home suggested that Malden was experiencing its own kind of wartime trauma. The construction of a nearby army air base brought in hundreds, and eventually thousands, of outsiders, both workers and servicemen, and housing became scarce. With Myers's younger brother Jimmy now at Annapolis, his parents rented out their rooms to soldiers. Almost at once, however, the presence of "colored" men at the base became a community issue. Malden was in the far southeastern "bootheel" of Missouri, only a few miles from the Arkansas line, and Jim Crow remained dominant. Montgomery's parents were Democrats and strong supporters of Franklin Roosevelt, but even Roosevelt had to tread lightly in dealing with the powerful segregationist traditions of the South. Black soldiers who attempted to patronize restaurants in Missouri were not only denied service but frequently set upon and beaten. At Camp Crowder in western Missouri, Black soldiers were denied entrance to the USO and took up a collection to buy their own building so they would have a place to go when off duty. Informed of the situation in Malden, Montgomery confessed to his parents, "I don't believe I had ever realized just how the situation was." A few days later, he wrote to ask if they had made any

230   ANNAPOLIS GOES TO WAR

progress "in taking care of those colored men." A solution to that problem, however, would not be found during the war.[15]

In the spring of 1943, Admiral Nimitz finally found a use for the old battleships. The year before, during the campaign for Midway, the Japanese had seized two island outposts in the Aleutian Islands: Attu, at the tail end of the archipelago, and larger Kiska Island, fifty miles further east. Often thought of as a diversion for the Midway expedition, the Japanese move was actually part of their continuing effort to establish a defensive perimeter around the western Pacific. The islands themselves were of little strategic value; Nimitz believed it would be best to let the Japanese garrisons stay there to suffer the terrible weather and burden Japan's already stressed merchant fleet with the need to supply them. On the other hand, the two islands were American territory, and popular sentiment demanded that they be retaken.[16]

The man Nimitz assigned to the task was Rear Admiral Thomas C. Kinkaid, a 1908 Academy classmate of both Richmond Kelly Turner and Bill Munroe, Montgomery's erstwhile tennis opponent. Kinkaid was a veteran of most of the Pacific battles to date, including Coral Sea, Midway, and Guadalcanal. It was he who suggested that because Kiska was more strongly held, with perhaps five thousand Japanese, it might be best to attack Attu first, which was thought to have a garrison of only about twelve hundred (though the true number was nearly double that). Because the Japanese were not likely to commit their battlefleet to defend these remote outposts, Nimitz concluded that gunfire support for the invasion could safely be entrusted to the older battleships. Those chosen for that task were the Pearl Harbor survivors, *Pennsylvania* and *Nevada*, plus the now-refurbished *Idaho*. Perhaps relieved to be able to gratify King's persistent demands, Nimitz wrote Kinkaid, "I am glad that the older battleships are going to have some really useful employment."[17]

On April 7, 1943, while British and American troops closed in on Tunisia in North Africa and fierce fighting continued in the Solomons, the three chosen battleships, with four destroyers as escorts, left San Francisco and turned north. Once they were well out to sea, the *Idaho*'s captain, Horace D. Clark, came on the "squawk box" to announce that they were headed for the Aleutians to kick the Japs off two islands they had captured. That night, Montgomery attended a crowded meeting in the junior officer's mess, where a model of Attu Island had been set up on a table. There, planning officers described the role the *Idaho* was to play in the forthcoming assault. First, there would be a preliminary bombardment to soften up the landing area, then the battleships would provide gunfire support during the fighting ashore. At last, the *Idaho* was going to war.[18]

As the ships headed north, the weather turned both colder and rougher; snow flurries became common. Montgomery was glad he had asked his family to send him his heavy bridge coat. After a short stop at Adak, the *Idaho* and *Nevada* set out on a circumnavigation of the Japanese-held islands, hoping to intercept a supply convoy. The weather remained daunting. In addition to the penetrating cold, the "ship rocked and pitched all night," making sleep difficult. One sailor on the *Idaho* was washed over the side by a rogue wave and froze to death before a destroyer could reach him.[19]

The invasion force of battleships, cruisers, destroyers, and transports, plus the escort carrier *Nassau*, left the Alaskan mainland for Attu Island on May 5. Though the day began with promising sunshine, fog soon rolled in again, cutting visibility to near-zero and bringing a damp chill to the air. The attack had been scheduled for May 7, but weather dictated otherwise, and it was on May 11—520 days after the Japanese attack on Pearl Harbor—that the *Idaho* fired its first salvo at the enemy. Orange flame erupted from her twelve new gun barrels, sending eight tons of explosive ordnance into the Japanese positions with each salvo. The concussion was so powerful that, as a sailor on the *Idaho* recalled, it would "blow your helmet and life jacket right off your body."[20]

The commander of the battleship group, Francis W. Rockwell, another 1908 Academy grad, stipulated that the initial rounds should be fired from a range of seven to nine miles. Kinkaid wanted him to move in closer. Rockwell resisted. Moreover, because the battleships fired those first rounds through a heavy fog, traditional spotting was impossible. On the other hand, the radar system that had been installed in Puget Sound allowed the *Idaho* to employ radar-guided ordnance. The *Idaho* maintained a steady fire for forty-five minutes, then, by prearrangement, lifted fire so planes from the *Nassau* could bomb the island. Montgomery could hear the bombs exploding ashore, but he could see nothing through the heavy fog.

The landings were unopposed. The defending Japanese had dug in on the upper slopes of the snow-covered hills that encircled the landing beach and from there defied the army soldiers (not marines) to come and get them. That forced the soldiers to spend the night ashore. The men had winter field jackets and leather boots, but they proved utterly insufficient for the appalling conditions. The surface of Attu was covered by a frozen spongy moss called "muskeg" that all but sucked the boots off their feet. Freezing rain soaked their jackets, and when night fell, the soldiers tried to sleep in shallow foxholes that soon filled with icy water. Many became incapacitated by frostbite. Even more than usual, Montgomery and his shipmates on the *Idaho* could be grateful for their hot showers, warm beds, and white tablecloths.[21]

The battleships resumed the bombardment the next morning. This time, Kinkaid convinced Rockwell to move in closer, and the *Idaho* fired salvo after salvo into the hills from all four of her turrets. The Japanese returned fire, but they had no heavy guns, and without radar they were firing blind. At one point a bold Japanese sub worked its way inside the destroyer screen to launch a torpedo at the *Idaho*. The escorting American destroyers went after it, depth charged it to the surface, and when its desperate crew clambered out of the hatch to man the deck gun, blasted it to pieces. There were no survivors.[22]

Montgomery and his crew remained at general quarters in Turret Two for most of the day, and the next day, too, as the big ship cruised back and forth in front of the target beach, firing first to starboard and then to port. Battered by the heavy naval guns and short on both supplies and ammunition, the Japanese launched a desperate and suicidal banzai charge on May 26. When it was over, only twenty-eight of the more than twenty-three hundred defenders were taken alive.[23]

The *Idaho* remained off Attu for several more weeks, taking wounded and frostbitten soldiers aboard, then made her way to Dutch Harbor, further up the Aleutian chain. There her crew was gratified when a navy tug came out to greet her with a band on board playing "Hail, Hail the Gang's All Here" and, of course, "Anchors Aweigh."[24]

In Dutch Harbor, the mail finally caught up with the *Idaho*, and Montgomery got a letter from his brother Jim, now a firstie at the Academy in the war-shortened class of 1943. Myers read with amusement his brother's description of his romantic misadventures. "He told me about another girl he was dragging," Montgomery reported to his parents. "I've lost track of them long ago." And then, with no apparent irony, he added: "Don't see how he keeps so many on the string at once." Montgomery included nothing at all in his letters about where he was or what he was doing, aware that the navy censors would cut all that out anyway.[25]

Kiska was next. Kinkaid had conceived of Attu as a kind of warm-up for the main event, since Kiska was both larger and reportedly more strongly defended. For a week, there were daily conferences on board the *Idaho,* where the officers went over "details of the invasion plans," and on the last day of July they finally set out. Montgomery sent off a letter to his family before sailing, in case it was the last one. He said nothing about the expedition, only that he was "keeping very much interested in my work, certainly no time to stop and worry about what to do next."[26]

The bombardment began on August 2, 1943, with the destroyers firing first and the *Idaho* and the other battleships joining in that afternoon. At night, Liberator bombers from Adak plastered the island from the air. For most of two weeks, navy ships and army planes delivered thousands of tons of high explosives onto the island. Finally on August 15, the soldiers went ashore.

There was no one there. "Nothing left," as one sailor put it, "but a few stray dogs." The Japanese had executed a stealthy withdrawal in late July without anyone in the American command being aware of it. Putting the best face on it that he could, Kinkaid decided that it had all been a large (and expensive) training exercise.

On August 28, the battleships left Dutch Harbor and headed south for San Francisco. The *Idaho* steamed back under the Golden Gate on September 6, 1943, which was Labor Day. Liberty call was sounded that night, and half the crew—nearly five hundred sailors—stormed ashore. Montgomery wrote his family that although he had "been working mighty hard," he was safe. The one thing he missed, he wrote, was sleep.

After several days in the Bay area, the *Idaho* headed south to Long Beach and more battle maneuvers. Over the next several weeks, more ships arrived in Long Beach, until there were literally hundreds of them. On October 30, they all put to sea, steaming in formation and heading west. The last time this had happened, it had been an exercise. Not this time.

PART IV

Valediction

We had spread out over the broad Pacific, from Panama to Palau, from New Zealand to Alaska, and we were ready to strike back at the Japanese... with all the fury of a people who have waited for their revenge.

—Reef Points, 1945

19

Semper Fidelis

In the early nineteenth century, the US Marine Corps had a number of semi-official mottos. The most common was *Fortitudine*, or "With Courage." Not until 1883 did the Corps adopt the motto employed during World War II and ever since: *Semper Fidelis*, or "Always Faithful." Every marine knows this motto and they will sometimes greet one another with it, often abbreviated as "Semper Fi." It was this institutional pride and self-awareness that encouraged twenty-five members of the Naval Academy class of 1940 to opt for the Marine Corps upon graduation.*

Afterward, all of them attended Marine Corps Basic School in Philadelphia, then underwent infantry training at Fort Indiantown Gap in Pennsylvania. After that, like their navy counterparts, they headed off in different directions and to separate commands with varying specialties. Some, like Otis Calhoun and Lobo Wolfe, went to flight school in New Orleans and became aviators; others, like Jocko Antonelli and George Herring, became infantry commanders and endured the meatgrinder of Guadalcanal; Steve Brody and Bob Wann landed on Bougainville and faced an equally challenging campaign there from November 1943 to March 1944. Leon Chabot, as we have seen, went to the Philippines and became an early prisoner of the Japanese. Most of the other marines from the class went to training commands, several of them at Camp Lejeune in North Carolina.

One of them was Fred Karch. The product of Carmi, a small town in southern Illinois fifty miles west of Evansville, Indiana, Karch attended the University of Illinois after high school. As with many of the Forties, it was his financially strapped father who encouraged him to consider starting over at the Naval

---

* The motto of the US Army is "This We'll Defend," though the motto of the Military Academy at West Point ("Duty, Honor, Country") is better known. The US Navy did not have an official motto until 1992, when it adopted "Honor, Courage, Commitment" as its motto, though "Anchors Aweigh," composed in 1907 and well known to the Forties, filled a similar niche.

Academy. His congressman named him his third alternate, and after the candidates ahead of him failed the entrance exam, Karch got the nod. He was happy to go and felt immediately at home in the regimented environment of the Academy, where he especially admired the clarity of expectations. There was, in fact, little nuance in Karch's worldview. During lengthy bull sessions in Bancroft Hall, he became notorious for taking uncompromising positions on all sorts of issues. According to his long-suffering roommate, Karch was seldom right, but he was never wrong. Even when confronted with evidence that contradicted his pronouncements, he would not budge or admit error. He had equally fixed views about personal discipline. He had only disdain for those classmates who looked upon Academy regulations as a challenge to overcome or who sought to cut corners. He took seriously the *Reef Points* axiom: "Thou shalt not criticize, but obey."[1]

During youngster cruise, Karch was within earshot when a navy lieutenant—a virtually godlike figure at the Academy—told an enlisted sailor to do a particular job. Already engaged in doing something else, the sailor nonchalantly responded, "I'll get to it." Karch was horrified. He decided right then that he wanted no part of a service where an enlisted man could address an officer like that. Noting the crisp military demeanor of the Marine Corps officers at the Academy, he aspired to be like them, and he was able to fulfill that ambition when he drew a low number in the lottery.[2]

After infantry training, Karch joined the Tenth Marine Regiment and was soon on his way to Iceland as part of the American occupation force. By 1943, however, he had been promoted to major and the command of the First Battalion (Artillery) of the Fourteenth Marine Regiment in charge of a battery of 75 mm pack howitzers. These were compact, short-barreled field guns that, despite weighing 1,379 pounds each, could be broken down and carried in jeeps or small landing craft to the combat zone to provide artillery support for marine infantry. In that capacity, he was soon swept up into what became the centerpiece of the US war against Japan: a drive across the central Pacific to the very doorstep of the Japanese Empire.

For thirty years and more, before any of the Forties had been born, US Navy strategists had begun to develop plans for a possible war against Japan, refining them over the years at the Naval War College and adding details as circumstances changed. What emerged was Plan Orange. Its basic outline was simple. As noted in chapter 10, American planners assumed that at some future date, the Japanese would attack the Philippine Islands. If they did—when they did—instead of trying to meet them on the beaches, American and Filipino forces would concentrate in the Bataan Peninsula, across the bay from the city of Manila, and hold out there for however long it took—perhaps six months— for the US Navy to fight its way across the Pacific and come to their rescue. As we have seen, General Douglas MacArthur's decision to meet the Japanese on the beach wrecked that plan, and the surrender of Corregidor in May 1942 rendered the whole concept obsolete. Nevertheless, because the idea of a Central Pacific Drive had been at the center of the navy's strategic planning for twenty years, it remained embedded in the institutional thinking of navy leaders.[3]

There was a lot of discussion about the route the fleet should take in its thrust to the Philippines. The most direct path, of course, was straight across the Pacific from Hawaii. Presumably, at some point, the Japanese fleet would come out to challenge the American advance, and the result would be a climactic naval battle somewhere in the Philippine Sea, which the Americans would win. This option was called the "Through Ticket to Manila." The difficulty with it (aside from its rosy assumptions) was logistical. Sustaining a large fleet of fuel-guzzling battleships all the way across the Pacific would be difficult if not impossible. Refueling while underway was still precarious at the time, and the navy didn't have enough oilers to do it anyway. So navy planners developed an alternate approach that called for seizing intermediate bases along the way. That meant conducting amphibious assaults against Japanese-held islands—in the Marshalls, the Carolines, and the Marianas.[4]

In recognition of that, in 1921 a Marine Corps major named Earl "Pete" Ellis wrote a study entitled "Advanced Base Operations in Micronesia." It explored the practical questions of how to get marines, their equipment, their supplies, and their artillery ashore onto a defended beach and hold it. Over the next two decades, the central mission of the US Marine Corps gradually shifted—from guarding navy bases to seizing enemy islands. By 1944, marines had landed on several islands in the South Pacific, including Guadalcanal. Now the concept would be applied to Japanese-held islands in the central Pacific.[5]

From the start, Plan Orange had assumed that the initial target of a Central Pacific Drive would be the Marshall Islands: twenty-nine coral atolls scattered over seventy square miles of the mid-Pacific. The Japanese had obtained those islands from Germany in 1919 under a League of Nations Mandate as their share of the spoils after World War I, when Japan had been a British ally. The agreement stipulated that the Japanese were not to fortify those islands, though US Navy planners assumed (correctly) that they had ignored that restriction.

240   ANNAPOLIS GOES TO WAR

After World War II began, some American strategists argued that it might be better to land first in the Gilbert Islands, five hundred miles southeast of the Marshalls. The Japanese had seized those islands from the British after the Pearl Harbor attack and had occupied them for only about two years. Since the Japanese had been in the Marshall Islands for more than two decades, Navy planners reasoned that the Gilberts would be a softer target for the initial offensive—a kind of warm-up for the main event.[6]

It proved otherwise.

The armada that set out from Long Beach on October 30, 1943 (including the *Idaho*) dropped anchor in the Gilbert Islands three weeks later. The principal American target there was Tawara Atoll and in particular the tiny island of Betio, which hosted the critical airstrip, with a secondary landing on the more lightly defended Makin Atoll 140 miles to the north. Along with the flagship *Pennsylvania*, the *Idaho* was assigned to support the Makin assault, and, as in the Aleutians, the attack began with a naval bombardment. At 6:00 a.m. on November 20, the *Idaho* raised her oversized battle flag and the main batteries opened fire at 6:40. In Turret Two, Myers Montgomery directed fire at targets ashore until 8:00, when the battleships lifted fire to allow planes from the escort carriers to bomb and strafe the island. Routine as it sounds, firing thousand-pound shells from fourteen-inch guns was both complicated and dangerous, even for an experienced crew. That was demonstrated by an accident on the *Idaho*'s sister ship *Mississippi*, when an internal explosion in Turret Two killed forty-three men and wounded nineteen others.[7]

The landing craft for the invasion were rectangular, flat-bottomed boats officially known as LCVP (Landing Craft, Vehicle and Personnel) but which were universally known as Higgins boats after their designer and builder, Andrew Jackson Higgins. At 8:00 a.m. on November 20, a flotilla of them carried the US Army's Twenty-Seventh Division, a reserve unit from New York, to the beach. After the landing, however, progress ashore was slow, and that kept the *Pennsylvania*, *Idaho*, and other big ships loitering off the island longer than initially planned. On November 24, a Japanese submarine worked its way inside the screen of US destroyers and sank the light carrier *Lipscomb Bay* with the loss of 644 officers and men—more than were lost in the conquest of Makin itself. One of those killed on the *Lipscomb Bay* was George V. Williams, an "eye unsat" from the class of 1940 who had been recalled to active service once the war began.

SEMPER FIDELIS 241

Some observers of the campaign for Makin Island, including the US ground commander, Marine Major General Holland M. Smith, blamed the loss of the *Lipscomb Bay* on the army for what he considered the army's reluctance to press the offensive more vigorously, which kept the support ships nearby. It was a viewpoint that would fester for months and sow the seeds of a subsequent dispute.

A hundred and forty miles to the south, the Second Marine Division landed on Betio Island, where progress was also slower than planned, partly due to the maritime geography. Many of the Higgins boats grounded on a shallow offshore coral reef while they were still a quarter mile or so off the beach. That compelled the marines to wade ashore through thigh-deep water under heavy machine gun fire. Though Betio was tiny—barely one square mile—Japanese resistance was ferocious. The Japanese commander there had bragged that his island fortress could not be taken by a million men in a hundred years. As the battle stretched into a second day and then a third, US commanders fed more men into the fight, including the Tenth Marine Regiment, which included another of the Forties, Captain Talbot "Tab" Collins, the unit's communications officer. When the island was finally secured, of the nearly five thousand Japanese defenders, only seventeen were taken alive. While it was an American victory, it had come at a sobering cost. Collins survived, but a thousand other US Marines were killed, and more than two thousand wounded. Widespread shock at such losses in so small a place suggested that another victory won at such a cost could undermine public support for the whole Pacific campaign.[8]

Partly because of that, members of Admiral Nimitz's staff argued that instead of moving immediately to the Marshall Islands and its citadel of Kwajalein Atoll, it would be better to take on a less challenging objective. Nimitz overruled them. He was convinced that the lessons learned in the bloodbath at Tarawa could be applied effectively to the invasion of the Marshalls. He ordered an attack on Kwajalein Atoll for January 1944, with the Seventh Division of the US Army assaulting Kwajalein itself at the southern end of the atoll, and the Second Marine Division, including Karch's Fourteenth Regiment, seizing the twin islands of Roi and Namur fifty miles to the north.[9]

Fred Karch was excited to get orders to the Pacific. First, though, he had to get his command across the country, from Camp Lejeune in North Carolina to Camp Pendleton in California. The regiment went by train, and as the men boarded the cars, Karch discovered that three of them were AWOL. A serious offense at any time, "missing movement," as it was called, was especially grave, and Karch wanted to ensure it never happened again. When the wayward men showed up, he sentenced all three of them to thirty days in solitary confinement on bread and water. He acknowledged that it was a stiff punishment, though he also noted that no one in his command ever missed movement again. It was, he said, exactly "the type of discipline that attracted me to the Corps to start with."[10]

Camp Pendleton was brand new in 1943. Dedicated by President Roosevelt just the previous September, the facilities were still fairly rudimentary, with unheated wooden barracks and not much else. The lack of creature comforts did not bother Karch; no one ever said war was supposed to be easy or comfortable. He was more concerned about not having enough space to conduct realistic live-fire exercises with his artillery. He found that shells fired into the nearby hills sometimes triggered brushfires, and he was annoyed that "a good part of the training time was spent putting out fires started by the shell bursts." To find a more suitable training area, the Fourteenth Regiment moved two hundred miles inland to remote Camp Dunlap in the Sonoran Desert, where the men slept in canvas tents. That would have been intolerable in summer, and it was pretty uncomfortable in December, especially at night, when the temperature regularly dropped into the low 20s. There was, however, plenty of room for artillery practice. The Fourteenth Regiment spent a busy week assembling, sighting, loading, and firing their 75 mm howitzers. Day after day, as one member of the command put it, "Shells were slammed into their breeches, breechblocks locked in place, and lanyards pulled."[11]

On January 1, 1944, the Fourteenth Regiment boarded transports in San Diego for the long trip to the mid-Pacific. There was one practice landing on San Clemente Island off the California coast. Though it did not go well, the pressing timetable did not allow for further training, and the invasion fleet set out for the Marshall Islands, forty-four hundred miles to the west.[12]

It took twenty-five days, and it was no pleasure cruise. The air was hot and stale below decks, and the men berthed in racks stacked eight high along the bulkheads; it was so crowded one could not turn over without disturbing all the others. Many of them also endured horrible bouts of seasickness. The invasion fleet stopped in Lahaina Roads off Maui to refuel and resupply, though the marines never got off the ships, and the invasion fleet continued westward after only a few days. It turned out to be the longest distance between a port of embarkation and a landing beach in the entire war. Finally, at the end of January 1944, the transports arrived off the target islands and dropped anchor.[13]

SEMPER FIDELIS 243

Now sporting a David Niven–like pencil mustache, Karch was tabbed as the operations and training officer for the regiment. Rather than supervise the guns of his battalion, his job was to oversee the deployment of all the batteries. Before leaving San Diego, the 75 mm guns had been preloaded into what were called Landing Craft, Tracked (LVTs), sometimes called "alligators," which were then loaded on board the transports. With their tank-like treads, LVTs could carry men, a jeep, or in this case a 75 mm gun over coral reefs without fear of running aground as the Higgins boats had done at Tarawa. Still, sending the guns ashore along with the infantry was problematic since it would be difficult to deploy them under fire. It was decided, therefore, to land the guns on smaller islands nearby and respond to requests for artillery support from there.*

As the transports carrying the Fourteenth Regiment's artillery approached the offshore islands, one marine noted how picturesque they were. "The plush green of the island vegetation outlined the bright white sand which ringed every islet, and provided a sharp contrast with the blue-green colors of the surrounding waters." Karch may not have noticed—or cared; he was focused on the task at hand, and it grew more complicated as the hours passed. Coordinating infantry, landing boats, and artillery off an enemy beach was stressful. There were delays in launching the LVTs into turbulent seas—two of them foundered, taking the guns they carried down with them. Not until late in the afternoon did Karch have five of the 75 mm guns ashore.[14]

Of course, the guns were useless without ammunition, all of which had to be hoisted up from the hold and then lowered down into the bobbing landing craft alongside. And once ashore, the fifteen-pound shells then had to be transported to the gun emplacements. The historian of the Fourteenth Regiment noted that "the first days ashore were tiring and hectic." More prosaically, one marine summed it up as "Operation Fubar."† It was full dark before all the guns were in position. The unloading and distribution of the ammunition went on all night. Karch never slept.[15]

A few minutes before 7:00 the next morning, February 1, 1944, Rear Admiral Richard Connelly, whose cool demeanor had so impressed Lieutenant Edelstein off Sicily, opened fire on Roi and Namur from his two battleships, plus the heavy cruiser *Louisville*. Karch ordered his guns to join in, though the impact of 75 mm ordnance was hardly discernible alongside the fourteen-inch shells of

---

* For the invasion of Kwajalein, the Army's Seventh Division also placed its artillery on adjacent islands to support the infantry assault.

† On the chance that some readers may be unaware of the acronym, still routinely used by GIs of all services, "fubar" stands for "F***ed Up Beyond All Recognition."

Connelly's battleships. Indeed, the naval bombardment was overwhelming, obliterating buildings, trees, bunkers, even sand dunes, so denuding the island that it reminded one marine of a bootcamp haircut. Karch noted approvingly that "the Navy had learned from the Tarawa Operation what it takes to soften up a beach."[16]

The fighting ashore was fierce. Amid the smoke-enshrouded confusion, Karch found it difficult to respond efficiently to requests for artillery support. More often than not, the marines on Roi and Namur used hand grenades, bangalore torpedoes, and satchel charges to work their way forward trench by trench. When one marine hurled a satchel charge into a bunker where the Japanese had stored torpedo warheads, the resulting explosion shook the whole island. After night fell, the marines on Roi and Namur bedded down where they were in hastily dug foxholes; Karch's men on the outlying islands did the same, sleeping alongside their guns. By the afternoon of February 2, both Roi and Namur were declared secure, and within days Marine Corps fighter planes were landing on the captured airfield.[17]

Fifty miles to the south, Montgomery's *Idaho* was one of several battleships assigned to the bombardment of Kwajalein. Montgomery was officer of the deck that day, and he maneuvered the *Idaho* so as to sustain fire support throughout the afternoon. On his watch alone, the *Idaho* fired four hundred rounds of high-capacity shells onto the island. The shelling finally ceased at 6:22 on the morning of February 5, when the island was declared secure, though mopping-up operations continued for several days. Nimitz's conviction that the lessons of Tarawa could be effectively applied in the Marshalls had proved valid.[18]

Karch was not satisfied. It was clear to him that "it took a lot more to be a regiment than a week's training in the desert." He thought that if the operation had gone on for another day, "the regiment would have lost control of the fire of the battalions." That conviction fed his determination to get out of staff work and back to the command of troops so that he could mandate more, and more serious, training.[19]

After a few weeks, most of the Fourteenth Regiment loaded onto transports and headed eastward, back to Maui. This time they got a hero's welcome. Schools on the island canceled classes, and children lined the road to cheer the returning marines. There were no facilities on Maui to house a division of seventeen thousand men, so the marines built their own, turning sixteen hundred acres of pastureland into what they dubbed Camp Maui. Eventually, it included twenty-one hundred tents, two mess halls, a post exchange, two softball fields, and a movie theater.[20]

Karch had no intention of settling down to such a benign existence. He went to the regimental commander, Colonel Louis DeHaven, and asked to be relieved as operations officer and returned to the command of a battalion. Asked why, Karch told him that the training for the recent operation had been inadequate and that he wanted to drill his men into a more effective fighting unit. The regimental XO, a lieutenant colonel with the serendipitous name of Randall Victory, backed him up and suggested that DeHaven should let him and Karch take over the training. If DeHaven was annoyed by that, he didn't show it: "If you think you can run this regiment better than I do, go ahead." So Karch remained operations officer after all, and when Colonel Victory asked him what he thought the regiment should do, Karch was ready with an answer: "We are going to move into the field and stay there."[21]

Determined to "whip this outfit into shape," Karch moved the Fourteenth Regiment out of Camp Maui, with its softball games and USO shows, and into the bush, where the men conducted maneuvers almost daily. The result was that by the time the unit received orders for the next operation in the spring, Karch was satisfied that "we were as hot an artillery regiment as there was in the Pacific."[22]

That new target was Saipan. The American high command had decided to bypass the Caroline Islands—including the Japanese base on Truk—and strike six hundred miles further west to the Marianas. What made the Marianas so critical is that they were within bombing range of the Japanese homeland, and from those islands the US Army Air Force could use its sleek new bomber, the B-29 Stratofortress, to hit Japanese cities almost at will.[23]

Unlike the tiny atolls in mid-Pacific, Saipan was not the outgrowth of a coral reef, but a full-sized island, thirteen miles long and five miles wide, with a substantial civilian population. It was also defended by thirty-one thousand Japanese soldiers. Because there were no offshore islands for Karch's batteries, the Fourteenth Regiment artillery remained on board the transports until called upon.[24]

The call came sooner than expected. Told that "the situation on shore was desperate," Karch received orders to land his guns that first afternoon. Some of the battalions in the Fourteenth Regiment had been equipped with larger 105 mm guns, and they were entrusted to a curious craft that was essentially a swimming truck that bore the acronym DUKW, but which everyone called "ducks."* One of them sank while heading to the beach, and another was blasted out of the water by a direct hit from Japanese artillery; the others made it to shore.[25]

The 75 mm guns were carried in smaller landing craft and assembled on the beach under fire. After supervising the landing, Victory and Karch established a regimental command post in a trench only half a mile inland, where they were under direct and nearly continuous fire from Japanese artillery on higher ground. One battalion was subjected to three hundred incoming artillery rounds that first day. As night fell, Karch was not certain the marines could hold the beachhead. He later recalled, "That night was probably the most critical of any that I went through in combat." The enemy shelling continued all night, and by eight o'clock the next morning, the Fourteenth Regiment had only two 75 mm guns that were still operational.[26]

Throughout the war—in both theaters—one difference between Allied and Axis forces was the ability of the Americans to extemporize and jury-rig repairs. Karch was full of praise for the divisional ordnance team—the men charged with maintaining and repairing the big guns. As the unit historian noted: "They worked miracles with the battered weapons they received. Howitzers came in with tails blown off, recoil mechanisms damaged, hydraulic cylinders punctured, sights damaged or missing, and cracked barrels," and somehow, the mechanics patched them up, repurposing or cannibalizing needed parts, and got the guns back into action.[27]

On D-Day plus 2, the restored 75 mm batteries began a rolling barrage ahead of the ground troops. That allowed the marine infantry to head inland. Yet expending all that ordnance had consequences. That afternoon, a courier came to Karch to tell him they had run out of ammunition and the 75s had to cease fire. The Japanese took advantage of the resulting pause to launch a counterattack. Karch got on the phone to a nearby 105 mm battery and ordered it to shift targets to staunch the break. He was gratified to see that the first salvo from the larger guns "landed right on the nose of the enemy penetration." He believed that salvo "saved us from disaster."[28]

Over the next few days, the marines of the Second Division moved inland, crossing to the island's eastern side and occupying the airfield en route. The Fourteenth Regiment went with them. Then the marines turned north to advance up the eastern shore. On the western side of the island, the Second

---

* The acronym was not intended to suggest ducks. Rather, each letter denoted a particular aspect of its design: the *D* indicated that it was produced in 1942; the *U* marked it as a utility vehicle; the *K* meant that it had all-wheel drive; and the *W* denoted that it had tandem rear axles.

Marine Division advanced up that coastline. In between them was the US Army's Twenty-Seventh Division, which held the center. The terrain there was especially daunting, with landmarks subsequently dubbed "Death Valley," "Hell's Pocket," and "Purple Heart Ridge." As a result, their progress was slower, and that threatened to expose the flanks of the fast-moving marines. The overall ground commander was, once again, Holland M. Smith, now a lieutenant general, whose initials (H. M.) suggested his nickname: "Howling Mad." Already skeptical of the army's combat prowess as a result of the fighting on Makin, he was infuriated by what he perceived as the army's foot-dragging on Saipan and decided to relieve the commander of the Twenty-Seventh Division, Major General Ralph Smith. For a marine three-star to relieve an army two-star for cause in the middle of an ongoing battle was unprecedented—even scandalous. Whether or not the move contributed to an acceleration of the campaign, this Smith-versus-Smith controversy, as it came to be known, left a lasting legacy of resentment in both services.[29]

Karch thought the decision was justified. He worked closely with an artillery regiment in the Twenty-Seventh Division and believed that, man for man, they were good soldiers. He was particularly impressed by Army Brigadier General Arthur M. Harper, who helped coordinate the artillery of both services. Karch credited Harper with "instilling a feeling of confidence, cooperation, and unity," between the army and marine artillerists. And Karch was gratified that army artillery units shared their equipment and ammo with the marines. All that led him to conclude that if there was a problem, it must be at the divisional level.[30]

Ralph Smith's dismissal did not immediately rectify the problem—if there was a problem. That very night, in fact, the Japanese launched a surprise counterattack on the Twenty-Seventh Division. Karch called his army counterpart to offer artillery support and was a bit annoyed when the army major replied that if he needed help he would ask for it. Later that night, Karch did get a call, though not the one he anticipated. An army brigade officer called to tell him that his artillery would not be able to support the planned morning offensive. "Why not?" Karch asked. "What's your problem?" The answer was unsettling: "We've been overrun." The Japanese had pushed the Twenty-Seventh Division back several miles, though after their attack lost its impetus, the men of the Twenty-Seventh counterattacked and recovered all the lost ground.[31]

In the midst of the fighting, Karch sent his forward observer, Hill Miller, up in a scout plane to look over the situation. Miller radioed back that what he saw was "unbelievable." Over on the eastern side of the island, the Japanese had somehow occupied an offshore reef and were firing into the flank of the marines of the Second Division. It was, in Karch's view, "a real fiasco." Yet that gambit, too, was soon overcome, and the American advance continued.[32]

By July 7, the Japanese defenders had been pushed back into the northern tip of the island. Miller, the forward observer, called Karch. "I need a battalion to shoot at a submarine." Karch was skeptical. "Don't tell me there's a submarine. Are you sure?" Miller confessed that he had never seen a submarine before, but it looked just like the ones he had seen in pictures. He suggested that it might be coming to evacuate the Japanese high command. Rather than commit an artillery battalion, Karch reported the sighting to the navy, which sent two destroyers to depth charge the area and chase the sub away. Whatever the sub's mission, it was not to evacuate the high command, for the Japanese naval commander, Admiral Chuichi Nagumo—the man who had led the attack on Pearl Harbor—had committed suicide the day before.[33]

There was one more tragic epilogue. The Japanese army had convinced the civilians on Saipan that the Americans would torture and rape them before killing them. Fleeing northward in terror, the civilians ran out of island when they reached the cliffs at Marpi Point. Unwilling to endure torture at the hands of the Americans, desperate parents threw their children over the cliff and then jumped after them. It was horrifying, Karch recalled. "A real bloody affair."[34]

A week later, Karch and his artillerists took part in the capture of Tinian, the island just south of Saipan. This time, the hypercritical Karch was fully satisfied. It was, in his view, "one of the great amphibious assault plans of the war." Rather than land at the obvious beach near Tinian Town, the Marines feinted there and landed on several small beaches on the other side of the island. It went off without a hitch, and Karch recalled that "we swept through Tinian with relative ease." After fending off a Japanese counterattack on July 24–25, the island was declared secured on August 1. A week later, the Fourteenth Marines boarded transports for the long trip back to Camp Maui.[35]

Despite spending twenty-four days at or near the front lines, Karch came though the fighting on Saipan and Tinian entirely unscathed. Indeed, though some three thousand marines had been killed on Saipan, none of them were from the class of 1940. Rather remarkably, in fact, though marines from the class fought on Guadalcanal, Bougainville, Tarawa, Saipan, and elsewhere, none of them received a mortal injury. Of the twenty-five Forties who had selected the Marine Corps, only one of them was killed in the war.

By the fall of 1944, Leon "Chab" Chabot had been a prisoner of the Japanese for more than two and a half years, first at Bilibud Prison, where he and the other POWs had clean water and even occasional showers, then at Camp Cabanatuan, sixty miles north of Manila, where conditions were more austere. Chabot soon appreciated that as bad as it was being a prisoner of the Japanese, it could have been far worse, for in June 1942, the survivors of the notorious Bataan Death March joined the inmates at Cabanatuan. They staggered into camp barely alive, and more than a thousand of them did die within a month.[36]

Each of the barrack buildings at Cabanatuan housed fifty POWs, divided into groups of ten. The barracks were made of wood with corrugated iron roofs and bamboo floors, and though rudimentary, they at least kept the rain off. The food, too, was basic, mostly salt-cured fish and rice. Entrepreneurial GIs set up a business of sorts, bribing the guards to obtain small cans of sardines, corned beef, and even native cigarettes and then selling them to the other prisoners. There was no clothing issue, and once their uniforms rotted away, they endured the interminable days wearing Ghandi-like loincloths. Virtually all of them lost weight; Chabot lost almost a third of his body weight. Disease also took a terrible toll: malaria, diarrhea, amoebic dysentery, yellow jaundice, scurvy, edema, and even beriberi were common. Men died every day, their bodies interred in the growing camp cemetery.[37]

There were a few escape attempts. Both soldiers and marines had been taught that if they were captured, it was their duty to try to escape, and a few did. The Japanese, however, quickly put an end to it. The prisoners were housed in groups of ten, and the Japanese announced that if any one of them escaped, the other nine would all be executed. After this happened once or twice, escape attempts ended.[38]

The only respite was work detail. Arising at dawn, the prisoners were transported by trucks to work sites where they grew food, built bridges, lengthened airport runways, and repaired war damage. In the rice fields, they worked in mud up to their thighs. At dusk they were trucked back to the prison compound. Hard as it was, it was at least a break from camp life, and the prisoners discovered that it was sometimes possible to find a piece of fruit or some other edible sustenance when they were engaged on work details.[39]

By 1943, however, the Japanese high command in Tokyo decided that this manpower resource was not being fully exploited. Prime Minister Tojo himself decreed that all ships returning to Japan from the Philippines should carry as many POWs as possible to work in Japanese war industries. This was a violation of the Geneva Convention, but since Japan had never signed it, no one in Japan

250   ANNAPOLIS GOES TO WAR

felt bound by it. Consequently, by 1944, large numbers of Allied POWs in the Philippines were being crammed into one or another transport ship and dispatched to work in factories in Formosa, Korea, Manchuria, and the Japanese home islands. Conditions aboard those ships were even worse than in the camps, and the men quickly dubbed them "hell ships." In September 1944, Chab Chabot was one of 750 American POWs ordered to board the *Shinyo Maru*, bound for Japan.[40]

Just getting aboard was an ordeal. The POWs had to climb a rope ladder to board the ship, and the weak and emaciated POWs found that daunting. They then had to descend another ladder down into an unlit hold. "As we went lower," one recalled, "the temperature rose, so the bottom was like a furnace." It was so crowded that there was no room even to sit down; the men had to stand, crammed up next to one another, sweating in their nakedness. The only toilet facility was a five-gallon drum in the middle of the hold.[41]

On August 22, 1944, Japanese guards on the *Shinyo Maru* stretched a canvas tarpaulin over the only hatch that allowed fresh air into the hold. Within hours, scores of prisoners passed out from the lack of oxygen.[42]

On that same day, the *Gato*-class submarine USS *Paddle* (SS-263) left Fremantle, Australia, for her fifth war patrol under the command of Lieutenant Commander Byron Nowell. Two weeks later, a few minutes after 6:00 a.m. on September 7, lookouts topside spotted a column of smoke on the horizon. As the *Paddle* closed the sighting, the stacks and masts of at least two large ships became visible, and Nowell went to periscope depth. It was soon clear that this was a Japanese convoy of at least five ships escorted by two small destroyer types, and as the convoy prepared to round Sindangan Point on the western side of Mindanao, Nowell maneuvered the *Paddle* into position for an attack. His primary target was the tanker in the lead, which was followed closely by a medium-size transport.

Just before 5:00 p.m., Nowell fired four torpedoes at the tanker, then fired two more at the transport. When one of the Japanese escorts turned toward the *Paddle*, Nowell went deep. As the sub descended, everyone on board heard the explosions of successful hits followed by "loud, characteristic, breaking up noises." The crew in the conning tower celebrated another successful sinking.[43]

Both of the torpedoes aimed at the *Shinyo Maru* struck her amidships, and it was immediately evident that she was sinking. The Japanese guards ripped off the tarpaulin covering the hatch and began machine gunning the semiconscious POWs below. With nothing to lose, those prisoners who could move fought their way up onto the deck, attacked the guards, and leaped over the side. Ships in the Japanese convoy launched small boats that picked up Japanese crewmen in the water and machine-gunned the POWs. Some of the POWs made it to shore; a few were recaptured; most were killed or drowned. Of the 750 American POWs on the *Shinyo Maru*, 688 died. One of them was Leon "Chab" Chabot, holder of the Academy 100-yard dash record and the only US Marine from the class of 1940 to die in the war.[44]

20

The Atlantic Again

The command of a ship at sea is the pinnacle of a naval officer's career. Regardless of rank, the commanding officer of a ship is always addressed as "captain," and he is all but sovereign. In the prewar years, fewer than 5 percent of career officers ever reached such a height, and then only after decades of serving in subordinate positions. By 1944, however, there were far more ships to command—hundreds more—and a number of the Forties reached that milestone early in their careers. As we have seen, John Claggett and several others commanded PT boats as ensigns as early as 1942, and P. T. Glennon had brief command of a *Gato*-class submarine in 1943, though only when it was tied up for repairs. Other Forties had commanded air squadrons, blimps, Marine Corps companies, even battalions. Still, when Henry "Hank" Vaughn assumed command of the brand-new destroyer escort USS *Seid* (DE-256) in July 1943 and Peck Greenbacker got orders to command the USS *Neunzer* (DE-150) two months later, it was a significant landmark for them and for the class. In only four years, at least some of the Forties had gone from being midshipmen who saluted anything that moved, to commanding a navy warship where everyone on board deferred to them. Greenbacker's assignment was especially noteworthy because his executive officer was another of the Forties, Virgil Gex ("It's Zhey, sir"), who, though he was a classmate, was junior to Greenbacker by five months because imperfect eyesight had delayed his commission.

The relationship between a captain and his exec is a singular one. The XO is the ship's second in command and responsible for converting the captain's wishes and intentions into orders: making out the watch bills, supervising the exercises, and scheduling drills. Often, he adopts the role of "bad cop" on the ship. While division officers could joke around with the men in their departments, the XO seldom has that luxury, since he is the one who has to enforce regulations, sometimes becoming unpopular in the process. The XO is also the

THE ATLANTIC AGAIN

one man on the ship with whom the captain can confer in confidence about all sorts of issues, from shipboard discipline to naval tactics. Since Greenbacker and Gex were also Academy classmates, theirs was a particularly close relationship—Gex called it "a congenial arrangement." Any time they were within earshot of another crew member, Gex was careful to refer to Greenbacker as "captain," though it is easy to imagine that in private they may have reverted to addressing one another as "Peck" and "Doc."

Technically, the *Neunzer* was not Greenbacker's first command, for he had previously captained a small (112-foot) British-built subchaser of a type known as a "Fairmyle." He had enjoyed some of the decorative touches on that vessel, such as the teak and mahogany woodwork, which made it feel more like a yacht than a warship. On the other hand, he had been appalled by its primitive air defense system: a mortar-like tube that flung an ordinary hand grenade up into the air to be used, apparently, against dive bombers. After that, Greenbacker spent a short tour as the executive officer of the USS *Stewart* (DE-238) before being tabbed as the initial commanding officer of her brand-new sister ship, the *Neunzer*.[1]*

The *Neunzer* was an *Edsall*-class destroyer escort, one of eighty-five built during the war specially designed for anti-submarine missions. In lieu of the five-inch guns on *Fletcher*-class destroyers, the *Neunzer* carried three-inch guns and fewer of them. They would be of minimal value against cruisers or even other destroyers, but they were plenty powerful enough to sink a submarine. And while the *Neunzer* carried conventional depth charges on her stern, she also had eight "K-guns" along her sides that could slingshot depth charges out away from the ship, plus a forward-throwing "hedgehog" on her foredeck that fired a pattern of seventy-pound bomblets out in front of the ship. All that made it possible for the *Neunzer* and her sister ships to assume the aggressor's role against submarines.

Greenbacker took command of the *Neunzer* in November 1943 (the same month marines went ashore on Betio Island), and in December he and the *Neunzer* formed part of the escort for a large transatlantic convoy to Britain. By now the Allied convoy system was working (in Greenbacker's words) "like clockwork." For one thing, there were a lot more escorts available, and many of

---

* The *Stewart* had a higher hull number (238) than the *Neunzer* (150) even though she had been launched first. The reason is that she was the first DE built by Brown Shipbuilding in Houston, which had the contract for ships numbered 238 to 255, and the *Neunzer* was among the last built by Consolidated Steel in Orange, Texas, which built DEs numbered 129 to 152. The *Stewart* floats still, as a museum ship in Galveston.

254 ANNAPOLIS GOES TO WAR

them carried new weapons like the K-gun and the hedgehog. In addition, many of the convoys now included a small escort aircraft carrier that gave the Allies eyes in the air. Another key factor was that the merchant captains had become accustomed to the discipline of convoy protocols, so herding them across the Atlantic was less stressful than it had been in 1942. Greenbacker noted that the "merchant masters were well trained," and that made convoys of seventy-five or even one hundred ships possible. And, finally, the U-boat threat had greatly diminished. Since 1942, Dönitz had lost many of his ace U-boat skippers, and the younger officers who replaced them were less experienced and less efficient. The December 1943 convoy to Britain arrived safely with no losses, and after returning to Norfolk, Greenbacker, Gex, and the *Neunzer* joined the escort force of another convoy to Gibraltar. There, however, the *Neunzer* was detached from convoy duty and assigned a special, and rather peculiar, mission.[2]

After the Allied conquest of Sicily in July 1943, Mussolini's fascist government collapsed, and the new Italian government opened secret negotiations with the Allies, hoping to change sides. Roosevelt's previously announced policy of "unconditional surrender" made that impossible, and in the end the Italians had to swallow the opprobrium of surrender after all. One stipulation the Allies made was that all the warships of the Italian navy, the Regia Marina, had to be turned over to the Allies. Italian naval officers had not been privy to the negotiations, and the announcement caught them by surprise. Nevertheless, in September 1943, the battleships and cruisers of the Italian navy crossed the Mediterranean and turned themselves over to the Allies either in North Africa or on the island of Malta. Five Italian submarines that were operating in the western Mediterranean surrendered to the British at Gibraltar, and they were still there when the *Neunzer* arrived in January 1944. Greenbacker got orders to escort them to the United States, where they would provide training for American destroyers in place of the old R-class boats. During the transatlantic crossing, the submarines would retain their Italian officers and crew, but they would be subject to Greenbacker's orders.[3]

They set out on January 27, 1944 (the same week US Marines went ashore on Roi and Namur). The *Neunzer* led, with the five Italian boats following her like baby ducks behind their mother. The little flotilla had barely cleared the straits, however, when the eight-hundred-ton *Tito Speri*, which had been built back in 1925, suffered an engineering failure, and the whole column returned to Gibraltar. There, a few Royal Navy officers speculated aloud that the Italians were inventing mechanical difficulties to avoid venturing out into the broad

THE ATLANTIC AGAIN

Atlantic. Greenbacker thought otherwise. He believed the Italians were eager to get away from both the war and the condescending remarks of the British. He thought that "the advantages of climate and likelihood of a more friendly reception farther from the war zone . . . provided adequate incentives" for the Italians "to get away from Gibraltar."[4]

After the *Speri*'s engine plant was repaired, they all set out again on January 29. There was no turning back this time, though the convoy's speed had to be reduced to seven knots to allow the *Speri* to keep up. During the crossing, Greenbacker conducted several anti-submarine drills with the Italian boats. For an hour each day, he had one or more of them submerge and try to avoid detection. Somewhat to his surprise, he discovered that they were quite good at it. As he put it later, "We found ourselves completely unprepared for the radical evasive tactics employed by the Italians." He was used to training with American R-class subs that maneuvered as best they could while submerged, but usually with unchanging speed. The Italians not only changed speed regularly but would back down into their own acoustic shadow and all but disappear. After discussing these tactics with the Italian skippers, Greenbacker summarized his thoughts in a report to the US submarine commander in Bermuda, urging changes to the training protocols. Current training, he wrote, "was simply inadequate." After they arrived in Bermuda, the submarine commander there treated Greenbacker's report as a personal criticism and in his endorsement asserted that Greenbacker not only had "violated safety precautions" but was probably "not fit to command." As Greenbacker put it later, "Fortunately, the type commander supported most of my observations."[5]

Well before that, when the little flotilla was still only about halfway to Bermuda, Greenbacker got another surprise when two of the Italian sub skippers reported they were so low on fuel that they would not be able to make it to Bermuda unless the flotilla slowed to five knots. American submarines, built for service in the broad Pacific, had a range of ten thousand miles or more, but Italian subs had been designed for service in the Mediterranean and had never had to cross an ocean. Greenbacker was astonished that no one had seen this coming. He mused drily that logistic planning for the trip "had been less than perfect."[6]

This new development provoked "consternation" on the bridge of the *Neunzer*. At five knots, the flotilla would arrive in New York too late to allow liberty for the ship's crew, something everyone had been counting on. Gex suggested that instead of slowing the whole flotilla to five knots, they should try to refuel the Italian submarines at sea. By now, underway replenishment (unrep) had become common in the surface navy, and the Germans had managed to resupply their submarines off the US East Coast, but the US Navy had never before tried to refuel a submarine at sea, especially a submarine of a different service. For their part, the Italians had never tried refueling at sea at all and found the whole notion little short of horrifying.[7]

There was plenty of fuel on the *Neunzer*, and only the two smallest subs had to be refueled, but making the transfer posed several problems. For one thing, *Neunzer* did not have any of the rigging necessary: no booms, lengthy hoses, or supporting cables, and the Italian sub skippers were leery of coming alongside while underway. Greenbacker and Gex decided that the only practical solution was to run a refueling hose off the stern to a submarine trailing behind. It was a protocol commonly used in the Royal Navy, so clearly it could be done, and it would allow the Italians room to maneuver if "extreme avoiding action" (Greenbacker's phrase) became necessary.[8]

It was not a perfect solution, however, for the *Neunzer*'s fuel hose bibs were amidships, and the fuel hoses were not long enough to run all the way to the stern and then down to the sub. Gex suggested using the ship's fire hoses. They were long enough, but the adapters did not fit. New couplings could be man-ufactured in the ship's machine shop, though that might take days, and with New York liberty calling, the whole crew got into the spirit of the project. The deck gang suggested detaching the fire hoses from the firefighting system alto-gether and using the bilge pump to move the fuel. Firefighting capability aft could be maintained by running a separate fire hose from the forward pump. Greenbacker approved the suggestion and the crew got to work.[9]

There was some concern that the Italians, unfamiliar with underway refuel-ing, would not prove up to the mark, but once the refueling began, Greenbacker noted, "The ship handling of the submarine captains was superb as they held their boats in perfect position." Over a two-hour period, each of the two smaller Italian subs took on seventy-five hundred gallons of fuel oil, and soon the flotilla was underway again, steaming at eight knots. Indeed, after a few hours, Greenbacker eased the convoy speed up to twelve knots. Arriving only one day late in New York, Greenbacker turned the subs over to Navy Yard offi-cials, and the *Neunzer* moored alongside the wharf on February 15, 1944. The crew got eleven days of liberty. Greenbacker attributed the innovative—indeed unprecedented—success of the fuel transfer to the eagerness of the crew for liberty, "the traditional preoccupation of sailors since time immemorial." In addition, however, it also highlighted "the celebrated American talent for improvisation." Even the Italians were impressed. The senior Italian naval

THE ATLANTIC AGAIN

officer, Commander Giuseppe Bartolo, told Gex: "To you, nothing is impossible. When something comes up you want to do, you simply go ahead and do it, whether it is impossible or not."[10]

In May, Greenbacker received orders to a new ship, and Gex fleeted up to command the *Neunzer*. It was a poignant moment as one member of the class of 1940 relieved another as commanding officer. The boatswain's whistle called the assembled ship's company to attention, and Greenbacker, in his service dress whites, read aloud the orders detaching him from the ship. Then Gex stepped forward to read his orders to command, after which he turned to Greenbacker, saluted, and said, "I relieve you, sir." Greenbacker returned the salute, said: "I stand relieved." Then they shook hands. It is unlikely either of them could have imagined such a scene during their plebe summer eight years earlier.

Both Greenbacker and Gex had held a number of assignments in the navy prior to their selection to command. That was a typical career path in the US Navy, where changing duty assignments every few years was commonplace. Bill Braybrook was an exception. He had reported aboard the heavy cruiser *Tuscaloosa* in Brooklyn two weeks after graduation, and he remained on board her throughout the entire war, indeed until she was decommissioned in December 1946. He never applied to flight school, or sub school, or gunnery school, or any other school, working his way up from assistant navigator to third division junior officer to first division officer to main battery assistant, which was the job he held in February 1944.

Soon after that, in April, the *Tuscaloosa* went into the yards at Boston to be supplied with special radio equipment, and only days later she was steaming east across the Atlantic to the Clyde Estuary in Scotland. There she engaged in more shore bombardment exercises. There, too, an army communications team came on board to establish secure ship-to-shore communications with US Army landing teams. By then, Braybrook and everyone else on board began to suspect that the *Tuscaloosa* had been tabbed to play a role in the long-awaited Allied invasion of Nazi-occupied northern France: D-Day.[11]

On June 3, the *Tuscaloosa* steamed out of the Clyde Estuary in company with several other Allied ships and headed south through the Irish Sea. Her sealed orders, opened only after she was well out to sea, indicated that she was to provide fire support for a landing on Utah Beach, the westernmost of five invasion beaches on the coast of Normandy.

The weather was terrible, and it remained so for three days. It was so foul, in fact, that the landings, which had been scheduled for June 5, had to be postponed by a day. Adjusting for that was easy for the *Tuscaloosa*, since it meant simply slowing down and maneuvering in the Irish Sea. Other elements of the invasion force, however, were already heading across the Channel. Radio orders recalling them went out from Allied headquarters, though one convoy of 138 vessels never got the word. Destroyers had to be dispatched from English ports to intercept them and bring them back.

One of the destroyers sent on that mission was the USS *Baldwin*, on which Ben Frana (Benjie to his classmates) was the gunnery officer. The *Baldwin* fought her way through the rough seas and caught up with the convoy of LCIs (Landing Craft Infantry), LCMs (Landing Craft Mechanized), and other ships in mid-Channel. Coming up alongside each ship, Frana or some other officer used a bullhorn to shout: "The operation has been cancelled. Return to base." Frana recalled later that the soldiers appeared to be desperately seasick, and while some may have been glad for the postponement, others no doubt simply wanted to get it over with. Their reprieve was short. Only hours after all the ships had been rounded up and were securely back in port, a mail boat approached the *Baldwin* and delivered an envelope containing terse orders: "Operation Overlord scheduled for June 6."[12]

Frana and the *Baldwin* accompanied the invasion force for Omaha Beach (Force O), escorting sixteen transports and participating in the preinvasion bombardment. The *Tuscaloosa*, with both Braybrook and another of the Forties, Bill Carpenter, on board, was part of the Utah Beach invasion force (Force U), as was the battleship *Nevada*, with another Forty, Allan "Cooky" Cook, as her first lieutenant and damage control officer. They all arrived off Utah Beach well before first light on June 6.

Braybrook was more than a little surprised to see the enormous stone lighthouse at Cape Barfleur still "flashing brightly." Were the Germans really so unaware of the mighty armada that was descending on them? It hardly seemed possible. Even before the sun rose, Bill Carpenter noted that "the surface radar screen showed literally thousands of surface ship echoes." As he watched, "a solid stream of allied aircraft" flew past overhead: "bombers, transports, transports towing gliders, and fighter cover." The German antiaircraft batteries "put on a fireworks display" that stretched "as far as the eye could see to the north and south," and the aerial drama was "punctuated with occasional aircraft falling in flames through the shell fire." Carpenter called it "the greatest show on earth."[13]

As main battery assistant, it was Braybrook's job to coordinate the preinvasion gunfire from the nine eight-inch guns of the *Tuscaloosa*. To execute that

THE ATLANTIC AGAIN   259

mission, he had been provided with a list of coded targets with specific coordinates. In the Pacific, naval gunfire prior to an invasion could last for several hours, even days. Here, however, in order to maintain the advantage of surprise, the Allied high command mandated a one-hour window for the naval bombardment. It was to begin at 5:50 a.m. and last until just before the soldiers landed at 6:40. Yet, short as it was, it would also be intense, with hundreds of naval guns, plus hundreds more bombers, saturating the five invasion beaches with heavy ordnance. It would not be enough to destroy enemy defenses; the hope was that it would demoralize the defenders, perhaps even stun them into submission.[14]

The commander of the Allied bombardment group off Utah Beach was US Navy Rear Admiral Morton Deyo, who used the *Tuscaloosa* as his flagship. In fact, he bunked in the same cabin FDR had used during his "fishing expedition" back in 1941. Deyo had all the ships of his command in position, six miles off the beach by 5:00 a.m. As soon as it was light enough to see, the Germans opened fire. None of the Allied ships was hit, though some of the shells came uncomfortably close. Braybrook described the German gunfire as "troublesome" and asked permission to return fire. Deyo told him no. He was to adhere to the schedule. Though other Allied ships responded with counter-battery fire, Braybrook waited until the scheduled hour.[15]

The targets were designated by numbers and map coordinates. That was just as well, because after the aerial bombing, the smoke and dust over the beach was so thick most of the gunfire was "unobserved." Relying on the predetermined target list, Braybrook directed the guns to hit sites designated only by their numbers: 7A, 9, and 14A. Once all the ships opened fire, it added to the blanket of dust and smoke, completely obscuring the landing beaches. That made it all but impossible to determine whether the ordnance was having the desired effect, or indeed any effect.[16]

The Higgins boats carrying the soldiers to the beach landed only a few minutes past the designated H-Hour of 6:40. After that, the naval guns directed their fire further inland to avoid hitting friendly forces. At 7:11, Braybrook sent twenty-four rounds into one German battery position, and thirteen minutes later he shifted fire to another. Both batteries were silenced, though it was not clear whether they had been destroyed or were playing possum. Braybrook had to write, "Believe target neutralized," and "Battery probably neutralized." The air spotters helped a little, but they, too, were hampered by heavy smoke and dust over the targets. At one point an air spotter identified a possible enemy battery and Braybrook sent twenty-one rounds of armor-piercing shells into it.

The pilot reported "many rounds in target area," but that was as specific as he could be. It would be better to be able to communicate with spotters on shore, but despite the presence of the army communications team on board, the radios with the landing teams had been wrecked during the landings, and it was late afternoon before the *Tuscaloosa* established radio contact with troops ashore.[17]

Meanwhile on Omaha Beach, the invasion had bogged down altogether. The brief preinvasion bombardment had failed to knock out German positions on the high ground behind the beach, and the invaders found themselves pinned down by a storm of artillery and machine gun fire. To break the stalemate, the navy brass offshore ordered the destroyers, with their shallow draft, to close the beach and provide fire support for the infantry. The *Baldwin* was one of a dozen destroyers that responded, and as gunnery officer it was Ben Frana who coordinated its effort to find and silence the German guns.

Then, as now, Omaha Beach slopes very gradually—only one foot of drop for each fifty feet of horizontal beach. Consequently, three hundred yards from the beach, the water was only eighteen feet deep. The *Baldwin* drew seventeen feet, and to get close enough to be effective, she had to risk grounding. Even so, she steamed in so close to the beach that she was being hit by rifle bullets. With his binoculars, Frana searched the high ground behind the beach looking for the well-disguised German gun positions, and whenever he saw something suspicious, he directed the *Baldwin*'s four five-inch guns to target it. At the Academy, Frana had received an award for "Excellence in Great Guns," and he put that skill to use now. The *Baldwin* fired into the hills as fast as possible, the brass casings of expended five-inch shells cascading into piles outside the gun mounts. The Germans fired back, of course, and two artillery shells struck the *Baldwin*, smashing up her whaleboat and blowing an eight-by-twelve-inch hole in her main deck. It did not slow the ship's firing.[18]

Back on the *Tuscaloosa*, Braybrook got orders to shift fire from his list of predetermined targets to a German battery that was shooting at the destroyers. Braybrook directed seventy rounds of high-capacity shells toward the new coordinates and was gratified when the battery stopped shooting.

Meanwhile, on the *Baldwin*, Frana maintained a relentless and continuous fire into the high ground. And it had an effect. A beachmaster on Omaha later testified, "You could see the trenches, guns, and men blowing up where they were hit." By 10:30, the soldiers who had been pinned down behind a low berm of shingle began to raise their heads, get up, and move inland. By noon, they had surmounted the bluffs and gained the high ground. This unanticipated role of the destroyers, including Frana's *Baldwin*, was a key to eventual success on Omaha Beach. Stanhope Mason, the chief of staff to Major General Clarence Huebner, commanding the First Division (the Big Red One), declared that "without that gunfire we positively could not have crossed the beaches."[19]

The *Baldwin* was the only American destroyer that was hit by enemy shellfire that day, though others were victimized by mines. One of them was the USS *Glennon* (DD-620), named for P. T. Glennon's grandfather, the man who had helped him study for the Academy entrance exam. On the afternoon of June 8, the *Glennon* was spotting for the *Tuscaloosa* and reporting the coordinates of German strongpoints. When the *Tuscaloosa* fired eight high-capacity shells and nine armor-piercing shells into a reported position, the *Glennon* radioed, "Target demolished." Soon after that, however, a German mine exploded underneath her and the *Glennon* reared violently out of the water. Though she remained afloat, she could not move. A destroyer escort, the USS *Rich* (DE-695), attempted to tow her off, until she, too, was damaged by a mine. Further attempts to tow off the crippled *Glennon* proved futile, and because she was stationary, she became an easy target for German artillery. Three shells hit her in quick succession, and they proved fatal. Her crew abandoned ship, and she sank on June 10.[20]

For several days after the initial landings, the *Tuscaloosa* and the other Allied heavy ships remained off the coast, responding to requests for fire support from the soldiers now moving inland. The spotters ashore now had working radios, and whenever the troops bumped up against a strongpoint—a pillbox, a troop concentration, or a group of tanks—they reported the coordinates to the ships offshore. Braybrook checked the coordinates on the map and passed the information to the turret officers. The eight-inch guns on the *Tuscaloosa* banged out a half dozen salvos until the radioman ashore reported, "Mission successful."[21]

Getting the troops ashore was only the first step. As the invasion of Guadalcanal had demonstrated, keeping them reinforced and supplied was at least as important and nearly as challenging. To land, maintain, and supply an army that would eventually number more than a million would require a working harbor for loading and unloading their supplies, equipment, and ammunition.* That is why the *Tuscaloosa*'s next target was the nearby French port of Cherbourg.[22]

By June 17 (D-Day plus 11), the army forces that had landed on Utah Beach had cut off the Cotentin Peninsula from the south, isolating Cherbourg. As the army advanced northward to attack the city from the landward side, navy ships sought to suppress the German batteries around the harbor. The naval force detailed to accomplish that consisted of three older battleships (*Nevada*, *Texas*, and *Arkansas*, the last two of which the Forties had ridden during their first class cruise), two heavy cruisers (*Tuscaloosa* and *Quincy*), plus two light cruisers and eleven destroyers, all under Morton Deyo. On June 25 they approached the German coastal batteries and opened fire.[23]

The German guns at Cherbourg were manned by gunners from the Kriegsmarine, veterans of the battleships and cruisers that Hitler had laid up, and they were terrifyingly accurate. With their first salvo, the Germans straddled the destroyer *Barton*, and in the next salvo, a German shell ricocheted off the water close alongside and crashed through the *Barton*'s engine room, coming to rest inside the ship. Thankfully, it was a dud and did not explode. Shells also landed all around the cruiser *Quincy*, and others landed within a hundred yards of the battleship *Nevada*. The *Nevada* maneuvered almost frantically to throw off the German gunners, and even so she was straddled at least six times. The gun duel lasted all afternoon, and while the navy ships managed to silence the smaller-caliber batteries west of Cherbourg, the larger guns to the east of the city remained defiant.[24]

Despite that, Braybrook considered the attack was a success. The *Tuscaloosa* had fired nearly two thousand eight-inch shells, and while that did not destroy the German batteries encased in their concrete revetments, it did significantly degrade the morale of the defenders. The German gunners were naval veterans, but many of the infantry solders were conscripts from conquered nations, and they were unwilling to fight to the death for Hitler. The city surrendered on June 29, and by mid-July Allied ships were unloading supplies and ammunition in the harbor.[25]

---

* Anticipating that, the Allies had arranged to construct two artificial harbors (called Mulberrys), one off Gold Beach and one off Omaha Beach. While they were engineering marvels, they were not a complete solution to the supply problem. For one thing, the artificial harbor off Omaha Beach was wrecked in a storm only a few days after it was completed, and in any case they had never been intended as more than a stopgap measure until an actual seaport could be captured.

THE ATLANTIC AGAIN 263

The Allied landings in Normandy marked the beginning of the end for Hitler's empire. Nearly a full year of hard fighting remained, but, after June 1944 the writing was on the wall. On June 22, the third anniversary of the German invasion of the Soviet Union, the Red Army launched Operation Bagration, a general offensive all along the eastern front. Between them, the Anglo-Canadian-American armies approaching from the west and Russian armies closing in from the east put Germany in a vice. Hitler ordered his generals to fight to the last man and the last bullet, and some did, but it did no more than increase the death toll. On August 15, other Allied forces, including a division of French troops, landed in the South of France. Ten days later, the Allies liberated Paris. There was a scare in December when the Germans tried to regain the initiative in what history has labeled the Battle of the Bulge. By the end of January 1945, however, that gambit had collapsed, and the Allies resumed their advance. In March they crossed the Rhine.

The war in the Pacific was also reaching a crescendo. Some of the bloodiest fighting there still lay ahead: the reconquest of the Philippines, Iwo Jima, and Okinawa. And all the while, American bombers assailed Japanese cities, and American submarines savaged Japanese shipping. The only question was how much punishment Japan would endure before its leaders acknowledged the reality of defeat. As Tom McGrath had told the Tucson Kiwanis Club back in 1942, "They are not afraid to be killed." It remained difficult to see how it all would end.

21

The Battle of Leyte Gulf

For more than twenty years, American planners—and Japanese planners, too—had been convinced that the outcome of any future war in the Pacific would be decided by a climactic naval battle somewhere in the western Pacific. Many thought that moment had arrived when the Japanese sortied their battlefleet to challenge the American invasion of Saipan. In what became known as the Battle of the Philippine Sea (June 19–20, 1944), or more prosaically, "The Great Marianas Turkey Shoot," American carrier-borne aircraft destroyed nearly four hundred Japanese planes (and, significantly, their air crews as well), and American submarines sank two of their aircraft carriers. The battle utterly eviscerated Japanese naval aviation, and the Japanese retreated in confusion.[1]

Yet some Americans, and especially the aviators, were disappointed that large elements of the Japanese battlefleet had escaped. Some blamed Admiral Raymond Spruance for that. In their view, Spruance should have been more aggressive with his carriers rather than keeping them near the beachhead on Saipan. Whatever the validity of those criticisms, the consequence was that when the forces of Nimitz and MacArthur converged on the Philippines that fall, the Imperial Japanese Navy, though greatly reduced, still posed a meaningful threat, and the final showdown was yet to come.

It occurred October 23–25, 1944, in the Battle of Leyte Gulf, though some of the Forties referred to it at the time as the "Second Battle of the Philippine Sea." Fought over three days by nearly three hundred warships spread out over a hundred thousand square miles, from the South China Sea to the northern tip of the Philippine Islands, the battle was characterized by miscommunication, misunderstandings, and errors on both sides, though it was also marked by extraordinary courage, bravery, and sacrifice. By the time it was over, the Imperial Japanese Navy had ceased to exist as a viable fighting force.[2]

THE BATTLE OF LEYTE GULF

The battle was touched off by MacArthur's long-promised, and long-anticipated, return to the Philippines, which took place on October 20. On that date, MacArthur walked down the ramp of a Higgins boat, splashed through knee-deep water, and stepped out onto a beach near Tacloban on the island of Leyte, one of the hundreds of islands that make up the Philippine archipelago. Leyte had been chosen in part because of the protected and commodious harbor offshore: Leyte Gulf, a body of water so large it could accommodate the whole of the American invasion fleet with room to spare. Indeed, as MacArthur looked about him on that October 20, he could see hundreds of ships: attack transports, cargo ships, ammunition ships, and the many amphibious ships known by their acronyms as LSTs, LCTs, LCIs, LSMs, plus, of course, the ubiquitous Higgins boats. Outside Leyte Gulf, well beyond MacArthur's line of sight, were half a dozen battleships and four heavy cruisers under the immediate command of Rear Admiral Jesse Oldendorf. The battleships were mostly prewar dinosaurs, though still capable of providing effective gunfire support against shore defenses. There were no fleet carriers; air cover was provided by eighteen small (and unarmored) "jeep carriers" that maneuvered off the entrance to the gulf. They were divided into three groups, identified by their radio call signs as Taffy One, Taffy Two, and Taffy Three.[3]

In addition to the invasion fleet, which was commanded by Vice Admiral Thomas Kinkaid, an entirely separate American fleet composed of the big fleet carriers and fast battleships plus their escorts maneuvered some two hundred miles to the north. This was the "Big Blue Fleet" of the US Navy—somewhat confusingly called the Fifth Fleet when it was commanded by Spruance (as it had been at Tarawa, Kwajalein, and Saipan) and the Third Fleet when it was commanded by Admiral William F. Halsey, as it was now. Halsey used the battleship *New Jersey* as his flagship, one of several powerful battleships built during the war. The striking power of the fleet, however, lay in the sixteen large-deck aircraft carriers under the command of Vice Admiral Marc "Pete" Mitscher that were also part of Halsey's Third Fleet. Halsey's job was to cover the northern flank of Kinkaid's invasion force. One problem with this command arrangement was that while Kinkaid reported to MacArthur, Halsey reported to Nimitz, which meant communication between the two fleet commanders was cumbersome.

By this time, many of the Forties had been promoted to lieutenant commander (or, like Fred Karch, to marine major). Even those who remained lieutenants held jobs with increased responsibilities, often as executive officers of ships,

266 ANNAPOLIS GOES TO WAR

squadrons, or battalions.* One of them was Lieutenant Donald F. Banker, the class practical joker from Duluth, Minnesota, who had been notorious at the Academy for "Grape Nutting" the bunks of his classmates. Despite this, no one could hold a grudge against Banker for long because, as his roommate put it, "His big pleasant grin and ready wit carry him gracefully though almost any situation." In his spare time, Banker liked to read books on philosophy and economics.[4]

Banker had completed his required two years of sea duty on the battleship *Idaho* with Myers Montgomery and Warren Smalzel, suffering with them through the Icelandic winter of 1940–41. He then applied for flight training, and after getting his wings in Pensacola, chose dive-bombers. By 1944 he was the executive officer of the bombing squadron (VB-19) on the USS *Lexington* (CV-16), named in honor of the carrier that had been lost in the Coral Sea two years earlier.[†]

Banker and his squadron mates flew the SB2C Helldiver, built by Curtiss-Wright. It was supposed to be an upgrade of the SBD Dauntless, which had been the standard dive-bomber in the fleet through 1943, and which had been responsible for sinking all four of the Japanese carriers at Midway. Yet while the new Helldiver had a greater payload of up to two thousand pounds, some of the performance attributes of the older SBD had been sacrificed to accommodate that. In fact, the Helldiver had so many flaws that the navy initially refused to accept it. Even after Curtiss-Wright made more than eight hundred modifications, the pilots themselves disliked it. One of the modifications was the enlargement of the plane's tail section that earned it its nickname as the "Big Tailed Beast," and some pilots insisted that its designation (SB2C) stood for "Son of a Bitch, Second Class."[5]

Dive-bombing was not for the faint of heart. To deliver their thousand-pound bombs, Banker and his squadron mates used the airplane itself as the aiming mechanism. Arriving over the target at between fifteen thousand and twenty thousand feet, from which altitude a ship was a mere hyphen on the sea's surface, the pilot opened the bomb bay doors, watched until that hyphen

---

* An interesting comment on the relative strength of the American and Japanese navies in 1944 is that even as the war was nearing a crescendo, with Japan literally running out of trained officers, especially pilots, the US Navy had sufficient reserves to send several of the Forties to graduate programs at civilian universities, including Bob Harris, John McMullen, and Warren Smalzel, all of whom went to MIT.

† In general, a squadron's number echoed the carrier to which it belonged: Thus VF-3 flew off the *Saratoga* (CV-3), and VF-5 was on the original *Yorktown* (CV-5). By 1944, however, it was no longer possible to sustain that tradition since squadrons often had to be moved from carrier to carrier as needed.

THE BATTLE OF LEYTE GULF

was just below the leading edge of his wing, then pushed over into a power dive. Diving at about an eighty-degree angle—almost straight down—the pilot deployed perforated wing flaps, called dive brakes, to keep the plane from going so fast that he lost control. As he plunged downward reaching speeds of nearly four hundred miles per hour, the target vessel grew nearer and larger, until at about fifteen hundred feet, the pilot released his bomb and pulled out of the dive. That abrupt maneuver generated enormous stress on both the airframe and the crew; the pilot and his radioman/gunner were pressed back in their seats with the force of eight or ten Gs—that is, eight to ten times the force of gravity.

During the summer of 1944, Banker flew multiple sorties off the *Lexington* in his Big Tailed Beast against Japanese targets on Guam as well as in the Palau Group further south. As American forces prepared for the invasion of the Philippines in October, he and his squadron mates were directed to focus on Japanese positions there. On September 21, they attacked a Japanese convoy of eleven ships that had just exited Manila Harbor and was headed north. In a demonstration of superb dive-bombing, they sunk all eleven ships; Banker was credited with one of them, in recognition of which he subsequently received the Distinguished Flying Cross. Exactly which plane sunk which ship was never established, which was just as well, for no one knew at the time that one of the ships they sank was a "hell ship" carrying 1,289 British and Dutch prisoners of war to Japan, more than a thousand of whom were killed.[6]*

In mid-October, as MacArthur, Kinkaid, and the American invasion convoy approached Leyte Gulf from the south, Banker's squadron on the *Lexington*, part of Halsey's Third Fleet, searched northward and westward to ensure that there was no interference from Japan's battlefleet. Though Halsey's primary job was to fend off any attempt to interfere with the invasion force, his orders also specified that if an opportunity arose to destroy the main Japanese fleet—which for him meant their aircraft carriers—that would become his primary mission. Halsey was one of those who believed that Spruance had lost a once-in-a-lifetime opportunity in the Philippine Sea, and he did not plan to make that mistake himself.

As for the Japanese, they were acutely aware that the loss of the Philippines would cut them off from the essential raw materials of South Asia and all but shut down their economy. After the virtual destruction of their naval aviation

---

* Altogether Allied forces sunk a total of seventeen "hell ships" between 1942 and 1945, including the *Shinyo Maru*, with Chab Chabot on board. Those sinkings resulted in the deaths of some nineteen thousand Allied personnel, more than died in the POW camps.

268   ANNAPOLIS GOES TO WAR

arm in the Philippine Sea, however, the only substantial weapon they had to hand was their fleet of battleships and cruisers, especially two oversize battleships, *Yamato* and *Musashi*, each of which displaced more than seventy thousand tons, and mounted nine 18.1-inch guns that could outrange anything the Americans possessed. The problem was getting them close enough to Leyte Gulf with no air cover to bring those guns to bear.

Faced with that conundrum, they concocted a truly desperate scheme.

The same afternoon that MacArthur splashed ashore at Leyte, a flotilla of Japanese ships under the command of Admiral Jisaburo Ozawa set out from Kure in Japan's Inland Sea, twenty-six hundred miles north of Leyte Gulf. It was an odd assembly of ships. There was one fleet carrier—the Pearl Harbor veteran *Zuikaku*—plus three light carriers, and two curious ships that had been converted into plane carriers by adding an abbreviated flight deck astern. A generous counting of airplane platforms therefore gave Ozawa a total of six carriers, though that was misleading because he had only about a hundred airplanes. His job was not to fight the Americans; it was to act as bait: to draw Halsey's carriers away from the beachhead so that Japan's battleships could thread their way through the Philippine Islands and attack the invaders in Leyte Gulf. As Ozawa steamed south, Japan's battleship force, commanded by Admiral Takeo Kurita, steamed north from its base near Sumatra. A much smaller Japanese surface force of two old battleships and two heavy cruisers under Admiral Kiyohide Shima would approach Leyte Gulf from the south. The Japanese hope was that the two surface forces would close like a vice on the American invasion force and destroy it altogether. It all depended, though, on getting the American carriers out of the way.

Kurita's powerful battleship force was dealt a heavy blow even before it got to the Philippines. On October 23, two American submarines, *Darter* and *Dace*, attacked and sank two of his heavy cruisers and damaged a third. One of the cruisers that went down was Kurita's flagship *Atago*, and that compelled Kurita to spend some time swimming for his life before he was rescued and transferred to the battleship *Yamato*. The experience did little to inspire confidence in the outcome of the coming battle.[7]

The next day was October 24, and search planes from Mitscher's carriers continued their patrols to the north and west. Don Banker led a trio of Helldivers over Manila Bay, where he spotted a Japanese heavy cruiser in the harbor. It was the *Nachi*, slated to join Admiral Shima's task force in attacking Leyte from the south. It was a prime target, but because he was on a scouting

THE BATTLE OF LEYTE GULF

mission, Banker's plane carried only five-hundred-pound general-purpose bombs, not likely to be decisive against an armored cruiser. Banker decided to execute a glide bombing attack, approaching the target at a sixty-degree angle, in the hope that his bombs could at least wreck some of the cruiser's superstructure. The *Nachi*, however, had been recently modified to carry forty-eight antiaircraft cannons, and she put up such a heavy volume of fire that Banker aborted the strike. He would come back later when he was carrying more appropriate ordnance.[8]

Other search planes flying over the Sibuyan Sea west of San Bernardino Strait reported a more substantial target: five battleships, nine cruisers, and thirteen destroyers coming from the west. This, of course, was Kurita's main force, and Halsey ordered an immediate strike. Wave after wave of American attack planes swarmed over them, and though one pilot reported that the Japanese "were shooting everything they could at us," Kurita's ships lacked effective air cover, which made them largely sitting ducks. Don Banker was credited with landing a bomb on a Japanese battleship, though with so many bombs raining down on so many ships, it was difficult to be certain of whose bomb hit what ship. Still, Banker's feat won him recognition in the form of a Silver Star. Many of the American pilots focused on Kurita's two big battleships, one of which, the *Musashi*, which was hit more than thirty times. The Japanese had proclaimed her "unsinkable," but no ship could survive that kind of abuse, and later that afternoon she sank after all. By 3:30, Kurita had seen enough. He ordered his command to turn around and retreat westward.[9]

This, the Battle of the Sibuyan Sea (October 24, 1944), marked a milestone for Don Banker, quite apart from his Silver Star. That is because en route to the target, the squadron commander, Dick McGowan, reported that his plane had suffered an electrical failure, and he broke off to return to the *Lexington*. As he made his approach to the carrier, his plane suddenly rolled to the right and crashed into the sea. McGowan was killed, and that made Don Banker the squadron's commanding officer.[10]

As the battle in the Sibuyan Sea played out, Ozawa and his decoy carriers continued to steam southward toward Halsey's fleet. When yet another American scout plane spotted and reported them, Halsey again reacted swiftly. Assuming that Kurita's battered surface force was no longer a serious threat, he abandoned his position off San Bernardino Strait and ordered the Big Blue Fleet to head north toward Ozawa's carriers.

270 ANNAPOLIS GOES TO WAR

Halsey was so eager to execute a battle of annihilation against Japan's carriers that he was dismissive of the news that Kurita's battleships reversed course and were again approaching San Bernardino Strait. Surely, Halsey concluded, Kinkaid should be able to handle any threat posed by the badly damaged Japanese heavy ships. Throughout the night of October 24–25, therefore, Halsey's Third Fleet—carriers, battleships, and all their escorts—steamed northward through the dark toward Ozawa's decoy fleet. Halsey went to bed convinced that the next day would bring the decisive naval victory over Japan that he and other navy senior officers had dreamed of for decades. The pilots were excited, too, and while Banker did not leave a record of his thoughts, one of the pilots in his squadron, Jack Meeker, no doubt spoke for many when he insisted that it was the moment they had been waiting for since Pearl Harbor. He was sure the next day would be "a day to remember."

At first light, Banker and his pilots all climbed into their planes and awaited the signal to launch. The omens were good. The weather, Meeker noted, "was perfect: clear, sunshiny, and not a cloud in the sky." The bombers from the carrier *Essex* launched first, followed at 6:30 by those from the *Lexington*. Soon deckloads of planes from other carriers filled the sky: bombers, torpedo planes, and fighters. Looking around, Banker could see at least three hundred navy planes winging toward the Japanese carriers. Meeker tried to imagine "what a sight it must have been for the Japanese" to see such a force coming at them. There would be no escape for them this time.[11]

At 8:00, with the American air armada about fifteen miles out from the target, the antiaircraft fire began: black puffs from exploding shells blemishing the clear blue sky. From twenty thousand feet, Banker picked out the largest of the aircraft carriers and circled overhead. As in the Sibuyan Sea, there were few Japanese fighters to worry about, and the American pilots were largely unmolested as they lined up on the target. The dive-bombers from *Essex* went first, and, watching them from above, Meeker estimated that as many as half of their bombs hit. That was impressive, though Meeker insisted that "our bombers did much better."[12]

Banker led the eighteen dive-bombers of VB-19 in the attack, and Meeker estimated that fifteen of them got a hit. Even allowing for exaggeration, the *Essex* and *Lexington* bombers between them may have hit the Japanese flattop (later identified as the *Zuikaku*) with as many as twenty thousand-pound bombs, that is, with ten tons of ordnance. Even without secondary explosions from embarked planes or munitions, it was devastating. One pilot in Banker's squadron, Ray Wicklander, noted that "we left it burning and engulfed in

THE BATTLE OF LEYTE GULF

271

smoke and . . . dead in the water." When Banker landed back on the *Lexington*, he learned that it had sunk. For that, Banker was one of thirty-two pilots that day recommended for the Navy Cross.[13]

Mitscher sent wave after wave of air attacks against Ozawa's dwindling fleet until only a few Japanese vessels remained afloat. Meeker called it "the largest fleet battle in history" and ranked it alongside Trafalgar and Midway as signature naval victories. Halsey thought so, too, and he planned to send the fast battleships ahead to clean up whatever cripples were left to ensure that the victory was complete.[14]

He didn't get the chance. All morning, beginning at about 8:00, just as Banker was approaching the *Zuikaku*, Halsey began receiving increasingly panicky radio messages from Kinkaid that the escorts guarding Leyte Gulf were under attack from Japanese battleships. Halsey's initial reaction was that Kinkaid should be able to handle it. He did not know that the battleships and heavy cruisers attached to Kinkaid's command had all gone south to deal with Shima's surface force in Surigao Strait and that, in any case, they had used up most of their supply of armor-piercing ordnance in that battle. As a result, the only American forces guarding Leyte Gulf were the small jeep carriers and their escorts.

At about 10:30, Halsey got another radio message, this one from Admiral Nimitz in Pearl Harbor, who had been listening in on the radio net and growing increasingly alarmed. Nimitz assumed that Halsey had left his battleships (Task Force 34) at San Bernardino Strait to guard Kinkaid's flank. Apparently, he had not. Though Nimitz was reluctant to interfere with an operational commander in the middle of a battle, he decided to ask Halsey a simple question: "Where is Task Force 34?" Though Nimitz merely asked a question, a radioman on Halsey's flagship failed to delete the terminal padding on the message so that when Halsey got it, it read: "Where is, repeat, where is Task Force 34. RR The world wonders." Halsey should have recognized that the double consonant (RR) meant the rest of the message was padding, but in the heat of the moment he took it as a sarcastic rebuke. Halsey exploded, flinging the message to the deck and offering many colorful imprecations. His chief of staff, Mick Carney, had to grab him by the shoulders to calm him down, and even then, Halsey sulked for an hour before reluctantly ordering the battleships and one carrier group to head south. For the rest of his life, he regretted giving that order, especially since, as it happened, they didn't get there in time anyway.[15]

When Kurita's battleships emerged from San Bernardino Strait around midnight on October 24–25, he expected to find Halsey's fleet there to meet him.

Instead, there was nothing but empty ocean. Astonished and perplexed, he turned south and headed for Leyte Gulf. Though he had lost the *Musashi* and several other ships, his command remained a powerful one. The *Yamato*, sister ship of the *Musashi*, was still intact, and he had three other large battleships, plus six heavy cruisers, three light cruisers, and fifteen destroyers. And there was nothing between him and the vulnerable invasion force in Leyte Gulf except a handful of jeep carriers and their destroyer escorts.

One of those destroyer escorts was the USS *Samuel B. Roberts* (DE-413), affectionately called the *Sammy B* by her crew. The executive officer on the *Sammy B* was another of the Forties: Lieutenant Everett "Bob" Roberts. A former enlisted sailor who had served two years "before the mast," Roberts had earned his ticket to Annapolis via the national exam. During plebe year, and especially plebe summer, his classmates had relied heavily on his fleet knowledge whenever an upper classman ordered one of them to discover the answer to some arcane question. Roberts did not play a sport at the Academy, but he was a serious tennis player who was seldom beaten. After graduation, he spent two years on the cruiser *Indianapolis* before transferring to small ships, serving two years as the XO of a subchaser before getting orders to the *Samuel B. Roberts*.[16]

Like Greenbacker's *Neunzer*, the *Sammy B* was a small ship, barely thirteen hundred tons, and designed for anti-submarine work. She had only two five-inch guns (as opposed to five on a *Fletcher*-class destroyer), plus 20 mm and 40 mm machine guns, eight K-guns along her sides, and a hedgehog on her foredeck. Her most effective anti-ship weapon was a trio of torpedo tubes amidships, though the torpedoes themselves had a range of less than ten thousand yards, which meant the *Sammy B* would have to get within four or five miles of a target before using them. As it turned out, however, getting close to the enemy would not be a problem.[17]

Like Gex and Greenbacker on the *Neunzer*, Roberts had a good relationship with his skipper, Lieutenant Commander Robert W. Copeland, a reserve officer who was half a decade older than he. Indeed, Copeland adopted the role of father figure to his mostly young crewmen, often asking them about their families and hometowns as he walked about the ship. He even participated in the "crossing the line" ceremony when the *Sammy B* headed into the South Pacific. It was (and is) a navy tradition that when a ship crosses the equator, those who had not previously done so (called "pollywogs") had to be initiated into the Kingdom of Neptune by those who had done so previously (called "shellbacks"). It generally involved a ceremony that included dressing up in silly outfits,

THE BATTLE OF LEYTE GULF

forcing the pollywogs to drink some obnoxious potion that might include fuel oil, and requiring them to crawl through garbage while being paddled by the shellbacks. A pollywog himself, Copeland accepted the humiliations in good spirits. That sacrificed some of his dignity but contributed to his popularity.[18]

Since Copeland adopted the mantle of paternal commander, it was left to Roberts to be the ship's enforcer. Not everyone on board appreciated that. Bud Comet, a seaman from West Virginia, thought Roberts was "strict, very strict . . . more strict than anybody else." And Lieutenant (j.g.) John LeClercq wrote home to his mother that "Mr. Roberts can go to blazes."[19]

Fall was typhoon season in the South Pacific, and while en route to the Philippines, the *Sammy B* ran into one on October 13. The small ship was tossed about like so much flotsam as towering waves washed completely over the open bridge, and Roberts was soaked to the bone, even through his oil-skins. The storm lasted for three days, and afterward, Roberts, like everyone else, was exhausted. Some in the crew hoped that that meant the worst was over.

During the late night hours of October 24, as Halsey's Big Blue Fleet steamed northward through the dark, Roberts and Copeland were on the bridge of the *Sammy B* off the entrance to Leyte Gulf listening to staticky radio messages from Oldendorf's battleships and cruisers that were engaged in a fierce night battle a hundred miles to the south in Surigao Strait. Based on the snippets of radio traffic that they could hear, it sounded like the Japanese were getting by far the worst of it. When Roberts overheard a message ordering the American ships to "polish off cripples," he turned to Copeland and said, "By God, I think we finally got 'em." Another officer admitted later, "I thought the Japanese were finished."[20]

Copeland and Roberts stayed on the bridge until just after first light, when Copeland left to get a cup of coffee, leaving Roberts in charge. The *Sammy B* was the northernmost ship of all the vessels guarding Leyte Gulf, and as the morning light grew, the chief quartermaster, Frank Cantrell, got out the telescope to scan the northern horizon. After a minute or two, he turned to ask Roberts if he had ever seen a Japanese battleship. Roberts took the telescope and studied the tiny dots on the northern horizon. He noted that a few of them did indeed seem to have the pagoda masts characteristic of Japanese battleships. The only possible explanation was that these were survivors of the Japanese fleet Oldendorf had beaten last night and they were fleeing northward. Nevertheless, Roberts sent word to Copeland that he should return to the bridge.[21]

274 ANNAPOLIS GOES TO WAR

When he arrived, Copeland took the glass, looked for a long moment, and agreed. They were Japanese warships all right, and, clearly, they were the survivors of last night's battle, running away. Roberts picked up the microphone of the 1MC loudspeaker and invited anyone in the crew who wanted to see enemy ships retreating to go to the fantail, from which they would have a good view.

The dots, however, didn't seem to be receding; indeed, they were getting larger. Copeland sent a TBS message to the commander of the jeep carrier force, Rear Admiral Clifton "Ziggy" Sprague, who had already received a report of ships to the north from his radar operator. Sprague asked the search plane pilots to have a look, and very quickly, one of them made a startling report: "four battleships, four heavy cruisers, two light cruisers, and ten to twelve destroyers" twenty miles away and approaching at high speed. That was so unlikely that Sprague asked the pilot to confirm it. He did.

Shocking as that was, Sprague cooly issued two orders at once. The carriers were to turn into the wind and "launch everything," and the small escort ships, including the *Sammy B*, were to make smoke to screen the carriers from the approaching battleships. Then he sent out the first of several radio messages that morning calling for help.[22]

Copeland sounded general quarters, and Roberts rushed down to his post in the CIC. Soon afterward, Sprague ordered the "small boys" to conduct a torpedo attack against the approaching warships. Copeland used the sound-powered phones to tell Roberts to calculate a course to put the *Sammy B* five thousand yards from the bow of the leading Japanese cruiser. Roberts was startled. "I wished he had ordered me to find a course that would be an escape route," he recalled later. He noted that his hands were ice cold, but it did not slow his work. Roberts calculated the course and sent it up to the bridge, and the *Sammy B* surged ahead, her whole frame vibrating from the increased speed. Copeland then picked up the 1MC to tell the crew that in order to protect the carriers, they were about to engage in "a fight against overwhelming odds from which survival could not be expected, during which time we would do what damage we could." Along with three destroyers, *Johnston*, *Hoel*, and *Heermann*, the *Sammy B* headed almost due north toward Kurita's battleships and cruisers.[23]

So far the Japanese gunners had focused mainly on the carriers they could see beyond the little destroyers, and when they did pay attention to the "small boys," they targeted the three destroyers. That allowed the *Sammy B* to survive longer than it otherwise might have and to get within torpedo range of the nearest cruiser, which was the Savo Island veteran *Chokai*. Near misses had

THE BATTLE OF LEYTE GULF

damaged the equipment in the CIC of the *Sammy B*, and Roberts had to determine the firing solution in his head; Copeland later said of him that he was "as fast as a slide rule and as accurate as a micrometer." When he was satisfied with the solutions, Roberts ordered the torpedomen to fire. The torpedoes arced through the air, splashed into the water, and began their run toward the target. Though the thick smoke made it uncertain, Roberts thought that at least one of them struck its target.[24]

Meanwhile, the destroyers *Johnston* and *Hoel* were being pummeled by repeated salvos from large-caliber guns, and it was soon evident that they were sinking. Only then did Japanese shells begin to target the *Sammy B*, yet because the Japanese were using armor-piercing shells, early rounds went right through the thin skin of the *Sammy B* without exploding. They did damage nonetheless, cutting the cables in the CIC and wrecking the radar and communication systems. That led Roberts to quit the CIC and head up to the bridge to join Copeland.[25]

Despite the heavy smoke, what he saw was terrifying. The Japanese battleships, hull up now and clearly visible, were approaching swiftly; both the *Johnston* and *Hoel* were on fire and sinking; the *Heermann* had also been hit. Worse, Japanese shells were walking their way up to the *Sammy B*, which was clearly next. Roberts later candidly admitted, "I was scared stiff." Copeland adopted the tactic of "chasing salvos": that is, steaming toward the location of the most recent shell splashes in the expectation that the Japanese gunners would adjust their aim and not hit the same spot again. The Japanese also carried torpedoes on their cruisers, and Roberts saw one of them headed directly for the *Sammy B*. Copeland called out "stand by for torpedo explosion," though instead of exploding, the torpedo passed under the ship and kept going. Just as the *Sammy B* was too thin-skinned to trigger an AP shell, she had too shallow a draft for Japanese torpedoes.[26]

Their luck did not last. Just before 9:00 a.m., a fourteen-inch shell from the battleship *Kongo* hit the *Sammy B* with a shattering whack. The ship convulsed like a rag shaken by a dog. Copeland and Roberts were knocked into a heap on the deck. Scores of men were killed outright, seawater rushed in through holes in the hull, and fires burned out of control. At 9:10 Copeland ordered abandon ship. He told Roberts to go down to the main deck and supervise the evacuation, adding that he should leave, too. Roberts balked. "Captain, I'm not leaving until you leave," he said. Copeland was annoyed. "I don't want you to be a damn fool and get heroic," he said. "You are my exec and my good friend, but this is an order. . . . I'm ordering you to leave the ship."[27]

276   ANNAPOLIS GOES TO WAR

Roberts scrambled down to the main deck, where he helped several of the wounded get into the water. Then, after checking for others, he jumped. It was 9:30, two and a half hours after Chief Cantrell had noticed the tiny dots on the northern horizon, and twenty minutes after Copeland ordered abandon ship. A half hour later, the *Samuel B. Roberts* sank. Copeland, Roberts, and the other survivors in the water watched her go down.* Their view of the battle was greatly restricted from sea level, and yet it seemed to Roberts that the Japanese ships had changed course and were withdrawing. Was that possible?

It was. Exhausted, perhaps confused, Kurita decided that he had pressed his luck as far as he could. He issued orders for his disorganized fleet to reassemble, and eventually the Japanese battleships and cruisers headed north. They returned the way they had come, back through San Bernardino Strait and the Sibuyan Sea. Halsey's battleships arrived too late to interfere.

The Battle off Samar on October 25, 1944, was one of the truly remarkable naval engagements of the entire war, and it has engendered heated arguments ever since: about Halsey's decision to leave San Bernardino Strait unguarded, about how close the Japanese came to wrecking the American invasion fleet, and about why Kurita decided to withdraw just as it seemed he was on the verge of victory. Most of all, though, it has drawn admiration for the handful of little ships, none of them smaller than the *Sammy B*, that sacrificed themselves against an overwhelming force to save the rest of the fleet.

Copeland, Roberts, and the 120 other survivors of the *Samuel B. Roberts* remained in the water for several days before they were rescued. After they were brought back to the States, it was Roberts's job to write letters of condolence to each of the families of the ninety men who had been killed. In time, he was awarded the Legion of Merit in recognition of his role in the battle. Copeland was awarded the Navy Cross.

Kurita's retreat effectively ended the fighting. As close as he may have come to a stunning and unlikely victory, the outcome was a disaster for the Japanese, who lost four carriers, three battleships, six heavy cruisers, four light cruisers, and thirteen destroyers. As Kurita's chief of staff acknowledged, "It spelled the end of our Navy."[28]

---

* In 1984, the US Navy launched another USS *Samuel B. Roberts*, a guided-missile frigate named in honor of the ship sunk in the Battle of Leyte Gulf. When that ship was severely damaged by an Iranian mine in the Persian Gulf in 1988, it triggered a massive US Navy response against Iran called Operation Praying Mantis.

Don Banker still had some unfinished business. He never forgot the cruiser *Nachi*, which had escaped him eleven days earlier because his planes had been armed with the wrong bombs. Now, with the Battle of Leyte Gulf over and the Leyte beachhead secured, he wanted to return to Manila Bay and find the *Nachi*. On November 5, 1944, he led a group of thirty airplanes in two divisions to Manila Bay, and, remarkably, the *Nachi* was still there. Though she had been tabbed to join Shima's doomed southern force in Surigao Strait, engine trouble forced her to return to Manila, which saved her from sharing Shima's fate. Her reprieve, however, was brief.

Banker led a dozen Hellcat dive-bombers that attacked from altitude, while six torpedo planes came in low. Banker's wingman, Lieutenant Donald G. Engen, watched Banker sustain his dive to the last second before releasing his bomb, which hit the *Nachi* amidships; then he pulled up "with white streamers coming from each wingtip," indicating that Banker was fighting the momentum of the dive. Engen watched as Banker tried to pull up, executing a series of snap rolls before hitting the water while his plane was inverted. Engen circled the spot where Banker had crashed, though he could see "nothing but boiling water and some shark chaser dye to mark the spot." The *Nachi* broke into three pieces and sank in a matter of minutes. Banker's body was never found.[29]

Don Banker had commanded VB-19 for exactly twelve days. In that time, he was credited with helping sink a battleship, an aircraft carrier, and a heavy cruiser. In recognition of that, he was awarded the Silver Star and two Navy Crosses. All three medals had to be awarded posthumously.

22

Iwo Jima and Okinawa

Doc Weatherup had dreamed of piloting a fighter plane in combat since he was a ten-year-old boy in Watertown, New York. In the spring of 1944, still six months before the American invasion of the Philippines, he got orders that promised to make that dream a reality. He was to report to Atlantic City, New Jersey, as a plank owner of a brand-new fighter squadron: VF-46. It was a replacement squadron, so its future service was still uncertain. Almost certainly, though, it meant active service against the enemy, and after a year as an instructor at Pensacola, Weatherup could hardly wait.

As it happened, because the squadron's designated commander, Carl W. Rooney (Naval Academy, 1934), could not report on the date specified, Weatherup stood in for him when the squadron was officially commissioned on April 15, 1944. After Rooney arrived, Weatherup became the squadron's executive officer. He and his squadron mates adopted the nickname "Men-O-War," after the frigatebird (also called a man-of-war), and they spent the summer of 1944 training in Groton, Connecticut. There the newer pilots completed their carrier qualifications on the escort carrier *Mission Bay*, doing so in brand-new F6F Hellcat fighters, faster and more robust versions of the F4F Wildcats that they had trained on. The Hellcat could outclimb, outmaneuver, and outperform the vaunted Japanese Zero, and Weatherup was eager to prove it.[1]

In addition to getting the newer pilots carrier-qualified, the training at Groton involved mastering complicated air tactics, including a maneuver known as the "Thach Weave," named for Jimmy Thach (Naval Academy, 1927) who had first employed it in the Battle of Midway. It required planes to fly in close proximity to one another and maneuver cooperatively, and because of that it occasionally led to accidents. During a training exercise on June 14, two of the Hellcats collided in midair at five thousand feet, and Lieutenant Arnold C. Harwood, an especially popular member of the squadron, was killed, a reminder that this was serious business. The pilots of VF-46 also competed in

IWO JIMA AND OKINAWA

279

gunnery exercises, shooting at towed target-sleeves or drones while flying at 350 miles per hour. Weatherup's yearlong experience as a pilot instructor contributed to his emergence as the squadron's gunnery ace. Finally, in September, the squadron received orders to report to San Diego for transportation to the South Pacific.[2]

It took them most of a month to get there. They flew across the country in stages to San Diego and then on September 25, they embarked on the escort carrier *Makassar Strait* for the voyage to Hawaii. There the squadron had to give up five of its experienced pilots in exchange for five rookies, a switch that Rooney protested, to no avail. Another acquisition was a squadron mascot, a dog they named "Frigate" (after the frigatebird), an animal who, the pilots claimed, had "unusual personality and intelligence," which it demonstrated by successfully completing two parachute jumps from the 225-foot tower on Ford Island. From Hawaii, they headed further west to Manus Island in the Admiralties group north of New Guinea. There they learned about the victory at Leyte Gulf, making them all the more eager to get back into the war.[3]

Despite their eagerness, action was not imminent. Indeed, the experience of VF-46 seemed to validate the adage that a lot of military service consisted of "hurry up and wait." After the planes of VF-46 flew ashore on Manus Island, it was almost as if the Navy Department forgot about them. It was a pleasant-enough interlude. There were weekly dances at the O Club, good chow in the officers' mess, and lengthy games of contract bridge in the wardroom. Still, Weatherup and the other pilots chaffed at the prolonged inactivity. The squadron's historian acknowledged that the five weeks they spent on Manus Island did not improve either their morale or their battle readiness. One reason for the hiatus was that the squadron had been slotted for service aboard the light carrier *Princeton*, an option that disappeared when the *Princeton* was sunk by the Japanese on October 24 during the Battle of Leyte Gulf.*

Not until early in the new year of 1945 did VF-46 get orders to a different light carrier, USS *Cowpens* (CVL-25). Like other Americans carriers (*Lexington* and *Yorktown*, for example, and *Princeton*, too, for that matter), the *Cowpens* had been named for a battle of the American Revolution, a relatively small skirmish in South Carolina. Despite that nod to historic events, her crew quickly nicknamed her "The Mighty Moo." Weatherup and the other pilots

---

* One of the Forties, William E. "Willie" Lamb, had been a pilot on the *Princeton*, though by the time of the Battle of Leyte Gulf, he was no longer on board because he had been shot down over Luzon in September. Rescued by Filipino guerillas, he spent several weeks dodging Japanese patrols and was eventually rescued by an American submarine.

280   ANNAPOLIS GOES TO WAR

were billeted separately from the rest of the crew, which was just as well since the aviators learned quickly that it was important to keep Frigate away from the captain's pet cat. In February 1945, the *Cowpens* and VF-46 left Manus and steamed nine hundred miles north to the commodious anchorage of Ulithi Atoll. As *Cowpens* eased into the harbor and dropped anchor, Weatherup marveled at the vista of more than four hundred American warships virtually filling the anchorage. "I looked out over the lagoon at Ulithi," he wrote later, "and saw what may have been the largest concentration of warships ever assembled."[4]

An isolated group of small islands twelve hundred miles southeast of the Philippines, Ulithi Atoll had become the principal American naval base in the South Pacific. Admiral Nimitz called it his "secret weapon." It was a place where US Navy warships and auxiliaries could rearm, resupply, and refuel and where the crews could have some R & R ashore. One of the islands of the atoll (charmingly named Mogmog) was set aside as a kind of South Pacific resort. While there were no nightclubs, hula dancers, or other such attractions, the officers and men could swim, play softball, and drink beer. A banner over the landing read, "Welcome to Mogmog, Paradise of the Pacific." Not every pilot was enchanted. As one put it, "Our R&R turned out to be a visit to the great Mog Mog Island where we would be deposited on a barren beach, handed two cans of lukewarm beer, and instructed to 'have a good time.'"[5]

At Ulithi, Weatherup burnished his growing reputation as the squadron's most proficient gunner and best navigator. At one point, he led a group of fighter planes to Biak, eight hundred miles almost due south of Ulithi over open water—a challenging navigational task. Not only did all the planes arrive within minutes of the official ETA, they returned exactly on schedule. In the wake of that, the squadron historian wrote admiringly, "The infallibility of 'Doc' Weatherup was again confirmed."[6]

This time, their stay in port was relatively short. On February 9, 1945, the *Cowpens* and a score of other ships departed Ulithi, heading north. The marines were scheduled to land on an island in the Bonins called Iwo Jima ten days later, and the *Cowpens* was one of several carriers assigned to cover the landings by striking targets on Japan's home islands. In his first combat action as a fighter pilot, Doc Weatherup would lead a squadron of fighter planes against the Japanese homeland.

Unlike Weatherup, Mike Hanley had failed to obtain his gold wings. After he was dropped from flight training in New Orleans, he got orders back to the

IWO JIMA AND OKINAWA

surface navy as the prospective executive officer of a new destroyer. To prepare him, the navy sent him to gunnery school in Washington, DC. Thus, in the summer of 1944, while Karch and his marines went ashore on Saipan, and Weatherup honed his pilot skills in Connecticut, Hanley studied theoretical and practical gunnery in the nation's capital. In the fall, as MacArthur closed in on Leyte and Weatherup headed to Manus Island, Hanley, now a lieutenant commander, got orders to report to the *Fletcher*-class destroyer USS *Dashiell* (DD-659) as her executive officer. Fulfilling those orders, however, turned out to be something of a challenge. That is because during World War II, the navy assumed that a resourceful naval officer should be able to get himself to his new duty station by means of his own devising.

A case in point was the experience of another of the Forties, "Pop" Dupzyk, who got orders to report to the USS *Stringham* as her new XO. It was not a prestige assignment. The *Stringham* had started life back in 1918 as a four-stack destroyer. Decommissioned after the Great War in 1920, she was reactivated in 1940 as a high-speed transport (APD-6). Prestigious or not, a promotion to lieutenant commander and an appointment as executive officer was gratifying to Dupzyk. Back in the summer of 1940, when he had reported to the battle-ship *West Virginia* as a brand-new ensign, he noticed that the senior officers on board were all pretty long in the tooth. The captain had been a naval officer for thirty-two years, the XO for twenty-four years, and the gunnery officer, a lieu-tenant commander, for twenty. How many years, Dupzyk wondered at the time, would it take for him to reach such heights? The answer, as it turned out, was four.[7]

Like Hanley, Dupzyk was expected to find his new ship and report aboard, though as with all navy ships, her location was technically a secret. To discover her whereabouts, Dupzyk consulted the local office of the Naval Intelligence Service (NIS) in San Francisco. Satisfied by his orders and his ID that he had a need to know, NIS officials informed him that the *Stringham* was in the Mare Island Navy Yard, where workers were finishing up some repairs. When Dupzyk got there, however, officials told him that the *Stringham* had com-pleted her repairs and gone to San Diego for underway training. So he took the overnight train to San Diego, where he once again had to convince local NIS officials that he was authorized to know the location of the ship. That com-pleted, he was informed that the *Stringham* had finished her underway train-ing and returned to San Francisco. So Dupzyk did, too. By the time he arrived back in the Bay Area, the NIS offices were closed, and he checked into a hotel hoping for better luck the next day. Suspicious by now of relying on official channels, he decided to try a different approach. That night, in the cocktail bar at the hotel, he struck up a conversation with several other naval officers, and in the midst of it casually asked, "Where is the Stringham?" "Oh," an officer replied, "she is moored at Pier 7." That was only one pier over from where he had first looked for her two days earlier.[8]

Dupzyk's pursuit of the *Stringham* was a mere diversion compared to Hanley's quest to find the *Dashiell*. When Hanley got his orders, all he knew for sure was that the *Dashiell* was in the war zone somewhere in the western Pacific. He had little difficulty getting himself from Washington to the West Coast and then out to Hawaii. From there he managed to catch a troop ship bound for Hollandia on the north coast of New Guinea. That took ten days, and when he arrived, he learned that the *Dashiell* had moved on to Leyte Gulf. So he caught a ride on a supply ship heading to the Philippines. In Leyte Gulf, however, he was informed that the *Dashiell* had left with the invasion fleet bound for Lingayen Gulf on the west coast of Luzon.

At this point, Hanley—like Dupzyk—got creative. He found a Landing Craft, Infantry (LCI) in Leyte Gulf that was scheduled to carry the mail to Rear Admiral Jesse Oldendorf's covering fleet for the Luzon invasion. He went aboard the LCI and told her skipper, a reserve lieutenant, that if he would let him bunk aboard, Hanley would agree to stand watches, thereby easing the burden on the wardroom, and to sweeten the deal, he offered to provide "certain alcoholic beverages," almost certainly several bottles of scotch. The skipper of the LCI agreed at once. So Hanley moved aboard and rode the LCI for another week, standing watches in regular rotation, until the LCI encountered a destroyer escort that was bound for Lingayen Gulf. Hanley transferred ships again, and on January 29, 1945, more than a month after he had received his orders, he reported aboard the *Dashiell* to assume duties as her executive officer.[9]

Not all orders to a new command required such exertions. When Connie Carlson got orders to report to the new destroyer *Douglas H. Fox* (DD-779) as her exec, he knew exactly where to look because she was still under construction in Seattle. While her captain, Commander Ray Pitts, supervised the final stages of her fitting out, Carlson took charge of the several hundred men who had been assigned as her initial crew. At the navy base on Treasure Island, in almost the exact center of San Francisco Bay, he supervised their training through the various division officers. The *Douglas H. Fox* was officially commissioned the day after Christmas in 1944 and, after a shakedown cruise off the California coast, headed for the Hawaiian Islands and the war.[10]

IWO JIMA AND OKINAWA   283

What Weatherup, Hanley, and Carlson all had in common, besides being classmates who now served as executive officers, was that they were each destined to play a role during the American invasions of both Iwo Jima and Okinawa.

As the American invasion force closed on Iwo Jima, Mitscher's carriers (labeled Task Force 58) were 750 miles to the north, approaching the Japanese homeland. Keyed up for their first mission, many of the pilots on the *Cowpens* were already awake when the early reveille sounded at 3:30 a.m. on February 16, 1945. Most of them immediately checked the weather. It could hardly have been worse: it was bitter cold, with a forty-knot wind driving snow and ice pellets across the flight deck. When they got to the ready room, their concern about the weather was all but erased by the news that "we were to take part in a carrier raid on Tokyo!" Thinking about his emotional reaction to that news years later, Weatherup struggled to articulate his thoughts. "Naturally, there was a feeling of apprehension," he wrote, but it also led to introspection. It was, he decided, "a time for prayer, meditation, and reflection." He thought back to the humiliation of the Pearl Harbor defeat, the terror of the middle-of-the-night combat in the dark waters off Guadalcanal, and the vista of the gigantic fleet he had seen at Ulithi. What a dramatic sea change had been wrought in only a few years. And it was not just the navy that had changed. He, too, had been transformed. And now he sat in the cockpit of a fighter plane preparing to lead an attack on the Japanese capital.[11]

On another of the carriers, the *Bunker Hill*, Ted Hill felt much the same. "There was some apprehension about the opposition we could expect over the heart of the homeland," he recalled, yet "there was also great enthusiasm and anticipation over being a part of the operation to put it to them at home." Hill had initially opted for dive-bombers, though by 1945 Japan's navy was literally running out of ships and the US Navy had more dive-bomber pilots than it needed. That led Hill to transfer to fighters, and for the raid on Tokyo he flew an F4U Corsair.[12]

Catapult launches from carriers had become common by now, yet the strong relative wind over the deck made them unnecessary on this occasion. Weatherup on the *Cowpens* and Hill on the *Bunker Hill*, as well as scores of other pilots on other carriers, revved their engines, holding the planes in place with the brake, until they got a signal from the landing signal officer. Then one after another, they released the brake, pushed the throttle forward, and surged toward the bow. Those launching first circled overhead until all the

284 ANNAPOLIS GOES TO WAR

planes joined up, and then they all headed inland in a series of V formations toward the airfields near Tokyo.

Over the land, atmospheric conditions were, if anything, even worse. Heavy clouds obscured terrestrial landmarks, and Weatherup looked desperately for a break in the clouds that would allow him to orient the squadron to the target. When at last he found one, he led his squadron down to ground level, found the airfield, and bombed and strafed Japanese planes parked on the runway. There was little opposition. The Japanese, desperately short of both fuel and pilots, had made a conscious decision to conserve both in anticipation of the expected invasion of their homeland. Weatherup, Hill, and the other fighter pilots dropped their five-hundred-pound bombs and expended all their .50 caliber ammunition, then formed up again and headed back to the carriers. Weatherup was enormously relieved that all the planes in his squadron returned safely. As the last of them caught a wire on the flight deck and jerked to a halt, he might have been forgiven a quiet internal celebration.[13]

They went back again the next day. In addition to payback for Pearl Harbor, Spruance wanted to demonstrate that carrier-based planes could perform a strategic bombing mission by wrecking Japan's war industries. For months, huge, sleek B-29 Superfortress bombers from Saipan, Tinian, and Guam had targeted Japanese factories with little success. The high winds and heavy cloud cover over Japan made precision bombing from altitude all but impossible. Spruance thought low-level carrier planes could do it better. So he ordered Mitscher's carrier planes to hit the Nakajima Aircraft Factory outside Tokyo. The result was disappointing. Once again, the weather was abysmal, so bad, in fact, that neither Weatherup nor anyone else could assess with any certainty what impact their strike had on the factory. Spruance called off further strikes and ordered the task force south, back to Iwo Jima, to provide more direct support to the invaders.[14]

The marines landed on the black sand beaches of Iwo Jima two days later, on February 19. Not a coral atoll, Iwo Jima was made up of volcanic rock and dust. Fred Karch, still with the Fourteenth Marines, remembered that "the black sand there was just impossible to move through." He and his men, indeed all the marines, encountered fierce resistance from an enemy dug deep into caves and tunnels all over the island. Bereft of vegetation to begin with, the island had been bombed from the air for months and shelled from the sea for weeks. When Weatherup and his squadron mates flew over the island, one of them described it as "a lunar landscape . . . pock-marked from Naval shells and aerial

IWO JIMA AND OKINAWA 285

bombs." All that punishment had not eroded Japan's defenses; enemy soldiers were so deep underground the marines were forced to go into the caves and fight it out with them hand to hand. The result was a lengthy and bloody battle that claimed over twenty thousand American casualties. It was also mentally and emotionally stressful. Karch noted an unusual number of what he called "crackups," a condition then called combat fatigue and known today as post-traumatic stress disorder (PTSD).[15]

While that sanguinary confrontation played out on Iwo Jima, Spruance again tried to demonstrate that carrier-based aircraft could perform the strategic bombing mission. On February 25, he sent another strike of 118 planes against Japan's military infrastructure. Initially, they were to hit the Nakajima Aircraft Factory, though weather forced a diversion to the Koizumi engine plant. Again, Weatherup and VF-46 were part of it. This time, the after-action assessment reported that the factory had been 90 percent destroyed. It is not clear what Army Major General Curtis LeMay, commander of the Twenty-First Bomber Command on Saipan, thought of that. He may have seen it as an attempt to usurp his mission, and if so, it may have been one factor in his decision to change tactics. In any case, he abandoned attempts to bomb precise targets in daylight from altitude and embraced a new strategy of low-level area bombing at night with incendiaries. On the night of March 9–10, 1945, he sent more than three hundred Stratofortress bombers to attack Tokyo. This time, rather than pinpoint factories, or indeed any particular target, the objective was to burn the city itself to the ground. The justification was that destroying the "housing units" of the workers would inhibit the production of aircraft as much as bombing the factories themselves. Whatever the merit of that argument, the raid ignited a literal firestorm that destroyed a third of the city, killed over one hundred thousand people, and left more than a million homeless. Perceived as a great success, the firebombing raids were soon extended to other Japanese cities.[16]

While Japan burned, American carrier planes continued to attack airfields and aircraft installations in the home islands, especially on the southern island of Kyushu. The four carriers of Task Unit 58.2—the *Essex*-class carriers *Hancock* and *Franklin* and two light carriers, *San Jacinto* and *Bataan*—maneuvered to within fifty miles of the home islands. Though the *Franklin* bore the hull number 13, her fighter squadron was designated Air Group 5 in honor of the planes that had flown from the martyred *Yorktown*, sunk at Midway. Its executive officer was Lieutenant Commander John Lacouture.

Lacouture had spent most of a year flying Hellcats and Corsairs at Navy bases from Fallon, Nevada, to Santa Rosa, California, before he joined the carrier *Franklin* as XO of the fighter squadron early in 1945. Because he had flown two sorties the day before, he was not scheduled to fly on March 19, and he was asleep in his stateroom when a single Japanese bomber that had somehow evaded the radar dropped out of the cloud cover and placed two bombs on the *Franklin*. One of them exploded among the thirty-one planes on the flight deck; the other penetrated to the hangar deck and exploded among the sixteen planes parked there. Some of the planes on the hangar deck were armed with new 11.75-inch rockets called "Tiny Tims," and when the flames reached them, they ignited, firing out in all directions. Lacouture leaped from his rack, pulled on his clothes, and raced up to the flight deck. The whole flight deck was aflame from the forward catapult to the center of the ship. It was so hot that some members of the crew jumped off into the sea and were never found. As fires raged out of control, the big flattop took on a pronounced list.

The cruiser *Pittsburgh* took her under tow, and slowly the twinned ships worked up to three knots, then four. All the time, damage control teams on the *Franklin* put out fires, patched holes, and worked to repair the steam plant. Finally, well beyond the reach of Japanese planes from Kyushu, the big carrier was able to restart her engines and make it to Ulithi under her own power.[17]*

Casualties on the *Franklin* were severe, including more than seven hundred dead. It was the largest number of men killed on a single warship since the *Arizona* had exploded in Pearl Harbor. Among them were sixty-one men from Air Group 5. Many had been burned beyond recognition; others could not be found at all. Though Lacouture had successfully transferred over to a cruiser alongside, he was formally listed as "missing," and for a full month his status— or even his existence—remained uncertain. Not until April 16, when a navy rescue ship arrived in San Francisco with survivors on board, did his wife Betty learn that he was alive and unharmed. As it happened, she had news for him, too: five days earlier, she had given birth to their daughter, whom they named Joan. Granted two weeks leave, Lacouture left for New Orleans to be with his wife and daughter.[18]

---

* There was an awkward aftermath to this tragedy. The strict and rigid Captain Leslie E. Gehres claimed that the men who had left the ship while it was under attack, even those who had leaped into the water to escape the fires, had "deserted," and he wanted to press charges against them. The navy decided otherwise, dropping the charges against the crewmen and sending Gehres to command the naval air station at San Diego.

IWO JIMA AND OKINAWA

Iwo Jima was declared officially secure on March 26, though many of the marines on the island would have disputed that designation, as they continued to encounter pockets of desperate resisters. Even so, the island appeared to be sufficiently under control that the navy brass could turn its attention to the next objective: the much larger Japanese island of Okinawa. The natives of Okinawa were not ethnically Japanese, and they spoke a separate dialect, yet in 1879, Japan had officially consolidated the island into the empire. As such, it was considered one of the five home islands and therefore sacred soil. The Japanese resolved to defend it even more ferociously—if that were possible—than they had Iwo Jima.

The American landings took place on April 1, 1945, and to the surprise of nearly everyone, they were virtually uncontested. Once again, the Japanese had withdrawn into caves and tunnels and defied the Americans to come and get them. The goal was to make the Americans pay in blood for every yard of Japanese soil in the hope that they would tire of their losses and open negotiations. In addition to the fierce fighting ashore, an existential threat to the invaders came from the air in the form of hundreds—and eventually thousands—of so-called *tokkotai* ("special attack") pilots popularly known as the *kamikaze* ("divine wind"). The Japanese had experimented with this tactic in the fighting for the Philippines, and its perceived success there convinced them that here was a weapon that could prove so devastating the Americans would decide that the cost of continuing the war was unsustainable.[19]

Aware of the threat, the admirals running the invasion—Raymond Spruance and Richmond Kelly Turner—established a picket line of radar-equipped destroyers fifty to sixty miles north of Okinawa as an early warning system. Because those destroyers would be the first enemy ships the kamikaze pilots would encounter as they flew south from Kyushu, it was a position of extraordinary danger. And it was there that several of the destroyers with executive officers from the Naval Academy class of 1940 were stationed. In the first two weeks of April 1945, a dozen or more of the Forties found themselves at the literal vortex of the war as they endured hundreds of attacks by thousands of airplanes in Japan's last, desperate effort to convince the Americans that the price of victory was more than they could tolerate.

One of the first picket destroyers was the USS *Dashiell*, with Mike Hanley as XO. Along with the USS *Harrison* (DD-573), she joined the picket line on April 6. That turned out to be the very day the Japanese launched their first full-scale kamikaze attack. The *Dashiell* had barely taken up its position on the picket line when she was assailed by the largest Japanese air strike of the war.

288 ANNAPOLIS GOES TO WAR

Some seven hundred airplanes took off from fields in Kyushu, half of them kamikazes, and half conventional bombers and fighters. Hanley's battle station on the *Dashiell* was in the CIC, one level below the bridge. There he would gather and collate input from the air and surface-search radars, the topside lookouts, and all radio transmissions to compile a tactical picture of the battle space and make recommendations to Captain Douglass Cordinier up on the bridge.[20]

Just before 1:00 p.m., a trio of planes, flying in a V formation, closed on the *Dashiell* and the *Harrison*. Two of them dove on the *Harrison*, while the third targeted the *Dashiell*. The starboard gunners on the *Dashiell* opened up, creating a virtual curtain of exploding ordnance. The gunners could see pieces of the plane's wing and tail assembly flying off as it was hit, but it kept coming. With the pilot almost certainly dead, what was left of the plane passed only a few feet over the ship's stack and crashed into the sea twenty yards off her port bow. Other US Navy ships were targeted that day, too. Three of the picket destroyers—*Bush*, *Calhoun*, and *Emmons*—were sunk with heavy loss of life, along with one LST, two Victory ships, and two ammunition ships. The destroyer *Haynsworth*, on which another of the Forties, Scott Lothrop, was XO, was also hit by a kamikaze and so badly damaged it had to return to California for extensive repairs. The *Dashiell* remained on station.[21]

A week later, on April 13, it was the turn of the USS *Zellars* (DD-777). Three suicide planes came at her from three directions at once, all flying about fifteen feet off the water. Gunners shot down the first two, but the third fought through the flak and struck the *Zellars* on her port side, with the plane's five-hundred-pound bomb smashing through several bulkheads and exploding in the ship's scullery. Twenty-nine men were killed outright and another sixteen died later of their wounds. Though the *Zellars* was dead in the water, her gunners continued to shoot at the swarming planes. That night, after the kamikazes left, the engineers got the engines started again, and the *Zellars* limped southward to the fleet anchorage at Kerama Retto, southwest of Okinawa.

The next day, a few minutes after one-o'clock in the afternoon, Hanley was back in CIC on the *Dashiell* when the radar picked up "groups of bogies closing from the north." Hanley remembered that, for the next hour, "the radar screen was full of bogies." The American fighters flying combat air patrol (CAP) shot down several of them, but there were just too many. The first dropped a bomb on the destroyer *McKee*, passed over the *Dashiell*, then crashed into the destroyer *Hunt*. Seven minutes later, another kamikaze closed from the north, "banked sharply, and crashed into the stern of the *Sigsbee*,"

IWO JIMA AND OKINAWA

289

sending a column of smoke and debris 150 feet into the air. Five minutes later, another kamikaze closed from the northwest, though it turned away in the face of heavy AA fire. Only two minutes after that, though, a Zero fighter "with a large red stripe" came in low, passed over the *McKee*, and headed straight for the *Dashiell*. The Zero was only yards away when it released a five-hundred-pound bomb that struck the destroyer forward and "shook the ship severely." The plane then crossed low over the bow and crashed into the sea ten yards off her port side. The bomb's explosion shut down the *Dashiell*'s main generator and started a leak in the condenser that compromised the engines.[22]

Within minutes, two more kamikazes attacked. One went into a steep dive from fifteen hundred feet; in the CIC, Hanley clocked its speed at 385 miles per hour. Every five-inch gun that could bear on it and all the ship's machine guns opened on it. At virtually the same time, another plane came in low off the starboard side. The plane diving from altitude crashed into the sea twenty-five feet off the starboard bow. The plane approaching low crashed, too, showering the crew with plane parts, oil, and "pieces of red tissue"—the remains of the pilot. Yet even with a dead pilot, the plane's momentum carried pieces of it, including the engine, into the *Dashiell*'s forward five-inch gun mount, starting another fire.[23]

Finally, at ten minutes after two, the attacks ceased. According to the official action report, "All hands on the Dashiell commenced breathing normally." She had been attacked by twenty planes in less than an hour, though it had seemed much longer. She had been badly damaged, and many in her crew had been killed or wounded; she was noticeably down by the head, yet she still floated. Just a mile or so away, the *Sigsbee* lay dead in the water, on fire and smoking. Crippled as she was, the *Dashiell* limped over to the *Sigsbee* and passed her a tow line. Barely moving at first, the paired ships worked their way southward, eventually achieving nine-and-a-half knots as they headed toward Kerama Retto.[24]

To slow the onslaught, American carrier planes flew missions against the airfields that hosted the kamikazes. On April 15, the day after the *Dashiell* and the *Sigsbee* were crippled, Weatherup, now on the USS *Independence*, got urgent orders to attack the airfields on Kyushu. In addition to the eight planes of his own squadron, he commanded twenty others from USS *Randolph* (CV-15). He led all of them north, into the yawning mouth of Kagoshima Bay at the southern tip of Kyushu, coming in lower than the proscribed thirty thousand feet because he was "hoping to catch several aircraft on the ground."[25]

290   ANNAPOLIS GOES TO WAR

And he did. Before he reached the airfield that was the official target, he spotted another field where eight to ten aircraft were in the process of taxiing for takeoff. He sent the planes from the *Randolph* on to the original target, and with a "follow me" gesture, led his own eight-plane group against the near target. He executed a wingover and dove directly at the lead aircraft, assuming that it was probably the squadron leader.* Weatherup waited until the target's wingspan filled his gunsight, then, just as the plane lifted off, he opened fire. The Japanese pilot saw the tracer fire and adjusted his turn so that Weatherup's first bullets flew wide. Weatherup adjusted, too, and he could see "little flicks of light" where his bullets careened off the plane's cockpit armor. Yet other bullets hit the unarmored wings and engine assembly, and the enemy plane began to nose over. Weatherup continued to fire until it cartwheeled on the tarmac and exploded. Pulling out of his dive, Weatherup saw another enemy fighter below him and attacked it, too. It also crashed. He had made two aerial kills in less than a minute. While that was happening, Weatherup's squadron mates had been strafing the planes lined up on the runway. With his pilots having expended all their ammunition, he abandoned the idea of rejoining the planes from the *Randolph* and ordered the eight planes in his squadron to return to the carrier. For his day's work, Weatherup was awarded the Distinguished Flying Cross.[26]

While American fighter planes attacked the kamikaze airfields in Kyushu and others flew CAP over the destroyers on the picket line, still others flew ground support for the soldiers and marines on Okinawa. One of the Forties, Arthur Maltby, flying a dive-bomber off the carrier *Shangri-La*, searched for targets on Okinawa itself.[†] He was surprised as he flew over the island that there was no enemy opposition. The Japanese had devoted everything they had to the suicide campaign and had nothing left to fend off American planes over the island. It was an odd feeling, Maltby wrote later, to be so utterly unmolested in the midst of a fierce battle.[27]

There was also news from Europe that week. An announcement on all the ships that night reported that Adolf Hitler had shot and killed himself in the Führerbunker in Berlin.

---

* Weatherup was correct. The squadron leader was Chief Petty Officer Shoichi Sugita, who, with seventy air-to-air combat kills, was Japan's third-ranking ace.
† The *Shangri-La* took its name from Franklin Roosevelt's quip after the Doolittle Raid back in 1942 that the American bombers had flown from a secret base in "Shangri-La," the locale of the mythical community at the center of James Hilton's 1933 novel *Lost Horizon*.

The news of Hitler's death had no impact on the battle for Okinawa. For another month—all through April and into May—hundreds of Japanese planes assailed the American fleet, concentrating on the picket destroyers. The Americans took considerable losses, but, heavy as they were, it was not enough to convince the high command to call off the invasion. For every ship on the picket line that was damaged—like the *Zellars*, *Dashiell*, and *Sigsbee*—others arrived to take their place.

Among them was the destroyer/minesweeper *Henry A. Wiley* (DD-749) on which Hershel Sellars was the XO. The *Wiley* stayed on the picket line for an interminable thirty-four days, during which time she was assailed by no fewer than sixty-four enemy planes, fifteen of which the *Wiley*'s gunners shot down, earning the ship a Presidential Unit Citation and Sellers a Bronze Star.

The *Wiley* also confronted an entirely new kind of Japanese weapon: a piloted rocket that was launched from long range by a Betty bomber and guided to the target by a suicide pilot. At five hundred miles per hour, they were too fast to shoot down, though they were also hard to control, which meant that they often missed. The Japanese called them *Ohka*; the Americans called them Baka, meaning foolish or stupid. On May 4, one of them approached the *Wiley*, coming in low and very, very fast. The pilot, either losing control or misjudging his altitude, hit the surface of the sea just off the *Wiley*'s starboard side, bounced over the ship, and exploded off her port quarter.

In May, two more destroyers, both of them with executive officers from the class of 1940, joined the picket line. One was the *Douglas H. Fox*, with Connie Carlson as XO; the other was the USS *Van Valkenburgh* (DD-656), with Bronx-born Joe "Otto" Treanor as XO. En route to Okinawa, the skipper of the *Fox*, Ray Pitts, had what Carlson thought was "a brilliant idea." He sent the ship's gunnery officer to the ordnance hangar in Pearl Harbor to claim six "spare" .50 caliber machine guns, which Carlson had bolted to the main deck amidships. Aware that torpedoes would be of little value in a battle against the kamikazes, he pulled the men of the torpedo gang off their duties and assigned them all to the Gunnery Division. When the *Fox* arrived at Ulithi, Carlson sent the former torpedomen ashore to requisition as much .50 caliber ammunition as they could carry. Consequently, as the modified *Douglas H. Fox* headed north for Okinawa, it literally bristled with antiaircraft guns. On May 17, the two destroyers occupied Radar Picket Station Number Nine, fifty miles north of Okinawa along with four small (250 ton) craft known as Landing Craft, Support (LCS), each armed with a single three-inch gun on the bow, plus several 40 mm and 20 mm antiaircraft guns.[28]

The first morning passed quietly, and the men on the *Fox*, especially the torpedomen now assigned to the .50 caliber batteries amidships, used the time to test their weapons. It was comforting to look up and see American fighter planes circling overhead to provide both eyes in the air as well as protection. With the coming of darkness, however, Pitts sounded general quarters, and Carlson headed down into the CIC. After a look at the air search radar screen, he got on the public address system to inform the crew: "There is a bogey seventy miles west of us." It was the first hint of the coming storm. Ten minutes later, as the sun dipped below the horizon, the American planes flying protective cover, which were not equipped for night flying, were recalled to the carriers. This time it was Pitts who got on the 1MC to announce: "All stations topside, if you will look on our starboard beam you can see our Combat Air Patrol. They are on their way home. We are on our own from now on. Heads up."[29]

Only ten minutes later, at 7:26, the radar scopes in CIC showed another bogey—or perhaps the same one—only twelve miles out now and flying very low. Carlson relayed the news to the gunners, who opened fire, and though the bogey maneuvered radically, it was hit and sent spinning into the sea.[30]

It may have been only a stalking horse, for within minutes the radar screen was a blizzard of white spots, all moving and coming in from different angles. Carlson marked the range and bearing of each contact on his plot while simultaneously checking the ship's heading indicator. Using a code he had worked out with the gunners, he employed the sound-powered phones to guide them: "Port 4, Up 2" or "Starboard, 12, up 4." The gun director above the bridge spun "like a whirling dervish" according to one witness, as the gunners adjusted to multiple threats from all directions. Pitts rang up thirty-five knots—as fast as the ship could go, later reporting that "the rapid flow of information from CIC was invaluable in analyzing the situation and determining the direction to turn."[31]

Despite the AA fire exploding all around them, the kamikazes pressed on recklessly. One crashed into the sea just off the *Fox*'s starboard bow; another splashed close off the starboard quarter. At 7:34, another approached from starboard. Bullets hammered it as it closed, and it disintegrated in midair, with pieces of it spattering the surface of the sea. What was left of the fuselage continued on its trajectory and smashed into the *Fox* between its two forward five-inch gun mounts. The bomb it carried penetrated the deck and exploded below, starting fires in several compartments. Pitts had to flood the forward magazine. There were no holes below the waterline, but the weight of the flooded magazine and the spill-off from fighting the fires pushed the *Fox* down by the head, reducing her speed. Another kamikaze approached from the stern. The gun crews fired continuously and the plane finally crashed into the sea only yards off the fantail. A laconic gunner declared, "Splash one Tojo."[32]

That was followed by a brief lull that allowed the *Van Valkenburgh*, which had not been as aggressively targeted, to come alongside and pass over medical supplies, including blood plasma. Too soon, though, Carlson reported another bogie, and the *Van Valkenburgh* sheared off. Both destroyers opened fire and the bogey turned away. By 8:30 the kamikazes were gone, and a half hour after that, the *Fox*'s crew got the last of the fires under control. The ship would survive. On the bridge, Pitts looked down "into the smoldering ruins of his new ship, [to] see the dead lying in mute rows along the passageways." He wondered if it had been his fault. Had he failed the ship, or worse, had he failed those dead men lying there?[33]

Herschel Sellars and the *Wiley* had remained on the picket line for thirty-four days; the *Fox* lasted only one. At 9:30 that night, under the dim light of a "sliver of moon," the USS *W. D. Porter* (DD-579) arrived to take her place and the *Fox* limped back to Kerama Retto under her own power to join the *Dashiell*, *Sigsbee*, *Zellers*, and many others. Carlson never forgot seeing "those damaged and burnt-out destroyers berthed all around the harbor." He counted them and concluded that "we became cripple number 32." They were among the 368 US Navy ships damaged by the kamikazes during the Okinawa campaign. Another 34 ships were sunk, 17 of them destroyers. More than four thousand American sailors were killed.[34]

As with many of the crippled destroyers, the damage to the *Fox* was too great for a local repair, and in a few days, having been in the warzone for less than a week, she began the long trip back to Pearl Harbor. There, the mail caught up with her. Carlson opened the most recent letter first, to learn that his wife had given birth to a baby girl. In the bloodiest month of the war, with death all around them, both John Lacouture and Connie Carlson returned to find new life.

23

Culmination

By the spring of 1944, Myers Montgomery had been on the battleship *Idaho* for nearly four years—literally all of his commissioned service. That finally changed in April. He was sitting in his stateroom on a Monday afternoon when an orderly stuck his head around the door and told him new orders had come in for him. They were somewhat enigmatic: He was directed and required to report to Washington, DC, as soon as possible. He threw his gear into a seabag and was off the ship and on his way by 7:45 the next morning. He flew across the Pacific to Hawaii, then to California, and finally to Washington, DC, where he arrived tired, dirty, and worn out. He went into a barbershop and ordered "the works."[1]

In Washington, he learned that his new assignment was as the main battery assistant (the same job Bill Braybrook had on the *Tuscaloosa*) on the heavy cruiser USS *Pittsburgh* (CA-72), a brand-new ship still under construction at the Fore River shipyard in Quincy, Massachusetts. First, though, he was to complete Gunnery School and several other schools in Washington over the summer. His well-worn khakis were too ragged for the nation's capital, it was simply too hot for his service dress blues, and he noticed that "no one at all wears whites in Washington," so he decided to commemorate this chapter in his career by purchasing a new uniform of gray gabardine. That option was available because the CNO, Admiral King, had embarked on a campaign to switch the entire navy into gray uniforms. Most officers hated it. Nimitz, for example, insisted that the gray uniforms made the officers look like bus drivers and the enlisted men like sanitation workers. In the end, King's sartorial experiment collapsed. Entirely unsuspecting, Montgomery went to the uniform shop and bought a complete new gray uniform, which he thought "looked real nice."[2]

All through a hot and steamy Washington summer, Montgomery attended Gunnery School, Firefighting School, and Ordnance School in his new gray

CULMINATION   295

uniform. The training was so fast paced that, as he put it, "if you drop a pencil, you'd fall behind." In the fall, having completed all the assigned schools successfully, he headed north to much cooler weather in Rhode Island, where, at the Education and Training Center in Newport, he supervised training for the *Pittsburgh*'s crew of twenty-eight officers and eight hundred men. Though it was a full-time assignment (including calisthenics at 5:30 every morning), Montgomery also attended radar school, which was sufficiently technical that he asked his family to send him his old slide rule from the Academy. Once a week, he went up to Quincy, Massachusetts, to visit the ship, which was nearing completion. "She really looks pretty now," he wrote his family, "getting all painted and cleaned up for commissioning." He kept up with the war news from the Pacific, including the Battle of Leyte Gulf, writing home that he was "anxious" about "all the fighting the Navy has been doing out there in the Pacific.... I wish we were out there helping out."[3]

The *Pittsburgh* was commissioned in October, and two weeks later Montgomery received official notification of his promotion to lieutenant commander. He was happy about the promotion and happy, too, with the "swell bunch of officers" on board, though he was taken aback by "all the extra duties thrown on me," which, in addition to main battery assistant, included senior watch officer, and service on the Court Martial Board. He confessed to his parents, "I really never knew what it was to have so many things to do at once." And it got even busier when the *Pittsburgh*'s executive officer transferred off the ship and everybody moved up a notch, making Montgomery the assistant gunnery officer as well.[4]

After several shakedown cruises off the East Coast, the *Pittsburgh* headed south to the Caribbean, through the Panama Canal, and across the Pacific to the war. In February 1945, she joined Mitscher's Task Force 58 at Ulithi, and Montgomery was excited to help make history when the *Pittsburgh* served as part of the escort for the carriers that conducted the first air strikes against the Japanese homeland, as discussed in the last chapter.

He was shocked on April 12 when he heard that President Franklin Roosevelt died. FDR had been president for so long, literally all of Montgomery's adult life, that it was almost disorienting. Montgomery took some satisfaction from the fact that it was a fellow Missourian, Harry Truman, who would handle the job now, though he suspected "it will take some time as he has to fill the place of such a great man."[5]

In May, when a Japanese plane landed two bombs on the carrier *Franklin*, the *Pittsburgh* dropped out of formation to pick up survivors. She then closed

296   ANNAPOLIS GOES TO WAR

the still-burning carrier, passed her a line, and prepared to tow her away. "That was a big assignment," Montgomery wrote his parents. "The Nips didn't want to see her get away so they really threw planes at her." He recalled later that towing forty thousand tons of inert steel that was on fire and smoking while under air attack was "quite an interesting experience."[6]

June 3, 1945, was the fifth anniversary of the Forties' graduation. It had been a remarkable—even historic—five years, unmatched in its impact on world events by any other half decade in history, save perhaps the years from 1914 to 1919. Few of the young men who had joyfully tossed their caps into the air on June 3, 1940, could have imagined all that the next five years would bring. Obviously, there was no class reunion, given that all of the Forties who remained alive were dispersed literally all over the world: from the coast of Japan to the Baltic Sea, and from the Aleutians to the Mediterranean. As Montgomery put it, "I have friends scattered all over the globe."[7]

The world was also a far different place in 1945 than it had been in 1940. Italy and Germany were defeated—both Mussolini and Hitler were dead (and Roosevelt, too, for that matter); and Japanese military power had been largely eviscerated. Yet the oceans remained dangerous, especially for the unwary, as Montgomery and the *Pittsburgh* were about to discover.

On that same June 3, Nimitz ordered Halsey to carry out a series of carrier raids against the Japanese home islands. With the battle for Okinawa winding down, the next likely operation was an invasion of Japan itself, and Nimitz wanted to "maintain unremitting military pressure" against the home islands. Eager to do exactly that, Halsey ordered the fleet to close within striking distance of Japan. As the fleet moved west, however, several of his task group commanders asked permission to change course to the east, away from Japan, to avoid an approaching typhoon.[8]

What are called hurricanes in the Atlantic and Northeast Pacific are called typhoons in the western Pacific though they are born of the same phenomena. Warm seawater causes the air to rise, and when it cools at higher altitudes, it is pushed aside by more warm air rising from below. The resulting low-pressure vacuum sucks air toward the center and creates the characteristic circular spin—clockwise south of the equator and counterclockwise north of it. Hurricanes or typhoons produce winds of up to a hundred miles an hour, and waves of forty feet or more. They are a reminder that for all the awesome power of a battleship or aircraft carrier, nature is more powerful still.

CULMINATION   297

Halsey's hallmark characteristic was his determination, and he was reluctant to yield to wind and weather. He had already dealt with one damaging typhoon back in December 1944, two months after the Battle of Leyte Gulf. On that occasion, to ensure that his ships were full of fuel and able to support MacArthur's pending invasion of Luzon, he had ordered a fleet refueling for December 17. He was frustrated when an approaching typhoon compelled him to postpone it. Typhoon or not, he tried again a few days later, mandating a fleet course that proved unrealistic in the appalling sea conditions. The typhoon tossed the smaller ships around like bathtub toys—three destroyers actually sank. Even the big ships were roughly handled, including Weatherup's former ship, the *Cowpens*, which was severely damaged when planes on her flight deck broke free of their restraints and crashed into one another, triggering raging fires even as giant waves continued to pound her. Altogether twenty-five ships suffered serious damage, and nearly eight hundred men were killed. Nimitz felt compelled to convene a board of inquiry, which subsequently found Halsey guilty of "errors of judgment," though it left him in command.[9]

Now, six months later, Halsey had an opportunity to redeem himself, though once again his determination to fulfill his orders overrode his judgment. He rejected the request to turn east and instead ordered a course to the northwest, to keep his ships nearer to the planned targets. It also put them in the path of the storm. The wind increased to eighty knots, and the task group commanders again requested a change of course. Again Halsey said no. On board the *Pittsburgh*, Montgomery wrote his grandmother that "today, we're trying to run out of the path of an approaching typhoon," adding, "Hope we're lucky." The ship's executive officer, Commander Horatio Rivero, could not understand "why we were barging into the damn storm."[10]

Subsequently named Typhoon Viper, the storm grew in strength, generating waves that crashed completely over the *Pittsburgh*'s foredeck and occasionally over her bridge. The *Pittsburgh*'s float plane was ripped from her catapult and smashed onto the deck. At 6:10 on the morning of June 4, the wind officially topped one hundred knots (115 miles per hour), and the whole ship began to bend and twist. Montgomery saw that some of the welded seams in her deck had begun to tear open, and the bow section seemed to move up and down independent of the rest of the ship. Captain John L. Gingrich, who remained on the bridge throughout, ordered all personnel out of the bow section and required the watertight doors to be dogged shut. It was just in time. At 6:33, with a grinding, tearing, sound, 104 feet of the cruiser's bow—a sixth of her length—broke off entirely, passed under the ship, and drifted away. The *Pittsburgh* remained afloat, though her hull now ended abruptly just forward of Turret One. Montgomery helped direct crewmen below decks who worked to shore up the forward bulkheads with timbers.[11]

The *Pittsburgh*'s bow section, only thirty to forty feet away, now constituted a hazard to navigation. Since the watertight doors had been secured, it did not sink; instead, it tossed about violently and unpredictably. Captain Gingrich had to maneuver creatively to avoid colliding with it. Only after the waning of the storm that afternoon was the *Pittsburgh* able to limp away southward toward Guam, where it arrived on June 10. A few days later, the bow section arrived, too, towed there by a destroyer. Sailors on the *Pittsburgh* joked that when her bow was still several hundred miles away, the *Pittsburgh* was the longest ship in the navy. In time, equipped with a temporary false bow, the big cruiser made her cautious way back to the States for a lengthy refit in Bremerton shipyard.[12]

Some thirty-two ships had been damaged in the storm—seven more than in Halsey's previous encounter with a typhoon. This time a board of inquiry recommended Halsey's removal from command. Such a penalty may have been justified, but Nimitz believed it would be a terrible blow to service morale and, for that matter, national morale, just as the war seemed to be reaching its culmination. Consequently, Halsey remained on duty, and eventually he would be awarded a fifth star as a fleet admiral.

For his part, Montgomery moved up to gunnery officer on the *Pittsburgh*, essentially the third-ranking officer on the ship. Even though she was now in drydock, Montgomery felt the increase of responsibility immediately. "It's a bit more difficult now," he wrote his father, "to have to make your own decisions than to have several officers senior to you to turn to for an answer." As it happened, the *Pittsburgh* remained in Bremerton for the rest of the war, which meant that Montgomery's war was effectively over.[13]

The violence continued in the western Pacific, though by now it was almost entirely one-sided because the Japanese had few tools left to fight back. They had lost 1,465 planes in their kamikaze onslaught north of Okinawa, and while there were still hundreds of planes left, there were few experienced pilots to fly them and virtually no gasoline to fuel them. The once-proud Imperial Japanese Navy had been reduced to a single capital ship: the battleship *Yamato*, which was sunk in April while heading toward Okinawa on what was essentially a suicide mission.

CULMINATION 299

Japan still had powerful armies on the Asian mainland in China, Burma, and elsewhere, though lacking sea transportation, they might as well have been on the moon. Meanwhile, the home islands absorbed unimaginable punishment from the air. All that summer, hundreds of B-29s from Saipan, Tinian, and Guam continued their relentless bombing of Japanese cities; Tokyo was so completely devastated it was removed from the target list. And during that same period, American submarines continued their campaign of destruction against what few Japanese transport ships remained afloat. The USS *Flasher* (SS-249), with Philip "P.T." Glennon as XO, cruised the South China Sea for seventy-seven days from February to April, looking for prey, and in all that time, she encountered only four vessels: one Japanese freighter of 2,000 tons, one small "sea truck" of 150 tons, and two tiny luggers of 50 tons each. The *Flasher* dispatched the freighter with three torpedoes and sank the three smaller ships with her four-inch deck gun. She returned to Fremantle, Australia, with most of her torpedoes still on board, having run out of targets.[14]

By July, Japan was a defeated nation, a passive victim unable to do much more than endure further punishment. Even so, the military leadership remained defiant, with a few senior officers insisting that it would be better for the Japanese race (their term) to die out entirely than to suffer the ignominy of surrender. American leaders wondered what it would take to secure final victory. On many of the Pacific islands, the Japanese had preferred death to surrender. Would it be necessary to invade the home islands and kill every Japanese who resisted? These were the circumstances in the first two weeks of August 1945, as the new president, Harry Truman, contemplated the cost of invasion—to both sides.[15]

This clash of cultural viewpoints—an unbridgeable gulf—had been evident from the start and had even played a role in the outbreak of war. Back in 1941, Franklin Roosevelt and his advisers had expected that the application of economic sanctions would encourage the Japanese to moderate their aggressive behavior in Asia; Japanese leaders had assumed that knocking out the American battlefleet would encourage the Americans to acquiesce in Japanese control of South Asia. During the war that ensued, Americans were stunned by the Japanese willingness to squander their human resources so profligately and to prefer death over surrender; the Japanese were amazed and appalled by those Americans who allowed themselves to be taken prisoner at all. Only rarely did men on either side have an opportunity to observe their foes in a noncombat environment, which meant there were few chances to glimpse, let alone

300 ANNAPOLIS GOES TO WAR

understand, the psyche of their opponents. Even when such a situation did occur, the result was generally bafflement rather than enlightenment.

In August 1945, Pete Peterson was the executive officer of the *Fletcher*-class destroyer *Charrette* (DD-581). After participating in the reconquest of Borneo in July, the *Charrette* was dispatched on a special mission to track a purported hospital ship that was crossing the Banda Sea between the Kai Islands and Java, both still held by the Japanese. On August 3, the *Charrette* closed on the ship in question, and the *Charrette*'s captain, Commander William H. Watson Jr., sent Peterson in a small boat with a twenty-five-man boarding party to inspect her. Armed only with a .45 caliber pistol, Peterson ascended the ship's accommodation ladder, and as his head reached the level of the deck, he was assaulted by a smell so powerful he had to stifle a gag reflex. He was met by a single officer, with no other person visible topside. Where was everyone? Were there armed Japanese soldiers below deck waiting to spring a trap? Through an interpreter, Peterson asked to see the commanding officer, and en route to the captain's cabin, he discovered why there was no one else about, as well as the source of the smell. The interior compartments on the ship were "totally covered with Japanese, half on the deck, and the other half on a low tier about 3 feet above the deck. They were packed in body to body and no aisles for walking among them."[16]

Arriving in the wardroom, Peterson explained to the captain, Kishiro Yasuda, that he needed to inspect the ship to ensure it was not carrying contraband. Peterson thought the captain was "a pretty nice fellow, not quite sure of all that was going on." In his subsequent report, Peterson wrote that the Japanese captain showed "great courtesy and willingness to oblige at all times." Peterson sent a search party below to look for contraband while he examined the ship's papers and passenger list. He read that the ship was the *Tachibana Maru*, a hospital ship carrying 1,562 patients, all of whom were Japanese officers and soldiers, to Surabaya in Java. It seemed pretty evident to him that the men crammed side to side on the deck were indeed patients, and not a combat battalion playing possum. "Most of them," he recalled, "didn't look too good." On the other hand, the search crew reported back to him that below decks they had found both weapons and ammunition—some .25 caliber machine guns, six or eight rifles, some hand grenades, and many boxes that were marked with a red cross but turned out to contain 70 mm artillery shells. That was more than enough for him to declare the vessel—hospital ship or not—a lawful prize. When informed that his ship was being impounded, the captain said

CULMINATION   301

nothing, though his face turned red, likely reflecting shame rather than fear. Peterson merely noted that "he looked very uncomfortable."[17]

When a prize crew arrived from the *Charrette*, Peterson stationed them to guard all the hatches, and he had barbed wire strung across the ship to discourage any attempt to retake her. That proved an unnecessary precaution, however, as over the next three days he met mostly with cooperation from the crew. There was some initial awkwardness, especially given the language barrier, though once routine protocols were established, the tension eased. "By the end of the first day," Peterson wrote, "most were becoming adjusted to the situation."[18]

The ship was crowded. It had been designed to carry seven hundred patients, and there were well over twice that number on board, as well as sixty or so caregivers and the ship's crew. For the most part, they all stayed on the job. Japanese engineers ran the power plant; Japanese corpsmen saw to the injured and sick; and Japanese cooks made the meals. Indeed, the most cheerful person on board was the Korean cook, who took it all in stride and seemed entirely unconcerned about the change in command. Members of the prize crew did not share the rice balls with fish that the cook prepared for the sick and the crew. Their food was sent over daily from the *Charrette*.

Peterson had difficulty reading the temperament of the Japanese. Several of the doctors, who were officers, felt obliged to explain to him that they chose to stay alive only to treat the patients, for otherwise they would have killed themselves rather than be taken prisoner. One Japanese officer approached an American sentry and begged to be shot, though whether the request was genuine or pro forma, Peterson could not tell. Only one Japanese officer expressed enmity to the Americans, and Peterson had him transferred to the *Charrette* just to be safe. To the others, Peterson explained that they were not really prisoners; the ship was being impounded for further investigation, and it was possible that they would all eventually be released. That explanation seemed to leave them perplexed.[19]

If the officers felt obligated to explain why they had not killed themselves, some of the enlisted men treated it as a lark. Several spent most of their time trying to learn English, periodically trying out newly learned words or phrases on the sentries. Others appeared to take quiet satisfaction at the discomfiture of the officers, whose staterooms they had been forced to clean. Some members of the crew Peterson could not read at all: "The purser," he wrote, "was one of the most willing of gents, but we never knew what he was thinking." Similarly, the helmsman was "a nice young kid but there again we got no indication of his thoughts."[20]

One thing Peterson found puzzling as he explored the ship was "the extraordinary large inventory of leather goods on board," as well as bottles of perfume, apparently acquired as gifts for family members. Moreover, every officer seemed to have a pet, including at least four monkeys and six cats, all of whom had the run of the ship. The officers' staterooms each contained a number of dolls intended, apparently, as decorations. The captain had four of them hanging on the bulkhead. The captain also had a small wooden shrine in his stateroom where he presumably prayed every night, as well as "two lovely small blue vases...each large enough to hold one small flower."[21]

The ship arrived without further incident at Morotai at 8:15 on the morning of August 6, 1945, and Peterson turned the ship, its crew, and the patients, over to the army. At that very moment, twenty-two hundred miles to the north, a B-29 named the Enola Gay dropped an atomic bomb on the city of Hiroshima.

Three days later, a second bomb devastated Nagasaki, and the Soviet Union declared war on Japan. Six days after that, on August 15, 1945, Emperor Hirohito announced Japan's surrender.

Bob Kaufman, from Clarion, Pennsylvania, had a "quiet, unassuming" personality and "an easygoing manner." Physically, his most prominent features were a pair of dark eyes and a truly impressive nose. Like two score others from the class of 1940, he had selected the submarine service in 1942 and spent most of the next year and a half on the *Gato*, the namesake of her class, for five war patrols—three of them as torpedo officer and two as executive officer. In March 1944, by then a lieutenant commander, he was selected to be the aide and flag lieutenant for the commander of all Pacific submarines, then Rear Admiral, and soon to be Vice Admiral, Charles A. Lockwood.[22]

In August 1945, Lockwood's headquarters were on the island of Guam near Admiral Nimitz's headquarters. On the last day of the month, Lockwood told Kaufman to pack a sea bag for a trip to Tokyo. Within hours, two seaplanes took off from Saipan's Tanapag Harbor. One of them contained Nimitz and his staff; the other carried Lockwood, Richmond Kelly Turner, and the senior Marine Corps general, Roy Geiger, and their staffs, including Bob Kaufman. During the sixteen-hundred-mile flight to Tokyo Bay, everyone was in a celebratory mood. Lockwood himself said, "We might easily have been bound for an Army-Navy game." En route, they overflew Iwo Jima, and Kelly Turner went forward into the cockpit and took the controls so he could circle Mount Suribachi. Later, as the two planes neared Japan, a squadron of navy fighters came out as an escort. Then, as the two planes approached Tokyo Harbor, in Lockwood's words, "The glorious sight of our Fleet, anchored below Yokohama, burst upon us! God, but it looked beautiful."[23]

Two days later, at nine o'clock in the morning on September 2, 1945, Lieutenant Commander Kaufman had what was very nearly a ringside seat standing behind his boss on the deck of the USS *Missouri* (BB-63). He watched as Douglas MacArthur and Chester Nimitz, each wearing an informal open-collar khaki uniform, walked together from the *Missouri*'s wardroom to stand near a small table on the quarterdeck that had been covered by a green baize cloth. The Japanese delegation, in full formal attire, came alongside the *Missouri* in an American destroyer, climbed the ladder to the deck, and formed up in an open space in front of the table. Then, at MacArthur's direction, they came forward one by one to sign the instrument of surrender.

It was five years and four months after the Forties had graduated from the Academy, and nine years and three months—3,366 days—since they had arrived in Annapolis in the sweltering summer of 1936.

It might as well have been a hundred years.

Epilogue

As shocking as the Pearl Harbor attack had been, the sudden arrival of peace was nearly as disorienting. Most of the Forties were still only twenty-seven years old, and the great adventure of their lives was now behind them. The war had dominated virtually all of their adult lives, from Hitler's reoccupation of the Rhineland in 1936 to Japan's surrender in 1945. For nine years, they had been directed by circumstance, authority, and a felt responsibility. They had served in different theaters, in different jobs, on different ships—or planes or battalions. Yet all of them had been forged, tempered, and tested. Every man in the class knew someone who had been killed in the war, and the sacrifice of their classmates was etched into their hearts.

The onset of peace offered another test. After nine years in a largely male environment, they went home to a world shared with women and children. Some of them, arriving home in 1945, met their own children for the first time. Men who had survived the terror of being in a submarine and hearing the pings of a hunting destroyer, now confronted the equally alarming cries of a newborn in the night. When civilian friends, or even members of their own family, asked them about the war, they generally deflected. They could talk about it with one another, but they had difficulty framing it for those who had not experienced it. Then, too, many hoped to spare their friends and family the horrors they had seen.

They had learned to live in the moment; now they had to think of the future. Nearly every member of the class of 1940 stayed in the navy (or Marine Corps) after the war was over. Even those who had chosen the Academy mainly to get a free education decided to stay. Partly, of course, they were motivated by a commitment to service. ("I do solemnly swear to support and defend the

Constitution of the United States against all enemies foreign and domestic...")
In addition to that oath, the brotherhood of shared experience and sacrifice
bound them.

They were older, changed in part by the simple passage of time and in part
by the war. The terror of a midnight engagement in Ironbottom Sound or
watching a kamikaze pilot line up on your ship were experiences never for-
gotten. And yet in many important and even fundamental ways, they
remained who they had been five years earlier when they left Annapolis and
the world of *Reef Points*. They still believed in personal and collective responsibility, in duty, hard work, and—even amid the elemental terrors of
combat—compassion. They honored the tradition of service. They felt they
had fought a just, honorable, and necessary war, and they never stopped
believing that.

For the next two decades and longer, they served in a wide variety of assignments throughout the world. For some of them, there was another war—in
Korea—and for a few a third war—in Vietnam. Throughout it all, they stayed
in touch with one another, attended class reunions when they could, and
caught the occasional Navy football game. In 1954 they commissioned a
stained-glass window in the Academy Chapel with the text: "They that go
down to the sea in ships...these see the marks of the Lord, and His wonders in
the deep." Eventually, they retired. Some took up a new profession; several
became teachers. But none of them ever forgot their trial by fire in World War II,
nor did they forget one another. They were always Forties.

EPILOGUE

Raymond A. "Hundy" Hundevadt was nine years old when he was captivated by the vista of navy battleships anchored in the Hudson River and decided then that he wanted to attend the Naval Academy. Fifteen years later, at age twenty-four, he watched Jimmy Doolittle's bombers take off from the *Hornet* to raid Tokyo, and only months after that, he was on the cruiser *Vincennes* when it was sunk during the Battle of Savo Island.

With the end of the war, Hundevadt returned to Annapolis to spend a year at the navy's Post Graduate School, followed by another year of postgraduate study at Cornell. Then he went to Little Creek, Virginia, to assume command of what was then called the navy's Underwater Demolition Teams, now called Navy SEALs. In 1951, he assumed command of the USS *Vogelgesang* (DD-862) serving mostly in the Mediterranean, before several tours ashore at the Bureau of Ordnance and the National War College. In 1963, he took command of the USS *Mulliphen*, an attack cargo ship.

Retiring from the navy in 1965, he, his wife Del, and their two daughters moved to Redlands, California, where he worked as a project engineer for Lockheed, developing systems for the retrieval of solid rocket boosters. He was active in a men's social group, the Fortnightly Club, and the First Congregationalist Church. He was a vocal "hawk" during the Vietnam War, writing letters to the local paper in support of a stronger defense. He died on April 17, 1992, a victim of lung cancer, at the age of only seventy-four.

Michael J. Hanley Jr. (formerly Joe Hanley) came to the Naval Academy to play basketball. Disenchanted by his first experience at sea during his youngster cruise, he grew to enjoy service on smaller ships. He never forgot his near-disastrous encounter with a downed PanAm airplane while in command of a navy blimp, nor could he forget the horrors of repeated kamikaze attacks near Okinawa.

After the war, Hanley commanded the destroyer escort USS *Scroggins* (DE-799) and then decided to make a second attempt at flight school. Successful this time, he became the commanding officer of the navy's first squadron of Douglas A-1 Skyraider attack planes (VA-65), on the carrier USS *Midway*. After stints in training commands and at the Armed Forces Staff College, he commanded Air Task Group 181, operating with several different carriers, mostly in the Mediterranean. He and his wife Chris had two daughters, Susan and Michelle.

Following a tour at the National War College in Washington, DC, he had one more staff job before taking command of the USS *Thetis Bay*, an escort aircraft carrier that had been converted into a helicopter carrier, and which bore the presidential helicopter of John F. Kennedy when he went to Berlin to deliver his famous speech in 1963. Hanley retired from the navy as a captain in 1970 and lived in London for several years before returning to the United States. Like many Academy grads, he enjoyed golf, tennis, and bridge and was an active member of the Army-Navy Country Club. Sadly, his retirement was marked by Alzheimer's disease, and he died on March 14, 2001, at Arlington Hospital, at the age of eighty-two.

John W. Myers Montgomery dated ("dragged") a dizzying number of young women before he finally met "the one." When the navy sent him to George Washington University Law School after the war, he met and married Mary Margaret Higgs of Washington, and they had three children between 1948 and 1955. After graduating from law school, Montgomery served on USS *Borie* during the Korean War and participated in the evacuation of American troops from Hungnam after the Chinese intervention. He then commanded the USS *Hank* (DD-702) in support of the Eighth Army's recapture of Seoul and Inchon. A tour of duty in the navy's JAG Corps (Judge Advocate General) followed. After duty on the staff of Supreme Allied Commander NATO and an XO tour on the cruiser *Norfolk*, he returned to Washington and the Pentagon, where he managed liaison with the House and Senate Appropriations Committees. After that he assumed command of the USS *Paul Revere*, an attack transport that carried elements of the US Marine Corps to Vietnam during that conflict.

In retirement, he worked for several companies, including National Paint and Coatings. In 1983, he became president of an insurance company, though he retired after only two years to devote himself full time to advising the Boy Scouts. His son, John B. Montgomery, graduated in the Naval Academy class of 1970, and his grandson graduated in the class of 1998. Myers Montgomery died on April 16, 2001, one month after Mike Hanley, at the Arleigh Burke Pavilion in McLean, Virginia, at the age of eighty-three.

Robert A. "Doc" Weatherup chose the Naval Academy because of his fascination with flying. Before the navy allowed him to go to flight school, however, he served on three different destroyers in the fierce fighting around Guadalcanal, earning a Purple Heart in the Battle of Cape Esperance. He then became a pilot, a squadron XO, and finally a squadron commander, flying his Hellcat fighter in combat over Tokyo, Okinawa, and Kyushu.

Like Hundy Hundevadt, he got orders to Post Graduate School after V-J Day. That was followed by a second year of postgrad education at Cal Tech in Pasadena, where he earned a master's degree in aeronautical engineering. Three children—Ann, Roy, and John—joined the family in short order. After a tour in the Office of Naval Research in Washington, Weatherup left for Korea to command air squadron VS-892 on the carrier *Badoeng Strait*, first defending the Pusan Perimeter and later flying cover for the marines during the Battle of the Chosin Reservoir.

When the Korean War ended, he headed back to Washington to head the Design Branch of the Bureau of Aeronautics. After a sea tour as the operations officer on USS *Boxer* (CV-21), he was pleased to get orders to the NROTC unit at MIT, where his title was Professor of Military Science.

In 1961 he went to work for the Douglas Aircraft Company in El Segundo, California, near Los Angeles. After retiring from that job, he and Kathryn continued to live in Southern California. His wife died in 1997, and Doc, then eighty-one, moved in with their daughter Ann and her husband in Portola Valley, near Palo Alto. He died there six years later on December 6, 2003, at the age of eighty-seven.

John E. "Peck" Greenbacker served on the carrier *Yorktown* in the Battle of the Coral Sea and was officer of the deck on that ship during the Battle of Midway. He was among the first in the class of 1940 to command a warship. He served the last few months of the war in command of the destroyer escort *Lloyd C. Acree* (DE-356), escorting convoys in the western Pacific and working with Chinese Nationalist forces in Shandong Province.

After the war, the navy sent him to law school at Georgetown, in Washington, DC, and after completing his law degree, he remained in uniform as a JAG officer. Between 1945 and 1949, he and his wife Carolyn welcomed four children (Susan, John Jr., Florence, and Christopher). In the 1950s he was the military personnel and legal officer for the battleship-cruiser force in the Atlantic. He had other sea commands, including that of a destroyer division in the early 1960s. He retired as a captain in 1969, accepting a position as senior attorney and treasurer of the Baltimore Gas & Electric Company, though he retired from that a few years later and moved to Halifax County, Virginia, where his wife had grown up. There he enjoyed practicing law with his son John Jr. Some years later, his son moved to Boston, and John was visiting him there in 2005 when he suffered a series of strokes and died at the age of eighty-seven. At the funeral, his son said of him: "He was always happiest when he was off at sea."

Frederick J. Karch remained the training officer of the Fourteenth Marine Regiment of the Fourth Marine Division until the division was disbanded in November 1945. He returned to the States for a reunion with his wife Mary Elizabeth (called Betty) and their son John Frederick (called Ricky). He was an artillery instructor at the Marine Training Center in Quantico, Virginia, when his second daughter, Kathy, was born. He commanded a battalion in the Tenth Marine Regiment before becoming executive officer of the regiment. In the mid-1950s he was serving with the Far East Command in Tokyo when a third child, Cindy, was born. Karch graduated from the Army War College in 1961 and earned a master's degree from George Washington University in 1963.

Promoted to brigadier general in 1964, he led the Ninth Marine Expeditionary Brigade ashore at Da Nang, South Vietnam, on March 8, 1965, to initiate direct US military involvement in Vietnam. Like most Americans at the time, he vastly underestimated the Vietnamese. "I thought that once they ran up against our first team they wouldn't stand and fight," he wrote later, "but they did." He admitted candidly, "I made a miscalculation."

Karch returned to Quantico in December 1965 to become the director of the Command & Staff College, and he remained in that job until his retirement in 1967. His marriage to Betty ended in divorce; his second marriage, to Virginia Zimmer, ended with her death in 1990. He then married Mary Lou Ruddy, who survived him. He died at his home in Arlington, Virginia, on May 23, 2009, at the age of ninety-one.

EPILOGUE

John E. Lacouture, the well-born, handsome, and supremely self-confident native of Boston and Hyannisport, cut a wide swath wherever he went. He competed with the Kennedy boys in sailing races, danced with Eleanor Roosevelt in the White House, and survived the sinking of the USS *Blue* in Ironbottom Sound. Once he earned his gold wings in 1942, he found his niche in the navy's aviation community. Despite a close brush with a fiery death on the *Franklin* in March 1945, he so loved to fly that by the time he retired in 1970 he had flown nearly six thousand hours in 173 different airplane types.

From 1945 to 1947, he was commanding officer of the "Red Rippers" (VF-4), with the call sign "Tiger One," and over the next two decades, he commanded three squadrons, three air wings, and two aircraft carriers, including the USS *Saratoga* (CVA-60). When not flying, he earned a degree in aeronautical engineering at Princeton and served as the US representative to the Strategic Air Command in Europe. He and his wife Betty had four children, though that marriage ended in divorce, as did his subsequent marriage to Jean Smith.

In retirement, Lacouture worked seven years for Ling-Temco-Vought (LVT), an aerospace conglomerate, before going to Cambridge University in England to earn an M.Lit. degree. After returning to the United States, he spent summers on Nantucket Island, writing occasional professional essays, including one in 2001 for the Naval Institute *Proceedings* suggestively entitled, "You Can Be Good and Be Colorful." He spent winters at his home in Williamsburg, Virginia, which is where he was when he died on August 16, 2010, at the age of ninety-two.

Philip "P. T." Glennon, was still only twenty-five, when he served as XO of the *Gato*-class submarine *Flasher*, which won six battle stars and was credited with sinking more than one hundred thousand tons of Japanese shipping, making it one of the most successful American submarines of the war. After the *Flasher* was decommissioned in 1946, her conning tower was removed and placed on display in Groton, Connecticut.

In late 1944, when the *Flasher* was in the yards in Perth, Australia, for a refit, Glennon met Australian Dorothy "Dottie" Leunig, and after a whirlwind romance, they married on January 13, 1945. Like his father and his grandfather, Glennon stayed in the navy for a full career. After commanding the *Baleo*-class submarine *Bergall* (SS-320), he became aide and flag lieutenant to Admiral Arthur W. Radford, commander of the Pacific fleet, though he had to leave that job early due to health problems. Glennon served two years as captain of the destroyer *C.O. Kepler* (DD-765) before moving his growing family to Norfolk, where he served on the staff of the Atlantic fleet commander. In 1959, a daughter, Ann, was born to join her three older brothers (Philip [called "PT"], Charles, and Richard). After two tours in the Pentagon, Glennon assumed command of a fleet oiler, USS *Truckee* (AO-147).

Retiring from the navy after thirty years, Captain Glennon moved to Tega Cay, south of Charlotte, North Carolina, where he took daily walks and served as chairman of the Beautification and Planning Committee. The community center there is named for him. He was happy in retirement, telling the local newspaper, "I've never been as contented as I am right here." He died two months after John Lacouture on October 25, 2010, at the age of ninety-one.

Conrad H. "Connie" Carlson, the former math major from Harvard who sang in the Academy choir, served in a variety of cruisers and destroyers during the war, including the *Astoria*, sunk from under him at Savo Island, and the *Douglas H. Fox*, assailed by a dozen kamikazes at Okinawa. After V-J Day, he briefly commanded the USS *MacDougal* (DD-358) before the Navy sent him to MIT in Cambridge, Massachusetts, his hometown, to earn a graduate degree in electronics. Carlson was thrilled, gushing, "How lucky can a man be!" Following staff duty in Norfolk, he commanded the USS *Brownson* (DD-868), a newer and larger (2,650 tons) *Gearing*-class destroyer. Once again, he felt lucky: "The years in Brownson were truly wonderful," he wrote. Shore assignments included working on the navy's Tactical Data System and serving in Norway as part of the Military Assistance Advisory Group (MAAG) to NATO. The Norway tour was "accompanied," meaning that his wife Alice and their two daughters went with him, and again he felt lucky: "Living in Oslo," he wrote, "was particularly nice."

He retired from the navy in 1962 and worked briefly for Raytheon, the company that developed the SG radar that had proved so valuable in Ironbottom Sound. Most of his retirement, however, he spent teaching math at a nearby independent school, a job he loved. He retired full time to Webster Lake, New Hampshire, where he played golf and avidly followed all Boston sports teams. In 2005, at age eighty-seven, he attended the sixty-fifth reunion of the class of 1940. It was his last. He died in 2011 at the age of ninety-three.

Ernest R. "Pete" Peterson, after his curious encounter with a Japanese hospital ship in the last days of the war, assumed command of the USS *Davison* (DD-618), after which he got orders to command the Gunner's Mate School in Great Lakes, Illinois. Like Connie Carlson, he was tabbed for service in Europe as a MAAG and sent to Copenhagen, Denmark, which allowed him, his wife Betty, and their children the opportunity to make weekend visits to scenic and historic places all over Europe.

Back in the States, he had a lengthy tour as a training officer in Norfolk before getting orders to command a destroyer. Before he could assume that post, however, he learned that Betty had been diagnosed with cancer, and he asked that his orders be changed so he could be with her. She survived that scare, though the cancer returned in 1957, and this time she did not survive. Pete remarried a year later, and a year after that he retired from the navy. Obtaining a master's degree from Fairfield University, he became a math teacher at the Hopkins School in New Haven, the country's third-oldest private school, retiring from that job in 1982.

During a long retirement in Cheshire, Connecticut, near New Haven, Peterson was an avid birder and community volunteer. He attended the funerals of many of his classmates until there were none left to attend. He died on April 14, 2016, at the age of ninety-nine, the last of the Forties.

Acknowledgments

Every Naval Academy class presents a gift to the institution as part of its legacy, usually at graduation. Sometimes there is an additional gift years later, when the graduates are more financially secure. Often it is something physical: a bench, a walkway, a fountain. Other gifts are more intangible. I benefited personally from the decision by the class of 1957 to create an endowed professorship in Naval History and Heritage, and I held the Class of 1957 Chair in Naval History during the academic year 2011–12.

The members of the class of 1940 were equally creative. During the 1980s, forty-some years after their graduation, they decided to create an archive containing as many of the personal stories of their 456 graduates as they could gather. The idea was that their experiences could benefit future generations of midshipmen, and, because of that, the contributors were encouraged to be especially candid in their observations and analysis. Not every graduate participated, and some who did submitted material that was largely pro forma, providing a list of assignments but omitting their thoughts and feelings. Still, quite a few took the assignment seriously and offered lengthy and thoughtful narrative accounts. That necessarily affected my selection of those who are featured here. And, of course, those who were no longer living in the 1980s could not take part at all. The archive that resulted from this project—nineteen boxes of personal histories and memories—tells a remarkable story. My first debt, therefore, is to those members of the Naval Academy class of 1940 who lived this story and contributed their memories and thoughts to the collection. It has become a hackneyed cliché of late, and I cringe when I hear it addressed to me, but it fits here: Thank you for your service.

Once they decided they wanted to create this archive, class leaders sought a Department of History faculty member at the Academy who could help them organize the material. The individual who performed that duty was my friend and colleague Robert William Love, Jr., who taught at the Academy for forty years and without whose involvement this archive would probably not exist.

After finishing my book on Fleet Admiral Chester Nimitz (*Nimitz at War*) in 2021, I thought about how to tell the story of World War II from the perspective of the junior officers who fought it. Profiling the members of the class of 1940 seemed a perfect way to do that. They arrived at the Academy only a few months after the German army marched into the Rhineland, and they graduated the week the British evacuated the beaches at Dunkirk. More than a hundred of them were in Pearl Harbor on December 7, 1941. I expressed this thought to my editor at Oxford University Press, Tim Bent, in the summer of 2022 while I was giving him and his son Fred a tour of the Academy. We were standing in front of Bancroft Hall, waiting for the beginning of noon meal formation, which I thought Fred would enjoy. Tim noticed a line of plebes standing at ease in a long row, all looking down at something in their hands. "Oh look," he said, "they're all staring at their phones." That would no doubt have been true at almost any other institution, but not this one. "No," I said smiling, "they're reading *Reef Points*." He looked at me quizzically and I explained what *Reef Points* was. "Well," he said at once, "there's your book title." Though it did not end up as the title, it did provide a through line for telling the story.

Particular thanks are due to the friendly and efficient staff in the Special Collections of Nimitz Library, who got used to seeing me and cheerfully brought out cartloads of Hollinger boxes. The Library Director, Larry Clemens, who retired during the project, helped me obtain access to the Yard when it was restricted for Covid. Jennifer Bryan, the Head of Special Collections, was involved in this project from the start and indefatigable in providing assistance, including scanning all the photos used in the book. Her efficient staff, Sam Limneos (who has since moved on to the History and Heritage Command in Washington), Adam Minakowski, and Jessica Scott, patiently supervised my lengthy stays in their domain.

Historical research, like history itself, can have moments of serendipity. One occurred during a reception at the US Naval Institute celebrating that institution's 150 years of service. I was idly sipping a glass of wine when a man initiated a conversation. He was a 1970 Academy grad and mentioned that his father had also attended the Academy. "Oh," I replied, "what class?" Of course it was the class of 1940. My interest rising, I asked if he had any surviving letters from him. "Oh, yes," John Montgomery told me. "He kept a diary and wrote home almost every day. I think I have over four hundred letters he wrote during his Academy days and during the war years." That is how Myers Montgomery came to be one of the characters whose life story helps propel this narrative. John Montgomery has since donated the entire collection of Montgomery Family Papers to the Special Collections of Nimitz Library, and he has been an enthusiastic and supportive champion of this project since.

ACKNOWLEDGMENTS

Other descendants of the Forties made contributions: Virginia Trimble, who coordinates news about the class for *Shipmate*, the magazine of the Alumni Association, shared stories of Joseph Weber; Neva Rountree shared material about her father, Thomas P. McCann; Charles M. Wood and George Wright (sons of Charles M. Wood and John H. Wright, respectively) each shared collected memoirs of their fathers; and Kevin and Dion Clancy (both Annapolis grads) generously sent me a complete copy of the diary and memoir of their father, Albert H. "Pat" Clancy. I am grateful to them for their thoughtfulness and their willingness to share their family stories.

No living person knows more about the history of the Naval Academy than James W. Cheevers, the now-retired curator of the Naval Academy Museum, who has been a friend for fifty years. Jim generously and carefully read the chapters of this book that cover the years 1936 to 1940, corrected a number of errors, and offered observations that led to new discoveries. Another Academy friend, retired Navy Captain Bill Garrett, who spent his naval career in submarines, generously reviewed my chapter on submarine warfare to ensure that I faithfully captured the character of that unusual and demanding service.

And, of course, in this, as in all my written work, and for that matter in all other aspects of my life, the brilliant and supportive Marylou Symonds was indispensable. She read every chapter, often more than once, doing so out loud, so that we could both hear what I was saying—or trying to say, and how I could perhaps say it more effectively.

Notes

PROLOGUE

1. E. M. Eller, "Navy Life Begins," USNI *Proceedings* (October 1935), 1515.
2. Myers Montgomery to his brother, August 22, 1936, John E. Montgomery Letters, USNA; Carroll S. Alden, "Officers and Gentlemen in the Making," USNI *Proceedings* (October 1935), 1497.
3. *Reef Points* (1936), 3.
4. Ibid., 14, 15.
5. Ibid., 176.
6. Ibid., 173.
7. William Lanier, "The Long Voyage of the Class of Forty," written for the Fiftieth Class Reunion (1990), Special Collections, USNA.

CHAPTER I: APPOINTMENT

1. US Treasury Department, *Statistics of Income for 1935* (Washington, DC: Government Printing Office, 1938).
2. A. H. Rooks, "Entrance Requirements of U.S. Naval Academy," USNI *Proceedings* (October 1935), 1472.
3. Ibid.
4. *Lucky Bag* (1940), 145; Philip T. Glennon file, box 3, folder 57, Class of 1940 Archive, USNA.
5. Ibid.
6. Robert Harris to R. W. Love, June 19, 1986, Robert Harris file, box 4, folder 31, Class of 1940 Archive, USNA.
7. Ibid.
8. Author interview of John B. Montgomery, August 2023; E. S. Montgomery to Orville Zimmerman, August 13, 1935, and John E. Montgomery to Zimmerman, August 30, 1936, both in John E. Montgomery Collection, USNA.
9. Robert Weatherup to Chief of the Bureau of Navigation, February 6, 1935, Records of the US Naval Academy (RG 405), Special Collections, USNA; Robert Weatherup to R. W. Love, May 30, 1986, Robert A. Weatherup file, box 15, folder 1, Class of 1940 Archive, USNA.
10. "Big Naval Fleet Sails for New York," *New York Times* (Apr. 23, 1927); Raymond A. Hundevadt, "Spindrift: Recollections of a Naval Career," 1–2, Special Collections, USNA.
11. Hundevadt, "Spindrift," 3.
12. John Lacouture file, box 8, folder 18, Class of 1940 Archive, USNA.
13. R. R. Dupzyk file, box 3, folder 10, Class of 1940 Archive, USNA.
14. Ibid.
15. Ibid.
16. Paul Desmond file, box 3, folder 3, Class of 1940 Archive, USNA.
17. Ibid.
18. Ibid.

322   NOTES TO PAGES 12–23

19. *Washington Post* (Feb. 24, 1935).
20. Michael J. Hanley file, box 4, folder 18, Class of 1940 Archive, USNA.
21. Robert Schneller, *Breaking the Color Barrier: The U.S. Naval Academy's First Black Midshipmen and the Struggle for Racial Equality* (New York: New York University Press, 2005), 15–27.
22. Ibid., 28–34.
23. Ibid., 34–41.
24. *Metropolitan News* (Chicago) (Oct. 24, 1936).
25. Schneller, *Breaking the Color Barrier*, 8.
26. Abraham Campo file, box 2, folder 12, Class of 1940 Archive, USNA.

CHAPTER 2: PLEBE YEAR

1. Anthony C. Benjes file, box 1, folder 6, Class of 1940 Archive, USNA.
2. *Reef Points* (1936), 22.
3. E. M. Eller, "Navy Life Begins," USNI *Proceedings* (Oct. 1935), 1524; *Lucky Bag* (1940), 57; A. G. Woodside file, box 17, folder 3, Class of 1940 Archive, USNA; John Montgomery Diary (Feb. 4, 1937), John E. Montgomery Papers, USNA.
4. A. G. Woodside file, box 17, folder 3, Class of 1940 Archive, USNA; Eller, "Navy Life Begins," 1521.
5. Ernest R. Peterson file, box 11, folder 9; Conrad H. Carlson file, box 2, folder 21, both in Class of 1940 Archive, USNA.
6. Diary of Albert Harrison (Pat) Clancy Jr. (July 14, 1936), courtesy of Kevin Clancy and Dion Clancy; John Lacouture file, box 8, folder 18, Class of 1940 Archive, USNA.
7. Harvey J. Smith file, box 13, folder 28, Class of 1940 Archive, USNA.
8. *Lucky Bag* (1940), 57–58.
9. Robert Harris to R. W. Love, June 19, 1986, Robert Harris file, box 4, folder 31, Class of 1940 Archive, USNA.
10. *Lucky Bag* (1940), 58.
11. Robert Harris to R. W. Love, June 19, 1986; John H. Wright, *That Jack the House Built* (privately printed, 1985), no pagination.
12. Michael J. Hanley file, box 4, folder 18, Class of 1940 Archive, USNA; and Robert Harris to R. W. Love, June 19, 1986.
13. Diary of Albert Harrison (Pat) Clancy Jr. (end-of-month note for July 1936, plus Aug. 2 and 9, 1936).
14. Montgomery to "Dear Daddy," undated letter, John E. Montgomery Letters, USNA; Wright, *That Jack the House Built*, no pagination.
15. A. G. Woodside file, box 17, folder 3, Class of 1940 Archive, USNA.
16. *Annual Register of the United States Naval Academy* (Washington, DC: Government Printing Office, 1932), 2; Jack Sweetman, *The U.S. Naval Academy: An Illustrated History* (Annapolis: Naval Institute Press, 1979), 189–91.
17. Diary of Albert Harrison (Pat) Clancy Jr. (end-of-month note, Sept. 1936); William Braybrook file, box 1, folder 23; and Conrad H. Carlson file, box 2, folder 21, both in Class of 1940 Archive, USNA.
18. Arthur A. Ageton, "Annapolis, Mother of Navy Men," USNI *Proceedings* (Oct. 1935), 1511; John Montgomery Diary (Nov. 28, 1939).
19. Robert Harris to R. W. Love, June 19, 1986; and William Braybrook file, box 1, folder 23, Class of 1940 Archive, USNA.

NOTES TO PAGES 24–37

20. *Reef Points* (1936), 150; Montgomery to his brother, no date, John E. Montgomery Letters, USNA; memoir of Albert Harrison (Pat) Clancy Jr., 18, privately held, courtesy of Kevin and Dion Clancy.
21. Robert Harris to R. W. Love, June 19, 1986.
22. *Reef Points* (1937); Ageton, "Annapolis, Mother of Navy Men," 1511.
23. Michael J. Hanley file, box 4, folder 18, Class of 1940 Archive, USNA.
24. Diary of Albert Harrison (Pat) Clancy Jr. (end-of-month note, Sept. 1936); John Lacouture file, box 8, folder 18; Ernest R. Peterson file, box 11, folder 9, both in Class of 1940 Archive, USNA.
25. Ernest R. Peterson file, box 11, folder 9, Class of 1940 Archive, USNA.
26. A. G. Woodside file, box 17, folder 3, Class of 1940 Archive, USNA.
27. *Reef Points* (1936), xx.
28. Robert Harris to R. W. Love, June 19, 1986.
29. *Philadelphia Inquirer* (Nov. 28, 1936), 18.
30. R. R. Dupzyk file, box 3, folder 10, Class of 1940 Archive, USNA.
31. John Montgomery Diary (Jan. 11, 1937).
32. Virgil Gex, "Inaugural Parade Memories," *Shipmate* (Apr. 1997), 20; John Lacouture file, box 8, folder 18; and Robert Harris to R. W. Love, June 19, 1986.
33. John Lacouture file, box 8, folder 18, Class of 1940 Archive, USNA.
34. Michael J. Hanley file, box 4, folder 18, Class of 1940 Archive, USNA.
35. Ibid.
36. Ibid.; *New York Age* (July 17, 1937); *Arizona Gleam* (July 30, 1937).
37. Michael J. Hanley file, box 4, folder 18, Class of 1940 Archive, USNA; John Montgomery Diary (Feb. 17, 1937).
38. *Metropolitan News* (Chicago) (Feb. 27, 1937); *New York Times* (July 7, 17, and 25, 1937).
39. *Washington Evening Star* (July 6, 1937); *Arizona Gleam* (July 23, 1937).
40. John Montgomery Diary (Feb. 22, 1937); Montgomery to "Dear Folks," undated letter, John E. Montgomery Letters, USNA.
41. Midshipman Records, class of 1940 (RG 405), Special Collections, USNA.
42. Hemley to his parents, June 12, 1937, Eugene Hemley file, box 18, folder 2, Class of 1940 Archive, USNA.
43. Ibid.

CHAPTER 3: YOUNGSTER CRUISE

1. *Lucky Bag* (1940), 62.
2. Ibid.
3. A. G. Woodside file, box 17, folder 3, Class of 1940 Archive, USNA.
4. *Lucky Bag* (1940), 62. Hemley to his parents, June 13, 1937, Eugene Hemley file, box 18, folder 2; Robert Harris, to R. W. Love, June 19, 1986, Robert Harris file, box 4, folder 31; and Mike Hanley file, box 4, folder 18, all in Class of 1940 Archive, USNA.
5. Hemley to his parents, June 13, 1937.
6. Michael J. Hanley file, box 4, folder 18; E. W. Dobie Jr. file, box 3, folder 7, both in Class of 1940 Archive, USNA.
7. Hemley to his parents, June 13, 1937.
8. Ibid.
9. Robert Harris to R. W. Love, June 19, 1986, Robert Harris file, box 4, folder 31, Class of 1940 Archive, USNA; Hemley to parents, June 20, 1937, Eugene Hemley file, box 18, folder 2, both in Class of 1940 Archive, USNA.

324   NOTES TO PAGES 37–47

10. Al Bergner file, box 18, folder 2, Class of 1940 Archive, USNA.
11. Ibid.
12. Ibid.
13. Bruce Rohn to Wendi Winters, August 28, 2008, Bruce Rohn file, box 18, folder 2, Class of 1940 Archive, USNA.
14. Raymond A. Hundevadt, "Spindrift: Recollections of a Naval Career," 4, Special Collections, USNA; John Lacouture, Oral History, Naval History and Heritage Command, 4; Robert Weatherup to R. W. Love, May 30, 1986, Robert A. Weatherup file, box 15, folder 1, both in Class of 1940 Archive, USNA.
15. Robert Weatherup to R. W. Love, May 30, 1986; Lacouture, Oral History, 5; Edward Rogers to Wendi Winters, March 3, 2008, Edward Rogers file, box 18, folder 2, both in Class of 1940 Archive, USNA.
16. R. K. John, "Hitler's Future Admirals," *The Log* (Dec. 8, 1939), 8; *Lucky Bag* (1940), 63; John H. Wright, *That Jack the House Built* (privately printed, 1985), no pagination; John Lacouture file, box 8, folder 18, Class of 1940 Archive, USNA.
17. John Lacouture file, box 8, folder 18, Class of 1940 Archive, USNA; *Arizona Daily Star* (Tucson) (Oct. 18, 1942).
18. John Montgomery Diary (June 16–29, 1937), John E. Montgomery Papers, USNA.
19. Ibid. (July 5, 1937).
20. Ibid. (July 10, 1937); John H. Wright, *That Jack the House Built* (privately printed, 1985), no pagination; Edward Rogers to Wendi Winters, March 3, 2008.
21. "Colorful Madeira Delights Tourists," *Kirksville* (Missouri) *Daily News* (June 13, 1937).
22. John Montgomery Diary (July 19, 1937).
23. *Lucky Bag* (1940), 65; Robert Harris to R. W. Love, June 19, 1986.
24. Robert Harris to R. W. Love, June 19, 1986; Edward Rogers to Wendi Winters, March 3, 2008.
25. Edward Rogers to Wendi Winters, March 3, 2008.
26. John Montgomery Diary (July 27, 1937).
27. *Torquay Herald and Express* (July 29, 1937).
28. John Montgomery Diary (Aug. 3, 1937).
29. Ibid. (Aug. 6, 12, 13, 17, 1937).

CHAPTER 4: YOUNGSTERS

1. John Montgomery Diary (Sept. 24, 1937), John E. Montgomery Papers, USNA; Robert Harris to R. W. Love, June 19, 1986, Robert Harris file, box 4. Folder 31; and Michael Hanley file, box 4, folder 18, both in Class of 1940 Archive, USNA.
2. A. G. Woodside file, box 17, folder 3, Class of 1940 Archive, USNA; John Montgomery Diary (May 22 and 25, 1938).
3. "Girls Punctual on Visits to Naval Academy," *Lock Haven* (Pennsylvania) *Express* (Jan. 18, 1940); A. G. Woodside file, box 17, folder 3; and John Lacouture file, box 8, folder 18, both in Class of 1940 Archive, USNA.
4. John Montgomery Diary (Dec. 25, 1937, Feb. 11, 12 and 13, 1938, and Mar. 2, 1938).
5. Michael J. Hanley file, box 4, folder 18, Class of 1940 Archive, USNA.
6. *Lucky Bag* (1940), 76; A. G. Woodside file, box 17, folder 3; and Robert A. Weatherup file, box 15, folder 1; both in Class of 1940 Archive, USNA; John Montgomery Diary (Oct. 22–23, 1939).
7. All nicknames are from *Lucky Bag* (1940).
8. Samuel E. Edelson file, box 3, folder 14, Class of 1940 Archive, USNA.

NOTES TO PAGES 48–57

9. Michael J. Hanley file, box 4, folder 18; Ernest R. Peterson file, box 11, folder 9; R. R. Dupyzk file, box 3, folder 10; and John Lacouture file, box 8, folder 18, all in Class of 1940 Archive, USNA.

10. Michael J. Hanley file, box 4, folder 18, Class of 1940 Archive, USNA.

11. Jack Sweetman, *The U.S. Naval Academy: An Illustrated History* (Annapolis: Naval Institute Press, 1979), 192; Ernest R. Peterson file, box 11, folder 9; R. R. Dupyzk file, box 3, folder 10; and Conrad H. Carlson file, box 2, folder 21, all Class of 1940 Archive, USNA.

12. A. G. Woodside file, box 17, folder 3, Class of 1940 Archive, USNA.

13. Philip T. Glennon file, box 3, folder 57; Robert Harris to R. W. Love, June 19, 1986.

14. Philip T. Glennon file, box 3, folder 57, Class of 1940 Archive, USNA.

15. Samuel E. Edelstein Jr. file, box 3, folder 14, Class of 1940 Archive, USNA.

16. *Honolulu Star Bulletin* (Aug. 30, 1937).

17. Richard B. Frank, *Tower of Skulls: A History of the Asia-Pacific War, July 1937–May 1942* (New York: W.W. Norton, 2020), 101–2; John Prados, *Combined Fleet Decoded: The Secret History of American Intelligence and the Japanese Navy in World War II* (New York: Random House, 1995), 48–51; *Boston Globe* (Dec. 25, 1937); John Montgomery Diary (Jan. 12, 1938).

18. Frank, *Tower of Skulls*, 46–58; *New York Times* (Dec. 18, 1937). A useful discussion of this by several authors is in Bob Tadashi Wakabayashi, ed., *The Nanking Atrocity, 1937–38* (New York: Berghahn Books, 2007).

19. Prados, *Combined Fleet Decoded*, 48–51; Douglas Peifer, "The American Response to the Sinking of the USS *Panay*, December 1937," in Brian VanDeMark, ed., *New Interpretations in Naval History: Selected Papers from the Twentieth McMullen Naval History Symposium Held at the U.S. Naval Academy 14–15 September 2017* (Annapolis: Naval Institute Press, 2023); *Boston Globe* (Dec. 25, 1937); John Montgomery Diary (Dec. 19, 1937).

20. Kent Bullfinch file, box 2, folder 4, Class of 1940 Archive, USNA.

21. John Montgomery Diary (May 1, 1938).

CHAPTER 5: BEAT ARMY

1. John Montgomery Diary (June 2 and 3, 1938), John E. Montgomery Papers, USNA.

2. Michael Hanley file, box 8, folder 18, Class of 1940 Archive, USNA; *Brooklyn Citizen* (June 23, 1937). The story of the Washington crew team at Berlin is dramatically chronicled by Daniel James Brown in *The Boys in the Boat: Nine Americans and Their Epic Quest for Gold at the 1936 Olympics* (New York: Penguin, 2014).

3. John Lacouture file, box 8, folder 18, Class of 1940 Archive, USNA.

4. John Montgomery Diary (June 6, 13, 14, and 15, 1938).

5. *Lucky Bag* (1940), 72; John Montgomery Diary (June 20, 1938).

6. John Montgomery Diary (June 25, 1938).

7. Michael Hanley file, box 4, folder 18, Class of 1940 Archive, USNA.

8. John Montgomery Diary (July 8, 13, 15, and 16, 1938).

9. Ibid. (June 18, 1938).

10. Ibid. (Aug. 1, 1938).

11. Ibid. (Aug. 8 and 11, 1938).

12. Ibid. (Aug. 19, 1938).

13. Ibid. (Aug. 20–21, 1938).

14. John Lacouture file, box 8, folder 18, Class of 1940 Archive, USNA.

15. John Montgomery Diary (Sept. 15, 1938).

16. Telford Taylor, *Munich: The Price of Peace* (New York: Random House, 1979) is a very detailed history. A shorter, more accessible account is David Faber, *Munich: The 1938*

326   NOTES TO PAGES 58–69

Appeasement Crisis (New York: Simon and Schuster, 2008). *Philadelphia Inquirer* (Oct. 2, 1938), 22; John Montgomery Diary (Sept. 19, 1938).

17. John Montgomery Diary (Sept. 29 and Oct. 12, 1938).
18. Ibid. (Oct. 31, 1938).
19. *Philadelphia Inquirer* (Nov. 27, 1938).
20. *New York Times* (Nov. 14, 1938); John Montgomery Diary (Mar. 14, 1938).
21. *Washington Star* (Dec. 29, 1938).
22. John Lacouture file, box 8, folder 18, Class of 1940 Archive, USNA.
23. *Baltimore Sun* (Dec. 20, 1938).
24. *Baltimore Sun* (Jan. 8 and Feb. 23, 1939).
25. Michael Hanley file, box 4, folder 18, Class of 1940 Archive, USNA.
26. Ibid.
27. *Baltimore Sun* (Feb. 26, 1939).
28. Michael Hanley file, box 4, folder 18, Class of 1940 Archive, USNA.
29. Ibid.
30. *Baltimore Sun* (May 28, 1939).
31. Bill Lanier and Cary Hall, "The Long Voyage of the Class of Forty," Class of 1940 Archive, USNA; *Baltimore Sun* (May 28, 1939).
32. John Montgomery Diary (Dec. 9 and 17, 1938, and May 29 and 30, 1939).
33. John Lacouture file, box 8, folder 18, Class of 1940 Archive, USNA.
34. *Richmond News Leader* (May 30, 1939).
35. *Baltimore Sun* (May 31, 1939).

CHAPTER 6: FIRSTIES

1. A. G. Woodhouse file, box 17, folder 3; Ernest R. Peterson Diary (May 27, 1939), box 11, folder 9, both in Class of 1940 Archive, USNA.
2. *Baltimore Sun* (June 3, 1939).
3. Ernest R. Peterson Diary (June 3, 1939); *Lucky Bag* (1940), 81.
4. Robert Weatherup to R. W. Love, May 30, 1986, box 15, folder 1, Class of 1940 Archive, USNA.
5. Ernest R. Peterson Diary (June 25, 1939).
6. John Lacouture file, box 8, folder 18, Class of 1940 Archive, USNA.
7. *Lucky Bag* (1940).
8. Ernest R. Peterson Diary (July 4, 1939).
9. Ibid. (Aug. 2, 1939).
10. John Montgomery Diary (Aug. 20, 1939), John E. Montgomery Papers, USNA.
11. Ibid. (Aug. 23 and 24, 1939).
12. *Baltimore Sun* (Aug. 31, 1939).
13. John Lacouture file, box 8, folder 18, Class of 1940 Archives, USNA.
14. *Buffalo News* (July 22, 1939); John Montgomery Diary (Aug. 23, 1939); *New York Daily News* (July 6, 1939).
15. *Washington Star*, extra edition (Sept. 1, 1939); Michael J. Hanley file, box 4, folder 18, Class of 1940 Archive, USNA; John Montgomery Diary (Sept. 1, 1939).
16. *Philadelphia Inquirer* (Sept. 2, 1939).
17. Ibid.; *Baltimore Sun* (Sept. 2, 1939); John Montgomery Diary (Sept. 3, 1939).
18. *Baltimore Sun* (Sept. 30, 1939); Bill Lanier and Cary Hall, "The Long Voyage of the Class of Forty," Special Collections, USNA; John Montgomery Diary (Oct. 6, 1939); Kent Bullfinch file, box 2, folder 4; and Michael J. Hanley file, box 4, folder 18, both Class of 1940 Archive, USNA.

NOTES TO PAGES 70–87

19. *Lucky Bag* (1940); John Lacouture file, box 8, folder 18, Class of 1940 Archive, USNA; John Montgomery Diary (Sept. 29 and Oct. 4, 1939).
20. John Montgomery Diary (Nov. 30, 1939).
21. *Washington Evening Star* (Nov. 29, 1939).
22. *Lucky Bag* (1940), 484–85; John Montgomery Diary (Dec. 3, 1939).
23. Philip F. Eckert file, box 3, folder 12, Class of 1940 Archive, USNA.
24. John Montgomery Diary (Dec. 9, 22, and 30, 1939).
25. *Baltimore Sun* (Jan. 25, 1940).
26. *Baltimore Sun* (Mar. 31, 1940).
27. Records of the U.S. Naval Academy (RG 405), Midshipman Records, USNA.
28. *New York Times* (June 1, 1940).
29. John D. Chase file, box 2, folder 36, Class of 1940 Archive, USNA; *Reef Points* (1942–43).
30. Craig L. Symonds, *World War II at Sea: A Global History* (New York: Oxford University Press, 2017), 39–57.
31. *Baltimore Sun* (May 19, 1940).
32. *Baltimore Sun* (May 28, 1940).
33. Symonds, *World War II at Sea*, 61–69.
34. *New York Times* (June 2, 1940).
35. *Baltimore Sun* (June 3, 1940).
36. *Baltimore Sun* (June 5, 1940).
37. Walter Lord, *The Miracle of Dunkirk* (New York: Viking Press, 1982); W. J. R. Gardner, ed., *The Evacuation from Dunkirk: Operation Dynamo, 26 May–4 June 1940* (London: Frank Cass, 2000).
38. *Baltimore Sun* (May 26, 1940).
39. *Baltimore Sun* (June 26, 1940).

CHAPTER 7: THE REAL NAVY

1. "Text of Roosevelt's Address," *New York Times* (June 11, 1940), 6.
2. Ernest R. Peterson Diary (June 28, 1941), box 11, folder 9, Class of 1940 Archive, USNA.
3. W. Crosswell Croft to Ed Sledge, August 29, 1986, box 2, folder 41, Class of 1940 Archive, USNA.
4. Robert Harris to R. W. Love, June 19, 1986, box 4, folder 31, Class of 1940 Archive, USNA.
5. David Nasaw, *The Patriarch: The Remarkable Life and Turbulent Times of Joseph P. Kennedy* (New York: Penguin, 2012), 468–72.
6. John Lacouture file, box 8, folder 18, Class of 1940 Archive, USNA.
7. George Kittredge file, box 8, folder 13, and Conrad H. Carlson file, box 2, folder 17, both in Class of 1940 Archive, USNA.
8. Robert A. Weatherup file, box 15, folder 9; William M. Braybrook file, box 1, folder 23; and John Lacouture file, box 8, folder 18, all in Class of 1940 Archive, USNA.
9. Robert H. White file, box 16, folder 14; John Lacouture file, box 8, folder 18; Robert A. Weatherup file, box 15, folder 3, all in Class of 1940 Archive, USNA.
10. John Lacouture file, box 8, folder 18, Class of 1940 Archive, USNA.
11. Craig L. Symonds, *World War II at Sea* (New York: Oxford University Press, 2017), 184.
12. R. E. Hill file, box 5, folder 17; and Robert Harris file, box 4, folder 32, both in Class of 1940 Archive, USNA.
13. Talbot F. Collins file, box 2, folder 40, Class of 1940 Archive, USNA; *A Score and Three More: Class of 1940* (entry of Charles Obrist), Twenty-Third Reunion book prepared by the

328   NOTES TO PAGES 88–99

Class of 1940, John E. Montgomery Papers, USNA; and Robert Harris file (July 10, 1986), box 4, folder 32, Class of 1940 Archive, USNA.

14. William Carpenter file, box 2, folder 28; John E. Greenbacker file, box 4, folder 12, both Class of 1940 Archive, USNA.

15. Jesse Worley file, box 17, folder 9; R.E. Hill file, box 5, folder 17, both in Class of 1940 Archive, USNA.

16. Warren Walker file, box 14, folder 20, Class of 1940 Archive, USNA.

17. Michael J. Hanley file, box 4, folder 30, Class of 1940 Archive, USNA; memoir of Albert Harrison (Pat) Clancy Jr., 31, privately held, courtesy of Kevin and Dion Clancy.

18. Memoir of Albert Harrison (Pat) Clancy Jr., 30; William Carpenter file, box 2, folder 28; Warren Walker file, box 14, folder 20, both in Class of 1940 Archive, USNA.

19. George Kittredge file, box 8, folder 13, Class of 1940 Archive, USNA.

20. Conrad H. Carlson file, box 2, folder 17, Class of 1940 Archive, USNA.

21. Michael J. Hanley file, box 4, folder 30, Class of 1940 Archive, USNA.

22. Michael J. Hanley file, box 4, folder 22, Class of 1940 Archive, USNA.

23. Ernest R. Peterson Diary (June 28, 1941); William Carpenter file, box 2, folder 28, both in Class of 1940 Archive, USNA.

24. R. R. Dupzyk file, box 3, folder 9; Class of 1940 Archive, USNA.

25. William Braybrook file, box 1, folder 23, Class of 1940 Archive, USNA; Symonds, *World War II at Sea*, 183.

26. Phil Glennon file, box 3, folder 42, Class of 1940 Archive, USNA.

27. John H. Wright, *That Jack the House Built* (privately printed, 1985), no pagination.

28. William Braybrook file, box 1, folder 23, Class of 1940 Archive, USNA.

29. Thomas A. Bailey and Paul B. Ryan, *Hitler vs. Roosevelt: The Undeclared Naval War* (New York: Free Press, 1979), 108–11.

30. Ernest R. Peterson file, box 11, folder 9, Class of 1940 Archive, USNA.

31. John E. Greenbacker file, box 4, folder 12, Class of 1940 Archive, USNA.

32. *Complete Presidential Press Conferences of Franklin D. Roosevelt* (New York: DaCapo Press, 1972), 17:285–86.

33. Bailey and Ryan, *Hitler vs. Roosevelt*, 147.

CHAPTER 8: THE CUSP OF WAR

1. Craig L. Symonds, *World War II at Sea: A Global History* (New York: Oxford University Press, 2017), 187–88; Thomas A. Bailey and Paul B. Ryan, *Hitler vs. Roosevelt: The Undeclared Naval War* (New York: Free Press, 1979), 171–3; Patrick Abbazia, *Mr. Roosevelt's Navy: The Private War of the U.S. Atlantic Fleet, 1939–1942* (Annapolis: Naval Institute Press, 1975), 223–31.

2. John Montgomery Diary (Sept. 9, 1941), John E. Montgomery Papers, USNA.

3. Ibid. (Sept. 12 and 14, 1941).

4. Montgomery to Dear Folks, October 6, 1941, John E. Montgomery Letters, USNA.

5. John Montgomery Diary (Sept. 26, 1941).

6. Ibid. (Sept. 26 and 27 and Oct. 10, 1941).

7. Ibid. (Sept. 8 and 12, 1941); Montgomery to "Dearest Dorothy," October 4, 1941, John E. Montgomery Letters, USNA.

8. Symonds, *World War II at Sea*, 189–91; Abbazia, *Mr. Roosevelt's Navy*, 270–72; Montgomery to Dear Folks, October 20, 1941.

9. John Montgomery Diary (Nov. 3, 4, and 14, 1941).

10. "Sinking Quickens Congress Action," *New York Times* (Nov. 1, 1941), 3.

11. John Lacouture file, box 8, folder 18, Class of 1940 Archive, USNA.

NOTES TO PAGES 100–117

12. Ibid.
13. *Honolulu Star Bulletin* (Aug. 9, 1941); John Lacouture file, box 8, folder 18, Class of 1940 Archive, USNA.
14. *Honolulu Star Bulletin* (Oct. 11, 1941); John Montgomery Diary (Oct. 11, 1941).
15. John Lacouture file, box 8, folder 18, Class of 1940 Archive, USNA.
16. *New York Times* (Nov. 2, 3, and 5, 1941).
17. Conrad H. Carlson file, box 2, folder 17, Class of 1940 Archive, USNA.
18. Gordon W. Prange, with Donald Goldstein and Katherine Dillon, *At Dawn We Slept: The Untold Story of Pearl Harbor* (New York: McGraw-Hill, 1981), 406; Roberta Wohlstetter, *Pearl Harbor: Warning and Decision* (Stanford: Stanford University Press, 1962), 228–46, 259.

CHAPTER 9: INFAMY

1. Irving J. Davenport file, box 3, folder 1, Class of 1940 Archive, USNA.
2. Sidney Sherwin, "Naval Academy '40 is 50 in 1990," in Michael J. Hanley file, box 4, folder 14, USNA.
3. Ibid.
4. Irving J. Davenport file, box 3, folder 1, Class of 1940 Archive, USNA.
5. Harvey Smith file, box 13, folder 28, Class of 1940 Archive, USNA.
6. Benjamin Frana file, box 3, folder 29, Class of 1940 Archive, USNA.
7. William C. Croft file, box 18, folder 2, Class of 1940 Archive, USNA.
8. Benjamin Hall in "Naval Academy '40 is 50 in 1990," Michael J. Hanley file, box 4, folder 14, Class of 1940 Archive, USNA.
9. Memo by R. D. Kirkpatrick for LCDR Dawson, in Warren Walker Jr. file, box 14, folder 21, Class of 1940 Archive, USNA.
10. Ibid.
11. "Statement of Warren Walker, Jr.," December 7, 1941, in Warren Walker Jr. file, box 14, folder 21; Crosswell Croft, "Naval Academy '40 is 50 in 1990," Michael J. Hanley file, box 4, folder 14, both in Class of 1940 Archive, USNA.
12. Warren Walker file, box 14, folder 21; and Crosswell Croft in Michael J. Hanley file, box 4, folder 14, both in Class of 1940 Archive, USNA.
13. R. E. Hill file, box 5, folder 17, Class of 1940 Archive, USNA.
14. Henry Davison file, box 3, folder 2, Class of 1940 Archive, USNA.
15. Ibid.
16. Bill Lanier and Cary Hall, "The Long Voyage of the Class of Forty," Special Collections, USNA; Virgil Gex file, box 3, folder 41, Class of 1940 Archive, USNA.
17. Virgil Gex file, box 3, folder 41, Class of 1940 Archive, USNA.
18. Henry Davison file, box 3, folder 2, Class of 1940 Archive, USNA.
19. Michael J. Hanley file, box 4, folder 8, Class of 1940 Archive, USNA.
20. Ibid.
21. John Lacouture file, box 8, folder 18, Class of 1940 Archive, USNA.
22. John Lacouture, Oral History, Naval History and Heritage Command, 16.
23. Ibid.

CHAPTER 10: RETRIBUTION

1. Ernest R. Peterson file, box 1, folder 9; Conrad H. Carlson file, box 2, folder 17, both in Class of 1940 Archive, USNA.
2. John Montgomery Diary (Dec. 7, 1941), John E. Montgomery Papers, USNA.
3. Michael J. Hanley file, box 4, folder 30, Class of 1940 Archive; Bill Lanier and Cary Hall, "The Long Voyage of the Class of Forty," Special Collections, both USNA.

330   NOTES TO PAGES 118–134

4. John Lacouture file, box 8, folder 18, Class of 1940 Archive, USNA.

5. John B. Lundstrom, *Black Shoe Carrier Admiral* (Annapolis: Naval Institute Press, 2006), 34–41.

6. John Lacouture file, box 8, folder 18; Robert A. Weatherup file, box 15, folder 3, both Class of 1940 Archive, USNA.

7. Harvey Vogel file, box 14, folder 12, Class of 1940 Archive, USNA.

8. Lundstrom, *Black Shoe Carrier Admiral*, 49–52; John E. Greenbacker file, box 4, folder 9, Class of 1940 Archive, USNA.

9. John Montgomery Diary (Dec. 9, 1941).

10. Ibid. (Dec. 10, 12, 14, and 27, 1941).

11. Winston S. Churchill, *The Grand Alliance* (New York: Bantam Books, 1950), 512.

12. Ernest R. Peterson file, box 11, folder 9, Class of 1940 Archive, USNA.

13. Ibid.

14. Craig L. Symonds, *Nimitz at War* (New York: Oxford University Press, 2022), 34–39.

15. Michael J. Hanley file, box 4, folder 30, Class of 1940 Archive, USNA.

16. Ibid.

17. Ibid. Hanley's memory of these actions is a bit muddled. He incorrectly placed the air attack on *Enterprise* as taking place after the Marcus raid.

18. John E. Greenbacker file, box 4, folder 9, Class of 1940 Archive, USNA.

19. Michael J. Hanley file, box 4, folder 30, Class of 1940 Archive, USNA.

20. John E. Greenbacker file, box 4, folder 9, Class of 1940 Archive, USNA.

21. Michael J. Hanley file, box 4, folder 30, Class of 1940 Archive, USNA.

22. Ibid.

23. James D. Hornfischer, *Ship of Ghosts* (New York: Bantam Books, 2006), 12.

24. *A Score and Three More: Class of 1940* (entry by John Hamill), Twenty-Third Reunion book prepared by the Class of 1940, no pagination, John E. Montgomery Papers, USNA.

25. Hornfischer, *Ship of Ghosts*, 217–18.

26. Ibid., 172.

27. Roy Maxwell Offerle, interview, March 2015, "Humanities Texas," Austin.

28. Bill Lanier and Cary Hall, "The Long Voyage of the Class of Forty," Special Collections, USNA; Gaylord Buchanan file, box 2, folder 1, both Class of 1940 Archives, USNA.

29. For a more detailed analysis of Allied strength on Luzon, see Richard B. Frank, *Tower of Skulls: A History of the Asia-Pacific War, July 1937–May 1942* (New York: W.W. Norton, 2020), 440–43.

30. Ibid., 513; Testimony of Lieutenant Engel, May 22, 1942, box 18, folder 8, Class of 1940 Archive, USNA.

31. Testimony of Elmer Long, box 2, folder 33; and Lieutenant Engel, box 18, folder 8, both in Class of 1940 Archive, USNA.

32. Raymond A. Hundevadt, "Spindrift: Recollections of a Naval Officer," 22, Special Collections, USNA.

33. Ibid., 25.

34. Hornfischer, *Ship of Ghosts*, 217–18.

CHAPTER 11: U-BOATS, CONVOYS, AND MATRIMONY

1. Craig L. Symonds, *World War II at Sea: A Global History* (New York: Oxford University Press, 2017), chapters 6 and 12.

2. Arnold Hague, *The Allied Convoy System, 1939–1945* (Annapolis: Naval Institute Press, 2000), 26–28.

NOTES TO PAGES 134–148

3. Ernest R. Peterson file, box 11, folder 9, Class of 1940 Archive, USNA.

4. Nicholas Monserrat, *Three Corvettes* (London: Cassell, 1945), 22; Ernest R. Peterson file, box 11, folder 9, Class of 1940 Archive, USNA.

5. John H. Wright, *That Jack the House Built* (privately printed, 1985), no pagination; Ernest R. Peterson file, box 11, folder 9, Class of 1940 Archive, USNA; Monserrat, *Three Corvettes*, 27.

6. Ernest R. Peterson file, box 11, folder 9, Class of 1940 Archive USNA.

7. Ernest R. Peterson Diary (Mar. 18, 1942), box 11, folder 9, Class of 1940 Archive, USNA.

8. Ibid.

9. Ibid.

10. Karl Donitz, *Memoirs: Ten Years and Twenty Days* (Annapolis: Naval Institute Press, 1959), 329.

11. Ernest R. Peterson Diary (Mar. 18, 1942).

12. Benjamin Frana file, box 3, folder 30, Class of 1940 Archive, USNA.

13. Sally C. Curtin, "Marriage Rates in the United States 1900–2018," National Center for Health Statistics, Centers for Disease Control and Prevention. Accessed September 5, 2023.

14. Raymond A. Hundevadt, "Spindrift: Recollections of a Naval Career," 18, 26, Special Collections, USNA.

15. W. Crosswell Croft to Ed Sledge, August 29, 1986, Crosswell Croft file, box 2, folder 41, Class of 1940 Archive, USNA; "Allan P. Cook's Account of the Attack on Pearl Harbor," Cook Family Papers, privately held.

16. John H. Wright, *That Jack the House Built* (privately printed, 1985), no pagination.

17. Robert Harris to Ed Sledge, October 26, 1986, Robert Harris file, box 4, folder 31; William Braybrook file, box 1, folder 23, both in Class of 1940 Archive, USNA.

18. Robert Harris to Ed Sledge, October 26, 1986.

19. Symonds, *World War II at Sea*, 262–63; Stephen W. Roskill, *The War at Sea, 1939–1945* (London: Her Majesty's Stationery Office, 1956), 2:12023, 127.

20. Robert Harris to Ed Sledge, October 26, 1986, 6.

21. Richard Woodman, *The Arctic Convoys, 1941–1945* (London: John Murray, 1994), 24–32.

22. Symonds, *World War II at Sea*, 263–66.

23. William Braybrook file, box 1, folders 18 and 23, Class of 1940 Archive, USNA.

24. Robert Harris to Ed Sledge, October 26, 1986.

25. *Los Angeles Times* (Apr. 19, 1942); *Albuquerque Journal* (May 5, 1942).

CHAPTER 12: THE CORAL SEA AND MIDWAY

1. John Prados, *Combined Fleet Decoded: The Secret History of American Intelligence and the Japanese Navy in World War II* (New York: Random House, 1995), 210–14; Edwin T. Layton, *And I Was There: Pearl Harbor and Midway—Breaking the Secrets* (New York: Morrow, 1985), 29, 32–33.

2. Craig L. Symonds, *Nimitz at War* (New York: Oxford University Press, 2022), 82–86.

3. John E. Greenbacker file, box 4, folder 9, Class of 1940 Archive, USNA.

4. Louis Saunders Diary (May 7, 1942), box 12, folder 18, Class of 1940 Archive, USNA.

5. Louis Saunders Diary (May 8, 1942); Joe Weber file, box 16, folder 1, Class of 1940 Archive, USNA.

6. Conrad H. Carlson file, box 2, folder 17, Class of 1940 Archive, USNA; Samuel E. Morison, *Coral Sea, Midway, and Submarine Action* (Boston: Little Brown, 1949), 43.

7. Joe Weber file, box 16, folder 1, Class of 1940 Archive, USNA; Louis Saunders Diary (May 8, 1942).

NOTES TO PAGES 149–164

8. John B. Lundstrom, *The First Team* (Annapolis: Naval Institute Press, 1984), 243–270; Morison, *Coral Sea*, 55.

9. Joe Weber file, box 16, folder 1, Class of 1940 Archives, USNA.

10. Morison, *Coral Sea*, 52–60.

11. Craig L. Symonds, *The Battle of Midway* (New York: Oxford University Press, 2011), 172; Joseph Weber file, box 16, folder 1, Class of 1940 Archive, USNA.

12. John E. Greenbacker file, box 4, folder 9, Class of 1940 Archive, USNA. A separate nineteen-page memo that Greenbacker wrote in 1966 in response to a query from Walter Lord is also included in box 4, folder 9. Hereafter cited as Walter Lord Memo.

13. H. P. Willmott, *The Barrier and the Javelin: Japanese and Allied Pacific Strategies, February to June, 1942* (Annapolis: Naval Institute Press, 1983), 286; Louis Saunders Diary (May 8, 1942).

14. Walter Lord Memo, 2.

15. Symonds, *Nimitz at War*, 98–101.

16. Walter Lord Memo, 2; Louis Saunders Diary (May 26, 1942).

17. Walter Lord Memo, 2–3.

18. Symonds, *The Battle of Midway*, 196–97.

19. Louis Saunders Diary (May 31, 1942).

20. Ibid. (June 4, 1942).

21. Ibid.; Symonds, *The Battle of Midway*, 245–308.

22. Walter Lord Memo, 4.

23. Symonds, *The Battle of Midway*, 316.

24. Conrad H. Carlson file, box 2, folder 22, and Herschel V. Sellars Diary, Herschel V. Sellars file, box 13, folder 11, both in Class of 1940 Archive, USNA. Like Greenbacker, Carlson also prepared a memo for Walter Lord in 1966, though it is much shorter. It is included in Conrad H. Carlson file, folder, box 2, folder 24. Greenbacker mistakenly believed that eight Japanese Val bombers got through the intercept to make the attack, though most sources agree that it was actually seven. See Symonds, *The Battle of Midway*, 313–17.

25. Walter Lord Memo, 5.

26. Ibid.

27. Symonds, *The Battle of Midway*, 321–25; Walter Lord Memo, 6–7.

28. Walter Lord Memo, 7; and John Greenbacker to Clark Reynolds, Dec. 19, 1967, both box 4, folder 9, Class of 1940 Archive, USNA.

29. Walter Lord Memo, 8.

30. Walter Lord Memo, 10–12; Conrad H. Carlson file, box 2, folder 24, Class of 1940 Archives, USNA.

31. Herschel V. Sellars Diary (July 5, 1942).

32. Walter Lord Memo, 15–16.

33. Ibid., 19; Earnest R. Peterson Diary (June 4, 1942), Ernest R. Peterson file, box 11, folder 9, Class of 1940 Archive, USNA.

34. R. R. Dupzyk file, box 3, folder 8, Class of 1940 Archives, USNA.

CHAPTER 13: SAVO ISLAND

1. The best overall account of the battle for Guadalcanal is Richard B. Frank, *Guadalcanal: The Definitive Account of the Landmark Battle* (New York: Penguin, 1990). The best account of the naval battles for Guadalcanal is James D. Hornfischer, *Neptune's Inferno: The U.S. Navy at Guadalcanal* (New York: Bantam Books, 2011).

2. Craig L. Symonds, *Nimitz at War* (New York: Oxford University Press, 2022), 140–43.

NOTES TO PAGES 164–178   333

3. Robert A. Weatherup file, box 15, folder 9, Class of 1940 Archive, USNA. The authority is James D. Hornfischer, *Neptune's Inferno*, op. cit.

4. G. E. Kittredge, "Broadside at Savo," *Saga* (Mar. 1954), 20, 23; John Lacouture file, box 8, folder 21, Class of 1940 Archive, USNA.

5. Kittredge, "Broadside at Savo," 23.

6. Ibid.; Frank, *Guadalcanal*, 78–79.

7. John Lacouture, "Remembrances of the Landings at Guadalcanal, the Battle of Savo Island, and the Sinking of the 'Blue,'" John Lacouture file, box 8, folder 21, Class of 1940 Archive, USNA.

8. Frank, *Guadalcanal*, 78; Conrad H. Carlson file, box 2, folder 20, Class of 1940 Archive, USNA.

9. Bruce Loxton with Chris Coulthard-Clark, *The Shame of Savo: Anatomy of a Naval Disaster* (Annapolis: Naval Institute Press, 1994), 73–85.

10. Raymond A. Hundevadt, "Spindrift: Recollections of a Naval Career," 44, Special Collections, USNA.

11. Conrad H. Carlson file, box 2, folder 20; Lacouture, "Remembrances"; Kittredge, "Broadside at Savo," 22.

12. Kittredge, "Broadside at Savo," 60.

13. John J. Domalgowski, *Lost at Guadalcanal* (Jefferson, NC: McFarland Press, 2020), 92.

14. Lacouture, "Remembrances."

15. Ibid., 16.

16. Craig L. Symonds, *World War II at Sea* (New York: Oxford University Press, 2017), 307; Frank, *Guadalcanal*, 99; Domagalski, *Lost at Guadalcanal*, 84; *Lucky Bag* (1940).

17. "A Wild Night," in Conrad H. Carlson file, box 2, folder 20, Class of 1940 Archive, USNA.

18. Ibid.

19. Ibid.

20. Hundevadt, "Spindrift," 45, 49–50.

21. Hornfischer, *Neptune's Inferno*, 70; Hundevadt, "Spindrift," 50.

22. Hundevadt, "Spindrift," 53.

23. Hornfischer, *Neptune's Inferno*, 76.

24. Hundevadt, "Spindrift," 54.

25. Ibid., 54–55.

26. Lacouture, "Remembrances."

27. John Miller, *Guadalcanal: The First Offensive* (Washington, DC: Department of the Army, 1949), 80–81.

28. Lacouture, "Remembrances." I took the liberty of adding exclamation points to Lacouture's rendition of his statements, which seemed appropriate given the circumstances.

29. Ibid., 25.

CHAPTER 14: IRONBOTTOM SOUND

1. The best account of this fighting is James Hornfischer, *Neptune's Inferno: The U.S. Navy at Guadalcanal* (New York: Bantam Books, 2011).

2. Craig L. Symonds, *World War II at Sea: A Global History* (New York: Oxford University Press, 2017), 332–33; Ben Blee, "Whodunnit?," USNI *Proceedings* (June 1982), 42–47.

3. Robert A. Weatherup file, box 15, folder 3, Class of 1940 Archive, USNA.

4. Ibid.

5. Symonds, *World War II at Sea*, 337–42.

6. Robert A. Weatherup file, box 15, folder 3, Class of 1940 Archive, USNA.

7. Ibid.

334 NOTES TO PAGES 178–191

8. Hornfischer, *Neptune's Inferno*, 169–88.
9. Tom Wells file, box 16, folder 4, Class of 1940 Archive, USNA; Hornfischer, *Neptune's Inferno*, 227–30.
10. Tom Wells file, box 16, folder 4, Class of 1940 Archive, USNA.
11. In his letter describing this battle, Wells noted to his classmates, "This letter is for you all to read and keep. It is not for publication.... It's what I saw or heard." I hope he would forgive my quoting from it here.
12. Symonds, *World War II at Sea*, 345–46.
13. Robert A. Weatherup file, box 15, folder 3, Class of 1940 Archive, USNA; Symonds, *World War II at Sea*, 367.
14. Dan Kurzman, *Left to Die: The Tragedy of the USS Juneau* (New York: Pocket Books, 1994).
15. Robert A. Weatherup file, box 15, folder 3, Class of 1940 Archive, USNA.
16. Conrad Carlson file, box 2, folder 19, Class of 1940 Archive, USNA.
17. Ibid.
18. *Lucky Bag* (1940), 197.
19. Robert J. Bulkley, *At Close Quarters: PT Boats in the United States Navy* (Washington: Naval History Division, 1962), 104–4; *A Score and Three More: Class of 1940*, Twenty-Third Reunion book prepared by the Class of 1940, John E. Montgomery Papers, USNA.

CHAPTER 15: FLIGHT TRAINING

1. "Text of President's Address," and "Roosevelt Asks Billion for Arms," both in *New York Times* (May 17, 1940), 10.
2. Archibald D. Turnbull and Clifford L. Lord, *A History of United States Naval Aviation* (New Haven: Yale University Press, 1949), 311–13.
3. "An Act To Repeal Certain Laws and to Amend Other Laws Relating to Naval Aviation Cadets" (July 6, 1942), US Congress, Committee on Naval Affairs (1942); R. E. Hill file, box 5, folder 17, Class of 1940 Archive, USNA.
4. David C. Wolfe file, box 17, folder 3, Class of 1940 Archive, USNA; John E. Montgomery to Dorothy Montgomery (sister), November 8, 1942, John E. Montgomery Letters, USNA.
5. Patrick Stephen and Robert Dupont, "Naval Air Station & University of New Orleans," *New Orleans Historical Magazine* (Apr. 2012), 143; D. C. Wolfe file, box 17, folder 3, Class of 1940 Archive, USNA.
6. Robert A. Weatherup file, box 15, folder 4, Class of 1940 Archive, USNA.
7. Raymond E. Hill file, box 5, folder 13, Class of 1940 Archive, USNA.
8. Michael J. Hanley file, box 4, folder 20, Class of 1940 Archive, USNA.
9. Robert A. Weatherup file, box 15, folder 4; Raymond E. Hill file, box 5, folder 13, both in Class of 1940 Archive, USNA.
10. Robert A. Weatherup file, box 15, folder 5, Class of 1940 Archive, USNA.
11. David C. Wolfe file, box 17, folder 3, Class of 1940 Archive, USNA.
12. John E. Montgomery to Dear Folks, November 20, 1942, John E. Montgomery Letters, USNA; Craig L. Symonds, *The Battle of Midway* (New York: Oxford University Press, 2011), 61.
13. David C. Wolfe file, box 17, folder 3, Class of 1940 Archives, USNA.
14. Symonds, *The Battle of Midway*, 61.
15. Raymond E. Hill file, box 5, folder 13, Class of 1940 Archive, USNA.
16. *Detroit Free Press* (Oct. 25, 1942), 51.
17. Robert A. Weatherup file, box 15, folder 4, Class of 1940 Archive, USNA.
18. Ibid.

NOTES TO PAGES 191–205

19. Ibid.; John Lacouture file, box 8, folder 18, also in Class of 1940 Archive, USNA.
20. J. Gordon Vaeth, *Blimps & U-Boats* (Annapolis: Naval Institute Press, 1992), 30–33.
21. Ibid., 23–25.
22. Ibid., 73–82.
23. Michael J. Hanley file, box 4, folder 21, Class of 1940 Archive, USNA.
24. Ibid.
25. Ibid.
26. Ibid.
27. Maury Klein, *A Call to Arms: Mobilizing America for World War II* (New York: Bloomsbury, 2013), 676–77.
28. Michael J. Hanley file, box 4. Folder 21, Class of 1940 Archive, USNA.
29. Bill Lanier and Cary Hall, "The Long Voyage of the Class of Forty," Special Collections, USNA.

CHAPTER 16: THE MED

1. Warren Walker Jr. file, box 14, folder 22, Class of 1940 Archive, USNA.
2. Ibid.
3. Corporal Walter Hausman, "Now It Can Be Told," Warren Walker file, box 14, folder 22, Class of 1940 Archive, USNA.
4. Warren Walker Jr. file, box 14, folder 22, Class of 1940 Archive, USNA.
5. Craig L. Symonds, *World War II at Sea: A Global History* (New York: Oxford University Press, 2017), 354–55.
6. Ibid.
7. Paul Auphan and Jacques Mordal, *The French Navy in World War II* (Annapolis: Naval Institute Press, 1959), 219; Symonds, *World War II at Sea*, 352.
8. Vincent P. O'Hara, *Torch: North Africa and the Allied Path to Victory* (Annapolis: Naval Institute Press, 2015), 188–89; Warren Walker, Jr. file, box 14, folder 22, and William M. Braybrook file, box 1, folder 23, both in Class of 1940 Archive, USNA.
9. "Now It Can Be Told," memo by Corp. Walter Hausman, no date, in Warren Walker Jr. file, box 14, folder 22, Class of 1940 Archive, USNA.
10. O'Hara, *Torch*, 188.
11. Ibid.; Auphan and Mordal, *French Navy*, 226–27.
12. "300 Killed by Fire," *New York Times* (Nov. 29, 1942), 1.
13. Sam E. Edelstein Jr. file, box 3, folder 13, Class of 1940 Archive, USNA.
14. *A Score and Three More: Class of 1940*, Twenty-Third Reunion book prepared by the Class of 1940, no pagination, John E. Montgomery Papers, USNA.
15. David L. Boslaugh, "The CXAM Goes to War," chapter 6 of *Radar and the Fighter Directors*, Engineering and Technology History Wiki, accessed November 23, 2023.
16. Robert Buderi, *The Invention That Changed the World* (New York: Simon & Schuster, 1997); Colin Latham, *Pioneers of Radar* (Thrup, Stroud: Sutton, 1999).
17. Robert Weatherup, "Discussion," in Robert A. Weatherup file, box 15, folder 7, Class of 1940 Archive, USNA.
18. R. P. Desmond file, box 3, folder 5, Class of 1940 Archive, USNA.
19. Samuel E. Edelstein Jr. file, box 3, folder 13, Class of 1940 Archive, USNA.
20. Ibid.
21. Ibid.
22. Ibid.
23. Ibid.

336   NOTES TO PAGES 205–217

24. Samuel E. Edelstein Jr. to his father, July 10, 1943, ibid.
25. Samuel E. Edelstein Jr. to his father, July 8 and July 10, 1943, ibid.
26. Samuel E. Edelstein Jr. to his father, July 10, 1943.
27. Samuel E. Edelstein Jr. file, box 3, folder 13, Class of 1940 Archive, USNA.
28. Eisenhower's report is in the *New York Times* (July 10, 1943), 1; Ernie Pyle, "The Roving Reporter," *San Bernardino County Sun* and other papers (July 20, 1943); Samuel E. Edelstein Jr. file, box 3, folder 13, Class of 1940 Archives, USNA; Symonds, *World War II at Sea*, 436.
29. Samuel E. Edelstein Jr. to his father, July 10, 1943.

CHAPTER 17: SUBMARINE WARFARE

1. Paul H. Grouleff, "Those Durable Submersibles," *Shipmate* (Sept. 1988), 25; Clay Blair, *Silent Victory: The U.S. Submarine War Against Japan* (Philadelphia: J.B. Lippencott, 1975), 40–41.
2. Blair, *Silent Victory*, 65.
3. Norman Friedman, *U.S. Submarines Through 1945* (Annapolis: Naval Institute Press, 1995), 206–8, 311.
4. US Submarine War Patrol Reports, 1941–1945, National Archives, RG 38 (M1752), USS *Greenling* (Report of First War Patrol), 3, 7.
5. Philip T. Glennon file, box 3, folder 52, Class of 1940 Archive, USNA.
6. See Joel Holwitt, *"Execute Against Japan"* (College Station: Texas A&M University Press, 2009).
7. Robert Gannon, *Hellions of the Deep: The Development of American Torpedoes in World War II* (University Park: Pennsylvania State University Press, 1996), 75–76; Blair, *Silent Victory*, 102–12, 141, 160, 169–71, 227–29.
8. Blair, *Silent Victory*, 879.
9. Philip T. Glennon file, box 3, folder 52, Class of 1940 Archive, USNA.
10. Ibid.
11. Ibid.; Blair, *Silent Victory*, 309–10.
12. The description of tedium is from Richard H. O'Kane, *Clear the Bridge: The War Patrol of the U.S.S. Tang* (New York: Ballantine, 1977), 216.
13. US Submarine War Patrol Reports, 1941–1945, National Archives, RG 38 (M1752), USS *Greenling* (Report of Second War Patrol), 7.
14. Ibid., 18.
15. Philip Glennon file, box 3, folder 52, Class of 1940 Archive, USNA; USS *Greenling* (Report of Second War Patrol), 33.
16. USS *Greenling* (Report of Second War Patrol), 10–11, 24–25; O'Kane, *Clear the Bridge*, 319.
17. USS *Greenling* (Report of Second War Patrol), 29.
18. Ibid., 16.
19. Interview of Glennon by the LeMoyne College (New York) newspaper *The Dolphin* (May 23, 1986); Philip Glennon file, box 3, folder 52, Class of 1940 Archive, USNA.
20. Commander Sub Force 42 to Commander Sub Force, Pacific, November 2, 1942, US Submarine War Patrol Reports, 1941–1945, National Archines, RG 38 (M1752), 1.
21. Theodore Roscoe, *United States Submarine Operations in World War II* (Annapolis: Naval Institute Press, 1949), 123; William Schumann, *The Big Spud: The U.S.S. Idaho in World War II* (Bennington, VT: Merriam Press, 2008), 160.
22. US Submarine War Patrol Reports, 1941–1945, USS *Greenling* (Report of Third War Patrol), National Archives, RG 38 (M1752), 10.
23. US Submarine War Patrol Reports, 1941–1945, USS *Greenling* (Report of Fourth War Patrol), National Archives, RG 38 (M1752), 6.

NOTES TO PAGES 218–230

24. Endorsement of *Greenling* Fourth Patrol Report, Commander, TF 42 to CinC, U.S. Fleet, February 2, 1943, National Archives, RG 38 (M1752), 1.
25. Philip T. Glennon file, box 3, folder 48, Class of 1940 Archives, USNA.
26. Philip K. Eckert, "Left Overboard from a Diving Submarine," *Shipmate* (June 1989), 17.
27. Ibid., 18.
28. Ibid., 17.
29. Ibid., 18.
30. Eckert recorded the conversations inside the sub, including Brockman's outburst, after talking with shipmates later. See Eckert, "Left Overboard," 18, and his earlier summary in Michael Hanley file, box 4, folder 24, Class of 1940 Archive, USNA.
31. Eckert, "Left Overboard," 18; US Submarine War Patrol Reports, 1941–1945 (USS *Nautilus* Fourth War Patrol Report), National Archives, RG 38 (M1752), 5.
32. *Lucky Bag* (1940), 329.
33. "McGrath Tells of Naval Fights," *Arizona Daily Star* (Oct. 23, 1942), 11.
34. US Submarine War Patrol Reports, 1941–1945, USS *Pompano* (Report of Third War Patrol Report), National Archives, RG 38 (M1752), 2–3. Other quotations are from McGrath's talk to the American Legion in Tucson on October 22, 1942, reported in the *Arizona Daily Star* (Oct. 23, 1942), 6. See also Blair, *Silent Victory*, 319–20.
35. USS *Pompano* (Report of Third War Patrol Report), 5.
36. "Biggest War That Ever Hit World, Lt. McGrath Calls It," *Arizona Daily Star* (Oct. 18, 1942).
37. Various articles in *Arizona Daily Star* (Oct. 19, 20, and 23, 1942).
38. USS *Pompano* (Report of Third War Patrol Report), 16; Blair, *Silent Victory*, 460–61.
39. Blair, *Silent Victory*, 229, 878; Roscoe, *United States Submarine Operations*, 112–13.

CHAPTER 18: "MOORED AS BEFORE"

1. Craig L. Symonds, *Nimitz at War* (New York: Oxford University Press, 2022), 156.
2. *A Score and Three More: Class of 1940* (entry of Edmund Gillette), Twenty-Third Reunion book prepared by the class of 1940, no pagination, John E. Montgomery Papers, USNA; William Schumann, *The Big Spud: The U.S.S.* Idaho *in World War II* (diary entry of June 5, 1942), 61–63.
3. Montgomery to Beatrice Montgomery, July 9, 1942, and to Dorothy, July 10, 1942, both in John E. Montgomery Letters, USNA.
4. Montgomery to Dear Folks, January 11, 1943, and to Mo, February 24, 1943, John E. Montgomery Letters, USNA.
5. Schumann, *The Big Spud* (diary entry of Aug. 9, 1942), 70.
6. Ibid. (diary entries of Aug. 14 and Sept. 10, 1942), 72, 76.
7. Ibid. (diary entry of Oct. 6, 1942), 79.
8. Ibid. (diary entries of Oct. 12 and 14, 1942), 81.
9. Montgomery to Dear Folks, October 14, 1942, John E. Montgomery Letters, USNA.
10. Ibid., October 27, 1942.
11. Ibid., November 21, 1942.
12. Records of the Bureau of Naval Personnel, Logbooks of Navy Ships, NARA, RG 24, log of USS *Idaho*, November 18, 1942.
13. John B. Montgomery to the author, February 8, 2024, author's collection; John E. Montgomery to Dear Folks, November 20 and December 8, 1942, John E. Montgomery Letters, USNA.
14. Montgomery to Dear Folks, January 16, 1943, John E. Montgomery Letters, USNA.
15. *Neosho Times* (Oct. 15, 1942), 5; Montgomery to Dear Family, March 23 and 25, 1943, John E. Montgomery Letters, USNA.

NOTES TO PAGES 230–245

16. Symonds, *Nimitz at War*, 196.
17. Gerald Wheeler, *Kinkaid of the Seventh Fleet* (Annapolis: Naval Institute Press, 1995), 295–308, 324. The quotation is from Nimitz to Kinkaid, April 20, 1943, and is quoted by Wheeler on p. 319.
18. Schumann, *The Big Spud* (diary entry of Apr. 7, 1943), 101.
19. Ibid. (diary entries of Apr. 21 and 23, 1943), 111.
20. Ibid. (diary entry of Aug. 2, 1943), 135.
21. John C. McManus, *Fire and Fortitude: The U.S. Army in the Pacific War, 1941–1943* (New York: Calibur, 2019), 372–75.
22. Schumann, *The Big Spud* (diary entry of May 12, 1943), 120.
23. McManus, *Fire and Fortitude*, 392–93.
24. Schumann, *The Big Spud* (diary entry of July 11, 1943), 131–32.
25. Montgomery to Dear Family, July 20, 1943, John E. Montgomery Letters, USNA.
26. Schurmann, *The Big Spud* (diary entry of July 30, 1943), 134; Montgomery to Dear Family, July 31, 1943, John E. Montgomery Letters, USNA.

CHAPTER 19: SEMPER FIDELIS

1. *Lucky Bag* (1940), 274; *Reef Points* (1936), 15.
2. Frederick Karch, Oral History, 6, Special Collections, USNA.
3. Craig L. Symonds, *World War II at Sea: A Global History* (New York: Oxford University Press, 2017), 487–91; Philip A. Crowl and Edmund G. Love, *Seizure of the Gilberts and Marshalls* (Washington, DC: Office of the Chief of Military History, 1955), 13–14; Henry I. Shaw et al. *History of the U.S. Marine Corps*, vol. 3: *The Central Pacific Drive* (Washington, DC: Headquarters Marine Corps, 1966), 3–13.
4. Edward S. Miller, *War Plan Orange: The U.S. Strategy to Defeat Japan, 1897–1945* (Annapolis: Naval Institute Press, 1991), 86–99.
5. Allan R. Millet, *Semper Fidelis: The History of the United States Marine Corps* (New York: Macmillan, 1980), 285, 325–26.
6. Crowl and Love, *Seizure*, 24.
7. William Schumann, *The Big Spud: The U.S.S.* Idaho *in World War II* (diary entries of Nov. 20, 21, 22, 1943), 163–66.
8. Joseph A. Alexander, *Across the Reef: The Marine Assault of Tarawa* (Washington, DC: Marine Corps Historical Center, 1993); Shaw et al., *The Central Pacific Drive*, 53–102; Bill Lanier, "The Long Voyage of the Class of Forty," 18, Special Collections, USNA.
9. Craig L. Symonds, *Nimitz at War* (New York: Oxford University Press, 2022), 263–65.
10. Karch, Oral History, 1.
11. Ibid., 6–7.
12. Symonds, *World War II at Sea*, 512.
13. Ronald J. Brown, *A Brief History of the 14th Marines* (Washington, DC: History and Museums Division, U.S. Marine Corps, 1990), 8.
14. Ibid., 14–15; Shaw et al., *The Central Pacific Drive*, 150–53.
15. Brown, *A Brief History*, 14.
16. Karch, Oral History, 6.
17. Ibid., 16.
18. Schumann, *The Big Spud* (diary entries of Jan. 26 and Feb. 1, 2, and 3, 1944), 179–83.
19. Karch, Oral History, 16.
20. Ibid., 28.
21. Ibid., 17.

NOTES TO PAGES 245–258

22. Ibid.
23. Symonds, *World War II at Sea*, 538–40.
24. Ian Toll, *The Conquering Tide: War in the Pacific Islands, 1942–1944* (New York: W.W. Norton, 2015), 459.
25. Brown, *A Brief History*, 26; Symonds, *World War II at Sea*, 429–30.
26. Brown, *A Brief History*, 30; Shaw et al., *The bCentral Pacific Drive*, 276; Karch, Oral History, 17.
27. Brown, *A Brief History*, 30.
28. Karch, Oral History, 18.
29. Symonds, *Nimitz at War*, 306–11.
30. Brown, *A Brief History*, 31.
31. Karch, Oral History, 20–21.
32. Ibid., 22.
33. Ibid.; Harold Goldberg, *D-Day in the Pacific: The Battle of Saipan* (Bloomington: Indiana University Press, 2007), 202.
34. Karch, Oral History, 22.
35. Brown, *A Brief History*, 36–42; Karch, Oral History, 24.
36. John Playter, *Survivor: A Personal Memoir* (Bolivar, MO: Southwest Baptist University, 2000), 81–82.
37. Ibid., 77–81; "U.S. Casualties and Burials at Cabanatuan POW Camp #1," Defense POW/MIA Accounting Agency, Washington, DC.
38. Playter, *Survivor*, 77.
39. Shields Goodman, "A Letter from Bilibud Prison," *Shipmate* (Nov. 1989), 1.
40. Elmer Long file, box 2, folder 33, Class of 1940, USNA.
41. Playter, *Survivor*, 121.
42. Ibid., 123.
43. US Submarine War Patrol Reports, 1941–1945, National Archives, RG 38 (M1752), *Paddle* (Report of Fifth War Patrol), 9.
44. Playter, *Survivor*, 125–27.

CHAPTER 20: THE ATLANTIC AGAIN

1. John E. Greenbacker file, box 4, folder 8, Class of 1940 Archives, USNA.
2. Ibid.
3. Craig L. Symonds, *World War II at Sea: A Global History* (New York: Oxford University Press, 2018), 443–54; John E. Greenbacker and Virgil E. Gex, "Refueling Submarines at Sea," *Shipmate* (Jan.–Feb. 1987), 17.
4. John E. Greenbacker file, box 4, folder 8, Class of 1940 Archive, USNA; Greenbacker and Gex, "Refueling Submarines at Sea," 17.
5. John E. Greenbacker file, box 4, folder 9, Class of 1940 Archive, USNA.
6. Ibid.
7. Greenbacker and Gex, "Refueling Submarines at Sea," 17.
8. Ibid.
9. Ibid.
10. Ibid., 18; Virgil Gex file, box 3, folder 40, Class of 1940 Archive, USNA.
11. "War Record of USS Tuscaloosa" (Aug. 12, 1945), 6, in William Braybrook file, box 1, folder 18, Class of 1940 Archives, USNA.
12. Benjamin Frana file, box 3, folder 31, Class of 1940 Archive, USNA.

340   NOTES TO PAGES 258–271

13. William Braybrook file, box 1, folder 19; William M. Carpenter file, box 2, folder 30, both in Class of 1940 Archive, USNA.

14. Craig L. Symonds, *Neptune: The Allied Invasion of Europe and the D-Day Landings* (New York: Oxford University Press, 2014), 258.

15. Ibid., 262; "Summary of Tuscaloosa Firing on June 6, 1944," William Braybrook file, box 1, folder 20, Class of 1940 Archive, USNA.

16. "Summary of Tuscaloosa Firing on June 6, 1944," William Braybrook file, box 1, folder 20, Class of 1940 Archive, USNA.

17. Ibid.

18. Symonds, *Neptune*, 298; *Lucky Bag* (1940), 263; Action Report, USS *Baldwin* (June 22, 1944), Special Collections, USNA.

19. Symonds, *Neptune*, 297; Omar Bradley, *A General's Life* (New York: Simon & Schuster, 1983), 251.

20. Symonds, *Neptune*, 313.

21. "Summary of Tuscaloosa Firing, June 7, 1944," in William Braybrook file, box 1, folder 20, Class of 1940 Archive, USNA.

22. Symonds, *Neptune*, 318–28.

23. Ibid., 313.

24. Samuel Eliot Morison, *The Invasion of France and Germany, 1944–1945* (Boston: Little Brown, 1957), 207.

25. William Braybrook file, box 1, folder 19, Class of 1940 Archive, USNA.

CHAPTER 21: THE BATTLE OF LEYTE GULF

1. General histories of the battle include Samuel E. Morison, *New Guinea and the Marianas* (Boston: Little Brown, 1964); William T. Y'Blood, *Red Sun Setting: The Battle of the Philippine Sea* (Annapolis: Naval Institute Press, 1981); and James D. Hornfischer, *The Fleet at Flood Tide* (New York: Bantam, 2016). See also Craig L. Symonds, *World War II at Sea: A Global History* (New York: Oxford University Press, 2018), 540–52.

2. General histories of the battle include Thomas J. Cutler, *The Battle of Leyte Gulf* (New York: Harper/Collins, 1994); and H. P. Willmott, *The Battle of Leyte Gulf: The Last Fleet Action* (Bloomington: Indiana University Press, 2005. See also Symonds, *World War II at Sea*, 562–88.

3. See the table of organization in Samuel E. Morison, *Leyte: June 1944–January 1945* (Boston: Little, Brown, 1958), 415–32.

4. *Lucky Bag* (1940).

5. Robert F. Dorr, "The Curtiss SB2C Helldiver: An Unpopular and Flawed Allied War Machine," *Warfare History* (Aug. 2014), 10.

6. Bill and Kathy Emerson, eds., *The Voices of Bombing Nineteen* (Dec. 2002), 71, http://www.emersonguys.com/bill/voices.pdf (accessed Nov. 7, 2024).

7. US Submarine War Patrol Reports, 1941–1945, National Archives, RG 38 (M1752), USS *Darter* (Report of Fifth War Patrol, Nov. 5, 1944), and USS *Dace* (Nov. 6, 1944).

8. Emerson and Emerson, *Voices of Bombing Nineteen*, entry by William Emerson, 76–77.

9. Ibid., 78.

10. Ibid., 80–81.

11. Ibid., 86.

12. Ibid., 87.

13. Ibid., 88.

14. Ibid., 89.

NOTES TO PAGES 271–285

15. Carl Solberg, *Decision and Dissent: With Halsey at Leyte Gulf* (Annapolis: Naval Institute Press, 1995, 154; Thomas Alexander Hughes, *Admiral Bill Halsey* (Cambridge: Harvard University Press, 2016), 370–71. See also Symonds, *World War II at Sea*, 584–85.

16. *Lucky Bag* (1940), 172.

17. James D. Hornfischer, *Last Stand of the Tin Can Sailors* (New York: Bantam Books, 2004), 29.

18. John Wukovits, *For Crew and Country* (New York: St. Martin's Press, 2013), 100–101.

19. Hornfischer, *Last Stand*, 22–23, 32–33, 35.

20. Ibid., 116; Wukovits, *For Crew and Country*, 121.

21. Wukovits, *For Crew and Country*, 130–31.

22. Symonds, *World War II at Sea*, 580.

23. From Copeland's Action Report, Nov. 20, 1944, quoted in Wukovits, *For Crew and Country*, 133.

24. Hornfischer, *Last Stand*, 254–55. The *Chokai* later sank, though postwar investigation showed that it was a number of five-inch shells, and not an American torpedo, that had done the damage.

25. Wukovits, *For Crew and Country*, 142.

26. Ibid., 167–69.

27. Ibid., 173, 183.

28. Symonds, *World War II at Sea*, 587.

29. Emerson and Emerson, *Voices of Bombing Nineteen*, 91–92.

CHAPTER 22: IWO JIMA AND OKINAWA

1. Hibben Ziesing, "History of Fighting Squadron Forty-Six" (1946), in *World War Regimental Histories* (New York: Plantin Press, 1946), 132:1.

2. Craig L. Symonds, *The Battle of Midway* (New York: Oxford University Press, 2011), 285–86; Ziesing, "Fighting Squadron Forty-Six," 4.

3. Nathan Canestaro, *The Mighty Moo* (New York: Grand Central, 2024), 268.

4. Ibid., 8–10; Robert A. Weatherup, "Meditations," in Robert A. Weatherup file, box 15, folder 5, Class of 1940 Archive, USNA.

5. Bill Emerson and Kathy Emerson, eds., *The Voices of Bombing Nineteen* (Dec. 2002), 71, http://www.emersonguys.com/bill/voices.pdf (accessed Nov. 7, 2024); Craig L. Symonds, *Nimitz at War* (New York: Oxford University Press, 2022), 339; Michael J. Hanley file, box, folder, Class of 1940 Archive, USNA.

6. Ziesing, "Fighting Squadron Forty-Six," 7.

7. R. R. Dupzyk file, box 3, folder 9, Class of 1940 Archive, USNA.

8. Ibid.

9. Michael J. Hanley file, box 4, folder 20, Class of 1940 Archive, USNA.

10. Conrad Carlson file, box 2, folder 25, Class of 1940 Archives, USNA.

11. Weatherup, "Meditations."

12. Raymond E. Hill file, box 5, folder 17, Class of 1940 Archive, USNA.

13. Ziesing, "Fighting Squadron Forty-Six," 9.

14. Robert A. Weatherup file, box 15, folder 5, Class of 1940 Archive, USNA.

15. Ziesing, "Fighting Squadron Forty-Six," 12; Fred Karch, Oral History, 28, 33, Special Collections, USNA.

16. Richard B. Frank, *Downfall: The End of the Imperial Japanese Empire* (New York: Random House, 1999), 3–19; Max Hastings, *Retribution: The Battle for Japan, 1944–45* (New York: Alfred A. Knopf, 2008), 296–305.

342 NOTES TO PAGES 286–299

17. John Lacouture, Oral History, Naval History and Heritage Command, 30.
18. "Four New Englanders Added to Growing List of Franklin Survivors," *Boston Globe* (May 20, 1945), 30.
19. Rikihei Inoguchi and Tadashi Nakajima, *The Divine Wind: Japan's Kamikaze Force in World War II* (Annapolis: Naval Institute Press, 1958).
20. Action Report, USS *Dashiell*, April 26, 1945, included in Michael J. Hanley file, box 4, folder 20, USNA.
21. Ibid.
22. Ibid.
23. Ibid.
24. Ibid.
25. "Details of the 15 April 1945 Raid," in Robert A. Weatherup file, box 15, folder 2, Class of 1940 Archives, USNA.
26. Henry Sakaida and Steve Blake, "The Last Flight of Shoichi Sugita," *Fighter Pilots in Aerial Combat* (Summer 1982), 2–18; Ziesing, "Fighting Squadron Forty-Six," 19–20.
27. Arthur Maltby file, box 9, folder 32, Class of 1940 Archive, USNA.
28. Conrad Carlson file, box 2, folder 25, Class of 1940 Archive, USNA.
29. Miles Lewis, "Destroyer Action," in Conrad Carlson file, box 2, folder 25, Class of 1940 Archive, USNA.
30. After Action Report, USS *Douglas H. Fox*, May 24, 1945, in Conrad Carlson file, box 2, folder 25, Class of 1940 Archive, USNA.
31. Ibid., 7.
32. Ibid., 3, 4.
33. Ibid., 9.
34. Conrad Carlson file, box 2, folder 25, Class of 1940 Archive, USNA.

CHAPTER 23: CULMINATION

1. Montgomery to Dear Family, April 1944, John E. Montgomery Letters, USNA.
2. Montgomery to Dearest Family, August 5, 1944, John E. Montgomery Letters, USNA.
3. Montgomery to Dear Family, September 2 and 30 and October 28, 1944, John E. Montgomery Letters, USNA.
4. Montgomery to Dearest Mother and Dad, November 3, 1944, and Montgomery to Dear Dottie, November 16, 1944, both in John E. Montgomery Letters, USNA.
5. Montgomery to Dearest Dottie, April 14, 1945, John E. Montgomery Letters, USNA.
6. Montgomery to Dearest Mother, May 22, 1945, John E. Montgomery Letters, USNA.
7. Montgomery to Dear Folks, January 16, 1943, John E. Montgomery Letters, USNA.
8. Craig L. Symonds, *Nimitz at War* (New York: Oxford University Press, 2022), 385–86.
9. Raymond Calhoun, *Typhoon: The Other Enemy* (Annapolis: Naval Institute Press, 1981), 208; Nathan Canestaro, *The Mighty Moo* (New York: Grand Central, 2024), 233–45; Craig L. Symonds, *World War II at Sea: A Global History* (New York: Oxford University Press, 2018), 600–602.
10. Montgomery to his grandmother, June 2, 1945, John E. Montgomery Letters, USNA.
11. Roger Barr, "The Pittsburgh's Typhoon Battle," *Naval History* (Oct. 2015), 26.
12. Ibid.
13. Montgomery to Dear Dad, June 24, 1945, John E. Montgomery Letters, USNA.
14. US Submarine War Patrol Reports, 1941–1945, National Archives, RG 38, USS *Flasher* (Report of Sixth Patrol, May 14, 1947).

NOTES TO PAGES 299–303

15. See, for example, Richard S. Frank, *Downfall* (New York: Random House, 1999) and Max Hastings, *Retribution* (New York: Knopf, 2008).
16. Ernest R. Peterson Diary (Aug. 4, 1945), Ernest R. Peterson file, box 11, folder 9, Class of 1940 Archive USNA.
17. "Statement of LCDR E. R. Peterson," August 24, 1945, Ernest R. Peterson file, box 11, folder 9, Class of 1940 Archive, USNA.
18. Ernest R. Peterson Diary (Aug. 4, 1945).
19. Ibid.
20. Ibid.
21. Passages from "The Seizure of the Tachibara Maru," Ernest R. Peterson file, box 11, folder 8, Class of 1940 Archive, USNA.
22. *Lucky Bag* (1940), 156; *A Score and Three More: Class of 1940*, Twenty-Third Reunion book prepared by the class of 1940, no pagination, John E. Montgomery Papers, USNA.
23. Charles A. Lockwood, *Sink 'Em All: Submarine Warfare in the Pacific* (New York: E. P. Dutton, 1951), 320.

Bibliography

PRIMARY AND OFFICIAL SOURCES

Annual Register of the United States Naval Academy. Washington, DC: Government Printing Office, 1936, 1937, 1938, 1939, 1940.

Bradley, Omar, with Clay Blair. *A General's Life*. New York: Simon & Schuster, 1983.

Brown, Ronald J. *A Brief History of the 14th Marines*. Washington, DC: History and Museums Division, US Marine Corps, 1990.

Complete Presidential Press Conferences of Franklin D. Roosevelt. New York: DaCapo Press, 1972.

Clancy, Albert Harrison, Jr. "Albert H. 'Pat' Clancy." A family memoir, courtesy of Kevin Clancy (USNA, 1969) and Dion Clancy (USNA, 1972), privately held.

———. Diary. Courtesy of Kevin Clancy (USNA 1969), and Dion Clancy (USNA 1972), privately held.

Class of 1940 Archive (19 boxes). Special Collections, Nimitz Library, US Naval Academy, Annapolis, MD.

Deputy Chief of Naval Operations (Air). *United States Naval Aviation, 1910–1980*. Washington, DC: US Government Printing Office, 1981.

Donitz, Karl. *Memoirs: Ten Years and Twenty Days*. Annapolis: Naval Institute Press, 1959.

Emerson, Bill, and Kathy Emerson, eds. *The Voices of Bombing Nineteen*. August 1993; August 1995; web version, December 2002.

Hundevadt, Raymond A. "Spindrift: Recollections of a Naval Career." Special Collections, Nimitz Library, US Naval Academy, Annapolis, MD.

Karch, Frederick, Brigadier General, USMC. Oral History, Special Collections, US Naval Academy.

Lacouture, John E. Captain, US Navy. Oral History, Naval Historical Foundation. Oral History Program, Naval History and Heritage Command, 2001.

Lockwood, Charles A. *Sink 'Em All: Submarine Warfare in the Pacific*. New York: E. P. Dutton, 1951.

Miller, John, Jr. *Guadalcanal: The First Offensive*. Part of "The United States Army in World War II." Washington, DC: Department of the Army, 1949.

John E. Montgomery Letters. Special Collections, Nimitz Library, US Naval Academy, Annapolis, MD.

John E. Montgomery Papers. Special Collections, Nimitz Library, US Naval Academy, Annapolis, MD.

O'Kane, Richard H. *Clear the Bridge: The War Patrol of the U.S.S. Tang*. New York: Ballantine, 1977.

Playter, John. *Survivor: A Personal Memoir*. Bolivar, MO: Southwest Baptist University, 2000.

Schumann, William. *The Big Spud: The U.S.S. Idaho in World War II. A War Diary*. Bennington, VT: Merriam Press, 2008.

Shaw, Henry I., Bernard C. Nalty, and Edwin T. Turnbladh. *History of U.S. Marine Corps Operations in World War II*. Vol. 3: *The Central Pacific Drive*. Washington, DC: Historical Branch, G-3 Division, Headquarters US Marine Corps, 1966.

346 BIBLIOGRAPHY

Solberg, Carl. *Decision and Dissent: With Halsey at Leyte Gulf.* Annapolis: Naval Institute Press, 1995.

US Naval Academy. *Lucky Bag* (1937, 1938, 1939, 1940).

US Naval Academy. Midshipman Records. National Archives and Records Administration, College Park, MD. Record Group 405.

US Navy Bureau of Naval Personnel. Logbooks of Navy Ships. National Archives and Records Administration. Record Group 24.

US Submarine War Patrol Reports, 1941–1945. Sub Operational History of WWII. National Archives and Records Administration, College Park, MD. Record Group 38.

US Treasury Department. *Statistics of Income for 1935.* Washington, DC: Government Printing Office, 1938.

Wright, John H. *That Jack the House Built.* Privately printed, 1985.

Ziesing, Hibben. "History of Fighting Squadron Forty-Six: A Log in Narrative Form of Its Participation in World War II." (1946) *World War Regimental Histories*, No. 132. New York: Plantin Press, 1946.

SECONDARY SOURCES: BOOKS

Abbazia, Patrick. *Mr. Roosevelt's Navy: The Private War of the U.S. Atlantic Fleet, 1939–1942.* Annapolis: Naval Institute Press, 1975.

Alexander, Joseph A. *Across the Reef: The Marine Assault on Tarawa.* Washington, DC: Marine Corps Historical Center, 1993.

Auphan, Paul and Jacques Mordal. *The French Navy in World War II.* Translated by A. C. J. Sabalot. Annapolis: Naval Institute Press, 1959.

Bailey, Thomas A., and Paul B. Ryan. *Hitler vs. Roosevelt: The Undeclared Naval War.* New York: Free Press, 1979.

Blair, Clay, Jr. *Silent Victory: The U.S. Submarine War Against Japan.* Philadelphia: J. B. Lippencott, 1975.

Boslaugh, David L. "The CXAM Goes to War." Chapter 6 of *Radar and the Fighter Directors*, Engineering and Technology History Wiki, accessed November 23, 2023.

Buderi, Robert. *The Invention That Changed the World: How a Small Group of Radar Pioneers Won the Second World War and Launched a Technological Revolution.* New York: Simon & Schuster, 1997.

Bulkley, Robert J. *At Close Quarters: PT Boats in the United States Navy.* Washington, DC: Naval History Division, 1962.

Burns, Russell, ed. *Radar Development to 1945.* London: Peter Peregrinus, 1988.

Canestaro, Nathan. *The Mighty Moo: The USS* Cowpens *and Her Epic World War II Journey from Jinx Ship to the Navy's First Carrier into Tokyo Bay.* New York: Grand Central, 2024.

Churchill, Winston S. *The Second World War.* 6 vols. New York: Bantam Books, 1950.

Faber, Frank. *Munich: The 1938 Appeasement Crisis.* New York: Simon & Schuster, 2008.

Crowl, Philip A., and Edmund G. Love. *Seizure of the Gilberts and Marshalls.* Washington, DC: Office of the Chief of Military History, 1955.

Cutler, Thomas J. *The Battle of Leyte Gulf.* New York: HarperCollins, 1994.

Domalgowski, John J. *Lost at Guadalcanal: The Final Battles of the* Astoria *and* Chicago *as Described by Survivors and Official Reports.* Jefferson, NC: McFarland Press, 2010.

Frank, Richard B. *Downfall: The End of the Imperial Japanese Empire.* New York: Random House, 1999.

———. *Guadalcanal: The Definitive Account of the Landmark Battle.* New York: Bantam Books, 1990.

BIBLIOGRAPHY

——. *Tower of Skulls: A History of the Asia-Pacific War, July 1937–May 1942*. New York: W.W. Norton, 2020.

Friedman, Norman. *U.S. Submarines Through 1945*. Annapolis: Naval Institute Press, 1995.

Gannon, Robert. *Hellions of the Deep: The Development of American Torpedoes in World War II*. University Park: Pennsylvania State University Press, 1996.

Goldberg, Harold. *D-Day in the Pacific: The Battle of Saipan*. Bloomington: Indiana University Press, 2007.

Guerlac, Henry E. *Radar in World War II*. New York: Tomash Publishers (American Institute of Physics), 1987.

Hague, Arnold. *The Allied Convoy System, 1939–1945*. Annapolis: Naval Institute Press, 2000.

Hampton, Dan, *Valor: The Astonishing World War II Saga of One Man's Defiance and Indomitable Spirit*. New York: St. Martin's Press, 2022.

Hastings, Max. *Retribution: The Battle for Japan, 1944–1945*. New York: Alfred A. Knopf, 2008.

Holmes, W. J. *Undersea Victory: The Influence of Submarine Operations on the War in the Pacific*. Garden City, NY: Doubleday, 1966.

Holwitt, Joel Ira. *"Execute Against Japan": The US. Decision to Conduct Unrestricted Submarine War*. College Station: Texas A&M University Press, 2009.

Hornfischer, James D. *The Fleet at Flood Tide*. New York: Bantam, 2016.

——. *Last Stand of the Tin Can Sailors: The Extraordinary World War II Story of the U.S. Navy's Finest Hour*. New York: Bantam Books, 2004.

——. *Neptune's Inferno: The U.S. Navy at Guadalcanal*. New York: Random House, 2012.

——. *Ship of Ghosts: The Story of the USS Houston, FDR's Legendary Lost Cruiser and the Epic Saga of Her Survivors*. New York: Bantam Books, 2006.

Hughes, Thomas Alexander. *Admiral Bill Halsey*. Cambridge: Harvard University Press, 2016.

Klein, Maury. *A Call to Arms: Mobilizing America for World War II*. New York: Bloomsbury Press, 2013.

Latham, Colin. *Pioneers of Radar*. Thrup, Stroud, United Kingdom: Sutton, 1999.

Layton, Edwin. *And I Was There: Pearl Harbor and Midway—Breaking the Secrets*. New York: Morrow, 1985.

Loxton, Bruce, and Chris Coulthard-Clark. *The Shame of Savo: Anatomy of a Naval Disaster*. Annapolis: Naval Institute Press, 1994.

Lundstrom, John B. *Black Shoe Carrier Admiral: Frank Jack Fletcher at Coral Sea, Midway, and Guadalcanal*. Annapolis: Naval Institute Press, 2006.

Martin, Adrian R. *Brothers from Bataan: POWs, 1942–1944*. Manhattan, KS: Sunflower University Press, 1992.

McManus, John C. *Fire and Fortitude: The U.S. Army in the Pacific War, 1941–1943*. New York: Calibur, 2019.

Miller, Edward S. *War Plan Orange: The U.S. Strategy to Defeat Japan, 1897–1945*. Annapolis: Naval Institute Press, 1991.

Millet, Allan R. *Semper Fidelis: The History of the United States Marine Corps*. New York: Macmillan, 1980.

Monsarrtat, Nicholas. *Three Corvettes*. London: Cassel, 1945.

Morrison, Samuel Eliot. *Coral Sea, Midway, and Submarine Actions*. Boston: Little Brown, 1949.

——. *The Invasion of France and Germany, 1944–1945*. Boston: Little Brown, 1957.

Nasaw, David. *The Patriarch: The Remarkable Life and Turbulent Times of Joseph P. Kennedy*. New York: Penguin, 2012.

O'Hara, Vincent P. *Torch: North Africa and the Allied Path to Victory*. Annapolis: Naval Institute Press, 2015.

348 BIBLIOGRAPHY

Prados, John. *Combined Fleet Decoded: The Secret History of American Intelligence and the Japanese Navy in World War II*. New York: Random House, 1995.

Prange, Gordon W. with Donald Goldstein and Katherine Dillon. *At Dawn We Slept: The Untold Story of Pearl Harbor*. New York: McGraw-Hill, 1981.

Roscoe, Theodore. *United States Submarine Operations in World War II*. Annapolis: Naval Institute Press, 1949.

Roskill, Stephen W. *The War at Sea, 1939–1945*. London: Her Majesty's Stationery Office, 1956.

Schneller, Robert J. *Breaking the Color Barrier: The U.S. Naval Academy's First Black Midshipmen and the Struggle for Racial Equality*. New York: New York University Press, 2005.

Symonds, Craig L. *The Battle of Midway*. New York: Oxford University Press, 2011.

———. *Neptune: The Allied Invasion of Europe and the D-Day Landings*. New York: Oxford, 2014.

———. *Nimitz at War: Command Leadership from Pearl Harbor to Tokyo Bay*. New York: Oxford, 2022.

———. *World War II at Sea: A Global History*. New York: Oxford, 2017.

Taylor, Telford. *Munich: The Price of Peace*. New York: Random House, 1979.

Toll, Ian W. *The Conquering Tide: War in the Pacific Islands, 1942–1944*. New York W.W. Norton, 2015.

———. *Pacific Crucible: War at Sea in the Pacific*. New York: W.W. Norton, 2015.

———. *Twilight of the Gods: War in the Western Pacific, 1944–1945*. New York: W.W. Norton, 2020.

Turnbull, Archibald D., and Clifford L. Lord. *History of United States Naval Aviation*. New Haven: Yale University Press, 1949.

Vaeth, J. Gordon. *Blimps & U-Boats: U.S. Navy Airships in the Battle of the Atlantic*. Annapolis: Naval Institute Press, 1992.

Wakabayshi, Bob Tadashi, ed. *The Nanking Atrocity, 1937–38*. New York: Berghahn Books, 2007.

Wheeler, Gerald E. *Kinkaid of the Seventh Fleet: A Biography of Admiral Thomas C. Kinkaid, U.S. Navy*. Annapolis: Naval Institute Press, 1995.

Willmott, H. P. *The Barrier and the Javelin: Japanese and Allied Pacific Strategies, February to June, 1942*. Annapolis: Naval Institute Press, 1983.

———. *The Battle of Leyte Gulf: The Last Fleet Action*. Bloomington: Indiana University Press, 2005.

Winston, Robert A. *Fighting Squadron: A Sequel to Dive Bomber*. Annapolis: Naval Institute Press, 1946.

Wohlstetter, Roberta. *Pearl Harbor: Warning and Decision*. Stanford: Stanford University Press, 1962.

Woodman, Richard. *The Arctic Convoys, 1941–1945*. London: John Murray, 1994.

Wukovits, John. *For Crew and Country: The Inspirational True Story of Bravery and Sacrifice Aboard the USS Samuel B. Roberts*. New York: St. Martin's Press, 2013.

Y'Blood, William T. *Red Sun Setting: The Battle of the Philippine Sea*. Annapolis: Naval Institute Press, 1981.

SECONDARY SOURCES: ARTICLES

Ageton, Arthur A. "Annapolis, Mother of Navy Men." US Naval Institute *Proceedings* (October 1935), 1499–1514.

Alden, Carroll A. "Officers and Gentlemen in the Making." US Naval Institute *Proceedings* (October 1935), 1494–98.

Barr, Roger. "The *Pittsburgh*'s Typhoon Battle." *Naval History* (October 2015), 24–30.

BIBLIOGRAPHY

Blee, Ben. "Whodunnit?" US Naval Institute *Proceedings* (June 1982), 42–47.

Curtin, Sally C. "Marriage Rates in the United States, 1900–2018." National Center for Health Statistics, Centers for Disease Control and Prevention.

Dorr, Robert F. "The Curtiss SB2C Helldiver: An Unpopular and Flawed Allied War Machine." *Warfare History* (August 2014), 8–11.

Eckert, Philip K. "Left Overboard from a Diving Submarine." *Shipmate* (June 1989), 17–18.

Eller, E. M. "Navy Life Begins." US Naval Institute *Proceedings* (October 1935), 1515–28.

Gex, Virgil. "Inaugural Parade Memories." *Shipmate* (April 1997), 20.

Goodman, Shields. "A Letter from Bilibud Prison." *Shipmate* (November 1980), 14–15.

Greenbacker, John E., and Virgil E. Gex. "Refueling Submarines at Sea." *Shipmate* (January–February 1987), 17–18.

Grouleff, Paul H. "Those Durable Submersibles: O, R, and S Boats." *Shipmate* (September 1988), 25–26.

Hall, Cary H. "Away the Boarding Party." *Shipmate* (September 1981), 31–33.

Hundevadt, Robert A. "The '40s Story." *Shipmate* (July–August 1988), 23–24.

John, R. K. "Hitler's Future Admirals." *The Log* (December 8, 1939), 8–10.

Kittredge, George W. "Broadside at Savo." *Saga* (March 1954), 20–23, 60–61.

Peifer, Douglas. "The American Response to the Sinking of the USS *Panay*, December 1937." In Brian VanDeMark, ed., *New Interpretations of Naval History*. Annapolis: Naval Institute Press, 2023.

Rooks, A. H. "Entrance Requirements of U.S. Naval Academy." US Naval Institute *Proceedings* (October 1935), 1468–81.

Sakaida, Henry, and Steve Blake. "The Last Flight of Shoichi Sugita." *Fighter Pilots in Aerial Combat* (Summer 1982), 2–18.

Stephen, Robert, and Robert Dupont. "Naval Air Station & University of New Orleans." *New Orleans Historical Magazine* (April 2012), 139–46.

NEWSPAPERS

Albuquerque Journal
Arizona Daily Star (Tucson)
Arizona Gleam
Baltimore Sun
Boston Globe
Brooklyn Citizen
Buffalo News
Detroit Free Press
Fairhope (Alabama) *Courier*
Hagerstown Daily Mail
Honolulu Star Bulletin
Kirksville (Missouri) *Daily News*
Lock Haven (Pennsylvania) *Express*
Los Angeles Daily News
Los Angeles Times
Metropolitan News (Chicago)
New York Age
New York Daily News
New York Times
Neosho (Missouri) *Times*

BIBLIOGRAPHY

Philadelphia Inquirer
Richmond News Leader
San Bernardino County (California) *Sun*
Torquay Herald and Express
Virginia Gazette
Washington Post
Washington Evening Star

The Forties Index

NOTE: The 128 members of the Naval Academy class of 1940 who are included in the narrative are listed in this index. A general index of people, places, concepts, and events follows.

Allsopp, Robert T. 147
Antonelli, John ("Jocko") 76, 165

Banker, Donald
  on USS *Idaho* 96
  as naval aviator 266, 268–69
  and Battle of Leyte Gulf 270–71
  and attack on the *Nachi* 277
Benbow, William 45
Bergner, Allen A. 37–38, 70
Blodgett, John 181, 183
Blough, Ira K. ("Ike") 169
Braybrook, William
  at USNA 23
  on *Tuscaloosa* 93, 98, 140, 142–43
  and the D-Day invasion 257–62
Bried, Joseph 195
Buchanan, Gaylord ("Buck") 77
  as POW 127, 131
Burgan, William ("Salty") 223

Calhoun, Otis ("Cal") 185–86, 189
Campo, Abraham ("Sparky") 77
  appointment to USNA 15
  homesick 27
  nickname 47
  and fencing 61, 73
  in Philippine campaign 128, 129n
Carlson, Conrad ("Connie") 19, 23
  plebe year 31
  academic performance of 73
  appearance of 89
  on USS *Astoria* 89, 101, 147
  in Battle of the Coral Sea 147
  in Battle of Midway 154, 157
  in Battle of Savo Island 164, 167, 169–70
  on USS *Foote* in Solomons 182–83
  on USS *Douglas H. Fox* at
    Okinawa 282–83, 291–93
  becomes a father 293
  post-war career and retirement 315

Carpenter, William 258
Chabot, Leon ("Chab")
  as track star at USNA 61, 73, 75, 76
  academic performance of 73
  in Philippine campaign 128–29
  as POW 130, 249–50
  death of 250–51
Champion, Richard 85, 109
Chase, John D. ("Charley") 74
Clagett, Henry 183, 252
Clancy, Albert H. ("Pat")
  at USNA 19, 21, 23, 25–26
  in Pearl Harbor 88–89
Cloues, Edward 112
Cochrane, Richard 182
Collins, Talbot ("Tab") 241
Cook, Allan ("Cooky") 139, 258
Croft, William ("Cros") 76, 82
  drive to West coast 85–86
  on USS *California* 88
  in Pearl Harbor attack 107–9
  marriage of 139

Darby, Marshall ("Darb") 105
D'Arezzo, Joseph 73, 76
Davenport, Irving J. 102
  at Pearl Harbor 103–5
Davison, Henry ("Dave") 102
  at Pearl Harbor 110–12
  in the Solomon Islands 182
Debie, William 35
Desmond, Ralph Paul ("Des")
  appointment to USNA 11–12
  and radar training 203–4
Donley, Edward 82
Dupzyk, Richard Robert ("RR") 91, 173
  appointment to USNA 10–11
  plebe year 27
  in Battle of Midway 158–59
  on USS *Stringham* 281–82
Durant, Dolive ("Schnozz") 46

THE FORTIES INDEX

Eckert, Philip F. 218–20
Edelstein, Samuel
  and eye trouble 50, 202
  as radar expert 203–5
  and the invasion of Sicily (1943) 204–7

Farrior, James ("Sinbad") 47
Frana, Benjamin ("Benjie")
  at Pearl Harbor 106–7
  on convoy duty 137
  and the D-Day invasion 258, 260–62
Freund, John F. ("Fritz") 74

Gex, Virgil ("Doc")
  at Pearl Harbor 110–11
  on USS *Neunzer* 252–57
  assumes command 257
Gillette, Edward ("Jug") 225
Glennon, Philip ("PT") 252
  appointment to USNA 4–5
  and eye trouble 49–50
  on USS *Cincinnati* 92
  and submarine training 55, 208–10
  on USS *Greenling* 212–18
  on USS *Flasher* 299
  post-war career and retirement 314
Gray, L. Patrick 96
Greenbacker, John E. ("Peck") 47, 70, 87
  in undeclared naval war 94
  on USS *Yorktown* 119–20
  and the Battle of the Coral Sea 146–51
  and the Battle of Midway 152–59, 158n
  commands USS *Neunzer* 252–57
  post-war career and retirement 311
Greene, William F. 166, 183
Guice, William L. ("Billy") 180, 183

Hall, Benjamin 85
  on USS *California* 88
  at Pearl Harbor 107–8
  death of 195
Hall, Cary 85
Hamill, John ("Ham") 126
Hanley, Michael Joseph 70
  appointment to USNA 12–13
  and basketball 25, 60–67, 72–73
  in FDR inaugural parade 28–29
  and racial issues 29–30
  and youngster cruise 35
  and youngster year 44

second class cruise 53–55
  and the coming of war 68–69
  academic performance of 31, 73
  on USS *Northampton* 89–91
  during Pearl Harbor attack 113–14
  and raid on Marshall Islands 122–24
  service in blimps 192–94
  in Okinawa campaign 287–89
  post-war career and retirement 308
Hanna, John 183
Hanson, Burton ("Ollie") 126n
Hanson, Harold ("Swede") 74
Hardy, John ("Jack") 116
Harris, Robert 70, 82, 266n
  appointment to USNA 5–6
  plebe year 20, 23, 28
  and youngster cruise 42
  and youngster year 44
  and eye trouble 50
  academic performance of 31, 73
  on USS *Pennsylvania* 86, 87
  on USS *Washington* 139–41, 143–44
  marriage of 139–40, 143–44
Healey, Vince ("Chet") 169–70
Hemley, Eugene
  and plebe year 32
  and youngster cruise 35–36
Herring, George 165
Hill, Raymond ("Ted") 109–10
  as naval aviator 185, 187, 189–90, 283
Hittorf, Joseph 105
Hundevadt, Raymond ("Hundy")
  appointment to USNA 8
  plebe year 26
  and youngster cruise 39
  academic performance of 73
  on USS *Vincennes* 89, 130–31
  marriage of 138–39
  in Battle of Savo Island 164, 167,
    170–72
  post-war career and retirement 307

Jarrett, Milton ("Mo") 195
Johnson, James Lee
  appointment to USNA 13–15
  harassment and dismissal of 29–30

Karch, Frederick 76, 237–38, 265
  and the Marshall Islands 241–44
  imposes training regimen 244–45

THE FORTIES INDEX

353

in battle for Saipan 245–48
lands on Tinian 248
and Iwo Jima 284–85
post-war career and retirement 312
Kaufman, Robert 302–3
Keating, William ("Slim") 47
King, David Lloyd George 182, 182n
Kirkpatrick, Robert ("Kirk") 108
Kittredge, George ("Keet")
on USS *Chicago* 89
in Battle of Savo Island 164–66, 168

Lacouture, John ("Lover") 70
appointment to USNA 9–10, 13
plebe year 19, 25, 28, 32
and youngster cruise 39–40
and youngster year 45
and second-class cruise 54
sailing in Hyannisport 56–57, 83
social life of 59, 65, 67, 84, 99–101
academic performance of 73
on USS *Saratoga* 83–85
on USS *Blue* 99–101, 173–74
and Pearl Harbor attack 114–15
and Wake Island rescue mission 117–18
engagement of 144
in Battle of Savo Island 166, 172, 173–74
and flight training 185–88
as naval aviator 286
marriage of 187–88, 188n
on USS *Franklin* 285–86
post-war career and retirement 313
Lamb, William ("Willie") 279n
Lanier, William 12, 69, 117
Lomax, Frank 112
Lothrop, Scott 288
Lowerre, Warren ("Sunshine") 47

Mallory, Fred 126
Maltby, Arthur 290
Mason, Richard ("Arky") 223
Matthews, William H., Jr. 195n
McElligott, Richard ("Moon") 164
McGrath, Thomas ("Tiny") 40, 47, 263
as regimental commander at USNA 70
as submarine officer 220–23
on leave in Arizona 222–23
death of 223
McMullen, John 266n
Merrill, Howard 112

Michaels, Frederick ("Mike") 202
Miller, John 186
Montgomery, John William Myers 54, 55, 70
appointment to USNA 6–7
plebe year 29
and youngster cruise 40–41, 42–43
and youngster year 44–46, 47
"running" plebes 55, 57–58
and second-class cruise 56
romantic adventures of 40, 43, 62, 67, 72, 82
academic performance of 73
reaction to Pearl Harbor 117
on USS *Idaho* 96–99, 226–29, 230–33,
240, 244
on leave in Missouri 227–28
on USS *Pittsburgh* 294–98
post-war career and retirement 309
Murray, Raymond 171, 183

Nelson, John B. ("Nelly") 125, 126, 131
Nethken, Alva ("AF") 126
Nicholson, Archibald Thomas
("Nick") 85
in Pearl Harbor 102, 107

O'Brien, Edward 223
Obrist, Charles ("Chick") 87

Peterson, Ernest ("Pete") 18–19
plebe year 26
first-class cruise 64–65
romantic adventures of 66, 82
on USS *Philadelphia* 91
on USS *Bristol* 116, 121, 134–37
on USS *Charrette* 300–2
post-war career and retirement 316

Rhodes, Arthur ("Dusty") 44, 55
marriage of 82
Roberts, Everett ("Bob") 272–76
Roddy, Thomas M. 181, 183
Rohn, Bruce ("Wouf") 38, 70
Rogers, Edward 39, 42

Sander, Carl ("Sandy") 167
Saunders, Louis ("Sandy")
in the Battle of the Coral Sea 146–51
in the Battle of Midway 152
Scheu, Donald 223
Sellars, Coleman ("Jim") 126

THE FORTIES INDEX

Sellars, Herschel ("Hershey") 154, 157
  in Okinawa campaign 291
Shaffer, Walter 223–24
Sherwin, Sidney 104–5
Smalzel, Warren 74, 96, 226, 266n
Smith, Charles D. ("CD") 126
  as POW 127
Smith, Harvey Jacob ("Snuffy") 105–6
Smith, Orville ("Smitty") 112
Spears, John 171, 183

Taylor, Thomas 109
Thompson, Irvin ("Igloo") 105
Treanor, Joe ("Otto") 291

Vaughn, Henry ("Hank") 252
Vogel, Harvey 119

Walker, Warren ("Hooky")
  at Pearl Harbor 89, 109, 196
  on USS *Massachusetts* (Operation
    TORCH) 196–201
Weatherup, Robert ("Doc") 54, 65, 70
  appointment to USNA 7
  and plebe year 25
  and youngster cruise 39
  academic performance of 73

on USS *Saratoga* 83–85
and Wake Island rescue mission 118
marriage of 187
and radar 203
and the Guadalcanal campaign 176–82
flight training 184–91
as naval aviator 187, 190–91, 278–80
attacks Tokyo factories 283–85
attacks Kyushu airfields 289–90
post-war career and retirement 310
Weber, Joseph 147
  in Battle of the Coral Sea 149–50
Weeden, Carl 112
Wells, Thomas 178–79
Whitehead, Ulmont ("Monty")
  and football 25, 70–71
  academic performance of 73
  at Pearl Harbor 112
Williams, George V. 240
Wilson, David Spencer 224
Wolfe, David ("Lobo") 186, 189
Wood, Emmet ("Punkin") 25, 47
  and football 58
Worley, Jesse 87–88
Wright, John ("Jack") 98, 134, 140

Young, Samuel 112

General Index

Aaron Ward (USN destroyer) 180, 181–82
ABDA command (American, British, Dutch, Australian) 125
aircraft carriers
 changing role of 74
 in Battle of the Coral Sea 146–51
 in Battle of Midway 151–59
 at Leyte Gulf 265, 267–71
 training regimen for 189–91
Aldrich, Clarence (USN officer) 155–56
Aleutian Islands campaign 230–33
Arizona (USN battleship)
 in Pearl Harbor attack 103, 110–12
Arkansas (USN battleship) 34, 64
Astoria (USN cruiser) 116
 delivers tanks to Philippines 101
 in Battle of Midway 157
 in Battle of Savo Island 169–70
Atlantic convoys, *see* Battle of the Atlantic

Baker, Henry E. (Black USNA candidate) 14
Baldwin (USN destroyer) 258, 260–61
Bancroft Hall x, 16, 18
Barbarosa (German invasion of USSR) 94–95
Bartolo, Giuseppe (Italian naval officer) 257
Barton (USN destroyer) 181
Battle of the Atlantic
 undeclared naval war with Germany 91–92, 133
 U-boat war against convoys 132–34, 132n, 253–54
 see also convoy protocols and PQ convoys
Battle off Samar (1944) 276
 see also Leyte Gulf
battleships
 pre-war assumptions about 88
 characteristics of 225–26
 wartime use of 230
Bennion, Mervyn (USN captain) 106
Bilibud prison (Japanese POW camp in Philippines) 130, 249

Bicycle Camp (Japanese POW camp on Java) 127, 131
Biscayne (USN command ship) 204–07
Black midshipmen at USNA 13–14, 29–30, 30n
blimps 191–94
Blue (USN destroyer) 99–101
 in Battle of Savo Island 168–69, 172
 sinks 173–74
Bode, Howard (USN captain) 168
Bristol (USN destroyer) 116, 121–22, 134–37
Brockman, William H. (USN sub skipper) 218–20
Brown, James (USN officer) 11
Brown, Wilson (USNA superintendent) 63
Bruton, Henry (USN officer) 210, 212, 215, 216–17
Buck (USN destroyer) 134–37
Buckmaster, Elliott (USN captain) 152–55
Bunker Hill (USN carrier) 283

Cabanatuan (Japanese POW camp) 249
California (USN battleship) 103
 in Pearl Harbor attack 107–08, 109
Canberra (Australian cruiser) 168
Cape Esperance, Battle of (1942) 177–78
Carney, Robert B. ("Mick") 88
Cherbourg (French port) 262
Chicago (USN cruiser) 167
Christie, Ralph Waldo (USN officer) 52
Churchill, Winston (British prime minister) 75, 121
Clark, Horace D. (USN captain) 230
codebreaking, *see* cryptanalysis
Connolly, Richard (USN admiral)
 and invasion of Sicily 204–07
 and invasion of Kwajalein 243–44
Conyers, John H. (Black USNA candidate) 13–14
Copeland, Robert W. (USN officer) 272–76
convoy protocols 121, 134–37
Coral Sea, Battle of (1942) 145–51

GENERAL INDEX

Cordinier, Douglas (USN captain) 288
Cowpens (USN carrier) 279–80, 283–84
cryptanalysis (codebreaking) 145–46
Czechoslovakia crisis, *see* Munich crisis

D-Day (Normandy invasion) 257–63
Dahlgren Hall (USNA) 17–18
Dashiell (USN destroyer) 281–82
and Okinawa 287–89
Depression, economic 3
Deutschland (German warship) 41
dive bombing protocols 266–67
Dönitz, Karl (German admiral) 132, 137, 211, 215n, 254
Doolittle Raid (1942) 130
Doorman, Karel (Dutch admiral) 125
Douglas H. Fox (USN destroyer) 282, 291–93
Draemel, Milo (USN admiral)
as USNA commandant 61–63
in Pearl Harbor 100
DUKWs (amphibious trucks) 245–46, 246n
Duncan (USN destroyer) 176, 178
Dunkirk, evacuation of 75, 76

Edison, Charles (Secy of Navy) 76
Eisenhower, Dwight D. (USA general) 201, 206
Elliott, Robert B. (Black USNA candidate) 13
Ellis, Earl ("Pete") 239
Engh, Helen Barbara ("Bobbie") 76, 82
Enterprise (USN carrier)
in Battle of Midway 152
in Guadalcanal campaign 180, 227

Fairbanks, Douglas (actor) 141
Farenholt (USN destroyer) 176–78
Flasher (USN submarine) 299
Fletcher, Frank Jack (USN admiral) 119–20, 118n
and Battle of the Coral Sea 146–51
and Battle of Midway 151–52, 153
flight training, *see* naval aviation
Foch, Ferdinand (French general) 81
Focht, Benjamin (US congressman) 6
Foote (USN destroyer) 182
Franklin (USN carrier) 285–86
Frost, Laurence (USN officer) 96

Gayler, Noel (USN officer) 11
Gehres, Leslie E. (USN captain) 286n
Giffen, Robert (USN admiral)
on USS *Washington* 140
Gingrich, John L. (USN officer) 297–98
Glennon, Harrison (USN captain) 5
Glennon, James Blair (USN captain) 5
Glennon, James Henry (USN rear admiral) 5
Glennon (USN destroyer) 261
Greenling (USN submarine) 209–10, 211–12, 213–15
Greer (USN destroyer) 96–97
Guadalcanal, Battle for 163–83

Haines, Preston (USN officer) 116
Halsey, William (USN admiral)
misses the Battle of Midway 152
and the Guadalcanal campaign 178–79
and the Battle of Leyte Gulf 265, 270–71, 276
and Typhoon Viper 297–98
Hammann (USN destroyer) 157–58
Harper, Arthur M. (USA general) 247
Harper, John S. (USN officer) 106
Harrison (USN destroyer) 288–89
Hart, Thomas A. (USN admiral)
as USNA superintendent 22
as commander of ABDA 125
Heermann (USN destroyer) 274–76
Helfrich, Conrad (Dutch admiral) 126
Helldiver (SB2C) dive bomber 266
Henry A. Wiley (USN destroyer) 291
Herbert (USN destroyer) 56
Huebner, Clarence (USA general) 261
Hitler, Adolf x, 38, 67–68, 81, 263
death of 290
Hoel (USN destroyer) 274–76
Hornet (USN carrier) 226
and Doolittle Raid 130–31
and the Battle of Midway 152–53
and Guadalcanal campaign 178–79
sinks 179–80
Houston (USN cruiser) 125–26
Hughes (USN destroyer) 157

Idaho (USN battleship)
in Iceland 96–99
returns to USA 120
an anchor in San Francisco 226–29

GENERAL INDEX

in Aleutian campaign 230–33
at Tarawa 240
at Kwajalein 244
Italian submarines 254–5
Iwo Jima, Battle for (1945) 283–85, 287

Japan
and war in China 50–51
Panay incident 51
and "Rape of Nanking" 51
invades Indochina 86
US sanctions on 101
Pacific war plans of 117
cultural differences with
USA 299–300, 301–02
circumstances of (1945) 299
Java Sea, Battle of (1942) 125–26
Johnston (USN destroyer) 274–76
Juneau (USN cruiser) 181

kamikaze attacks near
Okinawa 287–89, 291–93
Kasserine Pass, Battle of (1943) 201
Kearney (USN destroyer) 98
Kennedy, John F.
and sailboat races in
Hyannisport 56–57, 83
as PT boat commander 183
Kennedy, Robert F. 56–57, 83
Kennedy, Joseph P. (US ambassador to
Britain) 83, 83n
Kerama Retto (USN anchorage near
Okinawa) 288, 289, 293
Kiefer, Dixie, (XO on *Yorktown*) 154
Kinkaid, Thomas C. (USN admiral)
and the Aleutian campaign 230–31
and the Battle of Leyte Gulf 265, 271–72
Kimmel, Husband (USN admiral) 86, 113
King, Ernest J. (USN admiral and CNO) 92,
150–51, 163n
and Guadalcanal 163–64
advocacy of gray uniforms 294
Kurita, Takeo (Japanese admiral) 268–69, 276
Kwajalein, invasion of (1944) 244

Landing Craft, Tracked (LVTs or
alligators) 243
Landing Ship Tank (LST) 204
Layton, Edwin (Nimitz's intel officer) 145
Lejeune, John A. (USMC general) 5

LeMay, Curtis (USAAF general) 285
Lexington (USN carrier, CV-2) 146–51
sinks 150
Lexington (USN carrier, CV-16) 266–67
Leyte Gulf, Battle of (1944) 264–76
Lipscomb Bay (USN carrier) 240
lighter than air (LTA) craft, *see* blimps
Lindbergh, Charles A. (aviator) 7
Lockwood, Charles A. (USN admiral)
302–3
Lundeen, Ernest (US Senator) 72, 72n

MacArthur, Douglas (USA general)
and defense of the Philippines 128
escapes Philippines 134
returns to Philippines 265
and Japanese surrender 303
magnetic anomaly detector (MAD) 192
Marine Corps
motto 237
training program 237
change in mission 239
see also Tarawa, Kwajalein, and Saipan
Marshall, George C. (USA general) 201, 207
Marshall Islands
described 239–40
raid on (1942) 122–23
seizure of (1944) 241–44
Massachusetts (USN battleship) 196–201
and Operation TORCH 198–201
Mayo, Morton (USN admiral) 259
Midshipmen, origin of term 9
Midway, Battle of (1942) 151–59
McClennan, Alonzo (Black USNA
candidate) 14
Mikawa, Gunichi (Japanese admiral) 167
Miller, Doris ("Dorrie") 106, 106n
Mitchell, Arthur W. (US congress-
man) 14–15, 30
Mitscher, Marc ("Pete") (USN admiral)
in Battle of Leyte Gulf 265
mokes (*Reef Points*: "colored corridor
boys") 69–70
Momsen Lung (on submarines) 209
Monserrat, Nicholas (British novelist) 135
Morton, Dudley ("Mush") (USN sub
skipper) 215n
Munich crisis (1938) 57, 67
Munroe, William R. (USN admiral) 229
Musashi (Japanese battleship) 268

GENERAL INDEX

Nachi (Japanese cruiser) 268–69
Nassau (USN escort carrier) 231
Nautilus (USN submarine) 218, 218n
Naval Academy, United States
  founding of ix
  appointments to 3–15
  prep schools for 4, 5, 8–9, 13
  physical description of 16–17
  religious services at 17
  grading practices at 23
  drill maneuvers 20
  daily routine 23–25
  curriculum 22–23, 47, 57
  sports 25–27, 58, 70–71
  dating ("dragging") 44–45
  honor system 47–48
  movies filmed at 49
naval aviation
  training for 184–91
  dangers of 195
  see also, dive bombing protocols
Naval Battle of Guadalcanal (1942) 180–82
Nazi Germany 38–40, 59
Nelson, Oswald "Ozzie" (bandleader)
  66, 66n
Neosho (USN oiler) 147
Neunzer (USN destroyer escort) 252,
  253–57, 253n
Nevada (USN battleship) 110, 116
New Jersey (USN battleship) 265
New York (USN battleship) 34, 36, 64
  engineering plant of 65
Nimitz, Chester (USN admiral) 122
  and the Battle of the Coral Sea 145–46
  and the Battle of Midway 151–52
  and the Aleutians 230
  and Kwajalein 241
  and the Battle of Leyte Gulf 271
  and Japanese surrender 303
Normandy, invasion of, *see* D-Day
North Carolina (USN battleship) 175
Norway campaign (1940) 74–75
Nowell, Byron (USN sub skipper) 250

Okinawa, Battle for (1945) 287–89,
  291–93
  see also kamikaze attacks
Oklahoma (USN battleship) 103
  in Pearl Harbor attack 103–5
Oldendorf, Jesse (USN admiral) 265

Omaha Beach, *see* D-Day
Overlord, *see* D-Day
Ozawa, Jisaburo (Japanese admiral) 268

Paddle (USN submarine) 250
Patterson (USN destroyer) 167
Pearl Harbor
  pre-war social life in 88–89
  Japanese attack on 104–15
  conspiracy theories about 116
Pennsylvania (USN battleship) 86–87
  in Pearl Harbor 103
Pitts, Ray (USN officer) 291–93
Philadelphia (USN light cruiser) 91
Philippines
  political status of 128
  battle for (1942) 128–30
Philippine Sea, Battle of (1944) 264
pilot training, *see* naval aviation
Pittsburgh (USN cruiser) 286
  and Typhoon Viper 297–98
Plan Orange 238–40
Pompano (USN submarine) 220–23
PQ convoys 140–42
  PQ-17 convoy 142–43
Princeton (USN carrier) 279
Pye, William S. (USN admiral) 118–19

Quincy (USN cruiser) 164
  in Battle of Savo Island 171

racial issues
  in USN 13–14, 29–30, 30n, 69–70
  on the home front 229–30
radar
  pre-war rarity of 91, 124, 135
  in Battle of the Coral Sea 148
  in Guadalcanal campaign 164
  in blimps 192–93
  improvement of 202–03
  surface search (SJ) radar 217
Raeder, Erich (German admiral) 95
Ramsay, Bertram (RN admiral) 75
Reef Points x–xi
  quoted 1, 16, 69–70, 79, 161, 235, 238
Reifkohl, Frederick (USN captain) 139, 170–71
Reina Mercedes (station ship at
  USNA) xi, 12, 34
Reuben James (USN destroyer) 98–99
Reykjavik, Iceland 97–99

GENERAL INDEX

Reynaud, Paul (French prime minister) 75
Richardson, James O. (USN admiral) 86
Rochefort, Joseph (USN codebreaker) 145
  and the Battle of Midway 151
Rockwell, Francis W. (USN admiral) 231
Roberts, David W. (USN captain) 126
Rooks, Albert (USN captain) 125–26
Roosevelt, Eleanor 59
Roosevelt, Franklin 3, 53
  inaugural parade of (1937) 28–29
  and the war in Europe 68
  declares embargo on Soviet Union 71
  accelerates USNA graduations 77
  keeps fleet in Pearl Harbor 86
  cruise on USS *Tuscaloosa* 92–93
  and Lend Lease 93, 94–95
  undeclared war against U-boats 94, 95,
    96, 98–99
  calls for war preparations 184
  death of 295

Sable (USN training carrier) 190–91
Saipan, US invasion of (1944) 245–48
Samoa, reinforcement of 1
Samuel B. Roberts (USN destroyer
    escort) 272–76
San Francisco (USN cruiser) 177, 181
Santa Cruz Islands, Battle of (1942) 178–80
Saratoga (USN carrier) 83–85, 86
  and Wake rescue mission 117–19
  torpedoed 122
Savo Island, Battle of (1942) 167–73
Schuirmann, Roscoe (USN captain) 226
Scott, Norman (USN admiral) 176–78
Sellars, David (USNA superintendent) 22
Shinyo Maru (Japanese hell ship) 250–51
Shōhō (Japanese carrier) 14
Sicily, Allied invasion of 204–07
Sims (USN destroyer) 147
Singapore, fall of 128
Smith, Holland (USMC general)
  and the Gilberts campaign (Tarawa) 240
  and Saipan 247
  Smith vs. Smith controversy 247
Smith, Ralph (USA general) 247
Spanish Civil War 36, 41, 64
Sprague, Clifton ("Ziggy") (USN admiral) 274
Spruance, Raymond (USN admiral)
  on USS *Northampton* 90
  and Battle of the Philippine Sea (1944) 264

Stalin, Josef (Soviet leader) 143
Stark, Harold (USN admiral) 98
Stewart (USN destroyer escort) 253, 253n
Stribling Walk (USNA) 17
submarines
  R-class sub visits USNA 55, 208
  US policy of "unrestricted" warfare 210–11
  Gato-class submarines 209–10, 213
  hunting protocols 213–14
  casualty rate in US subs 224
  record of success 224, 299
  Italian submarines 254–57
Sunda Strait, Battle of (1942) 125–26
Surigao Strait, Battle of (1944) 273
Swanson, Claude (Secy of Navy) 30

Tarawa, Battle for (1943) 240–41
TBS (Talk Between Ships) short range
    radio 136
"Tecumseh" statue at USNA 47–48, 48n
Tennessee (USN battleship) 106–07
Texas (USN battleship) 64
Thatch Weave (aerial maneuver) 278–79
Thomas, Willis (USN sub skipper) 221–22
Tinian, Battle for (1944) 248
Tirpitz (German battleship) 140–41, 143
Tobin, Robert G. (USN captain) 176–78
Torch (invasion of North Africa) 196–201
torpedoes (US), problems with 211–12, 214
  torpedo data computer (TDC) 214
Truk Atoll (Japanese base) 210
Tullibee (USN submarine) 224
Turner, Richmond Kelly (USN
    admiral) 167, 302
Tuscaloosa (USN cruiser)
  hosts FDR on fishing trip 92–93
  in Iceland 98
  and Arctic convoys 140, 142, 143
  and D-Day invasion 257–62
Typhoon Viper (1945) 297–98

Ulithi Atoll (American base) 280

Vincennes (USN cruiser)
  in Doolittle Raid 130–31
  in Battle of Savo Island 167, 169–71
Vossler, F.A.L. (USNA commandant) 76

Wahoo (USN submarine) 215n, 223
Wainwright, Jonathan (USA general) 129

GENERAL INDEX

Wake Island rescue mission (1942) 113, 117–19
"War of the Worlds" radio broadcast 58
Washington (USN battleship) 139–40
Wasp (USN carrier) 175–76
Watchtower, *see* Guadalcanal
West Virginia (USN battleship) 105–6
Whiting, F.E.M. (USN captain) 197
Wildcat fighter plane (F4F) 190
Wilcox, John W. (USN admiral) 140
Wilson, Woodrow (US president) 210–11
Winant, John Gilbert (US ambassador to
    Britain) 121

Wolverine (USN training carrier) 190–91
Wyoming (USN battleship) 34, 40–41, 64

Yamato (Japanese battleship) 268
    sunk 298
Yorktown (USN carrier) 119
    in Battle of the Coral Sea 146–51
    in Battle of Midway 153–58

Zellers (USN destroyer) 288
Zimmerman, Orville (US congressman) 7
Zuikaku (Japanese carrier) 268